Kingship, Law, and Society

KINGSHIP, LAW, AND SOCIETY

Criminal Justice
in the Reign of Henry V

EDWARD POWELL

CLARENDON PRESS · OXFORD
1989

Oxford University Press, Walton Street, Oxford OX2 6DP
Oxford New York Toronto
Delhi Bombay Calcutta Madras Karachi
Petaling Jaya Singapore Hong Kong Tokyo
Nairobi Dar es Salaam Cape Town
Melbourne Auckland
and associated companies in
Berlin Ibadan

Oxford is a trade mark of Oxford University Press

Published in the United States
by Oxford University Press, New York

British Library Cataloguing in Publication Data
Powell, Edward
Kingship, law, and society : criminal justice in the
reign of Henry V.
1. England. Law, 1000–1600
I. Title 344.2'009
ISBN 0–19–820082–X

Library of Congress Cataloging in Publication Data
Powell, Edward.
Kingship, law, and society : criminal justice in the reign of
Henry V / Edward Powell.
p. cm.
Bibliography: p.
Includes index.
1. Criminal justice, Administration of—Great Britain—History.
I. Title.
KD7876.P69   1989   345.42'05—dc19   [344.2055]   89–31244
ISBN 0–19–820082–X

Typeset by Hope Services, Abingdon
Printed in Great Britain by
Courier International Ltd
Tiptree, Essex

To

MY PARENTS

Acknowledgements

I HAVE incurred many debts in the writing of this book. I am grateful to the Principal and Fellows of Lady Margaret Hall, Oxford, and the Master and Fellows of Downing College, Cambridge for making the work possible, and for providing such congenial environments for research and writing. Most of the source materials for this study are kept in the Public Record Office in Chancery Lane, and I am heavily indebted to many of the Assistant Keepers there: Dr R. F. Hunnisett and Dr J. B. Post taught me how to read and interpret medieval legal records, and the occupants of Room A23—Dr T. Chalmers, Dr D. Crook, Dr E. Hallam Smith, Ms S. Healy, and Dr A. Nicol—have offered me working space, hospitality, and considerable learning on many occasions.

I have profited greatly from the comments and criticisms of those who have read parts of the book in draft: Dr M. C. Carpenter, Dr M. J. D. Cooper, Dr G. L. Harriss, Dr A. M. Hudson, Dr P. C. Millett, and Mr J. Watts. I am very grateful, too, to my wife Alison, who has read large portions of the work and has never allowed me to get away with slack or imprecise expression.

My greatest debt, however, is to my parents, Ray and Avril Powell. It was they who first aroused my enthusiasm for history, and they have been unfailingly helpful and supportive throughout my academic career. My father read the entire book in draft and suggested innumerable improvements, most of which I have adopted. My mother has always been on hand to check PRO references for me, to transcribe documents, and to make sense of obscure passages of medieval Latin. Few historians can have been more fortunate in their choice of parents, and it is to them that I dedicate this book.

E. P.
Cambridge
April 1988

Contents

Abbreviations

AJLH	*American Journal of Legal History*
Aquinas	Thomas Aquinas, *De Regimine Principium*, tr. G. B. Phelan as *On Kingship to the King of Cyprus* (Toronto, 1949)
BBCS	*Bulletin of the Board of Celtic Studies*
BIHR	*Bulletin of the Institute of Historical Research*
BJRL	*Bulletin of the John Rylands Library*
BL	British Library
CCR	*Calendar of the Close Rolls, 1272–1485* (45 vols.; London, 1892–1954)
CFR	*Calendar of the Fine Rolls, 1272–1509* (22 vols.; London, 1911–63)
CIM	*Calendar of Inquisitions Miscellaneous, 1216–1422* (7 vols.; London, 1916–69)
CPR	*Calendar of the Patent Rolls, 1216–1509* (55 vols.; London, 1891–1916)
DKR	*Reports of the Deputy Keeper of Public Records* (120 vols.; London, 1840–1958)
EHR	*English Historical Review*
Glanvill	*The Treatise on the Laws and Customs of . . . England Commonly called Glanvill*, ed. G. D. G. Hall (London, 1965)
HMC	Historical Manuscripts Commission
LQR	*Law Quarterly Review*
NMS	*Nottingham Medieval Studies*
PBA	*Proceedings of the British Academy*
PPC	*Proceedings and Ordinances of the Privy Council of England*, ed. N. H. Nicolas (7 vols.; London, 1834–7)
Putnam, *Justices of the Peace*	B. H. Putnam (ed.), *Proceedings before the Justices of the Peace in the Fourteenth and Fifteenth Centuries: Edward III to Richard III*, Ames Foundation (Cambridge, Mass., 1938)
PRO	Public Record Office
RP	*Rotuli Parliamentorum, 1278–1503* (6 vols.; London, 1783–1832)

SKB   *Select Cases in the Court of King's Bench*, ed. G. O. Sayles,
      Selden Soc., 55, 57, 58, 74, 76, 82, 88 (7 vols.; London,
      1936–71)

TRHS *Transactions of the Royal Historical Society*

TSAS *Transactions of the Shropshire Archaeological Society*

A NOTE ON SOURCES

All manuscript references are to documents in the Public Record
Office unless otherwise specified.

Introduction: Towards a New Constitutional History of Late Medieval England

THE LAST twenty years have witnessed a remarkable revival of interest in the history of late medieval England. The fifteenth century in particular, from being 'the "Cinderella" of the centuries of English history', has become the most intensively studied of the entire middle ages.[1] The revival was heralded by the establishment of a regular conference on fifteenth-century history, first held in 1970, and by the posthumous publication of the lecture series given by K. B. McFarlane, notably *The Nobility of Later Medieval England*, which appeared in 1973.[2] Since then the reign of every fifteenth-century king of England has received detailed attention,[3] while the numerous volumes of conference proceedings and Festschriften reveal the breadth and vigour of current research.[4]

[1] S. B. Chrimes, C. D. Ross, and R. A. Griffiths (edd.), *Fifteenth-Century England, 1399–1509* (Manchester, 1972), p. vii; see also C. F. Richmond, 'After McFarlane', *History*, 68 (1983), 46; R. B. Dobson (ed.), *The Church, Politics and Patronage in the Fifteenth Century* (Gloucester, 1984), 9; R. L. Storey, *The End of the House of Lancaster* (London, 1966; 2nd edn., Gloucester, 1986), vii.

[2] K. B. McFarlane, *Lancastrian Kings and Lollard Knights* (Oxford, 1972); id., *The Nobility of Later Medieval England* (Oxford, 1973). The proceedings of the 1970 conference were published as Chrimes *et al.*, *Fifteenth-Century England*, and established the framework for much of the work which has since appeared.

[3] J. L. Kirby, *Henry IV of England* (London, 1970); G. L. Harriss (ed.), *Henry V: The Practice of Kingship* (Oxford, 1985); B. P. Wolffe, *Henry VI* (London, 1981); R. A. Griffiths, *The Reign of King Henry VI* (London, 1981); C. D. Ross, *Edward IV* (London, 1975); id., *Richard III* (London, 1981); S. B. Chrimes, *Henry VII* (London, 1972).

[4] J. R. L. Highfield and R. Jeffs (edd.), *The Crown and the Local Communities in England and France in the Fifteenth Century*, (Gloucester, 1981); C. D. Ross (ed.), *Patronage, Pedigree and Power in Later Medieval England* (Gloucester, 1979); R. A. Griffiths (ed.), *Patronage, the Crown and the Provinces in Later Medieval England* (Gloucester, 1981); Dobson, *Church, Politics and Patronage*; A. J. Pollard (ed.), *Property and Politics: Essays in Later Medieval English History* (Gloucester, 1984); M. Jones (ed.), *Gentry and Lesser Nobility in Late Medieval Europe* (Gloucester, 1986); C. H. Clough (ed.), *Profession, Vocation and Culture in Later Medieval England: Essays Dedicated to the Memory of A. R. Myers* (Liverpool, 1982); R. A. Griffiths and J. W. Sherborne (edd.), *Kings and Nobles in the Later Middle Ages: A Tribute to Charles Ross* (Gloucester, 1986).

Presiding over this historiographical renaissance has been the spirit of K. B. McFarlane, whose influence as a teacher and scholar is everywhere apparent.[5] His interests ranged widely across the late middle ages,[6] but the most important theme in his published work was the nobility, and its place in the society and politics of late medieval England. McFarlane's preoccupation with the nobility, which he chose as the subject of his Ford lectures in 1953, stemmed from his dissatisfaction with the institutional and administrative bias of English medieval history since the completion of William Stubbs's definitive *Constitutional History* in 1878.[7] Constitutional history, described by McFarlane as 'that far from helpful abstraction', dominated the study and writing of history until after the Second World War: its subject-matter was confined to the rise of Parliament and the development of the central institutions of royal authority, and its source material was restricted to the major chronicles and the records of the king's administration.[8] For McFarlane its inadequacy lay in its exclusive concentration on the central machinery of royal government, to the neglect of any serious study of the nobility and local society. Fundamental questions about the structure of power in medieval society, and in particular the means whereby the king exercised authority at the local level without the resources of a standing army and salaried bureaucracy, went unasked and unanswered. The role of the late medieval nobility in

[5] Ross, *Patronage, Pedigree and Power*, 8; Richmond, 'After McFarlane', 46.

[6] McFarlane, *Nobility*, pp. xxvii–xxviii; id., *England in the Fifteenth Century: Collected Essays* (London, 1981).

[7] W. Stubbs, *Constitutional History of England* (3 vols.; 5th edn., Oxford, 1903). Stubbs's work remained the fundamental textbook of English medieval history until after the Second World War: see H. M. Cam, 'Stubbs Seventy Years After' in ead., *Law-Finders and Law-Makers in Medieval England* (London, 1962), 188–211; G. T. Lapsley, 'Some Recent Advance in English Constitutional History', in id., *Crown, Community, and Parliament* (Oxford, 1951), 1–33; H. G. Richardson and G. O. Sayles, *The Governance of Medieval England from the Conquest to Magna Carta* (Edinburgh, 1963).

[8] McFarlane, *Nobility*, 1. Stubbs's work concentrated on the evolution of parliamentary institutions; with the opening up of the central administrative records at the PRO, attention shifted increasingly towards analysis of the machinery of government as the means of exercising royal authority: cf. T. F. Tout, *Chapters in the Administrative History of Medieval England* (6 vols.; Manchester, 1920–30). Traditional constitutional history continued to flourish in the late 1950s. See B. Wilkinson, *The Constitutional History of Medieval England, 1216–1399*, (3 vols.; London, 1948–58), iii, p. vii: 'The constitutional history of medieval England has, indeed, never been more significant as a subject of study, or more interesting.'

governing the kingdom was ignored, and magnates were dismissed as mere obstructions to the extension of royal power—selfish, factious, and stupid—a caricature which throughout his life McFarlane patiently sought to discredit.[9]

Although McFarlane's interpretations differed radically from those of his predecessors, his interests continued to focus on a central theme of constitutional history—the nature and exercise of political power. Furthermore the authority of his writings derives from his mastery of the traditional 'central' sources, for example the records of Parliament and the king's council, as well as the records of magnate and gentry families.[10] There can be no doubt, however, that his work has redirected late medieval historiography away from a narrowly constitutional and administrative perspective towards a broader analysis of political society based on meticulous study of the nobility collectively and individually.[11] In addition, intensive investigation of the nobility has confirmed McFarlane's belief in the importance of the gentry in central and local politics, and the fruits of detailed research into gentry communities, usually county-based, are beginning to appear.[12] Increasingly the political history of late medieval England is coming to be viewed in the light of local politics and social structures.[13]

[9] *Nobility*, 3, 228–9; *Fifteenth Century*, 232.

[10] See, for example, McFarlane, *Lancastrian Kings and Lollard Knights*, 78–101.

[11] Ross, *Patronage, Pedigree and Power*, 8; Griffiths, *Patronage, the Crown and the Provinces*, 9.

[12] McFarlane, *Fifteenth Century*, 20–1: 'The ramifications of that intricate network of personal relationships, constantly changing and forming fresh patterns, will never fully be traced, but as we make ourselves familiar with the lives and achievements of the country gentry . . . the main outlines of local and central politics may be expected to emerge.' Richmond, 'After McFarlane', 59–60; N. Saul, *Knights and Esquires: The Gloucestershire Gentry in the Fourteenth Century* (Oxford, 1981); M. C. Carpenter, 'Political Society in Warwickshire, c.1401–72', Ph.D. thesis (Cambridge, 1976); S. M. Wright, *The Derbyshire Gentry in the Fifteenth Century*, Derbyshire Record Soc., 8 (Chesterfield, 1983); M. J. Bennett, *Community, Class and Careerism: Cheshire and Lancashire Society in the Age of Sir Gawain and the Green Knight* (Cambridge, 1983); A. J. Pollard, 'The Richmondshire Community of Gentry during the Wars of the Roses', in C. D. Ross (ed.), *Patronage, Pedigree and Power in Later Medieval England* (Gloucester, 1979), 37–59.

[13] A similar trend is evident in the recent historiography of seventeenth-century England: see, for example, J. S. Morrill, *The Revolt of the Provinces* (London, 1976); A. Everitt, *The Community of Kent and the Great Rebellion* (London, 1966); A. Fletcher, *A County Community in Peace and War: Sussex, 1600–1660* (London, 1975).

McFarlane's influence has been so powerful and beneficial that the limitations of his published work have tended to pass unnoticed, or at least unchallenged. He concentrated on the practical and material concerns of the nobility, seeking to answer such questions as how they ran their estates, why they went to war, on what they spent their money, and how they passed on their lands. McFarlane showed very little concern, however, for the ideas and beliefs of the nobility. He showed that they were highly educated, that they possessed books and often wrote poetry,[14] but he did not explore the content of what they read and wrote.[15] He took for granted the chivalric ethos of aristocratic society without subjecting it to detailed scrutiny,[16] and interpreted Crown–magnate relations in terms of pragmatism, patronage, and personality rather than those of principle and ideology.[17]

A second limitation of McFarlane's writings on the nobility is that he made very little use of legal records as primary source material. The records of the central courts, the assizes, and the justices of the peace are conspicuously absent from his footnotes.[18] When he dealt with legal issues McFarlane showed his usual sureness of touch, as in his treatment of medieval land law and his references to maintenance,[19] but he did not pursue the implications of such insights, and consequently the workings of the legal system played only a peripheral part in his analysis of late medieval political society.

These limitations may seem trivial when set against the strengths of McFarlane's work, but they are significant because they reinforce the main features of the thorough reinterpretation of the political history of late medieval

[14] *Nobility*, 228–47.

[15] An exception is McFarlane's work on the Lollard knights, but even here his avowed concern was 'with people rather than ideas': *Lancastrian Kings and Lollard Knights*, 139.

[16] Cf. his comments on Henry Bolingbroke's career before 1399: ibid. 37–8. For an important study of chivalry, see M. H. Keen, *Chivalry* (London, 1984).

[17] *Nobility*, 119–21; *Fifteenth Century*, 19–21.

[18] In his book *John Wycliffe and the Beginnings of English Nonconformity* (London, 1952), repr. as *Wycliffe and English Nonconformity* (London, 1972), McFarlane did use the returns of judicial inquiries to throw light upon the participants in the Lollard revolt of 1414: see ch. 6 n. 3.

[19] *Nobility*, 61–82, 115; *Fifteenth Century*, 42.

England which he effected. Dismissing the discredited Stubbsian framework of Lancastrian constitutionalism and Yorkist autocracy,[20] McFarlane compared fifteenth-century politics with those of the eighteenth century, as analysed by Sir Lewis Namier:

The 'affinity' had little in common with the modern party; but it did, it seems to me, in many ways resemble the eighteenth century 'connection', so fully anatomised by Professor Namier. There was the same element of voluntary interdependence, the same competition for 'place' and the same absence of any separate fund of political principle. Held together by little else than the hope of gain, these affinities swelled with success and dwindled in adversity.[21]

According to McFarlane, English politics in the late middle ages did not turn upon the clash of principle between royal autocracy and baronial or parliamentary opposition; rather they functioned through personal connection, affinity, and patronage.[22]

Much recent research shares the limitations of McFarlane's published work, showing a lack of interest in ideology and in the workings of law as part of the structure of power. It is 'patronage' which has been the leitmotiv of the post-McFarlane revival of late medieval history, as is evident from the recent titles of conference proceedings and the chapter-headings of books.[23] Much of the behaviour of the landowning classes can be interpreted in this way, but there is a risk of over-simplification, of assuming that magnates and gentry were motivated only by economic rationalism expressed in the scramble for place and profit.[24] Quite apart from the obvious

[20] *Nobility*, 279–90.

[21] *Fifteenth Century*, 19; cf. Richmond, 'After McFarlane', 46.

[22] *Nobility*, 113–14, 119–21; *Fifteenth Century*, 18–21. McFarlane's views have been influential in redirecting research on fourteenth-century politics; recent analysis of the reign of Edward II, for example, has been conducted mainly through studies of individual magnates and prelates: J. R. Maddicott, *Thomas of Lancaster* (Oxford, 1970a); J. R. S. Phillips, *Aymer de Valence, Earl of Pembroke* (Oxford, 1972); R. M. Haines, *The Church and Politics in Fourteenth-Century England: The Career of Adam Orleton* (Cambridge, 1978); M. C. Buck, *Politics, Finance and the Church in the Reign of Edward II* (Cambridge, 1983).

[23] Ross, *Patronage, Pedigree and Power*; Griffiths, *Patronage, the Crown and the Provinces*; Dobson, *Church, Politics and Patronage*; Griffiths, *Henry VI*, chs. 4, 5, 14; Wolffe, *Henry VI*, ch. 7.

[24] Cf. Richmond, 'After McFarlane', 57: 'Men were not Pavlovian dogs, jumping at the chance of a fee, a rent charge, a stewardship here, a parkership there. No more

danger of adopting monocausal explanations to interpret complex phenomena, the concept of patronage is by itself a comparatively blunt analytical instrument, which McFarlane, that most skilled of historical surgeons, would have deplored. While it is fruitful to note the similarities between political society in different centuries, the historian must also look for the differences, which means exploring the institutional and ideological—as well as the economic—context in which systems of patronage functioned.

In short, the prevailing trend of historiography threatens to reduce our view of the late medieval polity to a shallow, two-dimensional image, devoid of ideological and constitutional content, in a way that McFarlane surely never intended. An understanding of magnate politics and local gentry society is of course essential, but it is not an end in itself; it should be complemented by investigation of the conceptual basis of late medieval kingship, and of the administrative resources by which the Crown exercised authority within the shires. There is an urgent need to integrate the new learning with the old,[25] in order to create a more complete constitutional history, in which analysis of the economic position of the landowning classes and the workings of power politics can be related to institutional and administrative changes, and to those developments in political theory which influenced relations between the king and his subjects.

This book is offered as a contribution to a new constitutional history of this kind. In many ways an exploration of the theory and practice of the legal system offers a promising starting-point for a more integrated analysis of late medieval society. To the medieval mind law was no mere human invention, but a fundamental body of principles through which God governed His Creation. The implementation of justice was one of the basic responsibilities of kingship, and the true king was distinguishable from the tyrant by his observance of law and custom. Since political authority in the middle ages was characteristically expressed in terms of jurisdiction, it was through the legal system that royal power was formally

were lords puppet masters manipulating their marionette retainers to dominate the provinces or pack parliaments.'

[25] Cf. McFarlane, *Nobility*, p. xxviii.

conveyed to the localities.[26] On a more mundane level, law embodied the customs and traditions of society, and provided the means whereby social relationships were ordered and the ownership of land—the primary economic resource—was regulated. The legal system, therefore, both mirrored the society it served and influenced the course of its development. Analysis of it may reveal much about the dynamics of English political society in the late middle ages.

A substantial body of work exists on late medieval legal history, from Professor Putnam's pioneering research on the justices of the peace to Dr Ives's recent study of the lawyer Thomas Kebell.[27] As yet, however, it remains a distinct and somewhat arcane discipline, bristling with technicalities. The value of legal records as an abundant source for the period is now well established,[28] but they tend to have been used piecemeal as repositories of raw data concerning aristocratic land disputes, rather than to illuminate the distribution of power between central government and the noble and gentry communities in the shires. In particular there is a need to reconcile the apparently contradictory conclusions reached by the historians of legal institutions and the historians of late medieval crime: whereas the former, through their studies of the central courts at Westminster, the provincial circuits of assize and gaol delivery, and the justices of the peace and coroners in the counties, have proved beyond doubt the precocity and sophistication of the late medieval legal system,[29] the latter have shown equally clearly that the courts were often incapable of keeping the peace or of doing justice. Indeed the period has long been notorious as one of widespread disorder.[30] This book represents an attempt to

[26] See ch. 2.
[27] *Proceedings before the Justices of the Peace in the Fourteenth and Fifteenth Centuries: Edward III to Richard III*, ed. B. H. Putnam, Ames Foundation (Cambridge, Mass., 1938); E. W. Ives, *The Common Lawyers of Pre-Reformation England* (Cambridge, 1983).
[28] Cf. Storey, *House of Lancaster, passim*.
[29] A few of the more important works are: *Select Cases in the Court of King's Bench*, ed. G. O. Sayles, Selden Soc., 55, 57, 58, 74, 76, 82, 88 (7 vols.; London, 1936–71); M. Blatcher, 'The Workings of the Court of King's Bench in the Fifteenth Century', Ph.D. thesis (London, 1936); M. Hastings, *The Court of Common Pleas in Fifteenth-Century England* (Ithaca, NY, 1947); R. F. Hunnisett, *The Medieval Coroner* (Cambridge, 1961).
[30] J. G. Bellamy, *Crime and Public Order in England in the Later Middle Ages* (London,

resolve that paradox, and to show that a knowledge of royal judicial policy and administration is central to our understanding of political society in England in the late middle ages.

The present work investigates the administration of criminal justice in the late middle ages using the reign of King Henry V as a detailed case-study. The enquiry falls into three sections, corresponding to the levels at which the subject has been approached: legal theory, legal institutions, and legal policy and administration. The first part, chapter 1, examines the theoretical foundations and expectations of the law in late medieval England, and the role the king was required to play in its administration. The second part, chapters 2, 3, and 4, analyses the machinery of royal criminal justice as it existed at the accession of Henry V, and explores its use in the wider context of dispute settlement within local society. The final part, chapters 5 to 10, offers a detailed investigation of judicial administration during Henry V's reign, assesses the king's success in restoring public order, and suggests the importance of justice as an instrument of royal policy.

There exists at present no other work devoted to the analysis of judicial policy and administration throughout a single reign. The nearest precedent is Professor Putnam's monograph on Chief Justice William Shareshull; that, however, was a study of Shareshull's career rather than of the reign of Edward III *per se*.[31] Owing to the wealth of judicial records for the late middle ages such a project is manageable only for a comparatively short reign.[32] Henry V offers an especially suitable case for study because that king formulated and enforced a clear judicial policy which is fully documented in the archives of the court of king's bench. His reign provides the opportunity to examine the workings of the legal system in favourable circumstances under a dynamic and powerful king

1973); E. L. G. Stones, 'The Folvilles of Ashby Folville, Leicestershire, and their Associates in Crime', *TRHS* 5th ser., 7 (1957), 117–36; Storey, *House of Lancaster*, *passim*.

[31] B. H. Putnam, *The Place in Legal History of Sir William Shareshull* (Cambridge, 1950).

[32] Equally it should be possible to study specific periods of intense judicial activity within longer reigns, for example the first decade of Edward I's reign, or the period between 1328 and 1332 under Edward III.

who was very conscious of his judicial responsibilities. The manner in which Henry administered justice and the limits of his success throw valuable light on the structural constraints on royal power to enforce the law in late medieval England.

THE GROWTH OF ROYAL CRIMINAL JURISDICTION, 1250–1400

During the century and a half before Henry V's accession, radical changes had occurred in the administration of justice in England, owing to the rapid expansion in the scope of the Crown's jurisdiction over criminal matters. The main outlines of those changes have been explored in many monographs and articles, but as yet there exists no satisfactory synthesis of this research. As a preface to the main body of the study, therefore, it may be useful to summarize the major developments in royal criminal jurisdiction and law enforcement between *c.*1250 and 1400.

The expansion of royal criminal jurisdiction during the late thirteenth and fourteenth centuries represented the third and final phase of the judicial revolution which transformed the governance of England between 1150 and 1400. At the beginning of that period the king's courts had dealt with little more than land disputes involving tenants-in-chief, and the most serious crimes; by the end they possessed a comprehensive civil and criminal jurisdiction. The first phase, coterminous with the reign of Henry II, had seen the establishment of standardized returnable writs for land actions and the regulation of procedure for the presentment of felonies. The second, which took place in the second half of the thirteenth century, witnessed the rapid growth of royal jurisdiction over personal actions, particularly trespass, and was marked by the increasing use of procedure by plaint and bill.[33] The third phase—the transformation of criminal

[33] F. M. Pollock and F. W. Maitland, *The History of English Law before the Time of Edward I* (2nd edn.; repr. Cambridge, 1968), i. 136–225, ii. 558–73; S. F. C. Milsom, *Historical Foundations of the Common Law* (2nd edn.; London, 1981), 11–59; J. H. Baker, *An Introduction to English Legal History* (2nd edn.; London, 1979), 11–33, 49–59, 198–204; A. Harding, 'Plaints and Bills in the History of English Law', in D. Jenkins (ed.), *Legal History Studies 1972* (Cardiff, 1975), 65–86; R. C. Palmer, *The County Courts of Medieval England, 1150–1350* (Princeton, NJ, 1982), 220–62.

justice—grew out of these developments, and gathered pace
during the later years of Edward I's reign.

The most striking symptom of change at this time was the
breakdown of the general eyre, whose last full visitation was
suspended in 1294.[34] The demise of the eyre has often been
seen as the prelude to the allegedly calamitous deterioration of
public order in the late middle ages,[35] and although recent
historians have debunked the myth of a golden age of public
order coinciding with that of the eyre, the latter still enjoys an
unduly inflated reputation in some quarters.[36] It is therefore
instructive to examine the extent of the eyre's criminal
jurisdiction and the reasons for its breakdown.

The general eyre was administered through itinerant
justices who travelled on county circuits throughout the
country at intervals which became progressively longer during
the thirteenth century as the business of the eyre increased.[37]
Justices in eyre were empowered to hear all pleas of writs, or
civil pleas, appointed before them, and all Crown pleas arising
since the last visit of the eyre.[38] The institution evolved in the
course of the twelfth century as a result of the increasing
concern of the royal courts for the administration of civil and
criminal justice, and was the instrument *par excellence* of
Angevin government. The civil pleas side dealt principally
with land litigation arising from the forms of action regularized
in Henry II's reign and available upon a chancery writ.[39] The
distinguishing feature of the eyre, however, was its jurisdiction

---

[34] D. Crook, 'The Later Eyres', *EHR* 97 (1982), 241–8.

[35] e.g. A. Harding, *The Law Courts of Medieval England* (London, 1973), 86–92;
H. M. Cam, *Studies in the Hundred Rolls*, Oxford Studies in Social and Legal History,
6 (Oxford, 1921) 82–3.

[36] Bellamy, *Public Order*, 1–2; Harding, *Law Courts*, 91–2. Cf. G. R. Elton, 'Crime
and the Historian', in J. S. Cockburn (ed.), *Crime in England, 1550–1800* (London,
1977), 10: 'It is really only from about 1660 that we again get the sort of continuous
record which the cessation of the great eyre terminated in the middle of the fourteenth
century.'

[37] Between 1176 and 1192 there were 11 visitations of the eyre, but only two
throughout the reign of Edward I: *Crown Pleas of the Wiltshire Eyre*, ed. C. A. F.
Meekings, Wiltshire Record Soc., 16 (Devizes, 1960), 4; D. W. Sutherland, *Quo
Warranto Proceedings in the Reign of Edward I* (Oxford, 1963), 25–30.

[38] *Crown Pleas of Wilts. Eyre*, 2.

[39] *The 1235 Surrey Eyre*, ed. C. A. F. Meekings, Surrey Record Soc., 31 (Guildford,
1979), 6, 26–87. For the records of the general eyre, see D. Crook, *Records of the General
Eyre* (London, 1982).

over Crown pleas, embodied in the *Capitula Itineris*, or articles of the eyre, upon which juries from the hundreds, boroughs, and liberties within a county were instructed to make returns.[40]

In the first half of the thirteenth century the articles of the eyre fell into three categories: the feudal and proprietorial rights of the Crown, such as wardships, marriages, and escheats; infringements of royal prerogatives and regulations, such as the rights of wreck and treasure trove, and the assize of wine; and presentments of death by felony or misadventure. The emphasis of the articles lay on the fiscal side and their criminal content was limited almost entirely to the presentment of homicide.[41] The eyre also heard appeals, or private accusations, concerning felony and trespass, and received indictments of suspected malefactors from the presenting juries.[42] The main purpose of the eyre was thus the enforcement of the Crown's financial rights; its effective criminal jurisdiction was confined largely to felony, and except in cases of violent death was far from systematic.[43] Much of the initiative for prosecuting even the most serious offences still lay with the private accuser.

The breakdown of the eyre was caused by the additional burdens thrust upon it in the second half of the thirteenth century.[44] The articles of the eyre were elaborated in 1254, and more extensively in 1278, to incorporate two areas of growing concern to the Crown: the unwarranted assumption of royal franchises, and the misdeeds of royal and seigneurial officials.[45] Such extensions of the eyre's competence brought a flood of new business. In particular, through the receipt of *querelae*, or plaints, against official abuses, a wide variety of lesser offences against persons and property was brought before the eyre and the central courts of the Crown. The scope of royal criminal

[40] Cam, *Studies in the Hundred Rolls*, 10; Sutherland, *Quo Warranto*, 35; *Crown Pleas of Wilts. Eyre*, 28–33.

[41] Ibid., 37–69; *Surrey Eyre*, 106; Harding, *Law Courts*, 66.

[42] *Crown Pleas of Wilts. Eyre*, 69–98.

[43] At the Shrops. eyre of 1256, for example, there were 30 appeals of felony, of which 4 resulted in conviction: 62 persons were indicted as suspected thieves or their accomplices, of whom 5 were convicted: Harding, *Law Courts*, 66–8; *Roll of the Shropshire Eyre of 1256*, ed. A. Harding, Selden Soc., 96 (London, 1980), pp. xvi–xvii.

[44] Harding, *Law Courts*, 86–8.

[45] Cam, *Studies in the Hundred Rolls*, 22–41; Sutherland, *Quo Warranto*, 17–28.

jurisdiction was thereby extended beyond felony to many trespasses.[46] Soon the eyre was entertaining plaints against offenders whether or not they were officials, and minor disputes which had formerly been settled in local courts came within the scope of central justice. This was a significant development, representing, in Professor Harding's words, 'the beginning of a second stream of English law'.[47]

The extra business soon became too much for the general eyre. In 1294 the second eyre of Edward I's reign was adjourned owing to the outbreak of war with France, and this proved to be the last such visitation attempted on a national scale. The eyre had been created in the twelfth century when its omnicompetence was appropriate to serve the needs of the Crown; with the rapid expansion of law and government in the following century it became increasingly unwieldy, and royal administration was driven to evolve more specialized institutions.[48]

The wars which began in 1294 lasted until the end of Edward I's reign. One of their chief domestic effects was a rise in violent disorder, which coincided with the demise of the eyre to precipitate a crisis of law enforcement in the early fourteenth century.[49] If the powers of the eyre have been exaggerated, its disappearance nevertheless left a gap in the judicial machinery which took over half a century of experiment and improvisation to fill.

Some measures had already been introduced during Edward I's reign in an attempt to relieve pressure of business on the eyre. By the early 1290s judicial commissioners were being organized on county circuits similar to the eyre, but with the more limited task of hearing assizes and delivering gaols.[50] Their work was complemented by the growing use of special oyer and terminer commissions for individual offences involving

---

[46] Harding, 'Plaints and Bills', *passim.*
[47] Ibid. 65–70.   [48] *Surrey Eyre*, 5.
[49] M. C. Prestwich, *War, Politics and Finance under Edward I* (London, 1972), 287–90; A. Harding, 'Early Trailbaston Proceedings from the Lincoln Roll of 1305', in R. F. Hunnisett and J. B. Post (edd.), *Medieval Legal Records Edited in Memory of C. A. F. Meekings* (London, 1978), 146–7; *Calendar of London Trailbaston Trials under Commissions of 1305 and 1306*, ed. R. B. Pugh (London, 1975), 2.
[50] R. B. Pugh, *Imprisonment in Medieval England* (Cambridge, 1968), 278–94. See ch. 2 n. 49.

trespass.[51] These measures provided only a partial solution, however, and in order to cope with the flood of plaints attracted by the Crown's new jurisdiction over trespass, the government resorted to general commissions of oyer and terminer. The aim was to relieve the pressure of business on the eyre in the hope that its visitations would be resumed.[52] In 1304 and 1305 the government, alarmed by the escalation of disorder throughout the country, issued numerous powerful oyer and terminer commissions which soon became known as 'trailbastons', after the gangs of malefactors armed with clubs who terrorized the countryside.[53] The trailbaston commissions were organized in five county circuits, and the justices heard private plaints as well as taking presentments from local juries. The articles of presentment were chiefly directed against violent breaches of the peace, especially organized violence involving extortion, and the abuse of legal procedure through bribery, maintenance, and intimidation.[54] The more serious 'enormous' trespasses were prosecuted at the king's suit, while persons indicted of lesser offences were released on security of good behaviour unless a private suit was brought against them.[55]

The trailbaston commissions were the first systematic attempt to deal with the expansion of royal criminal jurisdiction arising from the recognition of trespass as a Crown plea. Although trailbaston justices soon acquired powers of trying indicted felons at gaol delivery, most cases which came before them in their proper capacity were trespasses, often offences against the person not amounting to felony.[56] The petitionary nature of this jurisdiction emphasizes the dependence of the Crown on the private accuser.[57] The Crown

---

[51] R. W. Kaeuper, 'Law and Order in Fourteenth-Century England: the Evidence of Special Commissions of Oyer and Terminer', *Speculum*, 54 (1979), 734–84; E. Powell, 'List of Special Oyer and Terminer Proceedings, 1262–1443', unpublished PRO reading room list (1984).
[52] Harding, 'Trailbaston Proceedings', 149.
[53] *Cal. London Trailbaston*, 1–4; Cam, *Studies in the Hundred Rolls*, 74.
[54] Ibid. 75–6.
[55] Harding, 'Trailbaston Proceedings', 144–5; *Wiltshire Gaol Delivery and Trailbaston Trials, 1275–1306*, ed. R. B. Pugh, Wiltshire Record Soc., 33 (Devizes, 1977), 20–1.
[56] Ibid. 5–10.
[57] Cf. Harding, 'Trailbaston Proceedings', 150: 'It was assumed that behind all the presentments made to the inquests which the trailbaston oyer and terminer

characteristically exploited the situation: heavy fines for remission of imprisonment were the usual penalty imposed for trespasses, and trailbaston proceedings became notorious for their punishing financial exactions.[58]

In the wake of the trailbaston visitations, general oyer and terminer commissions became an established part of the judicial machinery.[59] During the fourteenth century the court of king's bench also came to be used in the suppression of disorder, setting out from Westminster to assume direct criminal jurisdiction over the shires through which it passed. King's bench assisted the trailbaston commissioners in the home counties in 1305, and was most active as an itinerant criminal court between 1320 and 1360.[60]

The measures so far discussed were short-term expedients designed to cope with immediate problems of law enforcement. The difficulties raised by the demise of the general eyre and the expansion of the Crown's criminal jurisdiction remained. At certain times both the oyer and terminer commission and the 'superior eyre' of king's bench seemed likely to become the cornerstone of a new judicial structure, but neither materialized as such.[61] What was required was a permanent staff of judicial officers in the localities, operating under central supervision. A solution was eventually found in the office of 'justice of the peace'.

The justice of the peace developed from the earlier 'keeper of the peace', whose functions had originally been chiefly of a military nature.[62] During the period of baronial reform

superseded there lay complaints from individuals . . . the private complainants were given a chance to prosecute trespasses before the justices . . .'.

[58] *Wilts. Gaol Delivery*, 24–5; *Cal. London Trailbaston*, 37–8; Cam, *Studies in the Hundred Rolls*, 73. Trailbaston commissions continued to be issued later in the fourteenth century, often in response to disorder with political overtones, as in 1321 and 1340. The term soon acquired a popular currency, however, and in the latter half of the century was used to denote any powerful oyer and terminer commission: ibid. 76–7; G. L. Harriss, *King, Parliament, and Public Finance in England to 1369* (Oxford, 1975), 280–7; Putnam, *Justices of the Peace*, p. xlvii.

[59] Kaeuper, 'Law and Order', 742–7; J. B. Avrutick, 'Commissions of Oyer and Terminer in Fifteenth-Century England', M.Phil. thesis (London, 1967), 12–42.

[60] See ch. 2 at nn. 86–91.

[61] Harding, *Law Courts*, 88–9; Putnam, *Justices of the Peace*, pp. xxxviii–xli; ead., *Shareshull*, 73, 134.

[62] A. Harding, 'The Origins and Early History of the Keeper of the Peace', *TRHS* 5th ser., 10 (1960), 85–91.

between 1258 and 1265 the keeper was given new functions, including the making of arrests and the hearing of inquests. The Statute of Winchester of 1285 invested him with regular police duties, so that by the end of the thirteenth century he was an important figure in the preservation of public order. He was therefore well qualified to receive on the Crown's behalf the trespass plaints which were flooding the judicial system at this time.[63] What the keeper could not do was determine the offences presented or bills submitted before him, and it was the acquisition of this power which transformed the keeper into the justice of the peace.

The course of this transformation has been traced by Professor Putnam.[64] Under Edward II regular commissions began to be issued to the keepers, and their numbers grew. At the same time their powers were increased to include the taking of felony indictments and the arrest of suspected malefactors.[65] The task of determining their presentments was assigned variously to supervisors of the keepers appointed for the purpose, or to regular gaol delivery justices.[66]

Although under Edward II some keepers were also appointed to gaol delivery commissions in the same county and thus acted as *de facto* JPs,[67] the Crown was reluctant to concede formal powers of determination to the keepers of the peace. In the mid-fourteenth century there was a protracted struggle between the central government and the magnates on one side, and the Commons in Parliament on the other, over the extent of the judicial powers to be granted to the keepers, later justices, of the peace.[68] The government and the magnates favoured a judicial system in the image of the general eyre, with authority firmly vested in the hands of itinerant professional justices, and expressed through powerful commissions such as those of trailbaston. They attempted to

---

[63] Ibid. 99–106.

[64] B. H. Putnam, 'The Transformation of the Keepers of the Peace into Justices of the Peace, 1327–80', *TRHS* 4th ser., 12 (1929), 19–48; ead., *Justices of the Peace*, pp. xxxviii–lvi.

[65] Ead., 'Transformation', 22–4; *Kent Keepers of the Peace, 1316–17*, ed. B. H. Putnam, Kent Records, 13 (Canterbury, 1933), pp. xv–xxi.

[66] Ibid.; *Rolls of Northamptonshire Sessions of the Peace*, ed. M. Gollancz, Northamptonshire Record Soc., 11 (Northampton, 1940), pp. xiii–xx.

[67] *Kent Keepers*, p. xxi. [68] Harriss, *Public Finance*, 401–10.

confine the keepers of the peace to a purely ancillary role,
working under the supervision of magnates and men of law.[69]
The Commons, representing the local gentry from whose
ranks the keepers of the peace were drawn, sought to gain a
greater say in the affairs of local government. They were
hostile to the unashamedly mercenary approach of the Crown
to its judicial responsibilities, and used their increasing
control over taxation as a bargaining counter to exact
determining powers for the keepers.[70]

The early years of Edward III's reign were the most
formative in the development of the office of JP. The keepers
of the peace were first granted powers of determination in
1329, only to have them withdrawn almost immediately when
Chief Justice Scrope attempted to restore public order
through trailbaston commissions and an abortive resurrection
of the general eyre.[71] During the 1330s the Commons
repeatedly attempted to secure for the keepers authority to
determine felonies and trespasses, but it was not until 1338
that powers of determination were restored to the peace
commissions. In 1344, under continued pressure from the
Commons, the Crown granted statutory powers of determination to the keepers when afforced by men of law. The
justices of the peace were finally established immediately after
the Black Death, when the shire gentry and the central
government were drawn together by a common interest in
enforcing the labour legislation, which, after 1359, the JPs
were called upon to administer.[72]

The judicial system which evolved in the middle of the
fourteenth century maintained a balance between local and
central interests, and this was reflected in the membership of
the peace commissions. JPs were chosen from three main
groups: magnates, gentry, and lawyers, marking the effective

[69] Putnam, 'Transformation', *passim*; ead., *Justices of the Peace*, pp. xxxviii–xlvii.

[70] Harriss, *Public Finance*, 401–2; see ch. 7 at nn. 98–102.

[71] Putnam, 'Transformation', 26–7; Crook, 'Later Eyres', 261–3; *The Eyre of Northamptonshire, 1329–30*, ed. D. W. Sutherland, Selden Soc., 97–8 (2 vols.; London, 1981–2) i, pp. xxii–xl.

[72] Putnam, 'Transformation', 27–46; Harriss, *Public Finance*, 403–5; E. Powell, 'The Administration of Criminal Justice in Late Medieval England: Peace Sessions and Assizes', in R. Eales and D. Sullivan (edd.), *The Political Context of Law* (London, 1987), 49–59.

amalgamation in the new office of the old keepers of the peace and their one-time supervisors.[73] Appointments were made by the chancery or the king's council, but were usually dictated by the realities of local politics: the ascendancy of a magnate in a county would be reflected in the number of his affinity serving on the peace commission.[74] Nevertheless the Crown did not totally lose control over local justice. Itinerant justices continued to operate on regular circuits for the holding of assizes, frequently in conjunction with the delivery of gaols. From 1330 responsibility for gaol delivery was permanently assigned to the circuit justices, who by this time were drawn from the judges and serjeants of the central courts.[75] The circuits soon proved their usefulness in providing the necessary administrative link between central and local justice. Besides delivering gaols and holding assizes, the justices performed a variety of functions.[76] From 1350 onwards they were also included in the peace commissions of each county within their circuit, and were invariably appointed to the quorum of those commissions—the inner circle of JPs, one of whom had to be present if cases of felony were to be determined.[77] Little study has been made of the connections between the JPs and the assize justices, but the co-operation between them was probably closer than has been assumed.[78] By 1370 the assize and peace commissions had emerged as the basic and complementary elements of the local judicial machinery of the Crown.

The development of this new judicial system was not achieved without difficulties, however, and the fourteenth century was a period of considerable turbulence. In particular

---

[73] Putnam, *Justices of the Peace*, pp. lxxix–lxxxiv; *Rolls of Northants. Sessions*, p. x.

[74] Putnam, *Justices of the Peace*, pp. lxxvi–vii; E. Powell, 'Public Order and Law Enforcement in Shropshire and Staffordshire in the Early Fifteenth Century', D.Phil. thesis (Oxford, 1979), 130–1. Only rarely was magnate influence upon the peace commissions challenged, as in Richard II's reign: see R. L. Storey, 'Liveries and Commissions of the Peace, 1388–90', in F. R. H. Du Boulay and C. M. Barron (edd.), *The Reign of Richard II: Essays in Honour of May McKisack* (London, 1971), 131–52.

[75] See ch. 2 at nn. 46–9.

[76] M. M. Taylor, 'The Justices of Assize', in J. F. Willard, W. A. Morris, and W. H. Dunham (edd.), *The English Government at Work, 1327–36* (3 vols.; Cambridge, Mass., 1940–50), iii. 219–47.

[77] Powell, 'Criminal Justice', 49–59.

[78] See ch. 2 at nn. 53–62.

the end of Edward II's reign and the first years of his sucesssor's were disorderly even by medieval standards. The breakdown of public order in the Midlands at this time has been documented through studies of criminal bands of gentry led by the Folville and Coterel families.[79] More generally the fourteenth century is notable for the suspicion and contempt in which royal justice was held and the hostility shown to its agents. Several royal judges met violent deaths: Roger Bellers was murdered by the Folvilles, Thomas Seton was stabbed to death in Fleet Street, Chief Justice Cavendish died at the hands of the rebels in 1381 and his successor Robert Tresilian at those of the Appellants in 1388.[80] Popular feeling was expressed in songs and ballads, where judges were portrayed as corrupt and oppressive, purveying false justice and quick to accept bribes from local magnates and prelates.[81]

This dissatisfaction with the legal system sprang from the disparity between the theory and practice of justice. The rapid expansion in the scope of royal jurisdiction from the reign of Henry II onwards was justified in terms of the higher standards of equity and impartiality available in the king's courts.[82] In practice royal judges systematically exploited their growing powers both to increase royal revenues and to amass private fortunes through fees and retainers from litigants. William Shareshull, who became chief justice of king's bench in 1350, was especially successful in extorting money through the courts.[83] Similarly royal judges exploited their position for their own enrichment. The retaining of judges by magnates and religious houses was already common in the thirteenth century, but as their influence extended with the boundaries of royal jurisdiction, the demand for their

[79] Stones, 'Folvilles', 117–36; Bellamy, *Public Order*, 69–88; S. L. Waugh, 'The Profits of Violence: The Minor Gentry in the Rebellion of 1321–2 in Gloucestershire and Herefordshire', *Speculum*, 52 (1977), 843–69.

[80] Stones, 'Folvilles', 119; *SKB*, vi, pp. xxvi–xxvii; vii, p. ix.

[81] Harding, *Law Courts*, 90–1; J. R. Maddicott, *Law and Lordship: Royal Justices as Retainers in Thirteenth- and Fourteenth-Century England*, Past and Present Supplement 4 (Oxford, 1978), 33–9; id., 'The Birth and Setting of the Ballads of Robin Hood', *EHR* 93 (1978), 285–6.

[82] *The Treatise on the Laws and Customs of . . . England Commonly Called Glanvill*, ed. G. D. G. Hall (London, 1965), 1–2; Palmer, *County Courts*, 141–2. See also ch. 4 at nn. 2–5.

[83] Putnam, *Shareshull*, 67. See ch. 7 at nn. 98–102.

services increased.[84] So also did popular outcry against the practice: the close association of many judges with a great lord or monastery was the cause of much of their unpopularity. It was no coincidence that the murder of Chief Justice Cavendish during the Peasants' Revolt in 1381 took place near Bury St Edmunds, for he had long been retained by the abbey.[85]

It is clear that there was a crisis of public order in fourteenth-century England, but it was associated with innovation and growth rather than degeneration. By 1370 a system for the administration of royal justice in the localities had emerged, based on the JPs and the assize circuits, which was to endure into the twentieth century.[86] By 1400 both the use of commissions as a fiscal weapon and the retaining of royal judges had largely disappeared. As to the commissions, it became customary for the king to lift the threat of a trailbaston or a renewed visitation of the eyre, or to issue general pardons, in exchange for regular parliamentary subsidies.[87] As to the retaining of judges, an intensive campaign against it was mounted in Parliament in the 1370s and 1380s. Popular hatred of corrupt judges was dramatically shown in the Peasants' Revolt, and retaining declined sharply in the 1390s.[88]

While it cannot be said that the problem of public order had been solved by the beginning of the fifteenth century, substantial advances had taken place since the breakdown of the general eyre. Far from marking a decline in the government's control over the localities, these developments strengthened it immeasurably, deriving as they did from a fundamental extension of the Crown's responsibilities for public order. One of the main instruments of change was the justice of the peace. The blatant self-interest of the magnates and gentry who served as JPs, and their readiness to exploit the peace commission as a weapon of faction in local politics, have been

[84] The problem was exacerbated by the laicization of the bench. By 1300 royal judges had largely ceased to be clerks content with benefices and were exploiting their wealth and expertise to accumulate large estates: Maddicott, *Law and Lordship*, 4–39.
[85] Ibid. 63–4.
[86] J. S. Cockburn, *A History of English Assizes, 1558–1714* (Cambridge, 1972), 1.
[87] Harriss, *Public Finance*, 405–9.
[88] Maddicott, *Law and Lordship*, 59–87.

widely condemned.[89] This cannot be denied, but it was
inevitable that, until such time as it had the resources to
maintain a standing army and police force, the Crown would
remain heavily dependent on the nobility and gentry for local
law enforcement. In those circumstances the king had to
tolerate a degree of crime and corruption among the governing
classes, and intervened only when a serious breach of the
peace occurred.[90] It is more significant that through their
inclusion in the peace commission the local gentry were
brought within the circle of government— a fitting acknowledgement of their role in the granting of taxation in
Parliament. Thereafter they were prepared to work increasingly
inside the judicial system, rather than to flout it directly, as
did the criminal gentry gangs at the beginning of Edward
III's reign. A streak of poacher remained in the gamekeeper;
but in the fifteenth century, as K. B. McFarlane observed, it
was safer and easier to subvert the law from within than to
break it outright.[91] A national framework of royal justice and
law enforcement had been established, and if the country
appeared more disorderly as a result, it was partly because
many offences hitherto outside the jurisdiction of the king's
courts were being brought before them. It is paradoxical that
the growth of royal jurisdiction should have given the late
middle ages such a bad name.

[89] Harding, *Law Courts*, 92–8; Bellamy, *Public Order*, 2; J. B. Post, 'Some
Limitations of the Medieval Peace Rolls', *Journal of the Soc. of Archivists*, 4 (1973),
633–9.
[90] B. A. Hanawalt, 'Fur Collar Crime: the Pattern of Crime among the Fourteenth-
Century English Nobility', *Journal of Social History*, 8, no. 4 (1975), 1–17.
[91] McFarlane, *Nobility*, 115–18.

PART I

Law, Justice, and Kingship

Concepts of Law, Justice, and Kingship in the Age of Henry V

WHILE IN exile with the defeated Lancastrians in France in the late 1460s, the former chief justice Sir John Fortescue wrote a treatise for Prince Edward, the son of Henry VI, instructing him in the laws of England. The *De Laudibus Legum Anglie*, written in the form of a dialogue between the judge and the prince, extolled the peculiar merits of English law by comparison with civil (or Roman) law, which, according to Fortescue, prevailed elsewhere in the world.[1] Much of the treatise is taken up with detailed examination of points of law and procedure where the two systems differed: inevitably the judge demonstrates that the laws of England are in every way more just and reasonable than civil law, so that the prince cannot help wondering 'why this law of England, so worthy and so excellent, is not common to all the world'.[2]

In view of his theme it is surprising that Fortescue's sources are not the classic texts of the common law. There are no references to 'Glanvill', 'Bracton', or *Fleta*, no commentary on Magna Carta or the statutes of Edward I. Instead Fortescue cites works and authors which place him firmly in the mainstream of political and legal theory in medieval Europe: the Bible, the *Institutes* of Roman law, Aristotle, St Thomas Aquinas, Giles of Rome.[3]

No doubt Fortescue's choice of sources was partly dictated by the purpose of his work. The education of a prince required

[1] John Fortescue, *De Laudibus Legum Anglie*, ed. S. B. Chrimes (Cambridge, 1942). The insular conceit that Roman law prevailed throughout the world except England appears to go back at least to the thirteenth century: *Bracton on the Laws and Customs of England*, ed. S. E. Thorne (4 vols.; Cambridge, Mass., 1968–77), ii. 19; cf. S. Reynolds, *Kingdoms and Communities in Western Europe, 900–1300* (Oxford, 1984), 44.

[2] Fortescue, *De Laudibus*, 66–7: in this passage the prince is referring to trial by jury.

[3] Ibid., pp. lxxxix–xc; cf. John Fortescue, *On the Governance of England*, ed. C. Plummer (Oxford, 1885), 96–100.

the inculcation of the general principles of law and justice rather than the technicalities of doctrine and procedure, which could be left to professional lawyers.[4] On the other hand Fortescue's extensive use of biblical quotation, and his reliance on the authority of Aristotle and Aquinas, reveal the theological and philosophical assumptions upon which English law continued to be grounded in the late middle ages.

The paradox of the *De Laudibus*, therefore, is that it stresses the unique character and superiority of English law while demonstrating that its foundations lay in a common European tradition.[5] In this respect the work is typical of much contemporary thinking in late medieval England about law, government, and kingship. Against the background of the broad intellectual inheritance based on Christianity, Roman law, and Aristotelianism, there was a growing sense, fostered by the emergence of Parliament and the depositions of 1327 and 1399, of the distinctiveness of English political and legal institutions.[6] Fortescue contrasted England's constitution as a *dominium politicum et regale*, where the king could make laws and levy taxes only with the assent of his subjects, with the *dominium regale* of France, where the king legislated and taxed his subjects at will.[7] French writers also discerned a contrast, but expressed it in terms less favourable to England. They dwelt upon the disconcerting frequency with which the English killed their kings, a point emphasized in fifteenth-century texts by illustrations showing royal corpses piled one on top of another.[8]

Fortescue attributed the special character of late medieval English institutions to the natural riches of the country and

[4] Fortescue, *De Laudibus*, 21–5, 135–7.
[5] Similarly Fortescue's famous discussion of the kingdom of England as a *dominium politicum et regale* derives from the continuator of Aquinas' *De Regimine Principum*, Ptolemy of Lucca: John Fortescue, *De Natura Legis Naturae*, ed. Lord Clermont (London, 1864), i. 16; id., *Governance*, 110–15; id., *De Laudibus*, pp. xciv, 25–33; M. Wilks, *The Problem of Sovereignty in the Later Middle Ages* (Cambridge, 1963), 202 n. 3.
[6] S. B. Chrimes, *English Constitutional Ideas in the Fifteenth Century* (Cambridge, 1936), 305.
[7] Fortescue, *Governance*, 109–18; id., *De Natura*, i. 16; Chrimes, *Constitutional Ideas*, 309–13.
[8] P. S. Lewis, 'Two Pieces of Fifteenth-Century Political Iconography', in id., *Essays in Later Medieval French History* (London, 1985), 191–2; cf. B. Guenée, *States and Rulers in Later Medieval Europe* (Oxford, 1985), 86–8.

the spirit of its inhabitants.[9] In fact it had more to do with the incessant financial demands of English kings and the precocious expansion of royal justice in the two centuries after 1150. The triumph of royal jurisdiction created the common law which Fortescue praised so highly. By concentrating judicial power in the king's hands to a degree unparalleled in the rest of Europe, however, it also posed acute problems regarding the exercise and limitation of royal power, for which the traditional authorities provided little guidance.[10]

The purpose of this chapter, therefore, is to examine the impact which the growth of royal jurisdiction had on theories of law and justice in England, and to assess contemporary opinion as to the powers and responsibilities of the king in the late middle ages. Much of the discussion will inevitably centre upon academic and legal treatises; the works of Fortescue, in particular, must form the basis of any analysis of fifteenth-century kingship.[11] An attempt will also be made to explore popular attitudes towards law and justice through sources such as contemporary literature, parliamentary petitions, and accounts of the Peasants' Revolt.

LAW AND JUSTICE IN LATE MEDIEVAL THOUGHT

During the late middle ages academic discussion of the nature of law and government was dominated by the thought of St Thomas Aquinas. Aquinas's great achievement, and the source of his influence throughout Western Europe in the fourteenth and fifteenth centuries, was to have reconciled Christian dogma with Aristotelian concepts of the natural origin of the state.[12] His success thus lay less in formulating

---

[9] Fortescue, *Governance*, 137–42; id., *De Laudibus*, 67–9, 177–9.

[10] See Reynolds, *Kingdoms and Communities*, 48–51. Some distinctive features of legal and political theory in late medieval and early modern England, such as Fortescue's explicit rejection of the Roman law maxim *quod principi placuit legis habet vigorem*, and the emerging doctrine of the king's two bodies, represent attempts to provide solutions to these problems: Fortescue, *De Laudibus*, 25; id., *Governance*, 112; E. Kantorowicz, *The King's Two Bodies* (Princeton, NJ, 1957), 3–23.

[11] Chrimes, *Constitutional Ideas*, 304–7.

[12] Wilks, *Problem of Sovereignty*, 118–48; *Aquinas*, x–xxiv. Unlike earlier Christian thinkers such as Augustine, Aquinas saw the institutions of government as necessitated not by the sinfulness of man but by nature. Following Aristotle, Aquinas saw man as naturally a social and political animal, and the state thus acquired

new concepts regarding law and the state than in restating traditional assumptions in Aristotelian terminology.[13] For Aquinas legal philosophy and political thought were merely subsidiary aspects of theology: the true end of man on earth was the attainment of salvation, and the function of government was to further that end by encouraging the virtuous Christian life.[14] It was a medieval commonplace that all law derived ultimately from the eternal law established by God for the ordering of His Creation, and this was Aquinas's starting-point. Mankind could not apprehend eternal law directly, but by applying reason might deduce a body of general principles based upon it, the law of nature, from which the positive law of human societies was derived.[15] Law was thus no mere human device, but divinely sanctioned, and positive law was invalid if it was not in accordance with natural, and thus eternal law.[16] In England 'Bracton' reached similar conclusions using the authorities of Roman and canon law, and later writers such as Fortescue and St German incorporated Aquinas's teachings into their own works.[17]

Aquinas's discussion of law emphasized the formal process of legislation by the authority of the ruling power. Thus the essence of positive law was that it should be enacted by the

validity and divine sanction as the fulfilment of man's earthly (though not his spiritual) end: ibid., 3.

[13] See Reynolds, *Kingdoms and Communities*, 319–26.

[14] Thomas Aquinas, *De Regimine Principum*, tr. G. B. Phelan as *On Kingship to the King of Cyprus* (Toronto, 1949) i. cc. 8–9, 14; cf. id., *Summa Theologica*, tr. the Fathers of the English Dominican Province (25 vols.; London, 1911–22), II. i, q. 91–2; *Aquinas*, xiv–v, 43–53, 73–7, 115–19; Wilks, *Problem of Sovereignty*, 122–6. Cf. Fortescue, *De Natura*, i. 44; id., *De Laudibus*, 11–15. Aquinas's assimilation of the Aristotelian concept of the state within the doctrinal framework of salvation is in marked contrast with the writings of William of Ockham and Marsilius of Padua, whose reading of Aristotle led them to see government as an end in itself, regardless of divine sanction, and to establish a sharp separation between man's terrestrial and spiritual ends: Wilks, *Problem of Sovereignty*, 84–117.

[15] Aquinas, *Summa Theologica*, II. i. qq. 91–7; *Aquinas*, 113–41.

[16] Aquinas, *Summa Theologica*, II. i. q. 93, art. 3; *Aquinas*, 121; cf. Fortescue, *De Laudibus*, 7–11; Wilks, *Problem of Sovereignty*, 210–17.

[17] *Bracton*, ii. 22–7. 'Bracton' adopts a broader interpretation of the law of nature than Aquinas, regarding it as applying to all animate creatures, rational and irrational. For Fortescue's views on the law of nature, see *De Natura*, i. 4–5; id., *Governance*, 116–18; Chrimes, *Constitutional Ideas*, 196–200; E. F. Jacob, 'Sir John Fortescue and the Law of Nature', *BJRL* 18 (1934), 359–76. Christopher St German, *Doctor and Student*, ed. T. F. T. Plucknett and J. L. Barton, Selden Soc., 91 (London, 1974), 8–37. See also *RP* v. 622–3.

ruler for the public good in accordance with natural law.[18]
Custom occupied a subsidiary, but still important place in his
scheme because its repeated practice was conducive to respect
for the law. New legislation which breached custom undermined the habit of observance and thus weakened the coercive
force of law. Aquinas also acknowledged some circumstances
in which custom could acquire the force of law if it was in
accordance with reason; notably where a community with the
power to enact its own laws through common consent
habitually observed a certain custom.[19]

English legal writers shared Aquinas's formalist view of law
and custom.[20] From 'Glanvill' onwards they drew the
distinction between law, as the positive enactment of the ruler,
and custom, as the body of traditional practices sanctioned
through long usage and implicitly confirmed by the ruler's
tolerance of them. Customs could be altered or abolished by
legislation if the ruler, in consultation with his subjects, saw
fit. Nevertheless all writers greatly respected the authority of
custom as an integral part of the laws of England. 'Glanvill'
and 'Bracton' took for granted the variety of local customs,
while Fortescue and St German regarded it, alongside
statutory legislation, as one of the main sources of common
law. The excellence of custom was invariably measured in
terms of its antiquity: in Fortescue's eyes English customs
were the best possible because they were older even than
Roman law and had been observed successively by the
Britons, the Romans, the Danes, the Saxons, and the
Normans.[21]

Aquinas's concept of justice followed from his analysis of
law: it was that quality manifested in the application of the
principles of natural law.[22] He quoted with approval the

[18] Aquinas, *Summa Theologica*, II. i, q. 95, art. 4; *Aquinas*, 131. See also ibid. 145: 'All
law proceeds from the reason and will of a legislator.'
[19] Aquinas, *Summa Theologica*, II. i, q. 97, art. 3; *Aquinas*, 145.
[20] *Glanvill*, 2, 139, 147; *Bracton*, ii. 19, 22; Fortescue, *De Laudibus*, 39–41; St
German, *Doctor and Student*, 45–55, 70–1.
[21] *De Laudibus*, 39–41; cf. *Bracton*, ii. 22: 'the authority of custom and long use is not
slight.' Cf. M. T. Clanchy, 'Remembering the Past and the Good Old Law', *History*,
55 (1970), 172; F. Kern, *Kingship and Law in the Middle Ages*, tr. S. B. Chrimes (Oxford,
1939), 149–80.
[22] Aquinas, *Summa Theologica*, II. ii, qq. 57–8; *Aquinas*, 163–7; Wilks, *Problem of
Sovereignty*, 210–11. Fortescue, *De Natura*, i. 36–8, saw justice as synonymous with the
law of nature.

Roman law maxim of Ulpian, 'justice is the constant and unfailing will to give each his right', which was also adopted by 'Bracton'.[23] Aquinas also saw justice as embracing the notion of equality and reciprocity, and it was this quality that Fortescue emphasized, citing the biblical equivalent of Ulpian's maxim, 'all things whatsoever ye would that men should do to you, do ye even so unto them, for this is the law and the prophets.'[24] During Fortescue's lifetime Bishop Stillington of Bath provided a more peculiarly English definition in his speech as chancellor to the Parliament of 1467: justice was the observance of the constitutional proprieties of the realm, and the discharge by each of the three estates of its responsibilities.[25]

Medieval ideas of law were closely bound up with the concept of reason, and this was a central element in Aquinas's thinking.[26] Eternal law was the application of divine reason to the universe, natural law the participation of rational creatures in the eternal law.[27] For Aquinas, therefore, human laws were just only in so far as they were reasonable. The identification of the two concepts was characteristic of legal theory and practice in England from the twelfth century onwards. The term *rationabilis* occurs frequently in the pages of 'Glanvill' and in Magna Carta, denoting custom, fairness, and proportion.[28] In the later middle ages natural law and reason were regarded as virtually synonymous, and were cited in the law courts as well as the treatises of Fortescue and St

[23] Aquinas, *Summa Theologica*, II. ii, q. 58, art. 1; *Bracton*, ii. 22–4; cf. Fortescue, *De Natura*, i. 35.

[24] Aquinas, *Summa Theologica*, II. ii, qq. 57, arts. 1–2; 58, art. 2; *Aquinas*, 163. The quotation, from Matt. 7: 12, the 'golden rule' which Fortescue took as the embodiment of the law of nature, was cited at the beginning of Gratian's *Decretum*: see Fortescue, *De Natura*, i. 4; id., *Governance*, 117; *Decretum Gratiani*, ed. E. Friedberg (Leipzig, 1879), *distinctio* 1; Chrimes, *Constitutional Ideas*, 199–200.

[25] *RP* v. 622–3: 'Wherfore first be asked, what is Justice? Justice is every persone to doo his office that he is put yn accordyng to his astate or degre, and as for this Lond, it is understoud that it stondeth by iij estates and above that oon principall; that is to witte Lordes Spirituell, Lordes Temporell, and Commons, and over that, State Riall above, as oure Soverayn Lorde the Kyng . . .'

[26] Kern, *Kingship and Law*, 153.

[27] Aquinas, *Summa Theologica*, II. i, q. 91, arts. 1–3; *Aquinas*, 113–15; cf. Fortescue, *De Natura*, i. 5; St German, *Doctor and Student*, 12–13.

[28] *Glanvill*, 2, 7, 13, 15, 108–12, 125, 138–9, 143, 145–7, 152; Magna Carta (1215), cc. 4, 5, 12, 15, 26 (J. C. Holt, *Magna Carta* (Cambridge, 1965), 316–37).

German.[29] Petitioners invoking the equitable jurisdiction of the king's council or the chancellor habitually requested the remedy demanded by law and reason.[30] In the political sphere the appeal to reason was made to legitimize acts of resistance or usurpation: the opponents of Edward II justified their actions by citing the king's departure from 'right reason',[31] while the alleged need to halt the subversion of the laws and customs of the realm, against all reason and justice, provided a pretext for Richard III's seizure of the throne in 1483.[32]

The abstract concepts of law, justice, and reason formulated by Thomas Aquinas may seem remote from the rough and ready practice of late medieval law courts, and indeed it is hard to imagine many JPs thumbing through the *Summa Theologica* after a hard day at the sessions. Nevertheless his definitions are relevant because they articulated principles fundamental to medieval thought. The beliefs that law was of divine origin, that it must accord with reason, and that justice entailed giving each man his right, were matters of more than academic interest. They provided a yardstick against which the everyday practice of law could be measured and its shortcomings exposed.

THE KING AND THE LAW

A medieval king had two fundamental duties: to defend his realm and to dispense justice. Just as he needed arms for defence against external enemies, so he needed laws to defend the realm against internal disorders.[33] In the early middle ages, however, the king's legislative and judicial functions were comparatively restricted. Legislation (or 'law-finding')

---

[29] See above, n. 17; Chrimes, *Constitutional Ideas*, 196–218; Fortescue, *Governance*, 206–7; St German, *Doctor and Student*, 12–19.

[30] *English Historical Documents, 1327–1485*, ed. A. R. Myers (London, 1969), 493–6; *Select Cases in Chancery, 1364–1471*, ed. W. P. Baildon, Selden Soc., 10 (London, 1896), 9, 23, 43, 51, 64, 81, 83, 104, 121, 124, 132; *Select Cases before the King's Council*, ed. I. S. Leadam and J. F. Baldwin, Selden Soc., 35 (London, 1918), 86, 95, 97, 119.

[31] *English Historical Documents, 1189–1327*, ed. H. Rothwell (London, 1975), 525–7; for the use of a similar justification by Richard the Marshal for his resistance to Henry III in 1233, see Kern, *Kingship and Law*, 88–9.

[32] *RP* vi. 240 (Chrimes, *Constitutional Ideas*, 197–8). For Edward IV's claim to the throne by the law of nature, see *RP* v. 464.

[33] *Glanvill*, 1; *Bracton*, ii. 19; Fortescue, *De Laudibus*, 3; id., *Governance*, 116.

and judgement were collective activities, undertaken by a community as a whole or its leading members. The king was the representative of the people he ruled, declaring law and passing judgement in consultation with his greatest subjects.[34] He was the custodian and guarantor of the laws of his people, not their creator.

Those traditional assumptions of the relationship between the king and the law contributed to the theories of kingship elaborated in academic and legal treatises from the twelfth century onwards. The king was judicially supreme within his kingdom; he had no earthly peer, but ruled under God and the law. He was therefore free from the sanctions of human laws, but not their obligations, for if he ignored them he undermined his own authority, since as 'Bracton' said, 'there is no king where will rules rather than law.'[35] The true king ruled according to law and for the common good, the tyrant according to his own will and private interests.[36] As long as the king did justice he was God's vicar on earth, his power within the kingdom analogous to that of God in the universe, but as soon as he fell into injustice he became the devil's minister.[37] Although the treatise writers emphasized the ruler's law-making powers at the expense of custom, the legislative process they outlined preserved his time-honoured obligation to consult the great men of the realm. The potentially absolutist maxim of Roman law, *quod principi placuit legis habet vigorem*, was defused in exactly this manner: what pleased the prince were not his own private whims but solemn deliberations conducted with his magnates.[38]

Important changes did, however, take place during the twelfth and thirteenth centuries which upset the traditional relationship between the king and the law. The revival of the study of Roman law and the rapid growth of canon law gave

[34] Kern, *Kingship and Law*, 70–5, 149–80; Reynolds, *Kingdoms and Communities*, 12–34, 250–62.

[35] *Bracton*, ii. 33, 305; F. Schulz, 'Bracton on Kingship', *EHR* 60 (1945), 151–65; B. Tierney, 'Bracton on Government', *Speculum*, 38 (1963), 303–5; Kern, *Kingship and Law*, 10.

[36] Aquinas, *De Regimine Principum*, i. cc. 1–3, 5–6, 14–15; *Bracton*, ii. 33, 305; Schulz, 'Bracton on Kingship', 151–3; Kantorowicz, *King's Two Bodies*, 143–59.

[37] *Bracton*, ii. 305; Aquinas, *De Regimine Principum*, i. cc. 12–13.

[38] See above, nn. 17–20; *Bracton*, ii. 305; Schulz, 'Bracton on Kingship', 153–6; Wilks, *Problem of Sovereignty*, 206–15; Kantorowicz, *King's Two Bodies*, 151–2.

new prominence to the legislative authority of the prince;[39] while the transition from oral to written record placed judicial procedure increasingly under the control of professional lawyers and judges, eroding collective forms of judgement. Nowhere were these changes more sweeping than in England, where the king had the administrative resources and the financial incentive to exploit his growing jurisdiction. The new common law of the royal courts soon gave the king a virtual monopoly of judgement; and although it grew out of feudal custom and made use of collective decisions in the form of juries, it was administered by a small group of legal experts answerable only to the king, giving him unprecedented control over justice.[40] By about 1200, therefore, the king had shaken off the traditional administrative and procedural constraints on his judicial power, and England had become one of the few regions in Europe where absolutism was regarded as a practical—and dangerous—possibility.[41]

The course of English politics over the following two centuries was determined by attempts to find a 'bridle' to limit the king's power and to subject it to the rule of law.[42] During the thirteenth century the baronial opponents of the king thought the solution lay in establishing a judicial body superior to the king to correct him when he deviated from the law. The essential principle of Magna Carta was that the king should observe the laws he had established, and the short-lived security clause of 1215 sought to create machinery to coerce the king by distraint if necessary.[43] During the reign of Henry III there was vigorous debate, culminating in the baronial wars of the 1260s, as to whether the king could legitimately be constrained by his subjects. The controversy was reflected in the pages of 'Bracton'. In one section of the work it was argued that the king had no peer, that he was under only God and the law, and that in imitation of Christ

[39] Kern, *Kingship and Law*, 71–2; Reynolds, *Kingdoms and Communities*, 39–50.
[40] Clanchy, 'Remembering the Past', 173–5; id., *From Memory to Written Record: England 1066–1307* (London, 1979), 1–57; R. V. Turner, *The King and His Courts* (Ithaca, NY, 1968), 56–166.
[41] Reynolds, *Kingdoms and Communities*, 48–51.
[42] Cf. *Bracton*, ii. 305: 'Let [the king] therefore temper his power by law which is the bridle of power.'
[43] Magna Carta (1215), c. 61; Holt, *Magna Carta*, 75–104, 239–43, 332–7.

his submission to law was a voluntary act. On the other hand in a later addition, the *addicio de cartis*, it was claimed that the king did have peers, namely the earls and barons of his *curia*, who should bridle him if he departed from the law.[44]

Henry III and his apologists reacted to the challenge to royal authority by restating the powers of kingship in the most exalted terms. Henry laid particular emphasis on the sacramental aspects of his office, promoting the saint's cult of Edward the Confessor, increasing the use of the liturgical *Laudes Regiae* in court ceremonial, and asserting his duty, as God's anointed, to direct the affairs of the Church.[45] The assumption of thaumaturgical powers by English kings, in imitation of the Capetian kings of France, may also have taken place during Henry's reign, and Edward I's use of the royal touch is well documented.[46]

The attempt to limit royal power by constraint using straightforward legal terminology and procedures foundered on the anomalous concept of the king being judged by his inferiors, and the practical difficulty that the king controlled the judicial system, a point trenchantly made by the baronial opponents of Edward II in 1308.[47] In this sense the conventional theoretical relationship between the king and the law propounded in thirteenth-century treatises proved an inadequate guide to the problem of restraining the king's new

[44] *Bracton*, ii. 33, 110, 305; G. T. Lapsley, 'Bracton and the Authorship of the "Addicio de Cartis" ', *EHR* 62 (1947), 1–19; Tierney, 'Bracton on Government', 313–15; Kantorowicz, *King's Two Bodies*, 154–9; Kern, *Kingship and Law*, 88–9, 130; M. T. Clanchy, 'Did Henry III Have a Policy?', *History*, 53 (1968), 203–16. The two sides of the argument, royal and baronial, are stated with admirable clarity in the Montfortian tract, *The Song of Lewes*, ed. C. L. Kingsford (Oxford, 1890), 16–31. For the view in Edward I's reign that the earls and barons were entitled to judge the king, see *The Mirror of Justices*, ed. W. J. Whittaker, Selden Soc., 7 (London, 1893), 7, 155–6; *Select Passages from the Works of Azo and Bracton*, ed. F. W. Maitland, Selden Soc., 8 (London, 1894), 125.

[45] Clanchy, 'Henry III', 206–14; E. Kantorowicz, *Laudes Regiae* (Berkeley, Cal., 1946), 176.

[46] M. Bloch, *Les Rois Thaumaturges* (new edn.; Paris, 1983), 98–104; F. Barlow, 'The King's Evil', *EHR* 95 (1980), 3–27; M. C. Prestwich, 'The Piety of Edward I', in W. M. Ormrod (ed.), *England in the Thirteenth Century* (Harlaxton, 1985), 124–7.

[47] 'It is not, however, possible by recourse to law to obtain redress, because there would be no other judges than royal judges, in which case, if the king's will was not accordant with right reason, the only result would be that error would be maintained and confirmed': *Select Documents of English Constitutional History, 1307–1485*, ed. S. B. Chrimes and A. L. Brown (London, 1961), 5; tr. in *Eng. Hist. Docs, 1189–1327*, 525–6.

judicial powers. The solution lay in another direction, in the developing concept of the Crown as an entity distinct from the person of the king and embodying the interests of the realm as a whole. In this way the king, whose jurisdictional supremacy had set him above and apart from his subjects, was reintegrated into the body of the community of the realm. It is no accident that whereas in the thirteenth century discussions of kingship centred on law, by the fifteenth century the emphasis was on the king as the head of the body politic.[48]

In England the concept of the Crown as embodying the inalienable possessions, powers, and rights held by the king to enable him to maintain his estate, goes back at least to the middle of the twelfth century.[49] It drew strength from comparison with the inalienability of the Church's estates under canon law, an analogy made explicitly by 'Bracton' in describing matters pertaining to the Crown as *res quasi sacrae*.[50] During the thirteenth century, apparently under prompting from the papacy, kings took an additional oath at their coronation to maintain the rights of the Crown.[51] This provided a powerful weapon in the king's hands, both to attack seigneurial franchises and to withstand papal claims.[52] Edward I in particular often referred to his oath to maintain the Crown, and in 1305 invoked it to secure his release by Pope Clement V from concessions he had made in the political crises since 1297, notably the *Confirmatio Cartarum* and the *Articuli Super Cartas*.[53]

This concept of the Crown was, however, a double-edged weapon, as the reign of Edward II demonstrated. In 1308 the terms of the coronation oath were changed to prevent future kings unilaterally defining the interests of the Crown to

[48] Kantorowicz, *King's Two Bodies*, 87–272; see below, n. 60.

[49] H. G. Richardson, 'The Coronation in Medieval England', *Traditio*, 16 (1960), 151–61; Kantorowicz, *King's Two Bodies*, 343–58; Holt, *Magna Carta*, 100–1.

[50] *Bracton*, ii. 57–8; Kantorowicz, *King's Two Bodies*, 164–89.

[51] Ibid. 350–7; H. G. Richardson, 'The English Coronation Oath', *Speculum*, 24 (1949), 48–51; id., 'Coronation in Medieval England', 160–3.

[52] See, for example, Henry III's address to the sheriffs at the exchequer in 1250, in which he instructed them not to allow alienations without warrant of rights pertaining to the Crown: Clanchy, 'Henry III', 216; see also Sutherland, *Quo Warranto*, 1–15, 182–4.

[53] Richardson, 'Coronation Oath', 48–51; *Foedera, Conventiones, Litterae*, ed. T. Rymer and R. Sanderson (20 vols.; London, 1704–35), ix. 978–9.

repudiate their undertakings as Edward I had done. Edward II was made to swear to uphold 'the laws and customs which the community of [the] realm shall have chosen'. A few months later the barons invoked the new oath to demand the removal of Piers Gaveston, justifying their opposition to the king on the argument that their allegiance lay rather to the Crown than the king's person, who might act against the Crown's interests.[54] The revision of the coronation oath and the drawing of the distinction between the king's person and his office demonstrated that the community of the realm was claiming an interest in the Crown, defined not merely as the king's inalienable rights, but as the corporate existence and welfare of the kingdom. By implication the king was part of the community of the realm himself, and answerable to it; he might therefore be removed if he broke his coronation oath and harmed the interests of the Crown.

Such ideas made possible the depositions of Edward II and Richard II. In both cases the king was deposed through armed force, but the distinction between the king and the Crown, and the king's legal obligations under the new coronation oath, justified the act of removal.[55] It is nevertheless striking that in 1327 and 1399 the intractable issue of judging the king, which had confounded thirteenth-century theorists and politicians, was evaded by presenting the depositions in the form of voluntary abdications, thus preserving the integrity of royal jurisdictional supremacy for the incoming king.[56]

The depositions of the fourteenth century therefore helped to redress the balance between king and law which had been upset during the reigns of the Angevin kings, but there were two other important contributory factors: the formalization of the common law and the rise of Parliament. During the thirteenth and fourteenth centuries royal judicial administration,

---

[54] *Select Documents . . . 1307–1485*, 5; tr. *Eng. Hist. Docs., 1189–1327*, 525–6.

[55] The charges laid against both Edward II and Richard II referred to the breach of their oaths and their dissipation of the Crown's resources: *Select Documents . . . 1307–1485*, 37–8; *RP* iii. 416–22.

[56] For the deposition of Edward II, see *Select Documents . . . 1327–1485*, 36–8, partly tr. in *Eng. Hist. Docs., 1189–1327*, 287–8; for that of Richard II, *RP* iii. 416–23, partly tr. in *Eng. Hist. Docs., 1327–1485*, 407–14. Cf. M. V. Clarke and V. H. Galbraith, 'The Deposition of Richard II', *BJRL* 14 (1930) 125–81, esp. 146–54. See below at n. 68.

like the exchequer, moved 'out of court'; that is to say it
became independent of the king's household and accumulated
a distinct body of rules, procedures, and precedents which
acquired statutory authority as 'due process of law', and with
which the king found it increasingly difficult to interfere.[57]
Indeed the expansion of royal jurisdiction helped to raise
expectations regarding the impartial administration of justice,
which stimulated the reform of judicial abuses in the
fourteenth century.[58] Secondly the emergence of Parliament in
the fourteenth century, both as the supreme judicial and
legislative authority of the kingdom and as a representative
tax-granting assembly, confirmed the king's obligation to seek
the assent of his subjects in matters of law and taxation, and
provided an institutional framework for the exercise of the
king's ancient duty to take counsel with the great men of his
kingdom.[59] It also gave physical expression to the concept of
the community of the realm, fostering the image of the
kingdom as a body politic with the king as its head.[60]

Sir John Fortescue's reflections upon the political and legal
institutions of fifteenth-century England thus represent the
fruit of over two centuries of constitutional struggle and
development. England was a *dominium politicum et regale*, where
the king ruled with the assent of his people. Laws were created
by king and subjects together, and the king swore to uphold
them by his coronation oath; as head of the body politic he
had no more power to change them than the head of a
physical body could change its nerves or deny blood to its
limbs.[61] The Roman law maxim *quod principi placuit legis habet
vigorem* had no place in English law, but applied only under

---

[57] By the mid-fourteenth century the rigidity of the rules of common law was such
as to precipitate the development of the equitable jurisdiction of the court of
chancery: see Baker, *Legal History*, 83–92; *The Reports of Sir John Spelman*, ed. J. H.
Baker, Selden Soc., 93–4 (2 vols.; London, 1976–7), ii. *84*; M. E. Avery, 'The History
of the Equitable Jurisdiction of Chancery before 1460', *BIHR* 42 (1969), 129–44.

[58] See Introduction at nn. 82–5; ch. 4 at nn. 117–22.

[59] See above, n. 34.

[60] Fortescue, *Governance*, 112; id., *De Laudibus*, 31–2; *Twenty-Six Political and Other
Poems*, ed. J. Kail, Early English Text Soc., 124 (London, 1904), 64–9. Chrimes,
Constitutional Ideas, 304–5; 322 n. 6; Kantorowicz, *King's Two Bodies*, 223–30. Harriss,
Henry V, 10.

[61] Fortescue, *Governance*, 110–13; id., *De Laudibus*, 25, 31–3, 79–81, 89–91;
Chrimes, *Constitutional Ideas*, 309–24.

dominium regale, as in France, where government was instituted
by the might of the prince alone.[62] The Crown was provided
with an inalienable endowment to enable the king to
discharge his responsibilities, foremost of which was justice:
not the least of the evils which flowed from the poverty of a
king was that he was driven to abuse his judicial powers to
raise money.[63]

Fortescue's analysis was of course couched largely in
mythological rather than historical terms. England was a
dominium politicum et regale, not because of the events of 1215,
1258, or 1327, but because the companions of Brutus had
freely chosen him to be their king when they made themselves
into a body politic called a kingdom.[64] In the *De Laudibus* there
are, however, references to kings of England who tried to
repudiate the laws of the land and introduce civil law;
references which perhaps echo the charges laid against
Richard II at his deposition.[65]

The picture which emerges from Fortescue's works, then, is
of a monarchy limited by law, Parliament, and the king's
coronation oath. Although kingship was the highest temporal
estate on earth, it was an office in which the king ministered
defence and justice to his subjects.[66] On the other hand
Fortescue did not imply that England was a constitutional
monarchy in the modern sense.[67] He perceived no alternative
to monarchy as a form of government. The ruler was an
integral part of the kingdom, and his selection was part of the
process whereby the body politic came into being: the king,
the law, and the kingdom all came into existence at the same
time as a result of the will of the people to provide for their

---

[62] Fortescue, *De Laudibus*, 25, 79; id., *Governance*, 112; Fortescue's rejection of *quod principi placuit* contrasts sharply with 'Bracton's' treatment of the maxim: *Bracton*, ii. 305; Chrimes, *Constitutional Ideas*, 324–8. A second Roman law maxim inimical to English law was cited in the charges against Richard II in 1399: see below, n. 65.

[63] Fortescue, *Governance*, 116, 119, 139–40.   [64] Ibid. 112.

[65] Fortescue, *De Laudibus*, 79–81, 89. See *RP* iii. 419 (33) for the accusation that Richard II refused to defend the laws and customs of the realm but claimed that the laws were in his own breast, and that he alone could change or establish the laws of the realm. Richard's alleged statement appears to follow the Roman law maxim, 'the prince has all the laws in the shrine of his breast': Kantorowicz, *King's Two Bodies*, 153.

[66] Fortescue, *Governance*, 127.

[67] What follows is drawn from Chrimes, *Constitutional Ideas*, 320–1; see also J. Gillespie, 'Sir John Fortescue's Concept of Royal Will,' *NMS* 23 (1979), 47–65.

common welfare. The body politic did not exist prior to the establishment of the king and therefore could not grant him powers or withhold them from him. Exercised within the limitations that we have noted, the king's power was absolute. Parliament and the king agreed on exactly this point at the beginning of the fifteenth century when, in the aftermath of Richard II's deposition, the Commons acknowledged that Henry IV should enjoy the same royal liberty as his predecessors; to which Henry replied that he would not use that liberty to turn the laws to his own will, as Richard II had done, but that he would uphold them in accordance with his coronation oath.[68]

Moreover it is clear that during the fifteenth century there was no slackening of belief in the sacramental and miraculous attributes of kingship. The king's touch continued to offer a cure for scrofula, and rings with healing powers were made from royal Good Friday offerings.[69] Indeed, one of Fortescue's arguments against the Yorkist claim to the throne through the female line was that a woman could not be anointed in the hands, and would thus lack thaumaturgical powers.[70] This may reflect the increasing significance attached to the use of unction at English coronations in association with the ampulla and holy oil of St Thomas of Canterbury, which was first used at the coronation of Henry IV.[71] In the thirteenth and fourteenth centuries the kings of England were anointed on the head, both with holy oil, and with the chrism in the manner of priests, despite papal prohibition.[72] In the course of the fifteenth century, however, this double anointing gave way to a single ceremony using the miraculous oil of St Thomas, which by legend had been given to the saint by the Virgin

---

[68] *RP* iii. 434.

[69] Bloch, *Rois Thaumaturges*, 89–183; see also Barlow, 'King's Evil', 3–27.

[70] Chrimes, *Constitutional Ideas*, 7–8; Bloch, *Rois Thaumaturges*, 111–12, 178, 223.

[71] Thomas Walsingham, *Annales Ricardi Secundi et Henrici Quarti*, in *Johannis de Trokelowe Annales*, ed. H. T. Riley, Rolls Ser. (London, 1866), 297–300; id., *Historia Anglicana*, ed. H. T. Riley, Rolls Ser. (2 vols.; London, 1863–4), ii. 239–40. For references to the use of the ampulla and holy oil of St Thomas at the coronations of Henry V and Henry VI, see J. W. McKenna, 'The Coronation Oil of the Yorkist Kings', *EHR* 82 (1967), 102–4.

[72] L. G. W. Legg, *English Coronation Records* (London, 1901), 93, 118–19; Kantorowicz, *King's Two Bodies*, 318–21; Richardson, 'Coronation in Medieval England', 116–17, 199–200.

Mary herself for the coronation of English kings.[73] Under the
Lancastrian and Yorkist kings, therefore, kingship retained,
perhaps even strengthened, its sacramental character.[74]

POPULAR ATTITUDES TOWARDS LAW AND JUSTICE

While it is easy to identify the medieval concepts of law and
justice formulated by theologians and legal theorists, and
promoted in official government sources, the attitudes of the
consumer—the litigant or defendant who experienced the
practical workings of justice—are far more elusive. Evidence
is not lacking for some groups in society, notably the shire
gentry, whose views were expressed in numerous parliamentary
petitions,[75] but lower down the social scale the sources are
fragmentary and difficult to interpret; we must rely largely on
popular songs and poems, particularly the outlaw ballads,
and the complaints thrown up by risings such as the Peasants'
Revolt and Cade's rebellion. Fortunately this is an area which
has received considerable attention from scholars, so that it
should be possible to draw some tentative conclusions.[76]

Of course there was no single authentic 'popular' attitude
towards justice in late medieval England. Many litigants were
also active participants in the administration of justice—a few

[73] W. Ullmann, 'Thomas Becket's Miraculous Oil', *Journal of Theological Studies*, 8
(1957), 129–33; McKenna, 'Coronation Oil', 102–4; T. A. Sandquist, 'The Holy Oil
of St Thomas of Canterbury', in M. R. Powicke and T. A. Sandquist (edd.), *Essays in
Medieval History Presented to Bertie Wilkinson* (Toronto, 1969), 330–44. For the origins of
the legend, see J. R. S. Phillips, 'Edward II and the Prophets', in W. M. Ormrod
(ed.), *England in the Fourteenth Century* (Woodbridge, 1986), 189–201. Bloch, *Rois
Thaumaturges*, 237–43, notes this as a pale imitation of the French legend of Clovis's
sainte ampoule.
[74] During the fifteenth century statements of the king's priestly character,
discredited by ecclesiastical writers since the twelfth century, again became
respectable: Bloch, *Rois Thaumaturges*, 210–11; see ch. 5 at nn. 68–70.
[75] M. C. Carpenter, 'Law, Justice and Landowners in Late Medieval England',
Law and History Review 1 (1983), 205–37, esp. 225–31.
[76] Ibid.; A. Harding, 'The Revolt against the Justices', in R. H. Hilton and T. H.
Aston (edd.), *The English Rising of 1381* (Cambridge, 1984), 165–93; R. W. Kaeuper,
'An Historian's Reading of the Tale of Gamelyn', *Medium Aevum*, 52 (1983), 51–62;
J. R. Maddicott, 'Poems of Social Protest in Early Fourteenth-Century England', in
W. M. Ormrod (ed.), *England in the Fourteenth Century* (Woodbridge, 1986), 130–44.
Something of a Robin Hood industry has grown up from analysis of the outlaw
ballads. The definitive work is J. C. Holt, *Robin Hood* (London, 1982), which provides
a full bibliography.

as officials, many more as jurors—whose attitudes depended on the stake they had in the legal system and the benefits they derived from it. The view of the landed gentleman, who served as sheriff or JP and who could exercise considerable influence in local courts through his social and political connections, contrasted radically with that of the unfree peasant caught in a pincer of exploitation between royal and manorial courts;[77] while the view of the clergy, who were subject to canon law as well as common law, differed from both. On some matters, however, there seems to have been universal agreement. Belief in the divine origin of law, in the equation of law and reason, and in justice as the intention to give everyone his right, which we have seen expounded by Aquinas and other writers, went virtually unquestioned. Such assumptions pervade the topical poems which have survived from the early fifteenth century,[78] and it was in similar terms that the Kentish rebels presented their grievances against Henry VI's favourites in 1450.[79] Equally universal were recognition and respect for the king as the ultimate guarantor of justice. In the outlaw ballads the king invariably appears in a favourable light. As Robin Hood proclaims in the *Gest of Robyn Hode*:

> I love no man in all the worlde
> So well as I do my kynge.[80]

The outlaws are in conflict, not with royal authority, but with corrupt local officials, and at the end of the *Gest*, as in the *Tale of Gamelyn* and *Adam Bell*, the king intervenes to pardon them and take them into his service.[81] In 1381 the password of the rebels was 'with King Richard and the true commons', and

[77] Cf. C. C. Dyer, 'The Social and Economic Background to the Rural Revolt of 1381', in R. H. Hilton and T. H. Aston (edd), *The English Rising of 1381* (Cambridge, 1984), 9–42.

[78] *Twenty-Six Political Poems*, 1, 9, 13, 18, 36, 45, 62–3, 65; J. Coleman, *English Literature in History, 1350–1400: Medieval Readers and Writers* (London, 1981), 98–109.

[79] HMC, *Eighth Report* (London, 1881), Appendix, 266–7: 'we crye dayly and nyztly that God of his ryztwysnesse schall take vengaunse on the false treytours of [the king's] ryall realme . . . he that is gylty wulle wrye azenst thus but schulle be aschamed to speke azenst resone.' Cf. R. Virgoe, 'The Death of William de la Pole, Duke of Suffolk', *BJRL* 47 (1964–5), 499–501.

[80] *Rymes of Robyn Hood*, ed. R. B. Dobson and J. Taylor (London, 1976), 107; cf. Holt, *Robin Hood*, 10–11.

[81] *Rymes of Robyn Hood*, 108–10, 269–70; *The Tale of Gamelyn*, ed. W. W. Skeat (Oxford, 1884), 33–4.

the Kentish rebels of 1450 saw themselves as the king's 'true liege men and best friends'.[82]

The popular consensus regarding the principles of justice was matched only by the unanimity with which all sections of society condemned the workings of the legal system; the former, indeed, provided the criteria for criticism of the latter.[83] The outlaw ballads, the innumerable verses on the 'abuses of the age', and the complaints of parliamentary petitioners all tell the same story of bribery and intimidation and of grasping, corrupt, and incompetent officials.[84] Contemporary sources stressed the degree to which the corruption of the legal system sprang from financial greed. Royal officials ruthlessly exploited the Crown's jurisdictional powers as a source of revenue, while the services of all judicial personnel could be bought and sold, from the king's judges who accepted retainers from powerful lords and institutions, down to humble jurors who could be bribed for a few pence.[85] A fifteenth-century poem, the *London Lickpenny*, compared the courts in Westminster Hall to market stalls, where litigants, clerks, and pleaders haggled over the price of justice.[86] It was not the law itself, therefore, which was seen to be at fault, but rather the manner of its application: the failings of the system sprang from the weakness and venality of the individuals by whom it was administered.[87]

Opinion varied as to how the defects of judicial administration might best be remedied. For sermon-writers, and the authors of 'abuses of the age' literature like John Gower, corruption of the law was part of a wider malaise. According to the prevailing social theory of orders or estates, society was an organic whole

[82] R. B. Dobson (ed.), *The Peasants' Revolt of 1381* (2nd edn.; London, 1983), 130; R. Faith, 'The "Great Rumour" of 1377 and Peasant Ideology', in R. H. Hilton and T. H. Aston (edd), *The English Rising of 1381* (Cambridge, 1984), 69; HMC, *Eighth Report*, App., 267.

[83] Kaeuper, 'Tale of Gamelyn', 58.

[84] Carpenter, 'Law, Justice and Landowners', 225–34; Kaeuper, 'Tale of Gamelyn', 54–9; V. J. Scattergood, *Politics and Poetry in the Fifteenth Century* (London, 1971), 320–3. For fuller discussion of the problem of judicial corruption in late medieval England, see ch. 4.

[85] See ch. 4 at nn. 111–20. Maddicott, *Law and Lordship, passim*; see also Coleman, *English Literature in History*, 66–7, 103–4, 113–17, 151–3; G. R. Owst, *Literature and Pulpit in Medieval England* (2nd edn.; Oxford, 1961), 338–49.

[86] *Historical Poems of the Fourteenth and Fifteenth Centuries*, ed. R. H. Robbins (New York, NY, 1959), 130–4.

[87] *Reports of Sir John Spelman*, ii. 83.

within which each estate had essential functions and duties. The failure of any estate to discharge its duties produced discord and tensions to which all the evils of the age were attributable.[88] Thus, according to Gower's *Vox Clamantis*, the turmoil of late fourteenth-century England was caused by the laxity and worldliness of the clergy, the greed and vainglory of the knights, the rebelliousness of the peasants, and the avarice of the lawyers.[89] The remedy for society's ills lay in moral and spiritual regeneration, a revival of Christian values throughout society.

At the other extreme from this religious idealism was what William Langland in *Piers Plowman* called 'Folville's laws', after the notorious Midland gang who murdered one royal judge and kidnapped another: this was the rough but true justice of the outlaw ballads, where the wronged man took the law into his own hands.[90] In the *Tale of Gamelyn* the hero, falsely outlawed, rescues his brother as he is about to be condemned to death by a corrupt judge and jury, and dramatically turns the tables:

> He ordeyned him a quest of his men so stronge;
> The Iustice and the scherreve bothe honged hye,
> To weyven with the ropes and with the wynde drye;
> And the twelve sisours (sorwe have that rekke!)
> All they were hanged faste by the nekke.[91]

In general, as Dr Carpenter has pointed out, such scenes were the 'fantasy of wish-fulfilment'.[92] Only in times of revolt or severe political breakdown, such as the late 1320s and early 1330s, during which the Folvilles flourished, were they played out in reality. Perhaps the most graphic image of the Peasants' Revolt is the macabre puppet-show enacted at Bury St Edmunds, where the rebels beheaded the prior of Bury and Chief Justice John Cavendish, whom they regarded as having been in corrupt alliance, and placed their heads on pikes:

---

[88] Owst, *Literature and Pulpit*, 210–374; Coleman, *English Literature in History*, 113–56; Scattergood, *Politics and Poetry*, 264–376.

[89] *The Major Latin Works of John Gower*, tr. E. W. Stockton (Seattle, Wash., 1962): Coleman, *English Literature in History*, 138–56.

[90] William Langland, *The Vision of William Concerning Piers the Plowman*, ed. W. W. Skeat (2 vols.; Oxford, 1886), i. 564–5 ('B' text, passus xix, ll. 239–41; 'C' text, passus xxii, ll. 245–7); Stones, 'Folvilles', 117–36.

[91] *Tale of Gamelyn*, 33.   [92] Carpenter, 'Law, Justice and Landowers', 231.

they put the head of the prior to the justice's head, now to his ear as though seeking advice, now to his mouth as though showing friendship, wishing in this way to make a mockery of their friendship and counsel which was between them during their lives.[93]

The defects of judicial administration were in fact too deeply engrained in the fabric of medieval society to be remedied by spiritual revival or violent self-help.[94] The real value of such debate and complaint lies in their revelation of contemporary expectations of the legal system. The fundamental paradox in popular attitudes towards justice in late medieval England—reverence for the principles of law and contempt for its practice—was reflected in numerous lesser contradictions. On one hand the shire communities constantly petitioned Parliament for firm action to maintain public order; on the other they were reluctant to accept the intrusions of the king's justices.[95] Aristocratic landowners looked to the king to uphold the highest standards of justice, while expecting him to bend the law in their favour.[96] Peasant communities might show a superstitious reverence for the authority of written records, as in 1377, when many of them obtained exemplifications of Domesday Book; whereas in 1381 they indulged in an orgy of documentary destruction.[97] Rebels and outlaws, even in their acts of defiance, mimicked the forms and procedures of law.[98]

Such ambivalence in popular attitudes towards justice was caused in part by tensions generated throughout English society by the rapid expansion of royal justice between 1150 and 1350.[99] The new procedures made available in the royal courts were undoubtedly very popular, in the sense that they were much used by litigants. On the other hand the expansion of royal justice threatened the autonomy of all local communi-

---

[93] Maddicott, *Law and Lordship*, 63, citing *Memorials of Bury St Edmunds*, ed. T. Arnold, Rolls Ser. (3 vols.; London, 1890–6), iii. 128–9.

[94] See ch. 4 at nn. 103–16.

[95] Harding, 'Revolt against the Justices', 171–3; Carpenter, 'Law, Justice and Landowners', 228–31.

[96] Ibid. 209–13.

[97] Faith, 'Great Rumour', 43–70; Dyer, 'Rural Revolt', 39–41; Harding, 'Revolt against the Justices', 178–80.

[98] For the mock trial of Justice William Shareshull at Ipswich in 1344, see ch. 4 at n. 10. For the writ of 'Lionel, king of the rout of raveners', see Stones, 'Folvilles', 134–5. See also the trial scene in the *Tale of Gamelyn*, 33.

[99] See Introduction at nn. 33, 82–8; Maddicott, 'Poems of Social Protest', 142–3.

ties, from the shire and lordship down to the village, undermining their ability to administer their own affairs without external intervention.[100] Furthermore the sweeping jurisdictional claims made on the Crown's behalf greatly exceeded its administrative resources, raising expectations of justice which could not be met.[101]

The landowning classes adapted very successfully to these changes. Although the growth of royal justice eroded their private, territorial jurisdictions, the king lacked the resources to administer the new system without their co-operation. They were able to exercise considerable influence over the development of royal judicial institutions, and moulded them for their own advantage. The interests and autonomy of the gentry communities of the shires, which had been threatened in the thirteenth and early fourteenth centuries, were thereby secured, and a durable *modus operandi* established between the Crown and the local landed power.[102]

The effects of judicial transformation were far more traumatic amongst the lesser communities of manor, village, and seigneurial town, which were least well placed to withstand the intrusions of royal justice or to profit from the professionalization of the law and the use of written records.[103] It has been persuasively argued that, in demanding observance of the 'law of Winchester' at Smithfield in June 1381, Wat Tyler was referring to the Statute of Winchester of 1285. This statute, with its local public order provisions, represented 'an ideal of communal self-policing' for the peasantry, an ideal which became increasingly remote with the judicial developments of the fourteenth century. The common law as yet afforded no protection of the rights of unfree tenants against manorial lords, whereas the latter enjoyed a growing armoury of legal resorts which enabled them to attempt the enforcement

---

[100] For the expansion of royal justice at the expense of local jurisdictions, see J. B. Post, 'Local Jurisdictions and Judgment of Death in Later Medieval England', *Criminal Justice History*, 4 (1983), 1–21; Palmer, *County Courts*, 141–262; Baker, *Legal History*, 21–5.

[101] Kaeuper, 'Tale of Gamelyn', 59; Carpenter, 'Law, Justice and Landowners', 213. See ch. 4 at nn. 2–21.

[102] See ch. 4 at nn. 2–7; Carpenter, 'Law, Justice and Landowners', 214–17, 226–30; Harding, 'Revolt against the Justices', 180–3.

[103] The following paragraph draws heavily on Faith, 'Great Rumour', 43–70, and Harding, 'Revolt against the Justices', 166.

of increased services and restrictions on wage levels and labour mobility, and to erode customary rights of common.[104] Many peasant and urban communities nevertheless fought tenacious rearguard actions, some lasting several decades, to defend their customary rights. The strength of such communities lay in their cohesion and the astonishing power of their collective memory, but they lacked the documentary evidence now required to prove their claims in court; hence their search for a single authoritative document, such as Domesday Book or the legendary charter of King Offa at Bury St Edmunds, which would vindicate their rights against the charters, deeds, and confirmations of their masters.[105] On rare occasions they might appeal directly to the king himself for justice, as the tenants of Crondall in Hampshire did successfully in 1364.[106]

It was obvious, however, that the law was stacked in favour of the landlords, not only by virtue of their participation in judicial administration, but also through their retaining of royal judges, which remained common until the 1390s.[107] Tenants' daily experience of the courts was a sour parody of their expectations of equity and justice, promoted by contemporary sermons and royal propaganda. The frustration and resentment this generated was expressed in the murders of central court judges, JPs, and jurymen and the destruction of legal records during the Peasants' Revolt. In this sense the rising was no mere outburst of aimless violence, but an eloquent statement by the peasant rebels and their artisan and urban allies that they too expected justice of the legal system, an expectation consistently disappointed over the previous generation.[108]

[104] Dyer, 'Rural Revolt', 23–32. Cf. N. M. Fryde, 'A Medieval Robber Baron: Sir John Molyns of Stoke Poges, Buckinghamshire', in R. F. Hunnisett and J. B. Post (edd.), *Medieval Legal Records Edited in Memory of C. A. F. Meekings* (London, 1978), 204–5; Maddicott, *Law and Lordship*, 37–9; J. H. Tillotson, 'Peasant Unrest in the England of Richard II: Some Evidence from Royal Records', *Historical Studies*, 16 (1974), 1–16.

[105] Faith, 'Great Rumour', 64–5; E. M. Hallam, *Domesday Book through Nine Centuries* (London, 1986), 100–4.

[106] Faith, 'Great Rumour', 56; for a similar appeal to Henry IV, see *PPC* ii. 110. The problems faced by peasant communities when forced into litigation to defend customary rights against local landlords is well illustrated by the dispute over tracts of common fenland between Crowland abbey and the neighbouring townships of Moulton and Weston, and Spalding and Pinchbeck, in the early fifteenth century: see E. Powell, 'Arbitration and the Law in England in the Later Middle Ages', *TRHS* 5th ser., 33 (1983), 58–9, and refs. there cited.

[107] See Introduction at nn. 84–8.   [108] Maddicott, *Law and Lordship*, 62–3.

PART II

The Machinery of Criminal Justice in Late Medieval England

The previous part examined the theoretical foundations of the law in medieval England and established its close association with the idea of kingship. The administration of justice was one of the king's main responsibilities, and his judicial powers grew rapidly during the middle ages. We must now look at the practical workings of the law. How extensive was royal criminal jurisdiction by the fifteenth century? What machinery was available to the king to enforce the criminal law, and how did it function? What was the broader impact of the judicial system on late medieval society? The following three chapters will attempt to answer each of these questions in turn.

2

Royal Jurisdiction over Crime, and the Structure of the Legal System

MODERN LAW takes for granted a simple conceptual distinction between criminal and civil law. Crime is an offence against the public authority, an act punishable by law as being forbidden by statute or contrary to the public interest; whereas tort, or civil wrong, is a matter of private redress for offences against individuals. The great legal treatises of the twelfth and thirteenth centuries, 'Glanvill' and 'Bracton', followed Roman law in drawing this distinction, at least in theory, and equated the public authority with the king's peace.[1] In practice, however, it was (and still is) notoriously difficult to draw the line between crime and tort in medieval English law.[2] 'Even at the present moment', wrote F. W. Maitland in 1895, 'we can hardly say that *crime* is one of the technical terms of our law', and his comment applies *a fortiori* to the middle ages.[3] The Latin word *crimen*, from which the English term, current in the middle ages, derives, was applied indiscriminately to both crime (in the modern sense) and sin. The adjective *criminalis* was frequently used with reference to mortal sin.[4] In medieval usage, therefore, crime had very broad connotations, implying an offence not merely against the public authority, but against the law of God. Crime did not, however, acquire a technical meaning in law: 'Bracton' sustained the distinction between crime and tort by

---

[1] *Glanvill*, 3–4; *Bracton*, ii. 282–3.
[2] Baker, *Legal History*, 411–12; Milsom, *Historical Foundations*, 403–4.
[3] Pollock and Maitland, *History of English Law*, ii. 573.
[4] See the relevant entries in R. E. Latham (ed.), *The Dictionary of Medieval Latin from British Sources* (Oxford, in progress); and S. Kurath and S. M. Kuhn (edd.), *The Middle English Dictionary* (Ann Arbor, Michigan, in progress).

concentrating on procedure rather than substantive law.[5] Some of the offences thus lumped together as criminal, notably the felonies, were obviously crimes in the broad sense: in the legal jargon they were *mala in se* as well as *mala prohibita*. Others, such as forgery and concealment of treasure trove, were included because of the infringement of the king's authority and interests. Criminal legal procedure was clearly distinguished by a greater rigour of process and by the bodily punishments involved: death, mutilation, or exile. In 'Bracton''s day, however, it was not yet possible to assume that crime was prosecuted by indictment at the suit of the Crown and tort at the suit of the party by writ or bill. Crime and tort were not mutually exclusive concepts: a crime was a private wrong as well as a public offence, and the Crown remained heavily dependent on private appeals of felony to bring such offences to its notice.[6]

The criminal law of the thirteenth century depicted in 'Bracton' was transformed by developments later in the middle ages, above all by the great extension in the scope of royal jurisdiction. Before 1250 minor wrongs, or trespasses, and some forms of theft, were deemed breaches merely of the sheriff's or the lord's peace, to be dealt with in local courts.[7] From the end of Henry III's reign, however, such offences came to be seen increasingly as contrary to the king's peace, giving rise to actions of trespass by writ or bill. All that was required to bring the case before a royal court was the allegation that the act had been committed with violence and in breach of the king's peace: *vi et armis et contra pacem*.[8] Trespass thus became a Crown plea and technically criminal, since the offence to the public authority was punished by a fine, even when the action was brought at the suit of the party.[9]

To view all trespass actions in such a light, however, would bring within the scope of late medieval criminal law much of

---

[5] *Bracton*, ii. 282–3, 290–1, 297–8; Pollock and Maitland, *History of English Law*, ii. 464–8, 499–501.

[6] *Bracton*, ii. 298.   [7] *Glanvill*, 4, 177; *Bracton*, ii. 409–11.

[8] Baker, *Legal History*, 56–9; Milsom, *Historical Foundations*, 285–92; Harding, 'Plaints and Bills', 65–71.

[9] Pollock and Maitland, *History of English Law*, ii. 464; Milsom, *Historical Foundations*, 287.

what is now considered tort, since the allegation of a violent breach of the king's peace soon came to be used as a fictional device designed to bring the matter within the jurisdiction of the royal court.[10] Here the mode of prosecution becomes significant for the first time. For whereas felony could be prosecuted equally well by the Crown or the individual, civil trespass at the suit of the party came to be distinguished from criminal trespass, or misdemeanour, brought at the king's suit by indictment. The beginnings of this bifurcation are visible in the trailbaston inquiries of the early fourteenth century, where in cases of 'enormous trespasses' defendants were made to answer at the king's suit if the individual failed to prosecute his complaint.[11] The process was hastened by the expansion of the royal machinery of criminal justice in the fourteenth century, and particularly by the rise of the justices of the peace with their quarterly sessions for receiving and trying indictments.[12]

Well before 1400, therefore, the king's criminal jurisdiction had grown from treason and felony, a select group of very serious crimes prosecuted either by indictment or at the suit of the party, to include a much larger range of offences normally prosecuted by indictment. The appeal of felony survived as a private criminal action after 1300, probably because of its usefulness to injured parties seeking compensation from the offender.[13] It is important, however, not to exaggerate the distinction between civil and criminal offences which arose as the result of the changes outlined above. There remained a considerable overlap between Crown prosecution and private litigation: as Professor Plucknett long ago suggested, the taking of chattels could be couched as felonious or trespassory, and prosecuted by an appeal of larceny, an indictment of larceny, an indictment of trespass, or a civil action of trespass.[14] Although the responsibility for the prosecution of crime fell

---

[10] With the emergence of trespass on the case in the late fourteenth century, the *vi et armis* fiction became unnecessary for non-violent wrongs to sound in trespass. See Baker, *Legal History*, 57–8; Milsom, *Historical Foundations*, 286–305.

[11] Harding, 'Plaints and Bills', 76.

[12] See Introduction at nn. 62–72.   [13] See ch. 3 at nn. 29–36.

[14] T. F. T. Plucknett, 'A Commentary on the Indictments', in B. H. Putnam (ed.), *Proceedings before the Justices of the Peace in the Fourteenth and Fifteenth Centuries: Edward III to Richard III*, Ames Foundation (Cambridge, Mass., 1938), pp. clviii–x.

increasingly upon the crown after 1300, the older assumption survived that the king and the injured party could both have an active legal interest in a case, and this helped to blur the distinction between criminal and civil law.

In the late middle ages royal criminal jurisdiction was divided into three categories: treason, felony, and trespass.[15] These were determined by the gravity of the offence, and were distinguished by the type of procedure and punishments involved. Treason was defined under the Statute of Treasons of 1352 as compassing and imagining the death of the king, his consort, or eldest son; violating his consort, or eldest unmarried daughter, or the wife of his eldest son; levying war against the king in his realm or adhering to his enemies; counterfeiting the great seal or the coinage; and slaying the treasurer, chancellor, or judges in open court.[16] It was extended by construction early in the reign of Henry IV to include the speaking of words intended to incite his subjects against the king.[17] The statute also defined petty treason as the slaying of a master by his servant, a husband by his wife, or a prelate by his clerical subject. Convicted traitors were dragged to execution on a hurdle; women were burned, men hanged and sometimes disembowelled or dismembered.[18] Offenders convicted of high treason forfeited their estates and goods to the Crown, while the estates of those convicted of petty treason passed to the immediate lord after the Crown had wasted them for a year and a day. The felonies— homicide, rape, robbery, larceny, arson, and breach of prison while under arrest for felony—were the ancient pleas of the Crown over which royal jurisdiction had been claimed as far back as the twelfth century or earlier.[19] All felonies were

---

[15] Pollock and Maitland, *History of English Law*, ii. 462–518; T. F. T. Plucknett, *A Concise History of the Common Law* (5th edn.; London, 1956), 424–505; J. B. Post, 'Criminals and the Law in the Reign of Richard II', D.Phil. thesis (Oxford, 1976), 204–66.   [16] 25 Edward III st. 5 c. 2.

[17] J. G. Bellamy, *The Law of Treason in England in the Later Middle Ages* (Cambridge, 1970), 116–23. For other extensions of the law of treason under the Lancastrians, see ch. 5. at nn. 64–6.

[18] Bellamy, *Law of Treason*, 149–58; id., *Public Order*, 188–9. For executions for treason in Henry V's reign see *SKB* vii. 237–9; KB 9 (court of king's bench, ancient indictments)/209, m. 27.

[19] Pollock and Maitland, *History of English Law*, ii. 478–511; H. N. Schneebeck, 'The Law of Felony in Medieval England from the Accession of Edward I to the Mid-

punishable by death, and a felon's estates escheated to his lord after the king's year, day, and waste. Criminal trespasses, or misdemeanours as they subsequently came to be termed, fell into two groups: common law trespasses, such as non-felonious taking of goods, and assault; and statutory trespasses enacted by Parliament, which covered a wide range of economic and administrative offences such as usury, bribery of officials, paying excessive wages, and using false weights and measures.[20] Process on trespass indictments began with summons and distraint rather than arrest, as in felony, and punishment almost invariably took the form of a fine.

THE JUDICIAL STRUCTURE

The starting-point for any study of the workings of justice in late medieval England, as the previous chapter has shown, was the person and office of the king. The central duty of kingship was the dispensation of justice. Perhaps the classic image of this function of a medieval king is provided by Jean de Joinville, who portrayed his master Louis IX of France sitting under an oak tree at Vincennes receiving petitioners and dispensing justice.[21] Such informality was no longer conceivable in late medieval England, although kings still presided occasionally in person over their courts in the late fifteenth century.[22] Joinville's description nevertheless exemplifies very well the importance of easy access to royal justice, which in the late middle ages, despite the rapid development of judicial institutions, continued to focus on the person of the king himself.[23] The simplest method of seeking justice was

Fourteenth Century', Ph.D. thesis (Iowa, 1973). The old felony of mayhem—inflicting an injury which reduced the victim's ability to fight—was still actionable by appeal, but as an indictable offence had been largely absorbed into trespassory assault. In 1414, during the superior eyre in Staffs, an indictment of felonious mayhem was reduced to trespass by the court: KB 9/113, m. 22.

[20] Pollock and Maitland, *History of English Law*, ii. 511–18; Putnam, *Justices of the Peace*, pp. cliv–clx; Harding, *Law Courts*, 86–98.

[21] Jean, Sire de Joinville, *The Life of St Louis*, in *Chronicles of the Crusades*, tr. M. R. B. Shaw (Harmondsworth, 1963), 177.

[22] Ross, *Edward IV*, 398, 401–2; Bellamy, *Public Order*, 12.

[23] One of the demands made by the rebels led by Jack Cade in 1450 was that all subjects should have free access to the king to seek justice: HMC, *Eighth Report* (London, 1881), 267, art. 6.

the written petition or plaint direct to the king, stating some wrong suffered by the petitioner and seeking redress.[24] At the highest levels—in Parliament, the king's council, the court of chancery, and subsequently in star chamber—justice was sought in this way by petition. The jurisdiction of chancery and star chamber soon became as institutionalized as that of the common-law courts, but in their origins they reflected the expectation of litigants that the king had the authority and the responsibility to provide an equitable remedy which could not be obtained elsewhere because of the shortcomings of the common law or the power of an opponent.[25]

The judicial authorities closest to the king, the council and Parliament, dealt with criminal matters as part of their general concern for the maintenance of law and order. The council could not impose sentences of loss of life or limb or forfeiture of property, but could imprison and levy fines. Owing to the sparsity of the surviving council records it is difficult to gauge the amount of judicial business which came before it, but it appears to have been particularly concerned with the investigation of treason and outbreaks of riot and serious disorder involving magnates and gentry.[26] Thus early in Henry IV's reign several friars who had been arrested for preaching the imminent return and restoration of Richard II were brought before the council for interrogation, while under Henry V Henry Ducheman was examined for seditious words he had spoken against the king's conduct of the siege of Rouen.[27] In 1392 the earl of Devon was summoned before the council to answer charges of maintaining criminals and obstructing royal justices, and was subsequently imprisoned.[28]

---

[24] The direct appeal to the sovereign survives as a regular legal procedure in the Channel Islands in the form of the *clameur de haro*: *Financial Times*, 29 Apr. 1985.

[25] Harding, *Law Courts*, 98–109; J. F. Baldwin, *The King's Council in England during the Later Middle Ages* (Oxford, 1913), 236–306; Avery, 'Equitable Jurisdiction', 129–44.

[26] Bellamy, *Law of Treason*, 151–6; Harding, *Law Courts*, 105–6. The council's jurisdiction in riot was recognized in the Statutes of Riots of 13 Henry IV c. 7 and 2 Henry V st. 1 c. 8.

[27] KB 27 (court of king's bench, plea rolls)/559, Rex, m. 20; 565, Rex, mm. 3, 4d, 5d; see ch. 5 at n. 12. Bellamy, *Law of Treason*, 117, 152–3.

[28] *Select Cases before the Council*, 77–81; M. Cherry, 'The Courtenay Earls of Devon: the Formation and Disintegration of an Aristocratic Affinity', *Southern History*, 1 (1979), 92.

The Bedford riots of 1437 and 1439 between supporters of
Lord Fanhope and Lord Grey were investigated in council in
Henry VI's reign, as were the early stages of the feud between
the earl of Devon and Lord Bonville in 1440–1.[29] The council
was also the forum in which matters of general policy were
discussed and judicial appointments considered.[30]

Parliament was the highest court of the realm, where the
decisions even of the court of king's bench might be reviewed
and overturned, where peers were tried before the House of
Lords and where, at times of political crisis such as 1376,
1386, and 1450, the king's ministers were impeached for
misconduct.[31] In routine criminal matters Parliament's function
was less judicial than legislative: parliamentary statutes were
instrumental in reshaping the machinery of criminal justice
through the establishment of the justice of the peace, and in
extending the criminal law through measures such as the
Statutes of Riots and Forcible Entry.[32] Occasionally extraordinary measures might be authorized in Parliament to deal
with specific outbreaks of disorder. In 1410, for example, a
petition from Staffordshire, cataloguing the attacks of Hugh
Erdswick and his followers upon Lancastrian retainers and
officials, was converted into an indictment and sent to king's
bench for determination. If they failed to appear the accused
were to stand convicted without trial and to forfeit all their
lands and chattels to the Crown.[33]

Beneath Parliament and the conciliar courts royal justice
was dispensed by a network of courts which administered the

[29] *Select Cases before the Council*, 104–7; *PPC* v. 35–9, 57–9, 158–61, 165, 173–5;
Storey, *House of Lancaster*, 87–92. The fullest treatment of the Bedford riots is to be
found in P. Maddern, 'Violence, Crime and Public Disorder in East Anglia, 1422–
1442' D.Phil. thesis (Oxford, 1985), 223–53.

[30] *PPC* i. 107–13; ii. 166; iii. 5, 25, 302.

[31] *The Memoranda de Parliamento of 1305*, ed. F. W. Maitland, Rolls Ser. (London,
1893), pp. lxxvi–lxxxix; Plucknett, *Common Law*, 200–5. For examples of king's bench
decisions reviewed in Parliament, see *RP* ii. 330; iii. 330–6, 461. Formal judgment
was rendered against Sir John Oldcastle, Lord Cobham, as a peer in the 1417
Parliament: ibid. iv. 107–9.

[32] Putnam, 'Transformation', 19–48; Bellamy, *Public Order*, 145, 190–1; see id.,
Criminal Law and Society in Late Medieval and Tudor England (Gloucester, 1984), for a
detailed but idiosyncratic study of the statutory extension of the criminal law in the
fifteenth and sixteenth centuries.

[33] *RP* iii. 630–1. The device was given statutory sanction at the Leicester
Parliament of 1414: see ch. 7 at nn. 28–9.

common law. At the centre of this network were the four great courts which sat at Westminster, all dating from the late twelfth century: chancery, exchequer, king's bench, and common pleas. Of these, only king's bench was involved to any extent in the administration of criminal justice. As the name suggests, the court was particularly associated with the person and interests of the king; proceedings before it were still recorded as taking place *coram rege*. It was the most senior of the royal courts, subordinate only to Parliament, and could correct errors in law and procedure made in lower courts, including common pleas. Otherwise the court's jurisdiction encompassed any case in which the Crown had an interest.[34] The court's business was divided into the plea side, where suits of the party were heard, and the Crown side, where actions were brought on the king's behalf, usually by indictment.[35] Apart from appeals of felony, which were dealt with on the plea side, criminal matters came before the Crown side of the court.[36]

The criminal business of king's bench fell into three broad categories: the prosecution of treason; its jurisdiction at first instance within the county in which it sat; and the supervision of lower criminal courts, which arose from the court's powers of review. King's bench was the only permanent common-law court empowered to deal with treason, and indictments or appeals from lesser jurisdictions such as gaol delivery and peace sessions which related to treason had to be determined there.[37] Cases investigated by the king's council were often referred to king's bench for determination.[38] Where treasonable offences were widespread the government responded by the

---

[34] *SKB* ii, pp. xl–xlii; Turner, *King and His Courts*, 36–9.

[35] This division of business was reflected in the organization of the king's bench plea roll, where the plea side membranes were placed at the beginning, followed by the Crown side, or 'Rex' section. Cases on the Crown side also included business relating to royal fiscal or territorial rights.

[36] For the continuing popularity of the appeal of felony in the fifteenth century, see ch. 3 at nn. 34–6.

[37] In Hilary term 1415 king's bench called up the record of the trial at gaol delivery of William Glover, indicted at Coventry for clipping coin. The trial had been suspended by a writ *nullatenus procedatis* the previous July: KB 9/204/3, mm. 33–5; 207/1, mm. 29–30; KB 27/615, Rex. m. 46d. Cf. JUST 3 (gaol delivery rolls)/188, m. 28.

[38] See above, nn. 26–7.

issue of commissions of inquiry returnable in king's bench, as for example in the wake of the Lollard revolt of 1414, or during the spate of counterfeiting provoked by the shortage of coin during Henry V's reign.[39] More often, however, treason prosecutions proceeded piecemeal upon the appeals of approvers—accusations made by confessed criminals who turned king's evidence and accused their associates.[40]

King's bench possessed criminal jurisdiction at first instance within the county where its sessions were being held, as a result of its powers as a 'superior eyre', acquired in the fourteenth century. Since its regular home was at Westminster, this usually meant Middlesex, and the court took presentments from juries of the county every term, periodically delivering the king's bench marshalsea prison of Middlesex offenders.[41] Elsewhere king's bench supervised criminal jurisdiction at one remove through its extensive powers of review, and there was a variety of writs, such as *certiorari* or *terminari*, that could be used to summon indictments from a local jurisdiction.[42] Some cases were referred to king's bench by the central court justices in their capacity as circuit judges and JPs. In Michaelmas 1412, for example, Hugh Huls, a justice of king's bench and assize judge on the Oxford circuit, returned into court the record of a Staffordshire peace sessions indictment against William de Herton and others for breaking into the king's park at Tamhorn.[43] In 1414 the assize judges of the northern circuit delivered to the court a large file of Yorkshire indictments taken before them at a joint assize and peace

---

[39] See ch. 6 n. 59; ch. 10 n. 55.

[40] F. C. Hamil, 'The King's Approvers', *Speculum*, 11 (1936), 238–58; Hunnisett, *Medieval Coroner*, 69–74. It is interesting to note how the content of approvers' appeals varied according to the anxieties of the government at any given time. Early in Henry IV's reign there were several appeals concerning Ricardian conspirators: e.g. *SKB* vii. 126–8, 133. Under Henry V approvers' appeals were a prime source of accusations against supporters of John Oldcastle: KB 9/205/1, m. 15; KB 27/631, Rex, m. 8; 652, Rex, m. 14.

[41] Middlesex indictments take up a substantial part of all king's bench term indictment files (PRO class KB 9). King's bench's trailbaston jurisdiction in Middlesex was of great future significance, since the bill of Middlesex, which brought a vast amount of litigation into king's bench after 1450, had its origins in the court's power to hear suits brought by bill from the county in which it sat: M. Blatcher, *The Court of King's Bench, 1450–1550* (London, 1978), 111–37. See below at nn. 86–91 for the role of king's bench as a superior eyre.

[42] Putnam, *Justices of the Peace*, pp. lxiv–lxxii.   [43] KB 9/200, mm. 21–2.

session in August of that year.[44] Most cases, however, probably came into court as a result of private initiative: defendants might pay to have a case removed to king's bench in the hope of securing release from prison or obtaining a favourable verdict.[45]

If the central courts at Westminster formed the heart of the judicial system, its arteries were the six circuits of assize and gaol delivery.[46] The assize judges were drawn from the judges and serjeants of the central courts, and went on circuit twice a year, usually in the Lent and summer vacations, dealing with both civil and criminal business.[47] The judges received their power under two separate commissions. The assize commission empowered the judges to hear all possessory assizes arising within the counties of their circuit. This was the original purpose of the assizes (hence their name), but in the late middle ages the judges' work on the civil side came to consist increasingly of *nisi prius* business (that is, cases delegated to them by the central courts as a matter of administrative convenience to avoid the delays involved in summoning juries to Westminster).[48] On the criminal side, the commission of gaol delivery empowered the judges to deliver the gaols within their circuits of prisoners arrested on charges of felony. The link between assize and gaol delivery commissions had been permanently established by 1330, but the two functions remained distinct: although general assize commissions covered the whole of a given circuit, gaol delivery commissions were always specific to a given gaol.[49]

The biannual assizes proved a highly successful vehicle for the transmission of central government to the provinces, and

[44] KB 9/205/1, mm. 1–14, at m. 11.

[45] Post, 'Criminals and the Law', 275–7; *SKB* vii. 109–11.

[46] For the organization of the assize circuits, see Powell, 'Criminal Justice', 58. There exists no study of the medieval assizes comparable with Cockburn, *Assizes*, for the early modern period. See Pugh, *Imprisonment*, 278–94; Taylor, 'Justices of Assize', 219–47; M. Gollancz, 'The System of Gaol Delivery as Illustrated in the Extant Gaol Delivery Rolls of the Fifteenth Century', MA thesis (London, 1936).

[47] The authoritative work on serjeants is J. H. Baker, *The Order of Serjeants at Law*, Selden Soc., Suppl. Ser., 5 (London, 1984). Parts of the northern circuit were visited only once a year: see Cockburn, *Assizes*, 19, 45.

[48] Taylor, 'Justices of Assize', 240; Cockburn, *Assizes*, 134–50.

[49] *Calendar of General and Special Assize and General Gaol Delivery Commissions on the Dorses of the Patent Rolls, 1377–99* (London, 1977), 1–31; Gollancz, 'Gaol Delivery', 85–95.

the duties of the assize judges were often augmented by *ad hoc* judicial or administrative commissions. In 1421, for example, the judges of the home, Oxford, and western circuits were commissioned to inquire into the escapes of felons or traitors.[50] Of more permanent significance was the association of the assize judges, from the mid-fourteenth century, with the work of the JPs as the latter gained the power to hear and determine indictments for felony. The determining powers of the JPs could be exercised only when members of the quorum, learned in the law, were present, and from 1350 onwards assize judges were appointed to the quorum of each county peace commission within their circuit.[51] In addition the peace commission reserved certain offences for determination by the circuit judges.[52]

Some evidence, such as the records of payments of JPs, suggests that the assize judges rarely sat at peace sessions, and it has been assumed that their supervision of the county peace commissions was largely a formality.[53] Professor Putnam found no significant link between their activities and those of the assize judges, and regarded the latter as 'competitors' of the JPs in a struggle over the local criminal jurisdiction of the Crown. It was only in the course of the fifteenth century, she argued, that assize judges were regularly appointed JPs in each county of their circuit, thus acquiring the threefold commission of assize, gaol delivery, and the peace which made them dominant in provincial government under the Tudors.[54]

There is evidence, however, that the links between assizes and peace sessions were much closer than Putnam suspected. The practice of appointing assize judges to the peace commissions of their circuit occurred as early as 1350, and from that time the determining powers of the JPs were regulated by the Crown through the use of the quorum, particularly as regards their felony jurisdiction.[55] Between

---

[50] *CPR, 1416–22*, p. 421.

[51] Powell, 'Criminal Justice', 49–59. Cf. Cockburn, *Assizes*, 87.

[52] Putnam, *Justices of the Peace*, pp. xxi, xxvi. Between 1418 and 1422 the peace commission reserved all difficult cases of felony for determination before the assize judges. See ch. 10 at n. 14.

[53] *The Victoria County History of Wiltshire*, vol. v., ed. R. B. Pugh and E. Crittall (Oxford, 1957), 34; Putnam, *Justices of the Peace*, p. lxxxiii.

[54] Ibid., pp. xxxvi–lvi.   [55] Powell, 'Criminal Justice', 49–59.

1350 and 1394 there were only two brief periods when JPs were empowered to determine felonies without the presence of one of the assize judges. From 1394, following a parliamentary statute, the quorum for felony was extended to include two men of law of the county as well as the assize judges, in order to ease the burden on the latter.[56]

While fifteenth-century JPs undoubtedly exercised their felony jurisdiction,[57] the more serious cases continued to be referred from peace sessions to the assizes, as is shown by the high proportion of cases at gaol delivery brought on indictments taken before the JPs.[58] It also appears that, as in the sixteenth century, joint sessions of the peace and gaol delivery were often held while the assize judges were out on circuit. This is suggested by anecdotal evidence, such as the letter written to Henry V by Robert Waterton in 1420, announcing his intention to recruit troops at the Yorkshire assizes: 'upon Wednesday next shall your justice sit at York upon the deliverance of the gaol there and a session of the peace also . . .'.[59] The suggestion is strengthened by the fact that peace sessions and assizes were often held at the same time. In Staffordshire, each year between 1409 and 1413, the judges at the summer assizes also presided over a session of the peace.[60] The records of the East Anglian circuit between 1422 and 1442 reveal thirty-six occasions upon which peace sessions were held at the time the assizes would also have been sitting, although in only twelve instances does a record of assize or gaol delivery survive.[61] Finally, entries on assize rolls show circuit judges taking recognizances for the maintenance of the peace in their capacity as JPs.[62] The evidence, while not

---

[56] 17 Richard II c. 10. The two periods were 1361–4 and 1380–2.

[57] See ch. 10 at nn. 12–13.

[58] During Henry IV's reign 47% of defendants tried at gaol delivery in Cambridgeshire, and 58% on the Oxford circuit, were arraigned on peace indictments: Gollancz, 'Gaol Delivery', 230.

[59] *Original Letters Illustrative of English History*, ed. H. Ellis, 1st ser. (3 vols.; London, 1824), i. 6–7 (spelling modernized). I am very grateful to Professor R. L. Storey for this reference.

[60] JUST 3/189, 197 (gaol delivery rolls, 1399–1422); JUST 1 (eyre rolls, assize rolls, etc.)/750–1, 814, 1515, 1525 (assize rolls, 1399–1422); JUST 1/815 (peace roll, 1409–14).

[61] Maddern, 'Violence, Crime, and Public Disorder', 113–14, 363–5.

[62] e.g. JUST 1/1502, mm. 70, 112, 160, 171, 190, 196, 201 (1390–6); 1521, mm. 4,

conclusive, confirms that assize judges periodically attended peace sessions, and implies that assizes and peace sessions functioned in association rather than in competition with each other.

The duties of the justices of the peace, the principal local agents of royal justice in the late middle ages, were defined by the peace commission which appointed them.[63] The opening paragraphs prescribed, in general terms, enforcement of the Statutes of Winchester, Northampton, and Westminster for the maintenance of the peace. More specifically it gave the JPs responsibility for implementing the Statutes of Labourers, the Statutes of Livery, and, by the end of Henry V's reign, for measures against Lollardy and coining. The succeeding paragraphs detailed the JPs' competence to hear and determine felonies and trespasses, and authorized them to take surety of the peace from those who threatened disorder or assault. Legislation of the reigns of Richard II and Henry IV also empowered JPs to deal summarily with riot and forcible entry, giving them particular responsibility for the arrest and punishment of rioters.[64]

Although the JPs were the junior partners of the assize judges in the administration of criminal justice, they shared responsibility with the latter for the trial of felons, both under the terms of the peace commission and under *ad hoc* gaol delivery commissions.[65] As we have seen, statutory provision was made in 1394 for gaols to be delivered by local men of law on the county peace commission, and in addition frequent commissions were issued, usually to a group of JPs, for the single delivery of a gaol.[66] There is clear evidence that between 1399 and 1422 gaols on the Oxford circuit were delivered by JPs outside assizes.[67] The suspension of the

---

13d, 23d, 35 (1408–11); 1530, mm. 16d, 18d, 20 (1414–22); 1537, mm. 8, 10d, 12 (1425–7); cf. *The Shropshire Peace Roll*, ed. E. G. Kimball (Shrewsbury, 1959), 116.

[63] Putnam, *Justices of the Peace*, pp. xx–xxix.

[64] 15 Richard II c. 2; 17 Richard II c. 8; 13 Henry IV c. 7. See also ch. 3 n. 9; ch. 7 at n. 26.

[65] Post, 'Criminals and the Law', 43–6; Putnam, *Justices of the Peace*, pp. xxxvi–liv.

[66] *Cal. Assize and Gaol Delivery Commns., 1377–99*, 29. See above at n. 56.

[67] Gollancz, 'Gaol Delivery', 63–4; B. H. Putnam (ed.), *Early Treatises on the Practice of the Justices of the Peace in the Fifteenth and Sixteenth Centuries*, Oxford Studies in Social and Legal History, 7 (Oxford, 1924), 88–9.

possessory assizes between 1415 and 1421 because of the French wars may have encouraged the practice by disrupting the routine of circuit visitations and thus of biannual deliveries at assizes.[68] Since gaol delivery commissions were not invariably entered on the patent rolls, it is not always possible to tell in such cases whether the justices had been specially commissioned or were, as men of law, acting by virtue of their powers as JPs. This may reflect a genuine uncertainty, which undoubtedly existed in the sixteenth century, as to the precise extent of their criminal jurisdiction,[69] and emphasizes the fluidity of relations between the assize judges and the JPs. If the former sometimes sat as JPs, the latter might equally deliver gaols. It would therefore be unwise to draw too sharp a distinction between their functions.

The meteoric rise of the JPs after 1350 overshadowed, though it did not entirely supplant, the functions of the two older officials concerned with the administration of criminal justice in the shires: the coroner and the sheriff. The office of coroner had originally been set up to serve the general eyre by keeping the record between visitations of all Crown pleas to be presented before it. The taking of inquests in cases of homicide and sudden death originally formed only a part of a coroner's duties. With the breakdown of the eyre at the end of the thirteenth century the office declined in importance, and in the late middle ages coroners' business was largely confined to inquests and to recording approvers' appeals and the abjuration of felons—the procedure whereby a felon confessed his crimes and was sent into exile through a designated port.[70] Coroners also had to attend the county court to record exactions to outlawry.[71] The coroners remained an essential part of the local judicial machinery: their responsibility for inquests necessitated that they be permanently resident in the county, and their regular attendance at gaol delivery meant they were often called upon to serve on trial juries.[72]

[68] See 9 Henry. V st. 1 c. 3; ch. 10 at nn. 5–13.
[69] Cockburn, *Assizes*, 87–93.
[70] Hunnisett, *Medieval Coroner*, 37–54. See also P. Brand, 'Chief Justice and Felon: The Career of Thomas Weyland', in R. Eales and D. Sullivan (edd.), *The Political Context of Law*, (London, 1987), 27–47.
[71] See ch. 3 at n. 50.   [72] Ibid., at n. 78.

The principal judicial duties of the sheriff, as distinct from his executive responsibilities for writ-serving and arrests, sprang from his presidency of the county court and supervision of the work of the hundred courts. In the late middle ages the county court continued to be the centre of a county's political life, where shire-knights were elected, parliamentary petitions prepared, and government proclamations read.[73] It also retained certain judicial functions: exaction to outlawry could only be carried out there, and appeals of felony recorded.[74] The court of the hundred was held every three weeks, and its business consisted of private litigation similar to that of the county court. The hundred bailiff, or in the case of a private hundred the lord's steward, presided over the sessions.[75] Twice a year the sheriff held his tourn, or view of frankpledge, in each royal hundred to review the organization of adult males into tithings, and to receive presentments from a hundredal jury for any offences which had occurred in the hundred since the last tourn. Fines were imposed on minor offenders, while process was issued for the arrest of accused felons for trial at gaol delivery.[76] The lords of private hundreds and liberties usually supervised view of frankpledge and some were entitled to hold biannual tourns, or courts leet, of their own.[77] Tourns and leets survived the advent of the JPs, but their importance as agencies of criminal justice was greatly reduced. The very fact that the sessions of the peace were quarterly, and the tourn biannual, must have enabled the former to absorb much of the business of the latter, and by the early fifteenth century trial at gaol delivery upon an

[73] J. R. Maddicott, 'The County Community and the Making of Public Opinion in Fourteenth-Century England', *TRHS* 5th ser., 18 (1978), 27–43.
[74] Hunnisett, *Medieval Coroner*, 56–61. The court also had jurisdiction over private personal actions, of which the commonest were trespass and debt: Palmer, *County Courts*, 141–306.
[75] H. M. Cam, *The Hundred and the Hundred Rolls* (London, 1930), 179–85; G. D. G. Hall, 'Three Courts of the Hundred of Penwith', in R. F. Hunnisett and J. B. Post (edd.), *Medieval Legal Records Edited in Memory of C. A. F. Meekings* (London, 1978), 169–96.
[76] The articles of presentment embraced both minor offences liable to amercement, and more serious crimes, upon which the sheriff would issue process returnable at gaol delivery: W. A. Morris, *The Frankpledge System* (New York, NY, 1910), 112–50. For the articles of the tourn, see 12 Edward 1 c. 4.
[77] Cam, *Hundred Rolls*, 185–7.

indictment from the tourn or leet was the exception rather than the rule.[78]

The machinery of criminal justice outlined above was not the only means available to the king for law enforcement. Extraordinary commissions issued in chancery were used to deal with particular cases, ranging from widespread public disorders such as the Peasants' Revolt to the individual complaints of private parties.[79] There was a great variety of such commissions, but the two main categories relating to criminal justice were commissions of oyer and terminer and of inquiry.[80] A commission of oyer and terminer empowered the recipients to hear and determine certain specified offences, and could be adapted to cover as broad a range of cases as necessary. The commission of the peace, which has been mentioned above, was one form of oyer and terminer. Such permanent adaptations apart, oyer and terminer commissions were extraordinary, *ad hoc* devices. They fell into two categories, special and general, which were distinguishable by their content and mode of issue.[81] Special commissions were issued to hear and determine specific offences, usually trespass. They were initiated at the suit of the injured party, and were available from chancery, like ordinary writs *de cursu*, on the chancellor's own authority.[82] General commissions were issued on the orders of the king and council to deal with a wide range of offences, which might include treason and

[78] Post, 'Local Jurisdictions', 13–14. Post suggests that the triumph of quarter sessions took place more quickly in counties with a few, mainly royal, hundreds, such as Warwicks., Leics., and Staffs., than in counties with numerous hundreds, many of them private, such as Hants and Glos. One of the most vigorous private jurisdictions was the liberty of the abbey of Bury St Edmunds in Suffolk, which continued to provide substantial numbers of felony indictments at gaol delivery in the fifteenth century: Maddern, 'Violence, Crime, and Public Disorder', 373. See, for example, JUST 3/220/1.

[79] *Guide to the Contents of the Public Record Office* (2 vols.; London, 1963), i. 23. For an excellent analytical study of special judicial commissions in the context of the Peasants' Revolt, see A. J. Prescott, 'The Judicial Records of the Rising of 1381', Ph.D. thesis (London, 1984).

[80] *Early Registers of Writs*, ed. E. De Haas and G. D. G. Hall, Selden Soc., 87 (London, 1970), esp. 383–4; BL Add. MS 35205; *Registrum Omnium Brevium Tam Originalium Quam Judicialium* (London, 1687).

[81] Powell, 'Special Oyer and Terminer Proceedings', 1–3; Kaeuper, 'Law and Order', 734–84; Avrutick, 'Commissions of Oyer and Terminer', 12–20.

[82] B. Wilkinson, 'The Authorization of Chancery Writs under Edward III', *BJRL* 8 (1924), 117–18.

felony, within a given county or group of counties. They empowered justices to receive cases either at the suit of the Crown alone, or at the suit of both Crown and party. The most powerful and comprehensive form of general oyer and terminer was the commission of trailbaston established at the end of Edward I's reign.[83]

Commissions of inquiry were equally wide-ranging: their origins lay in the sworn inquest used by the Anglo-Saxon and Norman kings, and they could be used to investigate any matter concerning the Crown or an individual complainant.[84] Since their findings were returnable into chancery without determination of the matters investigated, such inquiries afforded a greater degree of central supervision than oyer and terminer commissions: the king and council could inspect the record and decide what measures were appropriate. This was no doubt the reason why commissions of inquiry, passed on to king's bench for determination, were among the instruments preferred by Henry V in combating disorder.[85]

As an alternative to trailbaston and general oyer and terminer commissions in the fourteenth and early fifteenth centuries, the court of king's bench was sometimes used as a 'superior eyre' to suppress local disorders.[86] As early as 1304–5 king's bench was associated with trailbaston proceedings in the home counties, and from the closing years of Edward II's reign it often exercised itinerant trailbaston jurisdiction on its own account, assuming direct responsibility for the restoration of public order.[87] Regulating its powers at Kingston-upon-Thames in 1353, Chief Justice William Shareshull asserted that it enjoyed a jurisdiction higher than that of the old general eyre.[88] It could determine all manner of pleas at the suit of both the Crown and the private party, and its proceedings included a thorough review of the machinery of

---

[83] See Introduction at nn. 53–5.
[84] Pollock and Maitland, *History of English Law*, i. 143–4.
[85] See chs. 6–8.　　　　　　[86] See above at n. 41.
[87] Putnam, *Shareshull*, 73, 109–10; *SKB* iv, pp. xxxviii–xli, c–cv, 133–5; vi, 9; Harding, 'Trailbaston Proceedings', 150; E. Powell, 'The King's Bench in Shropshire and Staffordshire in 1414', in E. W. Ives and A. H. Manchester (edd.), *Law, Litigants and the Legal Profession* (London, 1983), 94–5.
[88] *Les Reports des Cases* (11 pts.; London, 1678–80), pt. 5; Liber Assisarum, Mich. 27 Edward III, pl. 1; Putnam, *Shareshull*, 109.

civil and criminal justice of the shire within which it was
sitting. Professor Putnam perhaps overstated the case in
describing the superior eyre as 'an almost revolutionary
instrument for law enforcement',[89] but it was undoubtedly a
powerful device which brought the full weight of royal judicial
authority to bear on a locality. King's bench was used as a
superior eyre most frequently under Shareshull in the 1350s
and again in Richard II's reign.[90] Henry IV on the other
hand, perhaps fearing the opposition such visitations might
provoke, never took his bench away from Westminster. It is
all the more striking, therefore, that Henry V chose to revive
the superior eyre as the centrepiece of his campaign for law
enforcement in 1414.[91]

[89] Putnam, *Shareshull*, 134.
[90] Ead., *Justices of the Peace*, pp. lx–lxiii; *SKB* vi, pp. vii, ix–xii, liii–lxi; W. M.
Ormrod, 'Edward III's Government of England, *c.*1346 to 1356', D.Phil. thesis
(Oxford, 1984), 185–221.
[91] See ch. 7 for detailed analysis of the superior eyre held by Henry V in the north-
west Midlands in 1414.

3

Criminal Legal Procedure: The Workings of the Courts

THE CHARACTER OF CRIMINAL LEGAL PROCEDURE

WE HAVE seen that fifteenth-century England possessed an extensive hierarchy of royal criminal courts; the present chapter aims to describe the workings of those courts. How were criminal prosecutions brought, what measures were taken to arrest offenders, and how were trials conducted? Before considering these questions, however, it is necessary to mention a fundamental feature of the system which determined the whole character of criminal procedure: the reliance of the Crown on the private party and the local community for the prosecution of crime.

Medieval criminal justice lacked two central elements taken for granted in modern legal systems: a full-time police force and a public prosecuting agency. It was the duty of the sheriff and his staff to carry out arrests of criminals who had been indicted or appealed before one of the criminal courts. They had no responsibility, however, for criminal investigations. The justice of the peace was, in later centuries, to acquire important investigative and prosecutorial functions, but in the fourteenth and fifteenth centuries his role in this regard was very limited.[1]

As a consequence the royal system of criminal justice in late medieval England may best be described not as active but as reactive. The Crown enjoyed a virtual monopoly of criminal jurisdiction, with the framework of courts to enforce that monopoly, but the identification of offenders was still left mainly to the wronged individual and the local community.

---

[1] J. H. Langbein, 'The Origins of Public Prosecution at Common Law', *AJLH* 17 (1973), 313–35; id., *Prosecuting Crime in the Renaissance* (Cambridge, Mass., 1974), 1–103. The Statutes of Riots of 1411 and 1414 gave JPs the duty to investigate allegations of riot: see below, n. 9; ch. 2 at n. 64.

The only exceptions were cases of treason, which were actively prosecuted by the council through king's bench or special commissions; and cases of homicide, where the coroner was required to hold inquests and return indictments.[2] Even in these matters the council often acted on private accusations, while coroners were assisted by local juries.

The ubiquitous agent of criminal justice was the jury; juries of presentment decided who should be brought to trial, and trial juries determined the guilt or innocence of the accused. During the middle ages the jury was a powerful instrument for the exercise of a community's influence and the expression of its values in criminal proceedings. Jury verdicts remained as inscrutable as those of the ordeal, and it was only at the end of the fifteenth century that questionable jury decisions in criminal cases came to be examined before the king's council.[3] The importance of the private accuser is seen in the continuing vigour of the appeal of felony, and there is evidence also that his presence in court was necessary for the successful prosecution of an indictment.[4] It is difficult therefore to overstate the extent to which the initiative for criminal prosecution lay with the individual and the community of shire, hundred, and township.[5]

MODES OF PROSECUTION

By 1400 the standard method of prosecution was the indictment. In its broadest sense an indictment was 'an accusation made by twelve or more laymen sworn to inquire in the king's behalf and recorded before a court of record'.[6]

[2] Hunnisett, *Medieval Coroner*, 9–36; see ch. 2 at n. 26.

[3] Plucknett, *Common Law*, 125–30; T. A. Green, *Verdict According to Conscience* (Chicago, Ill., 1985), 3–102; P. R. Hyams, 'Trial by Ordeal: The Key to Proof in the Early Common Law', in M. S. Arnold *et al.* (edd.) *On the Laws and Customs of England: Essays in Honor of Samuel E. Thorne* (Chapel Hill, NC, 1981), 90–126; *Select Cases in the Council of Henry VII*, ed. C. G. Bayne and W. H. Dunham, Selden Soc., 75 (London, 1958), 62–77.

[4] E. Powell, 'Jury Trial at Gaol Delivery in the Late Middle Ages: the Midland Circuit, 1400–1429', in J. S. Cockburn and T. A. Green (edd.), *Twelve Good Men and True: the English Criminal Trial Jury, 1200–1800* (Princeton, NJ, 1988), 105–9.

[5] M. T. Clanchy, 'Law, Government and Society in Medieval England', *History*, 59 (1974), 73–8; see ch. 4 at nn. 6–14.

[6] J. H. Baker, 'Criminal Courts and Procedure at Common Law, 1550–1800', in J. S. Cockburn (ed.), *Crime in England, 1550–1800* (London, 1977), 18.

With the expansion of criminal business in the king's courts, the content of indictments was becoming increasingly precise, no doubt in response to the higher demands of royal judges and the growing sophistication of pleading.[7] It was probably the central court judges who drafted the Statute of Additions of 1413, which stipulated that all indictments, as well as appeals and original writs on private suits, should give not only the name of the defendant but also his place and county of residence and his estate, degree, or 'mystery'.[8] By the late fifteenth century the rules governing the form and content of indictments were finally settled, and they could be declared insufficient at law unless technically precise in every detail.[9]

Juries of presentment might be drawn from a township, hundred, borough, liberty, or in the case of a grand jury, from the whole county. They were summoned before peace sessions, the sheriff's tourn, the coroner, or other judicial commissioners, to report on offences committed within their area.[10] Once sworn, the jurors were given the charge, or articles of presentment detailing the offences upon which they were empowered to make accusations.[11] They could make

---

[7] *SKB*, vi. 21–5, 106–9, 136–8, 149–52; *Year Books of Richard II: 11 Richard II, 1387–88*, ed. I. D. Thornley, Ames Foundation (Cambridge, Mass., 1937), 230–3; *Les Reports des Cases*, Hilary 14 Henry IV, pl. 63. For an ingenious piece of chicanery involving an imprecise indictment, see KB 9/206/2, mm. 23, 30 (1417).

[8] 1 Henry V c. 5.

[9] By 1500 indictments had five essential components: the name and 'addition' of the accused; the date and place of the offence; the name of the victim; details of the 'thing' involved (e.g. goods stolen, the type of weapon used); and the nature of the offence. See Thomas Marowe's 'Reading on the Peace' of 1503, in Putnam, *Early Treatises*, 383–94; J. S. Cockburn, 'Early Modern Assize Records as Historical Evidence', *Journal of the Soc. of Archivists*, 5 (1975), 215–31. The Statutes of Riots of the early fifteenth century empowered JPs to certify incidents of riot to the king's council without jury inquest, which certificates of riot had the authority of conventional indictments. In practice this procedure was used only when a riot had taken place in the JPs' presence; otherwise proceedings under the Statutes of Riots used juries of presentment in the normal way: 13 Henry IV c. 7; 2 Henry V st. 1 c. 8; KB 9/210, mm. 70–2; 223/2, mm. 37–8, 74; KB 27/617, Rex, m. 23; 658, Rex, m. 5d. See also ch. 2 at n. 64; ch. 7 at nn. 25–9.

[10] Putnam, *Justices of the Peace*, p. xcix; Post, 'Criminals and the Law', 103–13, 130–1, 143–8; Hunnisett, *Medieval Coroner*, 13–22.

[11] 12 Edward I c. 4 (articles of the sheriff's tourn); Putnam, *Justice of the Peace*, pp. 10–25 (charge to peace sessions jurors); *Les Reports des Cases*, pt. 5: Liber Assisarum, 27 Edward III, pl. 44 (articles of the superior eyre of king's bench). Cf. Pollock and Maitland, *History of English Law*, ii. 641–8; Cam, *Studies in the Hundred Rolls*, 22–41, 73–9.

indictments in two ways, either from their own knowledge or by confirming private bills of complaint submitted to them, endorsing them *billa vera*, or 'true bill'. In the late sixteenth century the treatise-writer William Lambarde distinguished a bill confirmed by a presenting jury, which he termed an indictment, from an accusation found by a jury of its own knowledge, that is a presentment.[12] By the time he wrote, the 'indictment' as thus defined had replaced the presentment as the standard mode of criminal prosecution.[13] How far this was already the case by the early fifteenth century is unclear. *Bille vere* formed a comparatively insignificant proportion of juries' returns during the superior eyre of king's bench in 1414, where only 30 out of a total of over 2,500 indictments originated in bills.[14] On the other hand bills were quite common among peace sessions records and the returns of Middlesex juries summoned before king's bench, while the Worcestershire JP's manual of Henry V's reign contains several forms of bill.[15] Certainly indictment by bill was not an unusual procedure, which suggests that by 1400 juries of presentment were no longer even technically self-informing bodies.[16]

Very little is known about how presenting juries secured the information upon which they based their indictments. Constables and townships had the responsibility of making offences known to them; constables frequently served as

[12] W. Lambarde, *Eirenarcha* (London, 1599), 467–9; Putnam, *Justices of the Peace*, pp. c–cii. In the following chapters 'presentment' will be used according to Lambarde's definition, 'indictment' as a generic term for any accusation produced by a presenting jury when the question of its origin is unknown or immaterial.

[13] J. S. Cockburn, 'Trial by the Book? Fact and Theory in the Criminal Process, 1558–1625', in J. H. Baker (ed.), *Legal Records and the Historian* (London, 1978), 60–71; in the sixteenth century bills were first vetted by judges and their clerks before submission to presenting juries: Cockburn, *Assizes*, 111; see also Putnam, *Justices of the Peace*, p. cii.

[14] Cf. ch. 7 table. 1. For examples of *bille vere*, see KB 9/113, mm. 3, 7–10; JUST 1/753, mm. 2(2), 3(1), 7(4,5).

[15] e.g. KB 9/71, mm. 8–11, 16–18; 208, mm. 35–45; 210, mm. 21–8; 222/2, mm. 34–7; 937, mm. 31–45; Putnam, *Early Treatises*, 237–41.

[16] Pollock and Maitland, *History of English Law*, ii. 642–4; J. B. Thayer, *A Preliminary Treatise on Evidence at the Common Law* (London, 1898), 90–1, 123–4; Langbein, 'Public Prosecution', 314; Green, *Verdict According to Conscience*, 13–17; cf. *RP* ii. 259.

jurors, and sometimes entire juries were composed of them.[17] Individual jurors had no hesitation about putting forward offences of which they themselves had been the victims. At Leicester in May 1414 a jury from Gartree hundred returned indictments before king's bench which included charges of robbery committed against three of its members.[18] Likewise powerful local interests, notably magnate and gentry land-owners, could influence presenting juries, and one scholar has concluded that peace sessions' indictments 'give at best a gentleman's-eye view' of crime.[19] In view of the continuing importance of the private accuser in criminal trial procedure the likelihood must be that, even where charges were not made in the form of a bill, juries relied on individual complainants for all but the most notorious of offences. This suggestion is confirmed by the evidence of actions of conspiracy for false indictment, where charges were brought against individuals rather than collectively against the presenting jury.[20] A good example is the case of Ralph Huse, esquire, of Derbyshire, indicted for felonious breach of the close of Thomas Dethick at Dethick. Huse was acquitted at gaol delivery in 1420, and subsequently brought an action of conspiracy against Dethick, and his brothers John and Roger, for false indictment.[21] This was merely one incident in a long-running dispute between the two families, and shows how criminal procedures could be used by private parties as an extension of civil litigation.[22]

A system so dependent on individual and local initiative was obviously vulnerable to manipulation. This is well illustrated in a remarkable case which appeared in king's bench in

[17] Pollock and Maitland, *History of English Law*, ii. 643; Putnam, *Justices of the Peace*, pp. xcix–c. Examples of constables' juries are at KB 9/204/2, mm. 23, 33, 35, 39–43 (Notts., 1414); 1056, m. 34 (Derby., 1419); 218/2, m. 43 (Derby., 1423).

[18] KB 9/206/1, m. 28; KB 37 (court of king's bench, *brevia regis* (crown side) files)/ 4/2/1, unnumbered membrane (Gartree jury list). The three were William Brown, Richard Christian, and William Mowsley.

[19] Post, 'Medieval Peace Rolls', 637.

[20] Plucknett, *Common Law*, 127: an action of conspiracy could not be brought against a jury as a whole.

[21] JUST 3/195, m. 43d; KB 27/640, m. 12.

[22] *Collections for a History of Staffordshire*, William Salt Archaeological Soc., 17 (London, 1896), 115; CP 40 (court of common pleas, plea rolls)/616, m. 7d; 619, m. 122; 621, m. 136; JUST 4 (eyre, assize etc., writ files)/8/2, m. 240. See also ch. 4 at n. 42.

1418.[23] Thomas Clare, an Oxfordshire gentleman, petitioned the 1417 Parliament that he had been maliciously indicted and outlawed in Northamptonshire by his opponents in a lawsuit over land in Oxfordshire.[24] An inquiry was ordered, and the JPs, jurors, coroners, and under-sheriff of Northamptonshire were summoned into king's bench for examination. The record of their testimony, and in particular the confession of the villain of the piece, John Thornton, revealed that Clare had indeed been 'framed' in a most ingenious way.

John Thornton was under-sheriff of Northamptonshire in 1417, and also a servant of Sir Thomas Green, a leading landowner of that county, against whom Thomas Clare had brought legal action over estates in Lillingstone in Oxfordshire. The dispute had been submitted to arbitration which failed. While riding home from the unsuccessful loveday, Green was met by a yeoman, John Wadupp, who alleged that Clare had stolen two oxen which he found straying in the forest. Green instructed Thornton to labour an indictment of felony against Clare on this charge in order to delay his legal action, and Thornton submitted a bill of indictment to a presenting jury at a peace session held at Rothwell. The jury would not endorse it, however, because Thomas Clare was styled a gentleman. Undeterred, Thornton got his clerk to draft another bill, describing Clare as a husbandman, and submitted it to the next peace session at Wellingborough. He handed it to the jury himself, saying, 'Sirs, affirm this, for I know it is true, and my master will give you good thanks to affirm it, and he will say to you that it is true when he speaks next with you.' Thus reassured, the jury indicted Clare for felony. The indictment was passed to the clerk of the peace, but before process could be issued, Thornton took the bill and made his clerk erase 'husbandman' and substitute 'gentleman' so that Clare would not be able to challenge it on the grounds of inaccuracy.[25]

This account is especially valuable for its description of the process by which indictments were procured. The social and

[23] KB 27/629, Rex, m. 9.

[24] Clare's petition does not appear in the printed Parliament rolls.

[25] KB 27/629, Rex, m. 9 (spelling modernized). For the later stages of the case, see below at nn. 49–50.

official status of both the accuser and accused were clearly crucial. A powerful and well-connected individual could secure an indictment of felony upon an unsubstantiated allegation against an unknown husbandman simply by a verbal assurance to the jury. Were the accused a gentleman, however, this would be insufficient. The jurors, who were probably gentlemen or substantial yeomen themselves, would have required firmer evidence before indicting one of their own class, who might have powerful connections.[26] Thornton's position as under-sheriff gave him ready access to the juries in court.[27] The case suggests that the finding of indictments in late medieval England was more a question of influence and access than the objective reporting of crime.[28]

The extent of the Crown's reliance on the individual for the prosecution of crime is confirmed by the continuing popularity of the appeal of felony.[29] It was a private action brought by the party on the Crown's behalf, and enabled the victim of felony, or in the case of homicide his next of kin, to accuse and prosecute offenders in the king's courts. In procedural terms, therefore, it lay half-way between the private blood-feud and criminal prosecution initiated by the Crown.[30] Until the thirteenth century appeals were decided by trial by battle, but as a result of active judicial discouragement this was extremely rare after 1300.[31]

Although the appeal was no longer a serious rival to the indictment in the late middle ages, it enjoyed a vigorous old age, and appeal proceedings continued to take precedence over those arising from indictment. It became customary,

---

[26] For the social status of peace sessions jurors, see Powell, 'Jury Trial', 92–6; Post, 'Criminals and the Law', 111–13, 143–8.

[27] Hastings, *Common Pleas*, 224–30. See *Paston Letters and Papers of the Fifteenth Century*, ed. N. Davis (2 vols.; Oxford, 1971–6), i. 314; ii. 33, 262, 299, for illustrations of the sheriff's influence over the judicial process.

[28] See above at n. 19.

[29] C. Whittick, 'The Role of the Criminal Appeal in the Later Middle Ages', in J. A. Guy (ed.), *Law and Social Change* (London, 1984), 55–72; D. R. Ernst, 'The Moribund Appeal of Death: Compensating Survivors and Controlling Jurors in Early Modern England', *AJLH* 28 (1984), 164–88.

[30] W. Holdsworth, *A History of English Law* (12 vols.; London, 1922–38), ii. 195–8; Milsom, *Historical Foundations*, 407–9.

[31] *Surrey Eyre*, 116–25; *Crown Pleas of Wilts. Eyre*, 69–92; Holdsworth, *History of English Law*, ii. 195, 257; *Placita Corone*, ed. J. M. Kaye, Selden Soc., Suppl. Ser., 4 (London, 1966), xxiv–xxvii; Whittick, 'Criminal Appeal', 57–8.

however, for appeals to be accompanied into court by an indictment for the same offence, both to discourage the lodging of malicious appeals and to allow the prosecution of the accused felon at the Crown's suit if the appellor defaulted.[32]

The frequency with which appeals were brought varied according to the locality. On the East Anglian assize circuit between 1422 and 1442 only 71 appeals are recorded out of a total of over 2,500 prosecutions, a proportion of 3 per cent. In three Midland counties between 1400 and 1430 the incidence of appeals is slightly higher, ranging from 5 per cent to 9 per cent of 500–650 cases per county.[33] A recent survey of the records of king's bench has suggested that the number of appeals there actually increased in the second half of the fifteenth century, and revealed that nearly 400 appeals were recorded in the court between 1485 and 1495.[34] The appeal survived because of the advantages it offered to the victims of crime, in particular in enforcing compensation and restitution. In an appeal of robbery the appellor was entitled to the return of the stolen goods if the accused were convicted and if he could show fresh suit, that is, if the appeal had been lodged immediately after the robbery. Appeals of rape, mayhem, and homicide were routinely used as means of exerting pressure on offenders to come to terms with the victim,[35] and the appeal of homicide continued to serve this function even in the sixteenth and seventeenth centuries.[36]

A variant of the appeal of felony was the approver's appeal, whereby an accused felon confessed his offences before trial and turned king's evidence.[37] The approver made his confession before a coroner and appealed as many of his accomplices as he could remember. Should any of his

---

[32] Whittick, 'Criminal Appeal', 65–71.

[33] Maddern, 'Violence, Crime, and Public Disorder', 373 (table 8); Powell, 'Jury Trial', 101–4.

[34] Whittick, 'Criminal Appeal', 55–6.

[35] Ibid. 63–5; E. Powell, 'Settlement of Disputes by Arbitration in Fifteenth-Century England', *Law and History Review*, 2, no. 1 (1984), 27–8.

[36] Ernst, 'Appeal of Death', 164–88.

[37] Hamil, 'King's Approvers', 238–58; H. Röhrkasten, 'Some Problems of the Evidence of Fourteenth-Century Approvers', *Journal of Legal History*, 5, no. 3 (1984), 14–22.

appellees be acquitted, the approver was immediately hanged as a confessed felon.[38] The approver's appeal was an archaic procedure, and was one of the few in which trial by battle was allowed and still took place regularly after 1300.[39] In the early fourteenth century it fell into disrepute as a primary method of prosecution owing to the ease and frequency with which it was abused.[40] Like the appeal of felony, however, it survived into the fifteenth century because of its continuing usefulness both to the approver and to the Crown. To the approver it offered procedural delay, while for the Crown it provided the means of prosecuting crimes which might otherwise have gone undetected. Approvers' appeals were most useful to the courts in two main areas. The first was in the breaking up of professional criminal gangs, particularly of highway robbers. A spectacular example of this was the appeal of William Rose of Hampshire in 1383. Rose was a veritable 'supergrass', appealing no less than fifty-four of his former criminal associates.[41] Appeals were also useful in dealing with sedition and treason, and it is striking how approvers' appeals reflected the anxieties of a regime at any given time. Thus at the beginning of Henry IV's reign there were several appeals for incitement to treason and seditious words; while in the early 1420s, as the kingdom suffered the financial effects of Henry V's wars, there were numerous appeals for counter-feiting.[42]

In addition to the indictment and the appeal, a third mode of prosecution was developing during the late middle ages: the information.[43] This was a bill of accusation brought as a

[38] The number of successful appeals that an approver was expected to make to win his freedom varied, but it appears to have been at least six: Hamil, 'King's Approvers', 246; M. T. Clanchy, 'Highway Robbery and Trial by Battle in the Hampshire Eyre of 1249', in R. F. Hunnisett and J. B. Post (edd.), *Medieval Legal Records Edited in Memory of C. A. F. Meekings* (London, 1978), 31. Three appeals were considered insufficient in king's bench in 1400, where the approver was sent back to think up further charges: KB 9/185/1, m. 53.

[39] Richard FitzNeale, *The Dialogue of the Exchequer*, ed. C. Johnson (London, 1950), 87–8; *Bracton*, ii. 429–35.

[40] Röhrkasten, 'Fourteenth-Century Approvers', 14–15.

[41] J. B. Post, 'The Evidential Value of Approvers' Appeals: The Case of William Rose, 1389', *Law and History Review*, 3, no. 1 (1985), 91–100.

[42] *SKB* vii. 126–8, 133–4; Bellamy, *Law of Treason*, 145–6. See ch. 10 at nn. 59–68.

[43] Baker, 'Criminal Courts', 20–1.

private action by an individual who sued both for himself and for the king—hence the term *qui tam* for such actions. Informations could be filed only in cases of statutory trespass, and their evolution is closely associated with enactment of innumerable penal statutes from 1300 onwards, most of which attempted to curb abuses of legal procedure or to regulate commercial and industrial activity.[44] In the fifteenth century such statutes regularly prescribed a specific financial penalty, allotting half to any party who successfully sued for the king.[45] Under the Tudors professional informers made handsome profits out of such actions, but there is no evidence for the earlier period of *qui tam* proceedings on such a scale.

SUMMONS AND ARREST

Once a prosecution had been initiated by indictment or appeal, the next step was the issue of process summoning the accused into court.[46] For cases of trespass the initial writ was one of *venire facias*, followed by a *distringas* ordering distraint of a certain sum on the offender's chattels. If this failed to produce the accused, or if he had no goods to be distrained, process moved on to a writ of *capias* or arrest, which was issued three times before the machinery of the exigent was set in motion. The accused was summoned at four successive county courts; if he failed to appear upon the final summons he was outlawed in the presence and by the record of the coroners, and his goods and chattels declared forfeit to the Crown.[47]

The procedure in felony was the same, except that it began with the *capias*, which by statute had to be served twice before the exigent could be issued.[48] Here again the confession of John Thornton, the under-sheriff of Northamptonshire, provides an illustration. After securing the malicious indictment against Thomas Clare,[49] Thornton took out two writs of

---

[44] Bellamy, *Criminal Law and Society*, 90–114.   [45] Ibid. 99–100.

[46] For arrest before indictment, see below at nn. 58–63.

[47] Hastings, *Common Pleas*, 169–81; Blatcher, 'Workings of King's Bench', 206–21; *Reports of Sir John Spelman*, ii. 83–92; Hunnisett, *Medieval Coroner*, 61–8; Putnam, *Justices of the Peace*, pp. ciii–civ.

[48] 25 Edward III st. 5 c. 14. In cases of treason, homicide, and robbery only one *capias* might be awarded: cf. M. Hale, *A History of Pleas of the Crown* (London, 1736), ii. 194.   [49] See above at nn. 23–5.

capias, followed by the writ of exigent, which was called at three successive county courts. At the fourth a parliamentary election was due to be held, which meant an unusually large attendance. Fearing that his chicanery might be discovered, Thornton ordered his clerk to call the exigents very early to ensure that no one queried Clare's outlawry. Only one of the four coroners was present at the time, and Thornton later admitted that as he came into court with two of the coroners, one reproved the clerk for calling the exigents before their arrival.[50]

The whole process, from initial summons to outlawry, took between six months and a year to complete. It sounds like a ponderous system, but it should be noted that the process of summons had been streamlined and shortened since the thirteenth century, and that contemporary parliamentary petitions often complained that process was expedited much too fast.[51] In March 1416, the Commons complained that process in king's bench on indictments for trespass was so hasty that defendants' attorneys were unable to plead in court before the exigent had been awarded. In 1427 it was alleged that malicious indictments, combined with the speed of process in king's bench, led to the outlawry of innocent people and the forfeiture of their chattels to the Crown.[52] Considerations of speed and efficiency therefore had to be balanced against the need to ensure due process and to avoid a miscarriage of justice.

The weakness of late medieval court process stemmed less from its duration than from the ineffectiveness of outlawry as a sanction to compel attendance. In the twelfth and thirteenth centuries outlawry had been a fearsome penalty involving the exclusion of the outlaw from society, the forfeiture of all possessions and property, and the withdrawal of the protection of the law. A captured outlaw could be hanged merely on proof of outlawry.[53] Like its canon law equivalent, excommunication, its terrors were diluted by over-use, in particular through its

---

[50] KB 27/629, Rex, m. 9d.
[51] D. W. Sutherland, 'Mesne Process upon Personal Actions in the Early Common Law', *LQR* 82 (1966), 482–96.
[52] *RP* iv. 80, 327.
[53] Pollock and Maitland, *History of English Law*, ii. 449–50.

extension in an attenuated form to process arising from civil actions of trespass.[54] By the fifteenth century outlawry had outlived its usefulness in the judicial process.[55] In the reign of Henry V it was possible for a clerk of king's bench, Henry Chorley, to be outlawed in that court for several years without suffering the slightest inconvenience.[56]

The serving of process and the making of arrests were the responsibility of the sheriff, and were most usually carried out by a hundred bailiffs or village constables on his instructions.[57] The law governing arrests which were not based on prior indictment or appeal remained obscure throughout the late middle ages. Over-zealous officials and victims of crime certainly risked amercement by the courts and actions of false imprisonment by their victims,[58] but Professor Putnam's assertion that 'the inherent weakness in medieval criminal law procedure [was] the inability to arrest *before* indictment' is misleading.[59] Felons caught in the act could of course be apprehended, though by 1400 their summary execution was no longer permitted;[60] the traditional procedure of the hue and cry made the township, led by the constables, responsible for the pursuit and arrest of offenders when a felony was discovered;[61] in addition the Statute of Winchester of 1285 and subsequent statutes authorized constables and others to

[54] Pollock and Maitland, *History of English Law*, ii. 580.

[55] Blatcher, *King's Bench*, 74–100; Hastings, *Common Pleas*, 176–81.

[56] KB 29 (court of king's bench, controlment rolls)/53, mm. 29d, 36. Chorley was outlawed for failing to produce in court defendants for whom he had acted as mainpernor. An attempt was made in the early fifteenth century to enforce outlawry more strictly, but the exercise seems to have been primarily fiscal in purpose: R. B. Pugh, 'Early Registers of English Outlaws', *AJLH* 27 (1983), 319–29.

[57] The fullest treatment of shrieval administration is Cam, *Hundred Rolls*, 53–223. See also ead., 'Shire Officials: Coroners, Constables and Bailiffs', in J. F. Willard, W. A. Morris, and W. H. Dunham (edd), *The English Government at Work, 1327–36*, (3 vols.; Cambridge, Mass., 1940–50) iii. 165–83; Palmer, *County Courts*, 28–55; Powell, 'Jury Trial', 92–3.

[58] Pollock and Maitland, *History of English Law*, ii. 582–3; *Year Books 30 and 31 Edward I*, ed. A. J. Horwood, Rolls Ser. (London, 1863), 584–5.

[59] Putnam, *Shareshull*, 63.

[60] Post, 'Local Jurisdictions', 11–12; for two Leics. cases of homicide by beheading during Henry IV's reign, which appear to represent informal (and illegal) instances of summary justice, see JUST 3/188, mm. 47, 49.

[61] Pollock and Maitland, *History of English Law*, ii. 578–9; Bellamy, *Public Order*, 102–3; cf. Thomas Smith, *De Republica Anglorum*, ed. M. Dewar (Cambridge, 1972), 107–8.

make arrests of suspicious strangers.[62] The frequency with which the latter powers were used is demonstrated by the substantial numbers of prisoners at gaol delivery who had been arrested on suspicion without indictment or appeal.[63]

TRIAL PROCEDURE

In spite of its imperfections, the medieval machinery of summons and arrest probably succeeded in bringing to court between 30 and 50 per cent of persons indicted.[64] During the late middle ages cases of felony were invariably determined through trial by jury, except for the very occasional trial by battle arising from an approver's appeal.[65] The history of late medieval criminal trial procedure is extremely obscure. Little is known as to what went on in court: all the plea rolls recorded was the indictment or appeal, the defendant's appearance and plea, the selection and swearing-in of the trial jurors, their verdict, and the sentence. The lack of evidence is tantalizing because important changes in trial procedure may have been taking place during the period, the effects of which only become clear to historians in the mid-sixteenth century.

It is generally assumed that the medieval trial jury was originally self-informing, in the sense that the jurors were drawn from the vicinity of a crime and came into court already apprised of the facts of a case through their own local knowledge, and ready to render their verdict. There was thus no need for the presentation of evidence in court by prosecution or defence, and in consequence trials were extremely short and perfunctory.[66] Self-informing juries controlled the amount of evidence revealed to the judge in court and the manner of its presentation. Professor Green has argued forcefully that juries commonly took advantage of that

---

[62] Statute of Winchester, c. 4 (*Select Charters*, ed. W. Stubbs (9th edn.; Oxford, 1913), 465); Cam, 'Shire Officials', 170.

[63] See for example the gaol delivery files for Notts. and Derby. in the early fifteenth century: JUST 3/56/8–27.

[64] Post, 'Criminals and the Law', 15; J. B. Given, *Society and Homicide in Thirteenth-Century England* (Stanford, Cal., 1977), 93–4. See table 5 in ch. 7.

[65] See above at n. 39.

[66] Powell, 'Jury Trial', 78–9, 98–9; R. B. Pugh, 'The Duration of Criminal Trials in Medieval England', in E. W. Ives and A. H. Manchester (edd.) *Law, Litigants and the Legal Profession* (London, 1983), 104–15.

control to render merciful verdicts which accorded with popular attitudes towards crime and punishment, but which effectively nullified the common law of felony.[67] By 1550, however, the transformation of jury trial towards its modern form was already well under way, a process greatly accelerated by the Marian bail and committal statutes of 1554–5, which provided for the recording of evidence and the binding of witnesses to appear to give testimony in court. By that time, clearly, juries were no longer self-informing and so required the formal presentation of evidence before them in court. Apparently the criminal trial underwent major change during the late middle ages whereby the jury ceased to be a self-informing institution, thereby necessitating the overhaul of prosecutorial and trial procedure in the later sixteenth century.[68]

Although we have little direct information, a certain amount of indirect evidence is available which makes it possible to approach the problems of late medieval trial procedure, and to assess how far it diverged from the classic medieval stereotype. It is clear, first of all, that routine criminal trials at gaol delivery continued to be very brief. Professor Pugh's estimate of ten to twenty minutes per prisoner for late thirteenth-century deliveries accords well with what we can deduce for the fifteenth century.[69] In such circumstances there can have been little time for the presentation of the case or the hearing of witnesses. Persons accused of felony were not allowed defence counsel, and we may suspect that many prisoners had very little idea of what was happening in court.[70] In 1413 Richard Young of Bath, who had been arrested on suspicion of clipping coin, was brought before king's bench. There, supposing himself to be condemned to death automatically without answer, he confessed and turned approver to prolong his life. On interrogation he was able to establish his innocence. As he had not been

---

[67] Green, *Verdict According to Conscience*, 3–102.
[68] Ibid. 105–52; Langbein, *Prosecuting Crime*, 1–103.
[69] Pugh, 'Criminal Trials', 108; Powell, 'Jury Trial', 98–9.
[70] Baker, 'Criminal Courts', 37–8; J. B. Post, 'The Admissibility of Defence Counsel in English Criminal Procedure', *Journal of Legal History*, 5, no. 3 (1984), 23–32. Defence counsel were not admitted in routine criminal trials until 1836.

indicted or appealed of any offence, Henry V granted him a pardon for his mistaken confession.[71]

The brevity of trials and the lack of defence counsel hint at the survival of active, self-informing juries. Closer analysis of the composition and case-load of juries at gaol delivery during the fifteenth century, however, reveals evidence of trial procedure inconsistent with truly self-informing juries.[72] A study of three Midland counties, Derbyshire, Leicestershire, and Warwickshire, between 1400 and 1430, found that defendants were no longer tried by juries drawn exclusively from the vicinity, that is, the hundred or wapentake in which an offence had occurred. The breakdown of the system of hundredal trial juries may have been linked with problems of securing the attendance of jurors. Although each of the three counties had between four and six hundreds, at no delivery during the period were more than three jury panels summoned. In Derbyshire there was without exception only a single trial jury for the whole county.

It was therefore unusual for prisoners to be arraigned individually before separate juries, and each jury tried an average of three to five defendants.[73] Sporadic efforts were still being made to ensure that juries in criminal trials were drawn from the neighbourhood where the offence had occurred, but those efforts were more successful in the few cases where prisoners were tried on their own or in pairs. Where three or more prisoners were tried together the geographical correlation between jurors and offences tended to break down. Administrative experience and social status were more important criteria for jury selection than place of abode. Many jurors served twice or more and were involved in other aspects of judicial administration, whether as officials—coroners, bailiffs, or constables—or as jurors at assizes, peace sessions, and the sheriff's tourn. In Leicestershire 24 per cent of trial jurors had served on presenting juries, in Warwickshire 37 per cent. Many trial jurors were drawn from the lesser gentry: in

---

[71] *CPR, 1413–16,* 151.

[72] The following paragraphs summarize the findings of Powell, 'Jury Trial', 78–115.

[73] Ibid. 84. In Derby., which used only a single county trial jury, each jury tried an average of eight to nine defendants.

Derbyshire 35 per cent of all jurors, and nearly 60 per cent of those who served more than once, were of gentle status.

These findings suggest that fifteenth-century trial juries were no longer self-informing. Once they ceased to be truly local, juries must have found it difficult to acquire knowledge of crimes before they came to court, particularly as they were expected to try several prisoners at a time. In consequence, evidence in some form must have been presented. Apart from the defendant, whose demeanour must greatly have influenced the jurors, there were two possible sources of evidence in court: the victim or victim's kin and other witnesses for the Crown; and royal judicial officials. Sir Thomas Smith's description of criminal trial procedure, written in 1565, emphasizes the victim's importance to the prosecution:[74] he acted as accuser and leading witness, and the centrepiece of the trial was the 'altercation' between accuser and accused. Several pieces of evidence suggest that this was already the case in the late middle ages. The sixteenth-century reform of trial procedure took for granted the existence of the private prosecutor. The Marian committal statute of 1555 assumed that private parties who made accusations too often failed to discharge their duty to follow them up in court.[75] For the late middle ages themselves there is explicit reference to the private accuser in the judge's precept to the sheriff ordering preparations for gaol delivery. The sheriff was instructed to make proclamation throughout the county summoning all who wished to prosecute prisoners about to be delivered, and there is evidence that on occasion the proclamation did produce a response.[76]

The pattern of conviction and acquittal in late medieval criminal trials also points to the importance of the private accuser. In the three counties studied there was a marked contrast in results between cases brought on appeal and those brought on indictment. Whereas cases brought on indictment show the high levels of acquittal common in medieval courts, those brought on appeal show very high levels of conviction.

[74] Smith, *De Republica Anglorum*, 114.
[75] Powell, 'Jury Trial', 107; Langbein, 'Public Prosecution', 317.
[76] Powell, 'Jury Trial', 107–8. For examples of gaol delivery justices' precepts to the sheriff, see JUST 3/31/1, m. 10; 68/1, m. 6 (Leics. and Warw., 1423).

In Leicestershire there was a remarkable 100 per cent conviction rate on appeal, as against the 7 per cent convicted and 75 per cent acquitted on indictment.[77] The reasons for this disparity are not clear. It is possible that appeals were brought only in cases where the defendant's guilt was manifest. On the other hand the correlation between procedure and outcome is so strong as to suggest that part of the explanation lies in the nature of the appeal itself—the presence of the victim or his kin in court as accuser, in direct confrontation with the accused.

The second possible source of evidence to inform the jury lay with officials involved in the processes of indictment and arrest—the JPs, coroners, bailiffs, and constables—who were obliged to attend gaol deliveries in the line of duty. In discharging their duties these officials probably became acquainted with the facts of most cases and with the parties involved. JPs in particular might have examined the defendant and his accuser before committal, although before the sixteenth century they had no obligation to record the examination in writing.[78]

In summary, it is probable that in the fifteenth century trial juries were not usually self-informing, but relied upon the presentation of evidence in court by the private accuser and the officers of the law. Apart from the requirement of written examinations by JPs laid down in the Marian statutes, procedure was similar to that outlined by Sir Thomas Smith in the mid-sixteenth century. The weakness of late medieval trial procedure lay not so much in the increasing inability of the jury to inform itself as in the lack of means to compel the attendance of the private prosecutor in court.[79] It was this which helps to explain the high levels of acquittal on indictment during our period,[80] and which accounts for the

---

[77] Powell, 'Jury Trial', 102. The numbers of those appealed were small, but because of the large proportion who were convicted they are not statistically insignificant. In Leics. those arraigned on appeal constituted only 6% of those accused but 49% of those convicted: ibid. 104.

[78] Langbein, *Prosecuting Crime*, 67–103; Bellamy, *Criminal Law and Society*, 8–32.

[79] Powell, 'Jury Trial', 105–11.

[80] Ibid., tables 10, 13, 16; R. B. Pugh, 'Some Reflections of a Medieval Criminologist', *PBA* 59 (1973), 89; Given, *Society and Homicide*, 92, 99; *Shrops. Peace Roll*, 42–4; Green, *Verdict According to Conscience*, 22–6, 59–60. See table 8 in ch. 7. Cf.

concern of the legislation of the 1550s to secure the accuser's appearance.[81] As in other areas of judicial administration, the effectiveness of the criminal trial depended upon the conscientiousness and integrity of the private party and the local community.

MITIGATION AND PARDON OF OFFENCES

We have noted that rates of acquittal were very high in medieval courts. Available data from the thirteenth to the fifteenth centuries suggests that roughly 70 per cent of indicted felons were acquitted.[82] As suggested above, the reluctance of juries to convict stemmed in part from the failure of the accuser to appear in court. Equally significant, however, was the severity of the law of felony established under the Angevin kings, with its near-universal capital penalty. After 1200 the criminal law was sharply at odds with popular attitudes, which endorsed the death penalty only for the most vicious and premeditated crimes. In consequence, as Professor Green has shown, trial juries effectively nullified the law in many cases where the accused was guilty of felony but did not, in their opinion, deserve execution.[83] They did so either by returning verdicts of outright acquittal or by finding the defendant guilty of a lesser, non-capital offence. For example, whereas all deliberate, unjustifiable homicides were technically capital, in practice juries distinguished aggravated or truly premeditated cases, where levels of conviction were very high, from slayings in the heat of the moment, for which

Smith, *De Republica Anglorum*, 113: 'If none come in to give evidence, although the malefactor hath confessed the crime to the Justice of the peace . . . the twelve men will acquite the prisoner . . .'.

[81] 1 & 2 Philip & Mary c. 13; 2 & 3 Philip & Mary c. 10. Langbein, *Prosecuting Crime*, 5–17. It is therefore my contention that the contrast between the medieval and Tudor trial procedure has been overstated, and that the early modern 'transformation' of jury trial was more gradual and protracted than commentators such as Langbein and Green have assumed. It is also possible that even in the earliest days of jury trial in the thirteenth century juries were never entirely self-informing in the strict sense in which the term has been interpreted, and that accusers and witnesses had always had the chance to inform the jury in court: see Powell, 'Jury Trial', 105–16.

[82] See above, nn. 77, 80.

[83] Green, *Verdict According to Conscience*, 28–64.

verdicts of self-defence were often contrived.[84] Thus, according to Green's argument, trial juries imposed the community's attitudes upon the formal rules of the king's courts. The death penalty may have served as a form of ultimate deterrent used to exert pressure on offenders to make amends to their victims, so facilitating their reconciliation to the community. During the sixteenth century this unofficial nullification came to be accepted and institutionalized through the extension of benefit of clergy. Originally designed to preserve offenders in clerical orders from the indignities of secular punishment, benefit of clergy became available during the late middle ages to all convicted felons who could read or recite the 'neck-verse', the formal test of literacy which was accepted by the courts from the mid-fourteenth century as proof of clerical status.[85] A series of Tudor statutes regulated the availability of benefit of clergy for convicted felons, formally endorsing the mitigation of the rigours of the law of felony which had been practised informally by medieval trial juries.[86]

The evolution of the rules governing benefit of clergy from the informal nullification of medieval trial juries illustrates neatly the tension between royal authority and local initiative which determined the shape and character of criminal judicial administration in England. That can also be detected, though somewhat less clearly, in relation to the granting of royal pardons. The king's prerogative of pardon was a central element of royal authority, and the exercise of mercy a fundamental quality of kingship. During the fourteenth century this prerogative came to be exploited for financial

---

[84] Ibid. 58. Green's work has contributed greatly to our understanding of medieval jury behaviour, particularly in showing how the practice of jury nullification came to modify the law of felony. His insistence, however, upon the community-based quality of jury verdicts raises as yet unanswered questions as to the precise 'community' the juries represented. Green appears to assume a very localized basis for the jury, perhaps at village level: ibid. 28–59. In view of the data relating to jury composition discussed above, it is possible that juries in fact represented substantial yeomen or lesser gentlemen on the fringes of the gentry county community: cf. Maddicott, 'County Community', 27–43.

[85] L. C. Gabel, *Benefit of Clergy in England in the Later Middle Ages* (Northampton, Mass., 1929), 64–78.

[86] Green, *Verdict According to Conscience*, 116–25; Bellamy, *Criminal Law and Society*, 115–64. Thus benefit of clergy was made available for those convicted of deliberate but sudden homicide, but denied to those found guilty of premeditated slaying, following the distinction observed by medieval juries.

ends by the periodic granting of comprehensive general pardons which could be sued individually out of chancery, and which exempted the beneficiary from a wide range of fiscal liabilities and remitted the king's suit for felony, trespass, and sometimes even treason.[87] Royal pardons could be obtained at any time, not merely after conviction, so that, unlike a claim of benefit of clergy, the presentation of a pardon upon arraignment entailed the defendant's immediate release without the necessity of undergoing trial.[88]

The attitude of the king's subjects towards such pardons was ambivalent, for while they were ready to take advantage of the financial relief thus offered, they were sensitive to the abuse of the Crown's prerogative of mercy, and concerned at the potentially detrimental effect of general pardons on the state of public order.[89] This led eventually to the Statute of Pardons of 1390 which excluded from general pardons those charged with aggravated homicide, treason, and rape.[90] The attempt to abridge the royal prerogative by statute was short-lived, however, since its provisions were ignored by Henry V in the general pardon issued in 1414, and were generally disregarded thereafter.[91]

The lavish and indiscriminate dispensation of pardons throughout our period vitiated the effectiveness of the machinery of criminal justice. The problem was particularly acute in time of war, when criminals and outlaws might be pardoned in return for military service: it has been estimated that Edward I pardoned and recruited over 2,000 felons in

---

[87] Harriss, *Public Finance*, 408–10; Powell, 'Public Order', 218–22; Storey, *House of Lancaster*, 210–16; Blatcher, *King's Bench*, 81–7.

[88] Pardons were obtainable from chancery for a fee of 16s. 4d. upon presentation of security to keep the peace. In cases of felony, pardons had to be accompanied by a writ of *non molestetis* certifying that security had been given and ordering the justices to proceed no further with the charges: *Shrops. Peace Roll*, 44; Storey, *House of Lancaster*, 212; C. A. F. Meekings, 'King's Bench Files', in J. H. Baker (ed.), *Legal Records and the Historian* (London, 1978), 103–4. The PRO class of chancery files C 237 (bails on special pardons) consists of securities given on receipt of special pardons.

[89] *RP* i. 444; ii. 171–2, 253. See also 10 Edward III c. 2; 14 Edward III c. 15. N. D. Hurnard, *The King's Pardon for Homicide before 1307* (Oxford, 1969), 311–26; T. A. Green, 'The Jury and the English Law of Homicide, 1200–1600', *Michigan Law Review*, 74 (1976), 457–62; Bellamy, *Public Order*, 195.

[90] 13 Richard II st. 2 c. 1.

[91] C 67 (chancery, patent rolls supplementary (pardon rolls))/37, m. 60; see ch. 7 at nn. 91–2.

the last decade of his reign.[92] Given the low levels of conviction in medieval courts it is likely that only a small minority of such offenders would have gone to the gallows had they been tried. The concern of the shire communities, reflected in their petitions to Parliament, was rather that large numbers of criminals were dispensed from submitting to trial, from placing themselves 'on the country' and putting their lives and reputations in the hands of a local jury. The large-scale use of pardons undermined the initiative and authority of the local judicial agencies by reducing the informal social pressures towards compensation or reform which a community could exert upon offenders under the threat of the death penalty.

[92] Hurnard, *King's Pardon*, 316–17. See ch. 9 at nn. 18–31 for Henry V's use of pardons for recruitment.

4

Law, Politics, and Dispute Settlement in Local Society

WE ARE on comparatively well-trodden ground when dealing with the structure and workings of the late medieval system of criminal justice. The voluminous records of court proceedings have received much attention from scholars, so that, while obscure areas remain, the terrain is for the most part well charted. Once we step outside the courtroom, however, we are on less familiar ground. Only recently have historians begun to investigate the social history of medieval law, and to consider what the content of litigation or the pattern of crime can reveal about society in general, or how the formal judicial procedures were used in the wider conduct of disputes and the containment of deviant behaviour.[1] This chapter attempts to explore such themes, giving particular attention to the relationship between central and local government, the characteristics of the disputing process, including arbitration, and the problem of judicial corruption.

Although we are concerned with the administration of criminal justice, it would be misleading to restrict the ensuing discussion to the criminal law. As previous chapters have attempted to show, prosecution had many procedural features in common with civil litigation, partly because of the active role of the victim. In some respects the criminal law was still a specialized branch of civil litigation in which the Crown took a particular interest. Moreover indictments and civil actions

---

[1] A. Harding, *A Social History of English Law* (Harmondsworth, 1966); R. C. Palmer, *The Whilton Dispute, 1264–1380* (Princeton, NJ, 1984); Given, *Society and Homicide*; B. A. Hanawalt, *Crime and Conflict in English Communities, 1300–48* (Cambridge, Mass., 1979). For methodological problems associated with approaching the social history of medieval law through quantification, see E. ·Powell, 'Social Research and the Use of Medieval Criminal Records', *Michigan Law Review*, 79 (1981), 967–78. For a recent survey of the social history of crime in the early modern period, see J. A. Sharpe, *Crime in Early Modern England, 1550–1750* (London, 1984).

were routinely used together as complementary weapons in the same dispute. The workings of criminal justice must therefore be considered in this wider context.

CENTRAL AUTHORITY AND LOCAL GOVERNMENT

The most important feature of late medieval legal history is the expansion of royal authority. Between 1150 and 1400 the jurisdictional balance shifted decisively in favour of the Crown, at the expense of local territorial courts and the baronial and seigneurial liberties.[2] The judicial system constructed by the Angevin kings and their successors created a framework of institutions and a body of common law which regulated a wide range of social relationships and transactions, particularly those governing land—the fundamental source of wealth, status, and power throughout the middle ages. A uniform system of legal machinery was constructed, based on the central courts at Westminster, the assize circuits, and the peace commissions, through which the king's authority was channelled into the shires.[3] The consequences of this shift were profound,[4] but they did not include a revolution in the social and political structure of England. In practice the king's power to enforce the law was limited because he lacked the resources to maintain a salaried magistracy, police force, and standing army. In addition, relatively poor communications between Westminster and the provinces, particularly in winter, tended to delay the receipt of royal instructions and thus blunted their effectiveness.[5]

The routine administration of justice was thus inevitably decentralized, and the Crown had to rely on the co-operation of the local communities, and above all on the landowning classes, the magnates and gentry who were the traditional rulers of the counties and who controlled the older territorial and feudal jurisdictions which were rapidly declining as royal

[2] See Introduction at nn. 33–78.
[3] See ch. 2.
[4] See below at nn. 6–21.
[5] Cf. Carpenter, 'Law, Justice and Landowners', 213. Until the nineteenth century the assize judges visited the northernmost counties of Northumberland, Westmorland, and Cumberland no more than once a year, and in the late middle ages there were complaints at the infrequency of their visits: Cockburn, *Assizes*, 19, 45; *RP* iii. 662.

justice expanded.[6] In order to preserve their economic, political, and social predominance they needed to establish control over the new machinery of justice in their localities. They succeeded in doing so chiefly because they were the king's natural partners in government: he needed their support to raise taxation, fight his wars, and run local government. Through their representation in Parliament they curbed the activities of central legal officials, and increased their own judicial role through the commissions of the peace.[7]

The administration of justice entailed a continuous dialogue beween central government and the localities. The machinery of royal justice would have broken down without the active co-operation of the king's subjects. On the other hand the king was the ultimate guarantor of the system, explicitly bound to uphold the laws and do justice by the terms of his coronation oath. If the dialogue was not always harmonious, it was because the expansion of royal authority injected a powerful and unpredictable new force into the shires, which could disturb the equilibrium of local, and even national, politics.[8] On occasion the exercise of royal judicial authority was actively resisted where it was seen to conflict with the best interests of the local community. Opposition was often financially motivated, as in 1297 when juries refused to co-operate with commissions investigating the concealment of wool stocks from the royal prise, or in 1381, when commissions of inquiry into the evasion of the third poll tax sparked off the Peasants' Revolt in Essex.[9] In the 1340s the financially punitive series of trailbastons and inquiries imposed by Edward III roused fierce hostility both inside and outside Parliament: at Ipswich in 1344, after the departure of William Shareshull, who had presided over sessions of oyer and terminer in the town, a royal informant was murdered and a mock trial held of Shareshull and his colleague William Notton.[10] In 1414 the attempts of Henry V's justices to

---

[6] Post, 'Local Jurisdictions', 1–21; Palmer, *County Courts*, 56–173, 220–306.

[7] See Introduction at nn. 68–75.

[8] Cf. Kaeuper, 'Law and Order', 747–51, 774–81.

[9] T. H. Lloyd, *The English Wool Trade in the Middle Ages* (Cambridge, 1977), 92–3; Dobson, *Peasants' Revolt*, 119–22.

[10] *SKB* vi, pp. xxvii, 37; Putnam, *Shareshull*, 66–7; Harriss, *Public Finance*, 287, 405–7.

investigate acts of piracy by Devonshire mariners were met by a wall of silence from the jurors of the county.[11]

Royal justice might therefore be an unwelcome intruder in the shires. Indeed Dr Clanchy has gone so far as to argue that it was a disruptive force, which, far from promoting law and order, could destabilize local society and foster disorder.[12] There is some evidence to support this line of argument, particularly in the use of special commissions of oyer and terminer as weapons in local politics.[13] It would be dangerous, however, to turn conventional wisdom on its head, and to assume that royal power was inherently disruptive; what made it so, above all in the fourteenth century, was its rapid growth and extension into the localities. As it took on institutional form and was assimilated into existing local power-structures, so its destabilizing effects diminished.[14]

The local gentry communities of late medieval England have been the subject of several detailed studies, concentrated mainly in the Midlands and North. They have revealed highly localized, close-knit societies, at once cohesive and competitive, as well as intensely suspicious of external intervention. Whether or not such communities were shaped by the institutional geography of shire or lordship, they were bound together by ties of service, marriage, landholding, and regional sentiment which may have fostered rather than inhibited their incessant territorial disputes.[15] Within these communities greater landowners played an important role as arbiters and as power-brokers between central government

---

[11] See ch. 8 at nn. 41–59.

[12] Clanchy, 'Law, Government and Society', 78; id., 'Law and Love in the Middle Ages', in J. Bossy (ed.), *Disputes and Settlements* (Cambridge, 1983), 64.

[13] See above, n. 8.

[14] Cf. S. Roberts, 'The Study of Disputes: Anthropological Perspectives' in J. Bossy (ed.), *Disputes and Settlements* (Cambridge, 1983), 1–19, for a valuable general discussion of the relationship between central authority and local communities regarding dispute settlement.

[15] Carpenter, 'Political Society in Warwickshire'; Wright, *Derbyshire Gentry*; Bennett, *Community, Class and Careerism*; id., 'A County Community: Social Cohesion amongst the Cheshire Gentry, 1400–1425', *Northern History*, 8 (1973), 24–44; Pollard, 'Richmondshire'; M. Cherry, 'The Crown and the Political Community in Devonshire, 1377–1461', Ph.D. thesis (Swansea, 1981); S. J. Payling, 'Political Society in Lancastrian Nottinghamshire', D.Phil. thesis (Oxford, 1987).

and the locality.[16] Their authority therefore depended not merely on the size and income of their estates, but also on their political skills and influence at court: whereas a magnate high in royal favour was virtually irresistible in his 'country', exclusion from royal counsels could have a disastrous effect upon his local standing.[17] Membership of the retinues or affinities of such magnates offered the benefits of 'good lordship' in terms of protection and patronage, and provided a ready-made network of associates and allies who could witness agreements, give legal advice, act as mediators or arbitrators in disputes, and provide suitable marriage partners.[18]

Law and politics were inextricably linked in such communities. The overriding concern of their members was the defence and consolidation of the estates which were the source of wealth and status. In consequence control and manipulation of the legal system were vital ingredients, not just of success, but of survival, dictating the search for good lordship, the holding of office, and the acquisition of political influence.[19] The growing complexity of the law of real property in the late middle ages, caused principally by the increasing use of the entail and enfeoffment to use, meant that landowners had to exercise constant vigilance in defence of their estates.[20] Late medieval England was an obsessively litigious society, and territorial disputes the essential matter of litigation.[21]

The law courts, however, were by no means the only weapon available in the pursuit of defence of title to land.

[16] e.g. the Stanley family in north-west England and the Conyers family in Richmondshire: Bennett, *Community, Class and Careerism*, 215–23; Pollard, 'Richmondshire', 53–6.
[17] M. Cherry, 'The Struggle for Power in Mid-Fifteenth Century Devonshire', in R. A. Griffiths (ed.), *Patronage, the Crown and the Provinces in Later Medieval England* (Gloucester, 1981), 123–44.
[18] M. C. Carpenter, 'The Beauchamp Affinity: A Study of Bastard Feudalism at Work', *EHR* 95 (1980), 515–32.
[19] Ead., 'Law, Justice and Landowners', 219–37.
[20] Ead., 'Beauchamp Affinity', 524; S. J. Payling, 'Inheritance and Local Politics in the Later Middle Ages: The Case of Ralph, Lord Cromwell and the Heriz Inheritance' *NMS* 30 (1986), 67–96; see also Holdsworth, *History of English Law*, ii. 416. Possibly the growth of royal jurisdiction also caused litigation to proliferate by creating new avenues of resort to law and by undermining the older certainties of title to land: S. F. C. Milsom, *The Legal Framework of English Feudalism* (Cambridge, 1976), 185–6.   [21] Ives, *Common Lawyers*, 7–22.

They were most commonly used in conjunction with other resorts such as self-help or informal negotiation. The workings of the law within local society cannot be understood in isolation, but must be considered in the context of a broader strategy of dispute settlement. The next section attempts to set the law in this wider context.

THE LAW COURTS AND THE DISPUTING PROCESS

The central task facing the social historian of the law is the interpretation of the legal records. Because of their 'official' character they have retained an aura of objectivity long ago stripped from medieval chronicles; and because of their bulk they convey an impression of completeness which has encouraged some scholars to attempt the compilation of crime rate statistics.[22] Both impressions are false. Bias and incompleteness are the hallmarks of legal records, along with the opaque formalism of legal procedure and terminology which obscures the distinct features of each case. As with any other source, such records can only be understood in relation to their purpose. Because the legal system was adversarial, civil suits and criminal prosecutions alike were not statements of fact but *ex parte* allegations of one disputant against another. Criminal indictments require especially careful scrutiny. Unlike fertility or mortality, crime is not an objective social phenomenon but the product of a complex series of human interactions and decisions; whether an act was defined as criminal and led to indictment depended upon considerations such as the relative social and official standing of actor and victim, prevailing norms of social behaviour, and the composition and sympathies of presenting juries.[23]

The most significant limitation of the legal records is that they present a very one-sided and incomplete view of the disputing process: only very occasionally do they hint at negotiations out of court.[24] Until recently this view was taken

---

[22] Given, *Society and Homicide, passim*; Hanawalt, *Crime and Conflict, passim*; C. I. Hammer, 'Patterns of Homicide in Fourteenth-Century Oxford', *Past and Present*, 78 (1978), 1–23.

[23] Powell, 'Social Research', 967–8. Cf. Elton, 'Crime and the Historian', 1–14.

[24] Roberts, 'Study of Dispute', 1–6; Clanchy, 'Law and Love', 50–1.

at face value, and legal history was written as if the law courts were the only available means of resolving disputes in medieval England; the inconclusiveness of most proceedings was seen as a sign of judicial inefficiency and governmental weakness.[25] To borrow the terms of legal anthropologists, medieval legal historians have been narrowly 'rule-centred' rather than 'processual' in their approach, viewing disputes in terms of breaches of social rules which the law courts existed to put right.[26] The inadequacy of this method is that it ignores extra-judicial proceedings and concentrates on the formal procedures and institutions of the law at the expense of the purposes for which it was used by individual disputants.[27] By contrast the 'processual' approach views conflict as an inevitable part of social interaction, as individuals compete to secure their objectives. Disputes thereby come to be studied from the standpoint of the disputants themselves, revealing the strategies they adopt to achieve their aims.

The 'rule-centred' and 'processual' approaches are complementary, although the latter has long been overlooked by medieval scholars, and therefore requires particular emphasis. Litigation and prosecution were not pursued in isolation, but as part of an overall strategy for dispute settlement. The law courts might thus be used tactically to exert pressure on an opponent to settle out of court rather than with the single-minded intention of forcing a judicial resolution.[28] Even where a lawsuit came to final judgment we must beware of assuming that this was the end of the story. As Dr Clanchy has shown in the case of Barnwell abbey against Henry Tuillet, the final outcome might be the reverse of the legal position.[29] Legal records cannot be studied in a vacuum, but must be related wherever possible to out-of-court proceedings.

The work of legal anthropologists is of value here in suggesting the choice of methods available for resolving

---

[25] Powell, 'Settlement of Disputes', 21–4.

[26] Roberts, 'Study of Dispute', 3–4.

[27] Ibid. 22.

[28] See below at nn. 50–2.

[29] Clanchy, 'Law and Love', 57–8. In 1286 Tuillet won an action of novel disseisin brought against him by the abbot for arrears of rent. Nevertheless the abbot subsequently managed to browbeat Tuillet into recognizing his liability for rent in return for pardoning half the arrears.

disputes.[30] They range from violent self-help, through direct negotiation and mediation, to arbitration and adjudication (i.e. resort to law). These methods fall into three categories, according to the level of third-party involvement: self-help and negotiation, where the parties seek to settle the dispute without outside help; mediation, where a neutral party helps to bring about a settlement; and arbitration and adjudication, where the parties submit their dispute to an umpire for his decision, thereby surrendering their power to negotiate a settlement directly.[31] In simple disputes only one such method may be adopted, but where several alternatives are available they can be used in conjunction and provide the scope for complex and sophisticated disputing strategies.

The relevance of this general theoretical framework to late medieval England is obvious when well-documented disputes come to light. The evidence points to a continuous interplay between litigation and extra-judicial manoeuvring and negotiation. A case from the Paston letters confirms how involved and intricate the disputing process could be.[32] The differences between William Paston and Walter Aslake in the 1420s allegedly began when Paston acted as legal counsel to the prior of Norwich in a suit between Aslake and the prior over the advowson of Sprowston in Norfolk. In August 1424 Aslake posted bills in Norwich threatening Paston's safety; Paston responded by demanding surety of the peace from Aslake before the Norfolk JP Sir Thomas Erpingham, and by lodging an action of trespass against him in the city court of Norwich. Aslake brought in the required surety before Erpingham, who tried to dissuade Paston from pursuing his trespass suit, arranging instead for the dispute to go to arbitration. Paston agreed to submit to this award, but insisted upon continuing his action, ostensibly for reasons of prestige, while promising, according to Aslake, 'that the said Walter should not be damaged in his body nor his goods, whatever the quest said'.[33] The accounts of Aslake and Paston differ on the course of the

---

[30] Roberts, 'Study of Dispute', 11–13; L. Nader and H. F. Todd (edd.), *The Disputing Process: Law in Ten Societies* (New York, NY, 1978), 8–11.

[31] S. Roberts, *Order and Dispute* (Harmondsworth, 1979), 69–71.

[32] Two conflicting versions of this dispute appear in *Paston Letters*, i. 7–12; ii. 505–7.

[33] Ibid. ii. 506.

lawsuit: Paston claimed that it proceeded in due and lawful form, while Aslake alleged that a packed jury was empanelled at dead of night with the assent of corrupt officials to ensure his conviction. Both versions agreed, however, on the outcome: the jury found for Paston and awarded £120 in damages against Aslake, who was committed to gaol in Norwich. As a result the attempted arbitration arranged by Erpingham broke down late in 1424.

After a lull of several months negotiations resumed between the parties, and in the spring of 1425 Erpingham persuaded the duke of Gloucester to arrange a second arbitration, which was to be concluded by August of that year.[34] Meanwhile Aslake secured his release from gaol through a writ of *corpus cum causa* in chancery, and in July submitted a petition against Paston to Parliament. Paston countered with a bill of account in the exchequer for the damages owed him by Aslake.[35] Despite this continued litigation, the arbitration arranged by Gloucester was completed at Norwich in August 1425. According to Paston's account, Aslake, newly released from gaol, refused to observe its provisions and took his grievances against Paston to the duke of Norfolk. This proved a most effective strategy, causing Norfolk, on Paston's own admission, 'to be heavy lord to the said William'.[36] On Norfolk's instructions Paston twice agreed to further efforts at arbitration in the spring of 1426, although both were unsuccessful. Having seized the initiative Aslake kept up the pressure, bringing actions against the jurors who convicted him on Paston's suit of trespass and petitioning the Leicester Parliament of 1426.[37] After a fifth inconclusive submission to arbitrators late in 1426,[38] the matter was finally settled by the award of the duke of Norfolk in June 1428: Paston was ordered to pay Aslake £50 in return for a release of all personal actions.[39]

The Paston–Aslake dispute bears comparison with other recently studied cases, such as the Ladbroke manor dispute and the Mountford case in Warwickshire, the Arundel–Talbot

---

[34] *Paston Letters*, i. 9.

[35] Ibid. ii. 506–7.   [36] Ibid. i. 10.   [37] Ibid. i. 11–12; ii. 505.

[38] Paston's memorandum to arbitrators in the dispute apparently survives from this attempt: ibid. i. 7–8.

[39] *CCR, 1422–29*, pp. 393–4, 406.

feud in Shropshire, Sir John Fastolf's litigation in East
Anglia, and the struggle over the Heriz inheritance in
Nottinghamshire.[40] From these studies the characteristics of
the late medieval disputing process are beginning to emerge.
The most significant features are the diversity of resorts
available to the parties; the involvement of third parties as
mediators and arbitrators; the importance of the political
influence and connections of the disputants in determining the
outcome of cases; and the pervasiveness of manipulation and
corruption in the legal process.

The diversity of resorts available is immediately apparent
in the Paston–Aslake case, where they ranged from the local
borough court to petitions in Parliament. The practice is
exemplified also by the Ladbroke manor dispute, which was
heard in king's bench and common pleas, at the assizes, in
chancery, by the king's council, and before the councils of four
magnates.[41] The abundance of different courts and forms of
action made the disputing process a complex enterprise
requiring great tactical skill, and disputants readily exploited
criminal as well as civil procedures. Indictment was a
particularly effective method of harassing an opponent because
of the involvement of the Crown as an injured party and the
rigorous legal process which it entailed; if successful, the
threat of outlawry and forfeiture could virtually neutralize an
opponent, which explains the lengths to which John Thornton
went to procure the indictment of Thomas Clare on behalf of
his master, Sir Thomas Green.[42]

The second principal feature of late medieval litigation is
the frequent intervention of third parties as intermediaries,
like Sir Thomas Erpingham in the Paston–Aslake dispute, or

[40] J. B. Post, 'Courts, Councils and Arbitrators in the Ladbroke Manor Dispute,
1382–1400', in R. F. Hunnisett and J. B. Post (edd.), *Medieval Legal Records Edited in
Memory of C. A. F. Meekings* (London, 1978), 289–339; Carpenter, 'Law, Justice and
Landowners', 219–25; A. Smith, 'Litigation and Politics: Sir John Fastolf's Defence
of his English Property', in A. J. Pollard (ed.), *Property and Politics: Essays in Later
Medieval English History* (Gloucester, 1984), 59–75; Payling, 'Heriz Inheritance', 67–
96; see ch. 8 at nn. 160–87.
[41] Post, 'Ladbroke Manor Dispute', 290.
[42] See ch. 3 at nn. 23–5. In the most extreme cases, such as the indictment of John
Bruyn during the Arundel–Talbot feud in Shropshire, it could be used to harass and
humiliate an opponent to the extent of driving him out of the county: see ch. 8
nn. 174–5.

as arbitrators. The importance of arbitration, and its place as an integral part of the disputing process, emerge quite clearly from the case studies mentioned above, and will be considered in more detail below.[43] A common form of third-party involvement in gentry disputes was intervention by a local magnate, usually at the request of one of the parties. Walter Aslake successfully appealed to the duke of Norfolk, just as Sir John Fastolf looked to Norfolk's son and successor for aid in settling his disputes over land.[44]

The status and political connections of the disputants were clearly vital in determining the outcome of cases, a factor most evident in major territorial disputes. The Mountford dispute in mid-fifteenth-century Warwickshire became a microcosm of wider political conflict, its course fluctuating with the national power-struggles in the 1450s; Sir John Fastolf's legal difficulties in the 1440s sprang largely from the opposition of the all-powerful duke of Suffolk and his adherents; while Ralph, Lord Cromwell's appropriation of the Heriz inheritance between 1430 and 1441, in the face of the much stronger claim of Sir Henry Pierrepont, would have been inconceivable but for his dominance of Nottinghamshire politics, stemming from his position as a royal councillor and treasurer of England from 1433.[45]

Closely related to the previous point is the most notorious characteristic of the late medieval disputing process: the manipulation and corruption of legal officials and procedure.[46] Case-studies confirm the anecdotal evidence of sources such as the Paston letters in showing that success in litigation depended upon the ability to exert pressure and influence on judges, sheriffs, and jurors—if necessary by bribery and intimidation.[47] Even if they did not resort to outright corruption, all self-respecting litigants knew how to exploit the

[43] Post, 'Ladbroke Manor Dispute', 294–7; Carpenter, 'Law, Justice and Landowners', 223–5; Smith, 'Litigation and Politics', 66–73.

[44] Ibid. 69–72; Post, 'Ladbroke Manor Dispute', 290–7; Carpenter, 'Law, Justice and Landowners', 220–5.

[45] Ibid. 222–3; Smith, 'Litigation and Politics', 73; Payling, 'Heriz Inheritance', 78–9, 94–5; cf. Post, 'Ladbroke Manor Dispute', 293–4.

[46] See below at nn. 96–122.

[47] H. S. Bennett, *The Pastons and Their England* (2nd edn.; Cambridge, 1932), 165–79; Ross, *Edward IV*, 389–95; McFarlane, *Nobility*, 117–18; Ives, *Common Lawyers*, 308–12.

technicalities of the law: a textbook example was Lord Cromwell's use of collusive legal actions to fortify his tenuous title to the Heriz inheritance; while in the Ladbroke manor dispute the Cardian family made the best of their slender claims by repeatedly defaulting in court, thus forestalling any definitive judgment in favour of their Catesby opponents and retaining their right to reopen the matter at a time when political circumstances might tilt in their favour.[48] Contrary to received opinion, however, physical violence was not used as a matter of course in late medieval disputes. As Dr Payling has pointed out, it was probably a matter of last rather than first resort for disputants, and played a comparatively minor part in the cases discussed. Threats or allegations of violence were much more common than violent acts, and the most notorious incidents tended to occur at times of serious political upheaval, such as the 1320s and 1330s, and the 1450s.[49]

ARBITRATION

There can be no doubt as to the importance of the law courts in the late medieval disputing process. It is difficult to imagine how a dispute could have been conducted without them, and for all their shortcomings there is no sign that frustrated litigants were avoiding recourse to the courts and seeking other remedies.[50] Nevertheless disputes were rarely settled through the courts alone. The fundamental feature of the process was the combined use of litigation and extra-judicial negotiation in an overall strategy for dispute settlement. Much legal action was therefore brought for secondary, tactical purposes—as a means to an end rather than an end in itself. Going to law might be a matter of social prestige and status, as William Paston asserted when pursuing his trespass action against Walter Aslake, or the means of obtaining a formal record of a claim with which to confront an opponent

---

[48] Payling, 'Heriz Inheritance', 75–85; Post, 'Ladbroke Manor Dispute', 294.

[49] Payling, 'Heriz Inheritance', 94–5; for the outrages committed by criminal gangs in the 1320s and 1330s, see Stones, 'Folvilles', *passim*; Bellamy, *Public Order*, 69–88. See Storey, *House of Lancaster*, 168–71, for the notorious murder of Nicholas Radford in Devon in 1455.

[50] Powell, 'Arbitration and the Law', 56–7.

out of court.[51] Most frequently it was a method of exerting pressure upon an adversary and persuading—or harassing—him to negotiate. Even today, as Dr Baker notes, 'the vast majority of cases commenced in the central courts never reach trial; the issue of a writ is as much an inducement to compromise as it is a threat to pursue the law to its conclusion.'[52]

The prevalence of extra-judicial forms of dispute settlement in late medieval England, and arbitration in particular, has by now been fully established.[53] Many historians had previously noted examples of arbitration, but it was generally assumed to have been a temporary expedient forced on litigants by the inadequacies of the legal system and above all by the collapse of royal authority during the Wars of the Roses.[54] Closer analysis has revealed, however, that throughout the middle ages and beyond, modes of compromise complemented legal procedures, and that 'love' often prevailed over 'law'.[55] Arbitration was, indeed, as characteristic of the disputing process as litigation, violence, or corruption.

The popularity of arbitration in late medieval England should occasion no surprise, for it possessed several advantages over litigation. As an antidote to the elaborate formalism of the common law and the delays and expenses this often entailed, arbitration offered a well-designed, adaptable procedure notable for its flexibility, simplicity, and speed. Since submission to arbitration—the *compromissio*—was a voluntary under-

---

[51] D. J. Guth, 'Enforcing Late-Medieval Law: Patterns in Litigation during Henry VII's Reign', in J. H. Baker (ed.), *Legal Records and the Historian* (London, 1978), 87.

[52] *Reports of Sir John Spelman*, ii. 91.

[53] Powell, 'Arbitration and the Law', 49–67; id., 'Settlement of Disputes', 21–43; Post, 'Ladbroke Manor Dispute', 289–339; id., 'Equitable Resorts before 1450', in E. W. Ives and A. H. Manchester (edd.), *Law, Litigants and the Legal Profession* (London, 1983), 68–79; Clanchy, 'Law and Love', 47–67; J. T. Rosenthal, 'Feuds and Private Peace-Making: a Fifteenth-Century Example', *NMS* 14 (1970), 84–90; I. Rowney, 'Arbitration in Gentry Disputes in the Later Middle Ages', *History*, 67 (1982), 367–76; C. Rawcliffe, 'The Great Lord as Peacekeeper: Arbitration by English Noblemen and Their Councils in the Later Middle Ages', in J. A. Guy (ed.), *Law and Social Change* (London, 1984), 34–54; M. A. Hicks, 'Restraint, Mediation and Private Justice: George, Duke of Clarence as "Good Lord"', *Journal of Legal History*, 4, no. 2 (1983), 56–71.

[54] Bellamy, *Public Order*, 118–19; Storey, *House of Lancaster*, 121–2, 155; Griffiths, *Henry VI*, 596.

[55] Clanchy, 'Law and Love', 47–51; Powell, 'Settlement of Disputes', 21–6.

taking, the participants enjoyed considerable discretion in arranging such details as the selection of arbitrators and the issues to be decided. With certain exceptions,[56] the legal system offered a very restricted choice of judges, whereas the choice of arbitrators was left entirely to the parties themselves.[57] Similarly, while the rigid structure of the forms of action constrained the judge to consider the facts of the case only in so far as they related to the legal issue at hand, the arbitrators could, if the parties so wished, examine the broader context of the dispute. In this respect arbitration offered a far better prospect of achieving a lasting settlement because it allowed disputants to air all their grievances and did not confine them to a single point of conflict which might merely be symptomatic of deeper divisions.[58]

The voluntary nature of arbitration was also important in shaping a simple and unencumbered mode of procedure. It was assumed from their free submission that the parties desired a quick resolution of the dispute, and for this reason no dilatory devices were permitted, nor any appeal allowed against the final award.[59] Here the backing of the courts was essential, for without their recognition resort to arbitration would have been futile. The common law provided unequivocal support by accepting the plea of arbitration as a bar to further legal action. In addition there were various legal remedies available, if necessary, to enforce the obligations incurred through arbitration.[60]

Simplicity of procedure made for speed of execution, and speed was essential in arbitration, both to prevent the escalation of disputes and to keep down costs. The *compromissio*, which in general took the form of mutual bonds with conditional defeasance,[61] usually set a term for the completion

---

[56] Kaeuper, 'Law and Order', 758–61.

[57] Cf. H. Janeau, 'L'Arbitrage en Dauphiné au Moyen Age', *Revue Historique de Droit Français et Étranger*, 4th ser., 24–5 (1946–7), 245–6; B. Guenée, *Tribunaux et Gens de Justice dans le Bailliage de Senlis à la Fin du Moyen Age* (Paris, 1963), 117–20.

[58] Cf. S. D. White, ' "Pactum . . . Legem Vincit et Amor Judicium": The Settlement of Disputes by Compromise in Eleventh-Century Western France', *AJLH* 22 (1978), 281–308.

[59] In certain circumstances appeal from arbitration to the ecclesiastical courts was permitted at canon law: Powell, 'Arbitration and the Law', 54 n. 35.

[60] Ibid. 63–6.

[61] Ibid. 63–4.

of the award.[62] There was of course the risk that the term might run out, and the arbitrators' powers thus expire, before the award had been completed. This was not uncommon, but in such cases new arbitration arrangements were usually made.[63] The cost of arbitration was also kept down by savings on court expenses and lawyers' fees. John Wheathampstead, abbot of St Albans in 1431, boasted that he had saved his house a thousand marks by avoiding litigation with William Fleet of Rickmansworth and opting instead for arbitration.[64]

Without question the use of arbitration also had its disadvantages, notably the problem of enforcing an award with which either party felt dissatisfied.[65] When informal social pressures were ineffective, awards could only be enforced through the courts, which of course the whole process was designed to avoid. Nor, according to contemporary observers such as Langland and Wyclif, was arbitration any more impervious to corruption and intimidation than the law.[66] Indeed there were occasions when lovedays degenerated into armed brawls between the supporters of the disputing parties.[67] Such hazards were not peculiar to arbitration, however, but were fundamental elements in the conduct of disputes as long as the coercive powers of the government remained relatively weak. The problem of enforcement and the ease with which disputes escalated into violence gave still greater urgency to the search for genuine conciliation and compromise which was the main function of arbitration.

Perhaps the most important feature of arbitration in late medieval England is the frequency with which it occurred in conjunction with litigation. Like war and diplomacy, the two went hand in hand. Legal proceedings, like a military campaign, might be protracted, costly, and inconclusive, but with the threat that a tactical error could bring total defeat;

[62] e.g. *CCR, 1409–13*, pp. 69, 187; *1413–19*, p. 369; *1429–35*, p. 157.

[63] As, for example, in the Paston–Aslake dispute: see above at nn. 32–9.

[64] John Amundesham, *Annales Monasterii Sancti Albani*, ed. H. T. Riley, Rolls Ser. (2 vols.; London, 1870–1), i. 273.

[65] Powell, 'Arbitration and the Law', 56–7 and n. 67.

[66] J. W. Bennett, 'The Medieval Loveday', *Speculum*, 33 (1958), 364–5.

[67] *Memorials of London and London Life, 1276–1419*, ed. and tr. H. T. Riley (London, 1868), 156–62; see ch. 5 at n. 20.

whereas arbitration, like diplomacy, offered the safer if less spectacular alternative of peaceful negotiation.

Not all disputants, then, embarked on legal action with the single-minded intention of pursuing the law to its conclusion. Their purpose might rather be to persuade the opposing party to negotiate by threatening him with the expenses, risks, and inconvenience of a lawsuit. A well-documented example, from Shropshire, concerns a dispute resolved by arbitration in 1427. Two gentlemen, John Bruyn of Bridgnorth and John Gatacre of Gatacre, had come into conflict during the previous year. The origins of the dispute are obscure, but in the autumn of 1426 it flared into armed confrontation. During a mêlée between the adherents of the two parties involving about fifty men, one Roger Lockwood was killed by an arrow allegedly fired by Thomas Chamberlain, a supporter of John Bruyn's. It is not certain that Lockwood was a follower of Gatacre's—he may have been merely an innocent bystander— but there is no doubt that Gatacre encouraged the appeal of homicide brought in king's bench by Lockwood's widow Isabella against Bruyn and his followers.[68] Bruyn and others, including Thomas Chamberlain, pleaded not guilty in Hilary term 1427, and a trial jury was summoned for the following term. Meanwhile, through the mediation of friends of both parties, the two sides submitted their dispute to a panel of four arbitrators: two prelates, the abbot of Shrewsbury and the prior of Wenlock, and two influential gentlemen, George Hawkstone and Hugh Burgh. The arbitrators were empowered to deal with all 'debates, dissensions, and discords' between the two parties, including the death of Lockwood.[69] Twenty-eight of Bruyn's supporters and twenty-five of Gatacre's were also party to the award, which was concluded shortly before Easter 1427, well in advance of the date set for the trial in king's bench.

The arbitrators' award, although brief, contains numerous provisions. The first clause stipulated that all parties 'should

[68] KB 27/663, m. 55.

[69] Nat. Lib. Wales, Pitchford Hall deeds, no. 2482: 'debatez, discenciouns et discordes'. Hawkstone and Burgh were leading members of the affinity of John Talbot, Lord Talbot (later earl of Shrewsbury) and prominent in Shrops. administration: A. J. Pollard, 'The Family of Talbot, Lords Talbot and Earls of Shrewsbury, in the Fifteenth Century', Ph.D. thesis (Bristol, 1968), 217–19, 233–4.

henceforth be good and loyal friends, without holding any rancour or hatred in their hearts for things which have been done before this time'.[70] Bruyn and Gatacre were each ordered to pay £4 for the maintenance of a chaplain for one year to celebrate masses for Lockwood's soul, any funds remaining to go to his widow. The arbitrators also decreed that Gatacre and Isabella Lockwood should expedite legal process on the appeal in king's bench, 'in order to secure the speedy delivery of the said John Bruyn and all the afore-mentioned persons of his party according to common law'. Bruyn and the others were indeed acquitted in Michaelmas term 1427.[71] Further, Bruyn and his associate Thomas Ashton, a gentleman from Groby in Leicestershire, were ordered by the arbitrators to make every effort to secure for Gatacre the good lordship of Lord Ferrers of Groby. This apparently unrelated provision reveals something of the background to the dispute: presumably Gatacre had tried unsuccessfully to win favour with Lord Ferrers and in some way blamed Bruyn for his failure. There followed a number of subsidiary clauses, including provision that any lesser disputes still unresolved between the parties be resubmitted to the arbitrators by a specific date for determination.

This award demonstrates the flexibility and informality that constituted the greatest advantages of arbitration over a legal decision. Whereas an appeal of homicide was capable of determining only the culpability of Lockwood's slayers, the arbitrators authorized a series of reciprocal acts which restored the peace and laid the basis for future harmonious relations between the disputants. In practice Isabella's appeal was only a tactical device to put pressure on Bruyn to come to terms. Above all the theme of the award was the re-establishment of amity and concord, as emphasized by the arbitrators' opening provision that all parties henceforth be good and loyal friends.

[70] Nat. Lib. Wales, Pitchford Hall deeds, no. 2482: 'soient bones amys et loiales desorenavaunt saunce ascun ranker ou envie tenier en lour coers pour nullez chosez devaunt ses heurez featez ou movez'.

[71] Ibid.: 'al esploit de hastif deliveraunce de dit John Bruyn et touz lez aultrez de sa part desuisnomez solonc la cours de comyn ley'; the acquittal is at KB 27/663, m. 55.

Arbitrations of this kind, intended primarily to repair the consequences of criminal violence, were commonplace in the fifteenth century,[72] but among the county gentry they were much less numerous than arbitrations involving property disputes. The records of Burton abbey in Staffordshire, for instance, show that during the fifteenth century the house several times resorted to arbitration in its incessant conflicts with the local gentry over land.[73] One such case was the long-running dispute between the abbey and Sir John Bagot over lands in Abbots Bromley in Staffordshire, which went back to at least 1405.[74] In 1414 the abbot petitioned the chancellor and the king concerning the oppressions and depredations committed by Bagot against the abbey,[75] but it was not until 1428 that the issue was finally resolved by arbitration. The arbitrators were the bishop of Coventry and Lichfield and the earl of Stafford, the leading spiritual and temporal peers of the county. Bagot and the abbey presented witnesses and written evidence to the arbitrators and their counsellors, many of whom were no doubt men of law.[76] Again the award is notable for its reciprocal character: the abbey's rights to the disputed land were confirmed and Bagot was ordered to desist from further litigation; in return the abbey was to pay Bagot £40, in effect buying out his claims. The arbitrators also decreed that the abbey should grant Bagot an annuity of twenty shillings for life from rents in Abbots Bromley. To reinforce the settlement the arbitrators provided for a collusive lawsuit. They ordered that an action of novel disseisin brought by Bagot against the abbey, and still pending at the time of the award, should be continued in Bagot's name by attorneys appointed and directed by the abbot, who was to conclude the lawsuit as he saw fit. In 1429 Bagot quitclaimed the lands in

[72] See, for example, Rosenthal, 'Feuds and Private Peace-Making', 84–90; Storey, *House of Lancaster*, 155.
[73] Burton-on-Trent Public Library, D 27 (Burton abbey deeds).
[74] In that year Bagot brought an action of novel disseisin against the abbey: Burton Pub. Lib., D 27/620–1.
[75] C 1 (early chancery proceedings)/6/50; Burton Pub. Lib., D 27/648–50.
[76] For the arbitrators' award, see Burton Pub. Lib., D 27/654. See C. Rawcliffe, 'Baronial Councils in the Later Middle Ages', in C. D. Ross (ed.), *Patronage, Pedigree and Power in Later Medieval England* (Gloucester, 1979), 87–108, for the role of lawyers on magnate councils.

question to the abbey, and the agreement was confirmed after Bagot's death by his son Richard.[77]

A noticeable feature of such fifteenth-century awards is their procedural uniformity. Arbitration procedure followed a well-defined pattern. While not implying direct judicial supervision of the practice, this undoubtedly reflects the influence of legal development, and the active participation of lawyers in many arbitrations.[78] The records of arbitration, though much less plentiful than legal records, are far more informative regarding procedure, and they enable us to reconstruct in some detail the stages which led to the making of an award.

Preliminary negotiations towards a settlement were usually carried out by mediators between the parties in dispute, as for example in the Bruyn–Gatacre award. Once both parties had agreed to submit to arbitration, the arbitrators were elected. If the parties could not find an arbitrator or panel of arbitrators that was mutually acceptable, each side would choose an equal number.[79] In such circumstances it was usual for an umpire to be nominated to make a final award if the arbitrators failed to agree. The parties then took out conditional bonds whereby each promised to pay the other a certain sum if he failed to observe the award, the bond being voided on fulfilment of the terms laid down by the arbitrators.[80] These bonds defined the arbitrators' terms of reference and gave them full powers to determine the matters submitted to them, generally within a specified time. Such bonds, as formal recognizances, were enforceable at common law, and sometimes gave rise to litigation.[81] When the bonds had been made

[77] Burton Pub. Lib., D 27/659, 674; for other arbitrations involving Burton abbey, see ibid., 622, 642; C 1/6/207–9; Wright, *Derbyshire Gentry*, 125–6.

[78] Ives, *Common Lawyers*, 126–30; N. Ramsay, 'Retained Legal Counsel, c.1275–c.1475', *TRHS* 5th ser., 35 (1985), 110–11.

[79] See, for example, the attempted arbitration in the Erdswick–Ferrers dispute: see below, n. 83.

[80] Such bonds were frequently enrolled on the dorses of the close rolls: e.g. *CCR, 1409–13*, pp. 56–7, 61, 69, 71, 85, 96, 187, 202, 204, 211, 227, 235, 319, 324–5; *1429–35*, pp. 65–6, 68, 96, 103, 118, 157, 161, 167–8, 184–5, 193–4, 221–2, 224–5, 230, 297, 302, 316, 349; *1447–54*, pp. 31, 63, 66, 136, 159, 173–4, 183, 189–90, 202, 276, 325, 326–7, 334–5, 355, 358–9, 360, 402, 431–2, 440, 448, 450, 502.

[81] A. W. B. Simpson, 'The Penal Bond with Conditional Defeasance', *LQR* 82 (1966), 392–422; Powell, 'Arbitration and the Law', 63–6.

they were entrusted to the safe-keeping of a third party, usually a cleric, and a loveday was assigned on which the award was to be made.

The loveday saw the formal confrontation between the disputants in the presence of the arbitrators. Each party was accompanied by a retinue of servants, advisers, and supporters, and there was a danger that one side would attempt to overawe proceedings with a show of armed force. This was what happened in the celebrated dispute between William, Lord Roos, and Robert Tirwhitt, justice of king's bench, in 1411.[82] To guard against intimidation the size of retinues was sometimes regulated.[83] In assessing the claims of the disputants the arbitrators accepted both oral and written testimony and might examine on oath the parties themselves. It was usual for each party to make a written submission to the arbitrators stating his grievances and replying to his opponent. A document of this kind survives among the Paston letters.[84] When the issues were complex the parties might present their memoranda and evidence before the loveday, so that the arbitrators could consider them at length.[85] At their most formal, arbitration proceedings resembled those of the law: the arbitrators were central court judges and appointed legal return days for their sessions, and the parties were represented by legal counsel.[86] Having completed their deliberations the arbitrators made the award, which was recorded in the form of a tripartite indenture—one copy going to each party, with a reference copy for the arbitrators.

Arbitration procedures in late medieval England thus bear the clear imprint of legal thought and practice.[87] The form and conduct of arbitration was inevitably affected by such factors as the prominence of lawyers and judges as arbitrators,

[82] See ch. 5 at n. 20.

[83] The terms of the attempted award between Hugh Erdswick and Edmund Ferrers specified that each party should be accompanied to the loveday by no more than 50 supporters, of whom not more than 4 were to be knights and not more than 20 gentlemen: CP 40/615, m. 342; calendared in *Collections for Hist. Staffs.*, 51; see ch. 9 at nn. 53–9.

[84] *Paston Letters*, i. 5.

[85] The award between Burton abbey and Sir John Bagot (above, n. 76) refers to several sessions at which the parties submitted evidence before the arbitrators and their counsellors.

[86] Powell, 'Settlement of Disputes', 37–9.   [87] See ibid. 34–7.

the use of collusive litigation to confirm an award, and the tendency of litigation to redefine the issues of a dispute by acquiring a momentum of its own, as in the dispute between William Paston and Walter Aslake.[88] It is arguable, indeed, that the methods of arbitration characteristic of this period, far from reflecting the failure of the legal system, as has sometimes been claimed,[89] represent rather a measure of its success. The widespread imitation of precise, legalistic formulae derived ultimately from canon-law arbitration[90] implies a recognition by disputants that a settlement made out of court would only endure if it proved unassailable to a subsequent challenge in court. The resources of the law were thus invoked to support arbitration. This helps explain the remarkable growth of documentary evidence for the practice which takes place after 1350.[91] The rising tide of paperwork does not prove that arbitration was becoming more popular; it may suggest, however, that greater formality and better record-keeping were required of the process as the law grew more complex, litigation more commonplace, and lawyers more sophisticated.

Although the form of arbitration shows the influence of legal models, its function remained fundamentally distinct.[92] Whereas legal procedure was adversarial, being designed to isolate the point at issue between two parties, and to determine it in favour of one side or the other, arbitration was essentially a matter of compromise and conciliation. This is partly explained by the local context of many arbitrations. Unlike royal justices at Westminster, the local community had to live with the settlement that was reached, and its primary concern was therefore to reconcile the disputants and re-establish peace and concord. Typically, the settlement between Bruyn and Gatacre was arranged through the mediation of mutual friends, and its opening provision insisted that the parties henceforth be good and loyal friends. The arbitrators' role as peace-makers led them inescapably towards framing a settlement acceptable to both sides. Unlike judges they were concerned less to apply objective rules of decision than to ensure that both parties were satisfied and

---

[88] See above at nn. 32–9.

[89] See above, n. 54.

[90] Powell, 'Arbitration and the Law', 53–6.

[91] Ibid. 55.

[92] Powell, 'Settlement of Disputes', 34–7.

that no one left empty-handed. The reciprocal quality of awards stands out quite clearly in the examples discussed above. In addition, such settlements sought to create new social ties between recently conflicting parties. Most disputants within local society had links of some kind with their opponents, whether by marriage, political affiliation, or, in the case of a monastic house, family association. The immediate issues in debate might therefore be comprehensible only in the light óf the longer-term relations between the two parties. A successful settlement was one which took these matters into consideration and attempted to redress them, allowing the disputants to establish relations on a new footing. It is notable that the award between Sir John Bagot and Burton abbey contained a stipulation that the abbey grant Bagot a twenty-shilling annuity—not a large sum admittedly, but a retainer of great symbolic importance in restoring Bagot to a position of friendship with the abbey after a lengthy dispute.[93]

The broader legal and political significance of arbitration and other forms of extra-judicial settlement has been revealed in studies of local gentry communities and aristocratic affinities.[94] Arbitration, whether by a magnate and his council, by local prelates, or by a panel of gentry, was one of the principal means whereby such communities sought to contain disputes within their ranks, thereby reducing the opportunities for outsiders like the king's judges to intervene in their affairs.[95] As well as being a force for peace-making and social harmony, therefore, arbitration was an essentially conservative phenomenon, reinforcing the traditional authority of the landed aristocracy upon whose support the king depended for the smooth running of local government.

CORRUPTION

In medieval England, as elsewhere in Europe, there was a wide disparity between legal theory and legal practice.[96]

---

[93] See above at nn. 76–8, 82–3.   [94] See above, n. 15.

[95] Arbitration fulfilled a similar role in medieval towns; the regulations of craft and parish guilds frequently included provisions for dispute settlement to avoid litigation between guild members: Post, 'Equitable Resorts', 73–4.

[96] J. T. Noonan, *Bribes* (London, 1984), 139–310. See ch. 1, esp. at nn. 83–7.

Formal statements in treatises, statutes, and proclamations show that the medieval mind clearly associated law with abstract concepts of equity and justice, and appreciated the need for impartiality in its administration. In the early twelfth century patristic statements condemning judicial bribery and corruption were assembled in Gratian's *Decretum*, perhaps the most influential lawbook of the middle ages; later in the century the author of the English treatise 'Glanvill' extolled the impartiality of the king's court, where 'a poor man is not oppressed by the power of his adversary, nor does favour or partiality drive any man away from the threshold of judgement'.[97] The same emphasis is clear in the oath taken by kings of England at their coronation,[98] while Edward III's judicial ordinance of 1346 provides a model for the impartial administration of justice.[99]

On the other hand the evidence for corruption in all its forms—bribery, maintenance, conspiracy, intimidation—is extensive.[100] The venality of twelfth-century law courts, as revealed in the *Policraticus* of John of Salisbury and the account of Richard Anstey's litigation, contrasts starkly with the ideals of the *Decretum* and 'Glanvill'.[101] Similarly the careers of fourteenth-century justices like William Thorp and William Shareshull belie the effectiveness of the 1346 ordinance.[102] Why, then, if the imperatives for the impartial administration of justice were expressed with such clarity, was the gulf between theory and practice so great?

The answers to this question lie deep in the fabric of medieval society. The first concerns the function of the law itself, as a formal framework regulating social relationships

---

[97] Noonan, *Bribes*, 147–9; *Glanvill*, 2.

[98] See ch. 1 at n. 54; ch. 5 at nn. 51–60. For a translation of the oath taken by Edward II at his coronation, which was the model for the oaths of later medieval kings, see *Eng. Hist. Docs., 1189–1327*, 525.

[99] *Statutes of the Realm, 1101–1713*, ed. A. Luders *et al.* (11 vols.; London, 1810–28), i. 303–6; Maddicott, *Law and Lordship*, 40–8. Cf. the oath taken by JPs on assuming office: Putnam, *Justices of the Peace*, 8–10.

[100] e.g. Bellamy, *Public Order*, 12–29; Hastings, *Common Pleas*, 211–36; Maddicott, *Law and Lordship*, 1–2.

[101] Noonan, *Bribes*, 156–8; P. M. Barnes, 'The Anstey Case', in P. M. Barnes and C. F. Slade (edd.), *A Medieval Miscellany for Doris Mary Stenton*, Pipe Roll Soc., New Ser., 36 (London, 1960), 1–24.

[102] Maddicott, *Law and Lordship*, 48–56.

and transactions, particularly those governing the possession of land. Decisions made in the courts might profoundly affect the economic, and therefore the political, standing of litigants.[103]

Such a function of law is of course common to all legal systems and is hardly sufficient in itself to explain the widespread corruption in medieval justice. Two further factors deserve consideration: the imperfect distinction between the public and private interest; and the importance of the profits of jurisdiction as a source of both royal and seigneurial income. As regards the confusion (from a modern perspective) between the public and private interest, the point is most obvious in the persistent identification of land ownership with the exercise of judicial authority. In the scheme of the three orders of society, the knightly order shared with the king the responsibility for justice as well as defence.[104] During the thirteenth and fourteenth centuries, as royal jurisdiction and financial demands expanded, a distinction came to be drawn between the person of the king and the office of the Crown which foreshadowed the separation of the private interest from the public.[105] This did not, however, imply the existence of a bureaucratic ethos of public service among the king's servants. The character of government remained intensely personal, inspired by loyalty to the king as lord rather than to an abstract conception of the state. The king's service was avidly exploited for personal profit, a practice that went largely unchecked in spite of attempts by Parliament to impeach the more egregiously corrupt and incompetent ministers of the Crown.[106]

The same factor applies *a fortiori* to local government. In the late middle ages the leading landowners of the shire continued to exercise the same degree of judicial control, through the peace commissions and other local offices, as they had done in earlier centuries through the courts of the *honor*, county, and hundred. Although they now did so increasingly by virtue of

[103] See Carpenter, 'Law, Justice and Landowners', 219–31.
[104] G. Duby, *The Three Orders* (Chicago, Ill., 1980), 293–307; Keen, *Chivalry*, 73, 75–6.
[105] See ch. 1 at nn. 47–54.
[106] G. A. Holmes, *The Good Parliament of 1376* (Oxford, 1975); J. S. Roskell, *The Impeachment of Michael de la Pole, Earl of Suffolk* (Manchester, 1984). Cf. L. Stone, *The Crisis of the Aristocracy* (Oxford, 1965), 463–504.

royal commissions rather than through claims of immemorial liberties, this did not immediately imbue them with a sense of public service. Those who controlled the local judicial machinery used it to defend their territorial and economic security and to promote the interests of their families and associates. Immediate social pressures—the demands of kinship and the ties of lordship and clientage—overwhelmed the elusive ideals of equity, justice, and service to the state.

The personal nature of royal service is shown by the frequency with which medieval kings continued to intervene in the courts on behalf of their own men. A striking example was Edward I's maintenance of his treasurer, Walter Langton, in the face of accusations of official malpractice prohibited by statute. The king allowed the repeated postponement of the case and eventually granted Langton a pardon which implicitly conceded the truth of the accusations, 'for the king is unwilling that [Langton] should henceforth be in any way inconvenienced or troubled'.[107] Equally blatant to the modern eye was the intervention of Henry VI in the Gresham manor dispute between John Paston and Lord Moleyns, where the king ordered the sheriff of Norfolk to empanel juries to acquit Moleyns and his servants upon indictments of riotous disorder committed during attacks on Gresham.[108]

Similar considerations governed the relations between lesser lords and their dependants, as is illustrated by the case of John Freeman, who was indicted in Henry IV's reign of breaking into the treasury of the receipt at Westminster and stealing bundles of feet of fines.[109] Freeman was a servant of John, Lord Lovell, a member of the king's council, who was involved in a property dispute with William Doyle. The purpose of the theft was to remove the record of a fourteenth-century agreement which was a vital element of Doyle's case against Lovell. In spite of the gravity of Freeman's offence, which was framed as treason, Lovell was able to protect him. Freeman appeared before a session of the king's council at which Lovell was present, and was granted bail, on Lovell's

---

[107] McFarlane, *Nobility*, 255–6; *SKB* iii. 175–8. Langton's accuser was John Ferrers, whose father had been disinherited of the earldom of Derby by Edward I.

[108] *Paston Letters*, ii. 477, 479.

[109] KB 9/192, m. 8; KB 27/567, Rex, m. 18d.

security, to appear in king's bench at Easter 1403. In the event
Freeman did not appear until Michaelmas 1404, and then
merely to present a pardon, no doubt obtained through
Lovell's intercession. At the local level, the interrogation of
John Thornton, the corrupt under-sheriff of Northamptonshire
during Henry V's reign, reveals how royal officials continued to
be motivated more by loyalty to their lords than by the public
interest.[110]

The profitability of justice for both king and magnates also
helps to explain the gulf between legal theory and practice.
The general eyre of the twelfth and thirteenth centuries was
primarily a device to investigate the king's rights and translate
them into money, and it did much to fill the coffers of the
Angevin kings.[111] In the fourteenth century trailbaston
inquiries became notorious for their punitive financial exactions,
and under Edward III Parliament consistently sought to buy
off the threat of eyres and trailbastons in return for grants of
taxation.[112] Such a direct financial interest obviously undermined the Crown's claims to impartiality in the administration
of justice, and in the fourteenth century it attracted increasing
hostility towards the king's judges.[113] Of course the profits of
justice were as much a part of seigneurial income as of the
Crown's. This was particularly true immediately after the
Black Death, when landowners sought to compensate for a
decline in other sources of revenue by increasing judicial
exactions in manorial courts, and when some lords were able
to appropriate for themselves the fines levied for breaches of
the Statutes of Labourers within their estates.[114]

In short, the explanation for the prevalence of corruption
and judicial malpractice lies in the nature of the social and
political structure of medieval England. The law was not a
closed system, but reflected the character and needs of the

---

[110] Thornton procured the forgery of an indictment before the JPs in order to
promote the interests of his master Sir Thomas Green. See ch. 3 at nn. 23–5.

[111] *Surrey Eyre*, 98–105, 128–40; J. R. Maddicott, 'Magna Carta and the Local
Community, 1215–1259', *Past and Present*, 102 (1984), 47. See ch. 7 at nn. 96–8.

[112] Harriss, *Public Finance*, 410–19. In 1333 the eyres proclaimed in Kent and
Durham owing to the vacancies of the archbishopric of Canterbury and the bishopric
of Durham were bought off with fines of 1,000 marks each: Crook, 'Later Eyres', 265.

[113] See below at nn. 120–1.

[114] Dyer, 'Rural Revolt', 28–30.

society it served. There is overwhelming evidence in the fourteenth and fifteenth centuries of attempts to pervert or at least influence the course of justice, but the methods principally employed sprang out of the traditional bonds of family, lordship, and service which still formed the bedrock of political society. Maintenance, which has traditionally been seen as the bane of the late medieval legal system, only became an offence in the reign of Edward I, and was historically one of the main obligations of lordship.[115] Bribery, the epitome of corruption in the twentieth century, was less easy to isolate and condemn in a society where legal officials were inadequately paid and where gift-giving was an essential courtesy.[116]

Nevertheless, although such practices remained widespread, there is evidence that in the late middle ages tolerance of them was diminishing, as expectations concerning the administration of justice altered. The fundamental dynamic of changing attitudes was the rapid expansion in the scope of royal justice which took place between 1150 and 1400. In both civil and criminal law royal courts acquired something approaching effective jurisdiction at first instance, at the expense of local and seigneurial courts. The growth of royal justice was accompanied by an assertion of royal control over private judicial franchises, and by a series of statutes against offences which sought to pervert the course of justice in the king's courts.[117] Both developments signalled the reshaping of justice and its centralization directly under the Crown. Statutes were enacted against maintenance and conspiracy not because those practices had suddenly become widespread, but because they were grounded in traditional practices of private associa-

[115] Fortescue, *Governance*, 14–30; Bellamy, *Public Order*, 5–9; McFarlane, *Fifteenth Century*, pp. xix–xx.

[116] The difference between an acceptable gift and a bribe to a judge or public official rests ultimately on the creation of an obligation upon the donee to reciprocate the favour, which overrides his obligations as a public official: Noonan, *Bribes*, pp. xi–xxiii. Late medieval correspondence such as that of Mayor Shillingford of Exeter and Lord Lisle reveal how the wheels of private and business life were oiled by a constant flow of gifts: *The Lisle Letters: An Abridgement*, ed. M. S. Byrne (London, 1983), xiv–xvi; *Letters and Papers of John Shillingford*, ed. S. A. Moore, Camden Soc., New Ser., 2 (London, 1871), 8–9, 23; Ives, *Common Lawyers*, 308–12. See Noonan, *Bribes*, 198–202, for the elaborate etiquette governing gifts at the papal curia.

[117] Sutherland, *Quo Warranto*, 16–70; Hastings, *Common Pleas*, 217–36; A. Harding, 'The Origins of the Crime of Conspiracy', *TRHS* 5th ser., 33 (1983), 89–108.

tion, notably lordship and clientage, which were incompatible with the new judicial system, based upon a unitary concept of royal sovereignty, which Edward I and his successors erected. The late middle ages therefore saw the beginnings of the transition from a society in which the administration of justice was decentralized and dependent upon more or less informal bonds of personal loyalty, to one in which it was conducted and guaranteed by a single, supreme public authority.

That transition took centuries to complete, and, as we have seen, the numerous late medieval statutes against bribery, maintenance, and conspiracy failed to curb such practices. The expansion of royal jurisdiction did, however, have the immediate side-effect of raising expectations of the judicial system, above all because of the close connection made between the royal monopoly of judicial authority and the most exalted standards of justice and impartiality. The king's justice was now an all-pervasive presence in the shires, where the lofty ideals of royal statutes and proclamations could be tested against the daily routine of judicial administration.

Rising expectations were not matched at first by rising judicial standards. Indeed, in the first half of the fourteenth century they may have deteriorated. Magnates, prelates, and boroughs and monasteries, faced with the erosion of their liberties and the growing power of the royal courts, sought to compensate by extending their influence over the royal legal machinery.[118] Moreover, the Crown could not resist the temptation to exploit its increasing judicial prerogatives as a source of income, a practice which reached its most refined form under Chief Justices Thorp and Shareshull in the 1340s and 1350s.[119] The result was an unprecedented upsurge of popular and parliamentary discontent with the administration of justice culminating in the Peasants' Revolt of 1381 and the removal of Richard II's justices in 1388. During the mid-fourteenth century, for the only time in the middle ages, royal judges went about their business in fear of assault, abduction, or murder.[120]

---

[118] Maddicott, *Law and Lordship, passim.*

[119] Putnam, *Shareshull,* 65–74; Ormrod, 'Edward III's Government', 194–209.

[120] Maddicott, *Law and Lordship,* 40–87; Harding, 'Revolt against the Justices', 169–83; *SKB* vi, pp. xvi–xxvii. See ch. 1 at nn. 83–94.

The 1380s may represent a watershed in the history of judicial administration. After 1390 it is difficult to find clear evidence of central court judges being retained by private individuals and corporations, and from the time of the Lancastrian kings the exploitation of justice as source of revenue became much less evident.[121] Thus the two most palpable abuses of the system, which had brought the law into such disrepute during the fourteenth century, do appear to have been checked. Dr Ives's study of serjeant Thomas Kebell suggests that by the end of the fifteenth century straightforward bribery of royal judges and serjeants was most uncommon, although they continued to be lavishly entertained by prospective litigants in the medieval equivalent of the business lunch.[122] Thus although the suborning of sheriffs and jurors remained commonplace, the vigorous and sometimes vicious campaigns against judicial malpractice in the fourteenth century did succeed in improving the ethical standards of the higher and more influential reaches of the legal profession.

[121] See ch. 7 at nn. 96–106.
[122] Ives, *Common Lawyers*, 308–29.

PART III

The Enforcement of Criminal Justice in the Reign of Henry V

5

England at the Accession of Henry V: The Legacy of Disorder

ENGLAND, 1370–1413

THE FORTY years before Henry V's accession were a period of profound social and political crisis.[1] A fundamental agent of change was the demographic collapse caused by the Black Death, the effects of which took a generation to work through the economy. The tensions it created within English society contributed to the popular unrest and religious dissent which challenged the authority of both secular and ecclesiastical hierarchies, erupting in the Peasants' Revolt and the Lollard movement. Military failure in France and the chaos of royal finances caused deep divisions between the king and the magnates, and aroused vociferous condemnation from the Commons in Parliament. The prevailing sense of malaise and the fear of imminent social breakdown is vividly conveyed in contemporary English literature of complaint, satire, and political lampoon.[2]

The second phase of the Hundred Years' War, which reopened in 1369 after the French repudiation of the treaty of Brétigny, saw a series of English reverses. During the dotage of Edward III and the minority of Richard II English forces were unable to repeat the great triumphs of the 1340s and 1350s. The French, fighting a war of attrition, steadily regained the territories ceded at Brétigny, so that by the end of the 1380s English possessions in France were reduced to a few coastal strongholds and a rump duchy of Guienne. Against this background of failure the heavy burden of war taxation provoked widespread unrest. In the Good Parliament of 1376 the Commons mounted an unprecedented attack on the king's

---

[1] See M. H. Keen, *England in the Later Middle Ages* (London, 1973), 169–349, for a thorough and stimulating survey of the period.
[2] Harriss, *Henry V*, 1–10.

ministers, using the procedure of impeachent to charge them with corruption and financial mismanagement. In 1381 the imposition of a poll tax, the third in four years, was the immediate cause of the Peasants' Revolt, the first widespread popular rising ever to have occurred in England.

The cycle of military failure and financial mismanagement was compounded by the volatile and authoritarian rule of Richard II, who assumed personal power soon after the Peasants' Revolt. A confrontation between the king and his baronial and parliamentary critics in 1386 sparked off an acute political crisis which ended with the military defeat of Richard's supporters and the condemnation of his favourites by the Lords Appellant in the Merciless Parliament of 1388. After this humiliation Richard painstakingly rebuilt his power until, in 1397, he was in a position to take revenge on his enemies. The duke of Gloucester was murdered in gaol, the earl of Arundel executed, the earl of Warwick imprisoned. The destruction of the Appellants ushered in the final phase of the reign, the period of Richard II's 'tyranny', culminating in the confiscation of the Lancastrian inheritance and Henry Bolingbroke's usurpation of the throne in 1399.

Henry V's immediate political inheritance was determined by the events of his father's reign after the usurpation.[3] During the early years of the reign Henry IV's hold on the Crown was very insecure. His dubious title to the throne precipitated a series of magnate revolts. In January 1400, within weeks of the usurpation, the earls of Huntingdon, Kent, and Salisbury led a conspiracy to restore Richard II. All three were killed in the rising. The rebellion of the Percies in 1403, perhaps the most serious threat to Henry IV's throne, was suppressed only after a pitched battle at Shrewsbury. Henry Percy, earl of Northumberland, avoided implication in this revolt, in which his brother and son died, but two years later instigated a second northern rising supported by Archbishop Scrope of York and the earl of Nottingham. The manifest weakness of Henry IV's position at home encouraged the outbreak of

---

[3] For general accounts of Henry IV's reign, see J. H. Wylie, *History of England under Henry the Fourth* (4 vols.; London, 1884–98); Kirby, *Henry IV*; McFarlane, *Lancastrian Kings and Lollard Knights*, 5–113; E. F. Jacob, *The Fifteenth Century* (Oxford, 1961), 1–121.

rebellion in Wales led by Owen Glendower, war with
Scotland, and threats to the overseas possessions of Guienne
and Calais from the kingdom of France. In short, Henry IV
was assailed on every front, and until 1407–8, when the worst
dangers of rebellion had been overcome, the regime was at full
stretch, financially and militarily.

At the beginning of his reign Henry IV promised to 'live of
his own' without recourse to taxation, but his heavy military
expenditure and profligate granting of annuities drove him to
seek frequent grants from Parliament.[4] Between 1403 and
1412 direct taxation of some sort was imposed annually,
except in 1406. The Commons granted these subsidies
reluctantly, and in return attempted to exert an unprecedented
degree of control over the financial affairs of the Crown. Their
attempts to do so sprang directly from their concern for the
defence and security of the realm. Parliamentary taxation was
granted on a special plea of military necessity, and the
Commons expected to see their money used to good effect.[5]
Henry IV supported his pleas for taxation by promising to
implement a policy of 'bone governance', meaning the
restoration of peace, public order, and sound financial
administration.[6] Peace was slow to come, however, and royal
demands for taxation continued. As the reign passed, the
king's inability to fulfil his promises of 'bone governance'
became a dominant theme of parliamentary complaint.
Although in 1404 large subsidies were granted for the defence
of the Welsh and Scottish Marches, Guienne, and Calais, as
late as 1410–11 Parliament was still petitioning the king to
take measures to restore peace and order to those areas.[7]
Henry's failure in this regard placed him at a permanent
disadvantage in his dealings with the Commons.

Parliamentary dissatisfaction with Henry IV's rule came to
a head in the Long Parliament of 1406.[8] The Commons
granted a further subsidy only on condition that a council

---

[4] Jacob, *Fifteenth Century*, 74–88; McFarlane, *Lancastrian Kings and Lollard Knights*, 93–4.

[5] Cf. G. L. Harriss, 'Theory and Practice in Royal Taxation', *EHR* 97 (1982), 811–19.

[6] e.g. *RP* iii. 567, 609.

[7] Ibid. 547, 610, 622–5, 663; Harriss, *Henry V*, 139–43.

[8] The following paragraph is drawn from Harriss, *Henry V*, 139–45.

should be appointed to control royal government and spending, with Prince Henry as its nominal head. This supervisory council survived until 1411, its authority fluctuating with the uncertain health of Henry IV and the struggles of rival factions within the Lancastrian establishment. Prince Henry was at first too busy campaigning in Wales to play much part in its deliberations, but after the final suppression of the Glendower rebellion in 1408 he became increasingly active at Westminster. The brief of the supervisory council was to implement the policies of 'bone governance' which Henry IV had promised. Prince Henry actively identified himself with those policies, and in 1410, aided by renewed parliamentary demands for improved defence and tighter financial manage- ment, he took control of the council and filled it with his own supporters. He led the council for nearly two years, winning the confidence of Parliament and establishing his credentials as an effective and energetic ruler. His armed intervention in support of the Burgundian faction in France, however, brought him into conflict with his father, and it was this quarrel which probably prompted the dismissal of the council in 1411 and the reassumption of power by Henry IV.[9]

During this period of rule in 1410 and 1411 Prince Henry concentrated his energies on financial administration and defence, rather than public order. The former were probably the most immediate priorities for the Lancastrian regime, given the nature of parliamentary complaint over the previous decade, but they were also more easily dealt with through conciliar government. Even as prince of Wales and head of the council, Henry perhaps lacked the authority to take a strong judicial initiative; it required the active commitment and determination of the monarch himself.

Henry IV showed little sign of such commitment. Until 1405 he was too preoccupied with the military challenges to his throne to spare much thought for the administration of justice. Even in the second half of the reign, however, he failed to take action to curb the widespread local disorders of which Parliament complained. The usurpation and its aftermath inevitably caused serious disturbances in many parts of the

[9] P. McNiven, 'Prince Henry and the English Political Crisis of 1412', *History*, 65 (1980), 1–16.

country. After the failure of the rebellion of the earls in 1400 the ringleaders were lynched by mobs in scenes reminiscent of the Peasants' Revolt.[10] The king's council met shortly afterwards to consider measures to restore order. A general pardon was issued to prevent malicious accusations of treason arising from the rebellion; those responsible for the deaths of the earls were to be arrested and brought before the council, and commissions were appointed in each county to disperse riotous assemblies, which were declared to be treasonable.[11]

These measures might have heralded the purposeful administration of justice under Henry IV had they been accompanied by the swift settlement of the realm and universal acceptance of the Lancastrian dynasty; but as revolt was followed by revolt and plot by plot, the maintenance of public order took second place to the detection of conspiracy and disaffection. The acute insecurity of the new regime is reflected in the number and diversity of its enemies who were prosecuted in the courts; for example Thomas Marks, the former bishop of Carlisle; the countess of Oxford and the abbots of Beeleigh, Colchester, and St Osyth in Essex; Welsh sympathizers of Owen Glendower at Oxford; and several Franciscan friars, who in 1402 preached that Richard II was still alive.[12]

During the second half of the reign, as the threats of rebellion and invasion receded, the Commons increasingly drew the attention of the king and council to the disorder prevailing over much of the country. In 1410 the Commons complained of disturbances through the North and Midlands and in Devonshire, and requested the issue of general oyer and terminer commissions as a remedy. Petitions were received at the same Parliament alleging a series of attacks on Lancastrian retainers and tenants in Staffordshire. The commons of Northumberland complained in 1411 of the prevalence of thieves and robbers in the county and nearby liberties, and deplored the infrequency of visitations by royal

---

[10] Wylie, *Henry IV*, i. 99–104. [11] *PPC* ii. 107–13; *Foedera*, viii. 124–5.
[12] *SKB* vii. 102–5, 123–4, 126–7, 151–5; KB 27/565, Rex, mm. 3, 4d, 5d, 11; E 163 (exchequer miscellanea)/6/28; Wylie, *Henry IV*, i. 265–80; I. D. Thornley, 'Treason by Words in the Fifteenth Century', *EHR* 32 (1917), 556–61; R. A. Griffiths, 'Some Partisans of Owain Glyn Dŵr at Oxford', *BBCS* 20 (1963), 282–92.

judges.[13] The Commons also showed concern over the unofficial war raging in the English Channel between English privateers and their contintental counterparts, which disrupted maritime trade and impaired good relations with strategically important powers like the duchies of Brittany and Burgundy.[14] Disorder was most serious and protracted along the Welsh Marches, which bore the brunt of the Glendower rebellion. Complaints about the depredations by the Welsh and the inhabitants of the Marcher lordships were constantly reiterated throughout Henry IV's reign.[15] Legislation was enacted to allow redress to the victims of border raids, but it appears to have been totally ineffective.[16]

Concern over the state of public order in the closing years of Henry IV's reign was vigorously expressed by Thomas Hoccleve in his *Regement of Princes*, addressed to Prince Henry.[17] The rule of law, he claimed, was virtually banished from the country. In every shire gangs of armed men were taking the law into their own hands, protected by the maintenance of great lords:

> Is ther no lawe this to remedie?
> I can no more; but, and this forth growe,
> This londe shal it repent and sore abye;
> And al such mayntenance, as men wel knowe,
> Sustened is noght by persones lowe
> But cobbes gret this ryot sustene;
> Correct it, gode is, whil that it is grene.[18]

If action were not taken quickly, Hoccleve warned, the kingdom would be lost.[19] His complaints are exemplified by the misconduct of Justice Robert Tirwhit of king's bench, which came to the attention of Parliament in 1411 through a petition submitted by William, Lord Roos.[20] The parties had been involved in litigation over rights of common claimed by Roos and his tenants in Tirwhit's manor at Wrawby in Lincolnshire. The dispute was referred to the arbitration of

---

[13] *RP* iii. 624, 630–2, 662; see ch. 8 at n. 95.   [14] *RP* iii. 610, 625.

[15] Ibid. 457, 474, 476, 508–9, 615, 624, 663.

[16] 2 Henry IV cc. 16–19; 4 Henry IV c. 26; cf. ch. 7 at nn. 79–82.

[17] Thomas Hoccleve, *The Regement of Princes*, ed. F. J. Furnivall, Early English Text Soc., Extra Ser., 72 (London, 1897).

[18] Hoccleve, *Regement*, 101.   [19] Ibid. 102.

[20] *RP* iii. 649–50; *SKB* vii, pp. xiii–xiv.

Chief Justice William Gascoigne, and a loveday was assigned for both sides to submit their claims before Gascoigne at Wrawby. On the appointed day, instead of attending with a small following of relatives and servants as agreed, Tirwhit appeared at the head of an armed band, which, according to Roos, was several hundred strong. Tirwhit was apparently attempting to overawe proceedings with a show of force, and the meeting broke up in confusion. His tactics ultimately proved counter-productive, however; he was summoned before Parliament, where he was made to accept the award of arbitrators nominated by Roos, and to offer him a formal apology.

Some impression of the character of disorder during Henry IV's reign may be gained from the records of the judicial commissions sent out by Henry V in 1414.[21] The shires of the north and west Midlands were particularly unruly: there the concentration of local power in the hands of Lancastrian retainers fostered resentment among the gentry excluded from influence, which led to feuding and violent confrontation. In Staffordshire resistance to Lancastrian domination was led by Hugh Erdswick, who attacked the estates of royal servants such as Sir John Blount and Sir Nicholas Montgomery. Erdswick recruited support through the illegal granting of liveries, a practice which became widespread in the region at the end of the reign. On the Welsh borders, even after the suppression of the Glendower revolt, public order had all but collapsed. Marcher captains and royal officials like John Wele, constable of Oswestry castle, and Thomas Barnby, chamberlain of the principality of Wales, were a law unto themselves. They dealt openly with the rebels and extorted money and provisions from the lands under their control. On the Shropshire Marches in particular, Wele and his associate Richard Lacon, constable of Clun, became notorious for the depredations of their troops upon neighbouring lordships. Yet their presence did not deter the frequent incursions of Welsh raiders and cattle thieves into Shropshire. At sea as well as on land the day-to-day defence of the realm relied on local forces over which the king had little control. In the south-west,

[21] For full discussion of those proceedings and the disorders they illustrate, see chs. 7, 8, and Appendix.

Devon suffered French raids early in the reign, and retaliated in kind with coastal attacks on France and the unauthorized seizure of French shipping in the Channel. Throughout the kingdom there was a perceptible slackening of royal control after 1399, and an increasing slide towards self-help.

Henry IV made no systematic attempt to deal with these disturbances, and so fulfil his repeated promises of 'bone governance'. It is noteworthy that unlike all his fourteenth-century predecessors, and his son, he made no use of the special authority of king's bench as a superior eyre to restore public order in the provinces.[22] Admittedly, several statutory measures were enacted during the reign which aimed at the sterner and more efficient administration of justice: for example the introduction of the death penalty for heresy, the consolidation of the Ricardian Statutes of Livery and Forcible Entry, and the statute of 1411 which provided JPs with summary powers for dealing with riots.[23] These were not, however, followed up by the energetic programme of law enforcement necessary after the usurpation and the years of rebellion and disorder which ensued.

Henry IV's failure to enforce law and order may be ascribed to a number of factors. The circumstances of his accession and the repeated challenges to his throne un-questionably undermined his judicial authority. After 1405 he suffered bouts of illness, which left him totally incapacitated for short periods, sapped his strength, and weakened his grip on all aspects of government.[24] His reluctance to intervene in local disorders may also have stemmed from a desire to avoid investigating the unlawful activities of his servants and supporters, some of which, involving the earl of Arundel's lieutenants in Shropshire and Thomas Barnby, the chamber-lain of north Wales, were to be revealed under Henry V.[25] Only when Lancastrian interests were directly threatened was the regime quick to take action: in 1410 special measures in

[22] See ch. 2 at nn. 86–91.
[23] 1 Henry IV c. 7; 2 Henry IV c. 15; 4 Henry IV c. 8; 7 Henry IV c. 14; 13 Henry IV c. 7.
[24] P. McNiven, 'The Problem of Henry IV's Health, 1405–13', *EHR* 100 (1985), 747–72.
[25] See ch. 8 at nn. 27–30, 172–84.

king's bench were ordered for the apprehension of those accused of attacking Lancastrians in Staffordshire.[26]

Some scholars have suggested that in his later years Henry IV carried a heavy burden of guilt for his usurpation and that this induced a loss of self-confidence and lack of resolution.[27] Such psychological analysis is difficult to substantiate, but it finds a hint of confirmation in the strangely apologetic wording of the general pardon issued by Henry in 1409. One of the reasons stated in the preamble for the issue of the pardon was 'in order that our subjects may bear more cheerful hearts towards us and our heirs, more truly to remain in faith and love'.[28] The contrast with the confident, authoritative tone of Henry V's pardons is striking.[29]

Henry IV's greatest achievement was survival. He withstood the threats to his Crown and lived long enough to pass it unchallenged to a mature adult heir; but he also bequeathed a legacy of disorder and political division.[30] The tasks awaiting his successor were formidable: the reconciliation to the Lancastrian dynasty of the heirs of the earls—Huntingdon, Northumberland, Nottingham, and Salisbury—who had rebelled after 1399; the rebuilding of Parliament's confidence in the king's ability to govern effectively and economically; the establishment of secure defences along the kingdom's borders and in its overseas possessions; and the restoration of public order.

HENRY V AND KINGSHIP

In 1413 Henry V was unusually well qualified to assume the burdens of kingship. After a series of arduous campaigns in Wales he had thrown himself into the affairs of the kingdom following the political crisis of 1406, and as head of the council

---

[26] *RP* iii. 630–2.
[27] Kirby, *Henry IV*, 253, 257; McFarlane, *Lancastrian Kings and Lollard Knights*, 55. McNiven is sceptical of these arguments: 'Henry IV's Health', 166.
[28] KB 27/564, Rex, m. 7 (pardon presented by Thomas Stansbatch of Herefordshire); C 67/34, m. 11. Henry IV was certainly the object of intense personal antagonism. One of the friars examined before the council in 1402 on charges of preaching that Richard II was still alive said that 'he did not love the present king at all, but hated him with all his heart and strength': KB 27/565, Rex, m. 3.
[29] See below, nn. 76, 87.   [30] Harriss, *Henry V*, 31–3.

he had wrested control of government from his father's hands during 1410 and 1411. As prince he had been so impatient to take power that in 1411 he attempted to compel his father to abdicate in his favour.[31] As king he ruled with remarkable vigour and sense of purpose, and achieved unprecedented success, leading one commentator, K. B. McFarlane, to describe him as 'the greatest man that ever ruled England'.[32] Before embarking on an investigation of the administration of justice during his reign, it may be instructive to examine Henry V's own ideas on kingship, and how the powers and duties of the king were presented under his rule.

Henry V's views on his royal office were naturally derived from the theories of kingship and law which prevailed throughout western Christendom during the middle ages.[33] Those theories were disseminated in the manuals of advice to rulers known as 'mirrors of princes' which formed an important genre of medieval literature.[34] The 'mirrors' dwelt at length upon the fundamental Christian values which the prince, above all men, should cultivate: justice, mercy, fortitude, chastity, magnanimity, and prudence. They also gave advice on statecraft, the choosing of ministers, the conduct of warfare, family life, and education. Henry V, as a particularly well-educated prince, was undoubtedly conversant with such literature. Thomas Hoccleve, who wrote a 'mirror' in English, the *Regement of Princes*, for Henry as prince of Wales, assumed his familiarity with three of the most popular works of the genre, which were widely read in fifteenth-century England:[35] the pseudo-Aristotelian *Secretum Secretorum*, Giles of Rome's *De Regimine Principum*, written in the late thirteenth century for the French king Philip IV; and Jacobus de Cessolis' *De Ludo Scaccorum*, a treatise on government and

---

[31] Wylie, *Henry IV*, iv. 40; McFarlane, *Lancastrian Kings and Lollard Knights*, 108.

[32] Ibid. 133.

[33] See ch. 1.

[34] *Four English Political Tracts of the Later Middle Ages*, ed. J.-P. Genet, Camden Soc., 4th ser., 18 (London, 1977), pp. ix–xix; Guenée, *States and Rulers*, 69–74; L. K. Born, 'The Perfect Prince: A Study in Thirteenth- and Fourteenth-Century Ideals', *Speculum*, 3 (1928), 470–504; W. Berges, *Die Fürstenspiegel des Höhen und Späten Mittelalters* (Leipzig, 1938).

[35] Hoccleve, *Regement*, 74–8; see also *Gesta Henrici Quinti*, ed. F. Taylor and J. S. Roskell (Oxford, 1975), 28–9, 40–3. Cf. McFarlane, *Lancastrian Kings and Lollard Knights*, 114–17.

society based on a description of the game of chess.[36] Hoccleve claimed to have written the *Regement* as a digest of those three works for the prince's convenience.[37]

By the time Hoccleve completed his work, in 1411, Prince Henry was hardly a novice in the arts of war and government. As Hoccleve acknowledged, the prince was in little need of advice.[38] On the contrary, there is good evidence that he had already formulated clear views on the practice of government, as represented in the programme of 'bone governance' advocated in the Parliaments of 1406–10.[39] In order to find favour with his patron it is likely that Hoccleve sought to reflect the prince's views through skilful exploitation and adaptation of his sources.[40] The *Regement* may therefore provide a useful guide to Prince Henry's principal concerns and priorities on the eve of his accession.

Seen in this light, the most noticeable feature of the *Regement* is its emphasis on judicial matters. A quarter of the entire work, and one half of the 'mirror' proper, is devoted to the observance of justice, the keeping of the laws, and the exercise of the king's prerogative of mercy.[41] There is a lengthy opening discussion of the importance of the coronation oath, and the king's obligation to keep his word in general:

> The othes that at your creacioun
> Shul thurgh your tonge passe, hem wel observe;
> Lat no coloured excusacioun
> Yow make fro hem slippe aside or swerve.[42]

---

[36] *Secretum Secretorum: Nine English Versions*, ed. M. A. Manzalaoui, Early English Text Soc., 276 (Oxford, 1977); the only modern edition of Giles of Rome is of the French translation, *Li Livres du Gouvernement des Rois*, ed. S. P. Molenaer (London, 1899); Jacobus de Cessolis, *The Game of Chess* (tr. and printed by William Caxton; repr. London, 1976). For the circulation of these works in late medieval England, see N. Orme, *From Childhood to Chivalry* (London, 1984), 94–7, 179–80.

[37] Hoccleve, *Regement*, 77.

[38] Ibid. 78: 'And although it be no maner of nede/Yow to counseile what to done or leve'.   [39] Harriss, *Henry V*, 140–3.

[40] In a similar way the personal tastes and interests of Henry VI are reflected in the 'mirror' written for him in about 1437, the *De Regimine Principum ad Regem Henricum Sextum*: see *Four English Political Tracts*, 41–4. For the manuscript history of the *Regement*, see M. C. Seymour, 'The Manuscripts of Hoccleve's *Regiment of Princes*', *Edinburgh Bibliographical Soc. Transactions*, 4, pt. 7 (1974 for 1968–71), 253–97.

[41] Hoccleve, *Regement*, 80–125 (stanzas 314–494). The entire poem is 780 stanzas long, but the proem, containing Hoccleve's dialogue with a beggar, occupies 288 stanzas.   [42] Ibid. 80.

A section on justice follows, Hoccleve citing St Anselm as authority for the commonplace that justice means giving each man his due.[43] To observe justice is the essence of virtue, for it is of the nature of God. Kings are established to maintain justice, and in doing so are at their most Godlike:

> . . . a king is by covenant
> Of ooth maad in his coronacioun,
> Bounde to justices sauvacioun.
>
> And a kyng, in fulfillinge of that, is
> To god lik, whiche is verray rightwisnesse.[44]

The poet assesses the qualities needed in a good judge, and concludes the section by comparing the function of justice in the kingdom to that of the soul in the human body.[45] He then proceeds to a discussion of the observance of the laws, beginning with a rousing exhortation to Prince Henry:

> Prince excellent, have your lawes chere;
> Observe hem, and offende hem by no wey!
> Bi oth to kepe it, bounde is the powere
> Of kyng; and by it is kynges nobley
> Sustened; lawe is both lokke and key
> Of suerte; while law is kept in londe,
> A prince in his estate may sikir stonde.[46]

He then launches into a bitter complaint against the state of lawlessness within the realm. Law has been virtually banished from the kingdom, and armed bands gather in every shire, maintained by powerful lords who escape prosecution:

> Right as lop-webbys, flyes smale and gnattes
> Taken, and suffre grete flyes to go,
> For al this worlde, lawe is rewyld so.[47]

There follow two linked sections on pity and mercy. Mercy is indispensable to the exercise of true kingship, for without it a ruler degenerates into tyranny.[48] Conversely the merciful king is most like God:

[43] See ch. 1 at nn. 22–3.   [44] Hoccleve, *Regement*, 91.
[45] Ibid. 99; cf. Giles of Rome, *De Regimine Principum*, I. ii, c. 11 (Molenaer edn., 46–8).
[46] Hoccleve, *Regement*, 100.
[47] Ibid. 102; for the source of this simile, see Born, 'Perfect Prince', 492, 499.
[48] Hoccleve, *Regement*, 123.

> He moost is like to god, as seith Bernard,
> That holdeth no thing more precious
> Than to be merciful . . .[49]

Yet mercy can be taken too far. It is a mistake to pardon murderers, for they will simply repeat their offence.[50] At length the *Regement* moves on to other matters unrelated to justice, and to virtues such as patience, chastity, and magnanimity.

Hoccleve's comments on justice are in large part thoroughly conventional, but their length indicates Prince Henry's concern with the issue, especially during the disorderly years at the end of Henry IV's reign. Hoccleve's complaints against lawlessness have the urgency of a current political problem, and one which Henry was to confront as king. Hoccleve also attached great weight to the coronation oath, which is unparalleled in the sources upon which he drew.[51] It has a section to itself in the *Regement* and is mentioned at least three times elsewhere in the poem.[52] Hoccleve's emphasis on the Godlike qualities of the king is also evident: the comparison is made three times, each in association with the royal dispensation of justice or the exercise of mercy.[53]

In attaching such importance to the coronation oath Hoccleve identified a central theme of early Lancastrian kingship. The essence of Bolingbroke's case against Richard II, as the deposition articles reveal, was perjury. The coronation oath was recorded at the head of the charges against Richard; in the course of the articles the king's breach of his oath was mentioned three times, and he was explicitly accused of perjury on ten more counts.[54] As a result Henry IV's own promises inevitably came under close scrutiny, especially in the early years of his reign. In his first Parliament Henry IV promised to exercise the traditional liberties of his office to uphold the laws and statutes of the realm in accordance with his coronation oath;[55] but as early as 1402–3 rebels and Ricardian sympathizers justifed their opposition to the king on the grounds that he had

[49] Ibid. 122.   [50] Ibid. 113–15.

[51] Mention is made in Hoccleve's sources of the need for the king to keep his word, but not in the specific context of the coronation oath, and not with the degree of emphasis assigned to the point in the *Regement*: see *Secretum Secretorum*, 43–4, 139–41; Cessolis, *Game of Chess*, II. i.

[52] Hoccleve, *Regement*, 80–9, 91, 100, 105.

[53] Ibid. 87, 91, 122.   [54] *RP* iii. 416–23.   [55] See ch. 1 n. 68.

failed to observe his oath and other undertakings to maintain the laws and avoid recourse to taxation.[56]

The justification for the Lancastrian usurpation was thus inextricably linked to the coronation oath, whereby the king swore to uphold the laws, to protect the Church, and to do right and equal justice to all. Henry V treated his oath almost as a manifesto, a programme for government:[57] in January 1414 he ordered measures against the Lollards in defence of the Church, 'as we are bound by the chain of our oath';[58] while in his speech to the Parliament of October 1416 the chancellor, Bishop Beaufort, reviewed the achievements of Henry V's first five Parliaments specifically in terms of the king's fulfilment of his oath.[59] Perhaps we may also see, in the legends of the dramatic change which came over Henry V at his coronation and the abandonment of the riotous ways of his youth, an echo of the importance he attached to the obligations he had assumed.[60]

The obligations did not all run one way. In return for preserving the peace and maintaining justice the king was entitled to the assistance of his subjects in his just struggle to recover the rights of his Crown overseas. Henry V made a point of not requesting a subsidy at the Leicester Parliament of 1414 when launching his campaign of law enforcement,[61] but at the Parliament of November 1415, after Agincourt, Bishop Beaufort preached on the text 'sicut et ipse fecit nobis ita et nos ei faciamus'.[62] The king, he said, had devoted himself since his coronation to the establishment of peace and justice and the enforcement of the laws. Now he was fighting

---

[56] Jacob, *Fifteenth Century*, 50–1. These accusations were reinforced by allegations of perjury committed by Bolingbroke on his path to the throne in 1399: ibid. 4; McFarlane, *Lancastrian Kings and Lollard Knights*, 49–58.

[57] Cf. Harriss, *Henry V*, 8–9, 141–5.

[58] KB 9/204/1, m. 84: 'prout vinculo juramenti astringimur'; cf. *Foedera*, ix. 119.

[59] *RP* iv. 94.

[60] Thomas Walsingham, *The St Albans Chronicle, 1406–20*, ed. V. H. Galbraith (Oxford, 1937), 69; *Thomae de Elmham Vita et Gesta Henrici Quinti*, ed. T. Hearne (London, 1727), 12–14; *The First English Life of King Henry the Fifth*, ed. C. L. Kingsford (Oxford, 1911), 17–19; *The Brut*, ed. F. W. D. Brie, Early English Text Soc., 131, 136 (2 vols.; London, 1906–8), ii. 494. Cf. McFarlane, *Lancastrian Kings and Lollard Knights*, 123–4.

[61] *RP* iv. 16.

[62] Ibid. 62: 'What he does for us we should do for him.' This may be a free adaptation of Matthew 7: 12: see ch. 1 at n. 24.

to regain his inheritance in France and needed financial support. Parliament responded handsomely with a full subsidy and a grant of the wool customs for life.[63]

Henry V thus recognized a framework of mutual obligation between king and subject. At the same time, however, he consistently exalted royal authority by promoting the judicial and sacramental powers of kingship. His high view of his royal dignity was reflected in the extension of the law of treason beyond the 1352 Statute of Treasons. In 1414 breach of royal truces and safe-conducts was declared to be high treason under the Statute of Truces.[64] In the following year Henry, Lord Scrope, was convicted and executed as a traitor for his part in the earl of Cambridge's plot. His offence, however, was merely concealment, or misprision, of treason, which was outside the scope of the 1352 statute, and which later in the fifteenth century incurred lesser penalties than high treason.[65] Finally, at the end of the reign, escape from prison while under indictment or suspicion of treasonable acts was held to be treason.[66] As for the promotion of the sacramental characteristics of kingship, the most remarkable illustration comes from Bishop Beaufort's parliamentary speech of 1416, which compared Henry's Parliaments to the days of the Creation.[67] Other Lancastrian publicists likened the king to Christ: in their treatment of the Lollard revolt Thomas Elmham and the author of the *Gesta Henrici Quinti* both presented Henry V as a Christ-like figure, withstanding the temptation of the satanic Sir John Oldcastle.[68] It is likely that Henry regarded himself as enjoying priestly status by virtue of the unction conferred upon him at his coronation. The point is

[63] Harriss, *Henry V*, 147. Law enforcement was a recurrent theme in chancellors' speeches to Parliament under Henry V: cf. *RP* iv. 106, 116, 129.
[64] See ch. 7 at nn. 16–19.
[65] T. B. Pugh, 'The Southampton Plot of 1415', in R. A. Griffiths and J. W. Sherborne (edd.), *Kings and Nobles in the Later Middle Ages* (Gloucester, 1986), 68–9; Bellamy, *Law of Treason*, 222–4.
[66] See ch. 10 at nn. 39–47. The creeping extension of the law of treason is a notable feature of the reigns of Henry IV and V, and may be partly attributable to the insecurity of the Lancastrian regime. See Bellamy, *Law of Treason*, 116–31.
[67] *RP* iv. 94; see also Chrimes, *Constitutional Ideas*, 16.
[68] *Gesta Henrici Quinti*, 8–12; Thomas Elmham, *Liber Metricus de Henrico Quinto*, printed in *Memorials of Henry the Fifth*, ed. C. A. Cole, Rolls Ser. (London, 1858), 82, 151, 158; A. Gransden, *Historical Writing in England c.1307 to the Early Sixteenth Century* (London, 1982), 209–10. See ch. 6 at nn. 132–3.

argued at length in a letter written to Henry by the French humanist Nicholas de Clémanges, probably between 1418 and 1420.[69] Such a view is consistent with the firm control Henry exercised over the affairs of the English Church, and his imperious treatment of Bishop Beaufort when the latter accepted a cardinal's hat from Pope Martin V without obtaining the king's permission.[70]

Certainly there is no mistaking Henry's sense of divine mission. He presented himself as the soldier of Christ, fighting to defend the Church and the Christian faith against heresy, as well as to recover his rights in France.[71] The dramatic victory at Agincourt against overwhelming odds reinforced· this image, and the king's apologists were quick to interpret it as a mark of divine favour.[72] It was this sense of mission that convinced Henry of the justice of his claims in France: the French were rebels, and their denial of his rightful claims was an offence against God and justice.[73]

As Hoccleve pointed out, the king was at his most Godlike in the dispensation of justice. Henry V combined the stern judgement of the God of the Old Testament with Christ-like mercy. The author of the *Gesta Henrici Quinti* compared the king's action in hanging a soldier who stole from a church on the march to Agincourt to the punishment of Zimri by

---

[69] Nicholas de Clémanges, *Opera Omnia* (Leyden, 1613; repr. Farnborough, 1967), 350: 'Ideo autem Regnum sacerdotale esse debere Dominus adstruit, quia propter sacram chrismatis unctionem Reges in Christiana religione ad similitudinem sacerdotum sancti esse debent Christoque consecrati, tanquam illi a quo sunt Christi digno praeclaroque titulo nuncupati.' The letter is not dated, but contains unmistakeable references to the king's victory at Agincourt and commends him for actively seeking a peace treaty with France. Clémanges, as a canon of Bayeux, submitted to Henry V in 1418: J. H. Wylie and W. T. Waugh, *The Reign of Henry the Fifth* (3 vols.; Cambridge, 1914–29), iii. 101.

[70] K. B. McFarlane, 'Henry V, Bishop Beaufort and the Red Hat', *EHR* 60 (1945), 316–48; repr. in McFarlane, *Fifteenth Century*, 79–114; Jacob, *Fifteenth Century*, 196–200; J. Catto, 'Religious Change under Henry V', in G. L. Harriss (ed.), *Henry V: the Practice of Kingship* (Oxford, 1985), 115.

[71] *RP* iv. 62; *Gesta Henrici Quinti*, 3–11, 79, 84–9, 100–11, 191; R. M. Haines, ' "Our Master Mariner, Our Soveraign Lord": a Contemporary Preacher's View of King Henry V', *Medieval Studies*, 38 (1976), 94; *Historical Poems*, 107–8, 119–20.

[72] *Gesta Henrici Quinti*, 90–5, 122–7; Haines, 'Contemporary Preacher's View', 92; Clémanges, *Opera Omnia*, 348–9; *First English Life*, 138; see also Walsingham, *St Albans Chronicle*, 121.

[73] *Gesta Henrici Quinti*, 14–17, 34–7, 52–3, 102–3, 122–3, 178–9; *First English Life*, 85, 134; *Foedera*, ix. 313, 378–80, 482–3; Enguerrand de Monstrelet, *Chronique*, ed. L. Douët-d'Arcq, Société de l'Histoire de France (6 vols.; Paris, 1857–62), iii. 78–81.

Phinehas in the book of Numbers;[74] elsewhere he likened the anticipated fate of Oldcastle to the punishment of Dathan and Abiram, whom the earth swallowed up for rebellion against Moses.[75] In dealing with the main bulk of the Lollard rebels, however, Henry showed his capacity for mercy. He issued a general pardon for them, 'not at the request of any supplicant, but from the pure impulse of our royal clemency, because we choose rather to pity and spare those who have erred than to punish and destroy the righteous with the unrighteous, the innocent with the guilty'.[76]

Henry V's views of kingship, like those expressed by Hoccleve and Sir John Fortescue, were formed by the interaction of the common European tradition of Christian and Aristotelian thought—distilled in the 'mirrors of princes' literature—with the distinctive political and constitutional history of medieval England.[77] His understanding of the relationship between the king and the law, and of the king's resemblance to God in the discharge of his office, were entirely in keeping with the teachings of Aquinas or Giles of Rome.[78] Yet Henry's insistence upon the fulfilment of his coronation oath to keep the peace and do justice reveals the influence of his father's usurpation on his view of kingship. There is more than a hint of dynastic insecurity in this stress upon the king's performance of his duties, a sense of striving for legitimacy, which is also evident in the unremitting drive with which Henry applied himself to his French campaigns. His concern, as king, for justice and order was calculated to win the support of his subjects; but the implied existence of a manifesto for

[74] *Gesta Henrici Quinti*, 68–9; Numbers 25: 6–14. A later biographer of Henry V compared this act to the judgement of Joshua on Achan: *First English Life*, 44–5; Joshua 7: 18–26. During his campaigns in France Henry V frequently invoked the Old Testament 'Deuteronomic law', which stipulated that a prince should give a town the opportunity to surrender peacefully before laying it under siege; if the offer were refused, all men within the town might be put to the sword when it fell: *Gesta Henrici Quinti*, 34–5, 48–9, 154–5; Monstrelet, *Chronique*, iii. 79; Deuteronomy, 20: 10–14.

[75] *Gesta Henrici Quinti*, 8–9; Numbers 16: 12–33. For the use of Old Testament texts on justice in parliamentary speeches, see Chrimes, *Constitutional Ideas*, 16, 20–1, 165.

[76] *Foedera*, ix. 119–20. [77] See ch. 1.

[78] For Giles of Rome on law and kingship, see *De Regimine Principum*, I. i, c. 13; I. ii, cc. 10–12; III. ii, cc. 25–9 (Molenaer edn., 25–6, 43–52, 349–61). For Aquinas, see ch. 1, nn. 36–7.

government, even one so closely tied to the traditional duties of kingship, reinforced growing assumptions that the king was answerable to his subjects. Here, as in so many areas, the strengths of Henry V's rule were to be transformed into liabilities under Henry VI, as the Lancastrian regime disintegrated in the 1440s and 1450s.[79]

THE ACCESSION OF HENRY V

Henry V succeeded to the throne on 21 March 1413.[80] On that day the sheriffs were ordered to proclaim the new king's peace. All riots, armed gatherings, and breaches of the peace were forbidden, and the sheriffs instructed to arrest all those who ignored the proclamation.[81] New commissions of the peace were issued for all counties, and orders issued to elect coroners.[82] A few days later William Gascoigne, who had served as chief justice of king's bench throughout Henry IV's reign, was replaced by William Hankford.[83] It was unusual for a justice to be removed from office by an incoming king; the most likely explanation is that Gascoigne had fallen out with Henry during his rule as head of the council during 1410 and 1411.[84] The remaining central court justices were reappointed a few weeks later.[85]

Henry V was crowned at Westminster on 9 April 1413. To commemorate the event the king issued a general pardon for all treasons, rebellions, and felonies committed during his father's reign. The pardon was proclaimed in terms which signalled the king's determination to pacify the realm and heal the divisions of the preceding generation:[86]

Whereas we are mindful of the many great misfortunes which have arisen out of faction in the time of many kings (the result, we

---

[79] Harriss, *Henry V*, 209–10.   [80] Wylie and Waugh, *Henry V*, i. 1–11.

[81] *Foedera*, ix. 1; *CCR, 1413–19*, pp. 63–4. See KB 9/205/1, m. 5, for an indictment for breach of the proclamation of the king's peace.

[82] *CPR, 1413–16*, pp. 416–26; *CCR, 1413–19*, p. 1.

[83] Ibid. 10; *SKB* vi, pp. xliii–xliv.

[84] *SKB* vii, p. xiv. There is no contemporary foundation for the sixteenth-century legend that Gascoigne ordered the imprisonment of Prince Henry for contempt in king's bench when he tried to force the release of a servant indicted of felony: Wylie, *Henry IV*, iv. 94–7; Baker, *Serjeants at Law*, 285–6, 300.

[85] *CPR, 1413–16*, p. 3; Wylie and Waugh, *Henry V*, i. 15–19.

[86] Cf. Jacob, *Fifteenth Century*, 128.

suppose, of the prevalence of sin in our realm of England), and which, sad to say, has caused the greatest destruction of its lieges; now because the King of peace and Lord of lords has recently raised us, although unworthy, to the height of the royal dignity, and through the grace of his mercy has stilled the storms of discord throughout the realm with the banners of peace and quiet; we have firmly resolved, since it would be pleasing to God and most conducive to the preservation of order, that as God's pardon has been freely bestowed on us, we should allow all the subjects of our kingdom of England, Wales, Scotland, and Ireland who so desire, to drink from the cup of our mercy.[87]

The pardon was made available until Christmas 1413 for all those who wished to sue for it in chancery.[88]

The king ordered the summons of Parliament the day after his accession, and it assembled at Westminster on 15 May.[89] The new chancellor, Henry Beaufort, delivered the opening address, taking as his theme the text 'ante omnem actum consilium stabile'.[90] He announced that the king had called Parliament to take counsel with the Lords and Commons on three particular matters: the provision of adequate sustenance for the royal estate; the good governance and maintenance of the laws; and the support of the kingdom's allies and the resistance of its enemies. The issues raised had of course been the subject of much debate in the Parliaments of the previous reign, and the chancellor's address drew an immediate response from the Commons. Through their speaker they pointed out that they had frequently requested Henry IV to restore 'bone governance' to the kingdom, and that he had made many promises to do so; 'but how those promises were later upheld and performed the king himself well knows'.[91] They now pressed Henry V to implement 'bone governance',

[87] *Foedera*, ix. 3–4; *CCR, 1413–19*, p. 67; C 67/36, m. 1.

[88] The original deadline of 8 August 1413 was extended in Parliament in June: *CCR, 1413–19*, pp. 84–5. Some 750 pardons were issued in the course of the year: C 67/36.

[89] *CCR, 1413–19*, pp. 60–1; *RP* iv. 3. The proceedings of the Parliament of Feb. to Mar. 1413, which was sitting when Henry IV died, were annulled: F. M. Powicke and E. B. Fryde (edd.), *Handbook of English Chronology* (2nd edn.; London, 1961), 529.

[90] *RP* iv. 3: 'There should be wise counsel before every act.' The text is from Ecclesiasticus 37: 20 in the Latin Vulgate (37: 16 in modern translations).

[91] *RP* iv. 4: 'mes coment y feust tenuz et perfourne en apres, mesme nostre Seigneur le Roy ad bone conisance'.

referring to a number of matters which required the king's special attention: the defence of the Scottish Marches, Calais, Guienne, and Ireland; the safe-keeping of the sea; the pacification of the Welsh rebels and the settlement of disorder in the Welsh Marches; and the enforcement of the law.[92] They showed their willingness to assist the king in these tasks by granting a full lay subsidy and the tax on wool for four years. In return the king extended the general pardon issued at his coronation to include a wide range of trespasses and fiscal penalties.[93]

The Parliament of 1413 was primarily concerned with the defence of the realm, but a number of measures were enacted to improve the administration of justice. The Statute of Additions stipulated that persons cited in a writ or indictment should be described according to their place and county of residence and their profession. This eased the sheriff's task of locating and identifying defendants, and reduced the likelihood of mistaken identity.[94] Other acts were framed to prevent the forgery of title deeds and to curb the extortions of shrieval officials by limiting their term of office to one year.[95] At the same time, on the advice of the central court judges, the king's council established stricter regulation of the return of writs to the court of king's bench. Under Henry IV sheriffs had apparently often failed to return writs which they had been instructed to serve on behalf of king's bench.[96]

During the early months of the reign, while representing himself as a commanding but merciful ruler, Henry V watched intently for any hint of sedition or invasion.[97] He perceived the main threat as being from Scotland, with whom relations had been uneasy since 1399. The Scots harboured fugitives from Lancastrian rule and maintained the pseudo-Richard II, Thomas Ward of Trumpington, as a useful

---

[92] Ibid. The Commons also referred to riots in Cirencester resulting from a dispute between the citizens and the priory; cf. *CPR, 1413–16*, pp. 33, 38, 168.

[93] *RP* iv. 6–7; C 67/36, m. 6.

[94] 1 Henry V c. 5; for the background to the Statute of Additions, see Powell, 'Public Order', 187–9.

[95] 1 Henry V cc. 3, 4.

[96] KB 29/52, m. 4. Sheriffs were ordered to confirm in writing that they had received the writs sent to them by king's bench, and a record was kept for every return day of the number of writs returnable by each sheriff.

[97] Harriss, *Henry V*, 34.

diplomatic weapon. The Scottish king, James I, was held
captive in England, along with his cousin Murdoch Stewart,
son of the duke of Albany, the governor of Scotland.[98] Henry
feared a conspiracy between the Ricardian exiles and their
Scottish hosts to foment rebellion and rescue the royal
captives. During the Parliament which was sitting when
Henry IV died, bills had been circulated in London alleging
that Richard II was alive in Scotland, and one of Henry V's
first acts as king was to transfer James and Murdoch to the
Tower, where they remained for most of the next two years.[99]
A few weeks later he ordered the arrest of a group of
conspirators, including Henry Talbot, John Whitelock, and a
Scottish knight, Andrew Hake. The king's council reviewed
the defence of the Scottish Marches, and ordered that
reinforcements should be sent from the northern shires until
the Scots' intentions were known. In June Whitelock was
captured with two accomplices in sanctuary at Westminster,
and committed to the Tower.[100] They were speedily indicted,
and brought for trial in king's bench the following month.

Whitelock appeared on 5 July accused of plotting rebellion,
planning the death of Henry V and his father, adhering to the
king's enemies in Scotland, and honouring Thomas Ward, the
pseudo-Richard II, as the true king of England.[101] The
indictment alleged that he had returned from Scotland with
Sir Andrew Hake shortly before Easter 1413 to spread the
rumour that Richard II was still alive and would soon return
to England; during Henry IV's last Parliament, and that of
May 1413, he had broadcast his claims by putting up bills on
church doors in London, Westminster, and Bermondsey.[102]
Whitelock pleaded not guilty, and was returned to the Tower
for two days to await jury trial. Within that brief period,
however, he managed to escape.

[98] R. Nicholson, *Scotland: The Later Middle Ages* (Edinburgh, 1974), 218–32; Wylie, *Henry IV*, i. 266–9.
[99] *SKB* vii. 212–15 (KB 27/609, Rex, m. 14); E. W. M. Balfour-Melville, *James I, King of Scots, 1406–37* (London, 1936), 55–7. See above, n. 89.
[100] *CPR, 1413–16*, p. 35; Wylie and Waugh *Henry V*, i. 34–5. Henry Talbot was subsequently convicted for the abduction of Murdoch Stewart in 1415 as part of the earl of Cambridge's plot, and executed in 1417: see ch. 10 at n. 33.
[101] *SKB* vii. 212–14.
[102] One of Whitelock's original bills survives, attached to his indictment. These

The king reacted angrily to this lapse of security. He immediately deprived the duke of York of the office of constable of the Tower and appointed his own warden, Robert Morley; York's deputy, Simon Kampe, was committed to the Fleet ·prison and fined a thousand marks. Two servants implicated in the escape were outlawed and one, Robert Bache, subsequently executed for treason.[103] Whitelock was never recaptured, and continued plotting; in 1417 he was suspected of having links with Lollard conspirators.[104]

Whitelock left behind his accomplices, Thomas Clerk and Sir Ellis Lynet, in the Tower, and they appeared in court soon afterwards, accused of distributing seditious bills and planning rebellion in league with the Welsh and Scots. Clerk was acquitted of treason, but found guilty of writing the bill John Whitelock had posted at Westminster. He was sent back to the Tower.[105] Lynet was granted a pardon in return for unspecified services to be performed on the king's behalf, perhaps in the hope that he could be used as a double agent. Later in the year he went on a secret mission to arrest certain persons named to him by the king by word of mouth.[106]

The Whitelock conspiracy shows that the shadow of Richard II still lay across the Lancastrian dynasty. It may well have prompted Henry V to arrange the ceremonial reburial of Richard's body in Westminster abbey in December 1413.[107] Superficially it appears a trivial affair, exaggerated out of proportion by the regime because of its discovery in the first few weeks of the new reign. Yet Henry was right to be wary of the threat from the Scots and the Ricardians. The events of the spring of 1413 foreshadowed the much more serious conspiracy led by the earl of Cambridge in 1415,

documents have been incorrectly placed in the king's bench indictment file for Hilary term 1424: KB9/203, mm. 1–4. They should be in KB 9/993, the file for Trinity 1413.

[103] *SKB* vii. 215 (KB 27/609, Rex, m. 14d); Bellamy, *Law of Treason*, 131. Kampe's fine was later remitted at the request of the Commons: *CPR, 1413–16*, p. 191. Such escapes were embarrassingly frequent in Henry V's reign: see ch. 6 n. 40; ch. 10 at nn. 40–1.
[104] KB 27/624, Rex, mm. 9, 12; see ch. 10 n. 29.
[105] KB 9/993, mm. 32–4; KB 27/609, Rex, m. 17; KB 29/52, m. 7d.
[106] Ibid.; *CPR, 1413–16*, p. 149.
[107] Wylie and Waugh, *Henry V*, i. 209–11; Jacob, *Fifteenth Century*, 128–9.

which involved the abduction of Murdoch Stewart and the intended use of the Scottish pseudo-Richard.[108]

PUBLIC ORDER

It was some months before the king began to address the problem of public order, as he had promised in the Parliament of May 1413. The first part of the country to which he turned his attention was Wales and the Welsh Marches. Although the Glendower rebellion had effectively been suppressed as an organized revolt in the second half of Henry IV's reign, the settlement of the region—the restoration of public order and the re-establishment of civilian administration—had yet to be achieved. During the early summer of 1413 powerful commissions of oyer and terminer were appointed for north and south Wales, led by the earl of Arundel and the justices of king's bench and common pleas. The king also ordered a commission of justices in eyre to hold sessions in the duchy of Lancaster lordships in the March of south Wales. During the summer and autumn, and again in the spring of 1414, these groups of justices sat throughout Wales. They received rebels who submitted to the king's grace, sold confiscated lands, reconciled to the Crown communities which had risen in revolt (usually on payment of a corporate fine) and heard complaints against corrupt officials.[109]

Outside Wales the new king had done little to reduce the level of disorder by the end of 1413. Plans to hold sessions of the central courts at Lincoln in Michaelmas term had to be abandoned owing to the lack of food supplies in the town.[110] Lawlessness continued unchecked in many parts of the country, particularly in the Midlands.[111] In Staffordshire the disputes between Hugh Erdswick and Edmund Ferrers escalated into armed confrontation, while in Shropshire the feuding between adherents of the earl of Arundel and John Talbot, Lord Furnival, became so serious that in November the king took the drastic step of imprisoning Talbot, and

[108] Ibid. 146–7; Pugh, 'Southampton Plot', 65; see ch. 10 at nn. 26–7.
[109] See ch. 8.
[110] *CCR, 1413–19*, pp. 91–2, 96–7.
[111] Jacob, *Fifteenth Century*, 127–8. See chs. 7–9.

imposed huge recognizances on the parties to keep the peace.[112] Elsewhere the Devonshire mariners continued to ignore the king's truces with impunity, and parliamentary elections provoked riots at Norwich.[113] It was disorder of a new kind, however, which forced the king to confront directly the problem of public order and prompted him to initiate a far-reaching programme of law enforcement: this was the Lollard revolt of January 1414, led by Sir John Oldcastle.

[112] See ch. 8 at nn. 171–2.
[113] Ibid. at nn. 42–7; *CPR, 1413–16*, p. 176; KB 9/205/1, mm. 37–8.

6

The Lollard Revolt

THE LOLLARD revolt, led by Sir John Oldcastle, took place in January 1414, only nine months after Henry V's accession. It was an event of immense significance in shaping Henry V's practice of kingship. The king's prompt and decisive suppression of the rising showed him in the most favourable light, discharging his three principal duties of protecting the Church, defending the realm, and enforcing the law. Victory over the Lollards bestowed upon him the aura of divine approval which Henry exploited to extend his authority over the English Church.[1] The king's response to the threat to public order posed by the Lollards set the tone for a programme of law enforcement which was introduced later in the year.[2] The revolt must indeed have encouraged the implementation of such a programme by confirming the anxiety about law and order expressed by the Commons in the Parliament of 1413.

This chapter offers a reassessment of the Lollard revolt. The last detailed study, by K. B. McFarlane, was published in 1952, and did not include a systematic analysis of the legal proceedings arising from the revolt, as will be done here.[3] There is a pressing need, moreover, to examine the revolt in the light of recent research. The traditional view of Lollardy as a purely religious movement, lacking cohesion and organization and influenced only indirectly by the writings of John Wyclif, is no longer tenable. McFarlane's own work on the Lollard knights, published posthumously, confirmed the existence of a close-knit circle high in the favour of Richard II

---

[1] Harriss, *Henry V*, 97–115.   [2] See ch. 7.

[3] McFarlane, *John Wycliffe and the Beginnings of English Nonconformity*. McFarlane was the first to use the records surviving from the judicial commissions issued in the wake of the revolt, but in other respects his account is heavily dependent upon the pioneering article of W. T. Waugh, 'Sir John Oldcastle', *EHR* 20 (1905), 434–56, 637–58.

and Henry IV who were at least sympathetic to Lollardy.[4] Some members of this group, like Sir Thomas Latimer, actively promoted the movement and harassed its opponents, yet until Oldcastle's trial in 1413 none was prosecuted for heresy. McFarlane's conclusions have been taken a stage further by Dr Wilks, who has argued persuasively that Wyclif was attempting to achieve a reformation of the Church not by pressure from below but through the king and his court.[5] The substantial corpus of Wycliffite writings has been illuminated by Dr Hudson.[6] Her studies of the manuscripts of two principal Wycliffite texts—the sermon cycle and the compilations known as the *Floretum* and the *Rosarium*—have established a clear and direct link between Wyclif's theological writings and popular Lollardy. They suggest also that these texts had an official standing within the movement, and that many fine and accurate copies were produced in the years leading up to the revolt, suggesting that Lollardy was a wealthy and well-organized movement with some form of central direction.[7] Finally, Dr Aston has elucidated the social and political context of Lollardy, revealing in particular the connection between religious dissent and political sedition.[8]

Aston's work on the politics of ecclesiastical endowment is especially relevant to an understanding of the revolt. The idea of expropriating the temporal lands and revenues of the Church for secular uses was not peculiar to the Lollards. It had been suggested as far back as the 1350s, and was obviously attractive to laymen during the period of heavy taxation between 1370 and 1420.[9] Wyclif's espousal of

[4] McFarlane, *Lancastrian Kings and Lollard Knights*, 139–232.
[5] Ibid. 192–6; M. Wilks, 'Royal Priesthood: The Origins of Lollardy', in *The Church in a Changing Society: Proceedings of the CIHEC Conference, 1977* (Uppsala, 1978), 63–70; id., '*Reformatio Regni*: Wyclif and Hus as Leaders of Religious Movements', in D. Baker (ed.), *Studies in Church History IX* (Cambridge, 1972) 109–30.
[6] *Selections from English Wycliffite Writings*, ed. A. M. Hudson (Cambridge, 1978); *English Wycliffite Sermons*, vol. i, ed. A. M. Hudson (Oxford, 1983); ead., *Lollards and Their Books* (London, 1985).
[7] Hudson, *Lollards and Their Books*, esp. 13–29, 181–91.
[8] M. Aston, 'Lollardy and Sedition, 1381–1431', *Past and Present*, 17 (1960), 1–44; repr. in ead., *Lollards and Reformers* (London, 1984), 1–44.
[9] M. Aston, ' "Caim's Castles": Poverty, Politics and Disendowment', in R. B. Dobson (ed.), *The Church, Politics and Patronage in the Fifteenth Century* (Gloucester, 1984), 49–57; ead., 'Lollardy and Sedition', 19–24. C. Kightly, 'The Early Lollards:

disendowment was, however, condemned as heretical in 1382, and thereafter the proposal became increasingly identified with the Lollard cause. Between 1395 and 1413 there was a determined campaign inside and outside Parliament in favour of disendowment, which was countered by increasingly urgent demands by the Church for action against Lollardy. During Henry IV's reign both sides competed for the king's support. In the southern convocation of October 1399, the petitions of the clergy complained of the hostility of those knights in the concurrent Parliament who, encouraged by Lollard propaganda, were planning to introduce statutes—presumably involving disendowment—to the detriment of the Church.[10] In the convocation of 1401 the clergy secured the death penalty for heresy in return for a grant to the king of a large subsidy. The point was forced home by the trial of William Sawtry before convocation, his conviction as a relapsed heretic, and his exemplary execution in March 1401 while Parliament was still in session.[11] At the Coventry Parliament of 1404, according to the chronicler Walsingham, knights in Parliament again put forward plans for disendowment, proposing that the temporalities of the Church be alienated for one year to provide for the king's needs.[12] During the 1406 Parliament the Lollard William Taylor preached at St Paul's Cross, condemning ownership of temporal possessions by the clergy and arguing that in certain circumstances they could legitimately be deprived of them by lay lords.[13] This immediately provoked a strongly worded petition sponsored by the prince of Wales and the spiritual and temporal lords.[14] It denounced heretics who sought to turn the hearts of good Christians against the Church and who advocated disendowment, and emphasized the threat to secular lordship if the

A Survey of Popular Lollard Activity in England, 1382–1428', Ph.D. thesis (York, 1975), 59–60, 195, 209, 278–83, 411–12, 439.

[10] Lambeth Palace Library, Register of Archbishop Thomas Arundel, vol. i, fo. 53^v, vol. ii, fo. 5^r (*Concilia Magnae Britanniae et Hiberniae*, ed. D. Wilkins (4 vols.; London, 1737), iii. 242); see also Walsingham, *Annales Ricardi Secundi et Henrici Quarti*, 289.

[11] Reg. Arundel, vol. ii, fos. 2^v, 178^r–86^v (*Concilia*, iii. 255–62); *RP* iii. 459, 466–7.

[12] Walsingham, *Annales Ricardi Secundi et Henrici Quarti*, 391–4.

[13] Reg. Arundel, vol. ii, fo. 118^v; Walsingham, *St Albans Chronicle*, 1–2.

[14] *RP* iii. 583–4.

clergy were stripped of their temporalities. The petition indirectly associated the Lollards with the supporters of Richard II, and requested that judges should be given the power to indict and arrest those who preached Lollardy and disendowment, or claimed that Richard II was still alive. These demands were not met in 1406, but they foreshadowed the Statute of Lollards enacted after the revolt in 1414.[15] At Oxford in 1407 Archbishop Arundel issued thirteen constitutions against unlicensed preaching, study of Wyclif's writings, and unauthorized translations of the Bible. Subsequently Arundel waged a determined and ultimately successful battle with Oxford University to secure its submission to his jurisdiction and the comprehensive condemnation of Wyclif's errors.[16]

Despite the opposition of the clergy, the campaign for disendowment lost none of its impetus in the later years of Henry IV's reign. The fullest manifesto of the campaign, the Lollard disendowment bill, is usually associated with the Parliament of 1410, although there is evidence that it had existed in some form since the 1390s.[17] The bill may have been formally presented to Parliament: Walsingham states that it was submitted to the king by knights in Parliament.[18] It detailed the income of the English bishoprics and major religious houses, and purported to show how disendowment could be used to provide for 15 earls, 15,000 knights and esquires, 15,000 priests, 100 almshouses, and £20,000 a year for the king's treasury. It was perhaps no coincidence that the convocation of 1410, sitting at the same time as Parliament, tried and convicted John Badby, only the second Lollard to be burnt for heresy since the introduction of the death penalty in 1401.[19]

---

[15] Aston, 'Lollardy and Sedition', 28, 42. See below, n. 103.

[16] McFarlane, *Wycliffe*, 140–3; G. Leff, *Heresy in the Later Middle Ages* (2 vols.; Manchester, 1967), ii. 570–3; *Snappe's Formulary*, ed. H. E. Salter, Oxford Historical Soc., 80 (Oxford, 1924), 90–180.

[17] *Selections from Wycliffite Writings*, 135–7, 203–7; Aston, ' "Caim's Castles" ', 54–6.

[18] Walsingham, *St Albans Chronicle*, 52.

[19] Reg. Arundel, vol. ii, fos. 17^r–18^r. The record of Badby's trial is immediately followed by the enrolment of the statute *De Heretico Comburendo*. See P. McNiven, *Heresy and Politics in the Reign of Henry IV: the Burning of John Badby* (Woodbridge, 1987), 158–219.

Henry IV resisted the temptation to plunder the Church as a means of easing his acute financial difficulties. He was described in the convocation of 1408 as 'the most Christian and most faithful athlete of the Church'.[20] Yet there is evidence of anti-clericalism and support for disendowment not merely among the knights in Parliament but also within the households of the king and the prince of Wales. Apart from the careers in Lancastrian service of such Lollards as Oldcastle, Richard Colfox, and Sir John Cheyne,[21] there are several instances related by Walsingham. He records twice, under the years 1403 and 1405, how Henry IV demanded a subsidy from the clergy at Worcester to finance campaigns against the Welsh rebels. The clergy pleaded poverty, and the knights and esquires present with the king urged that their horses and money be seized to aid the war effort.[22] At the time of the Coventry Parliament of 1404, when proposals for disendowment may have been made, Archbishop Arundel berated the king for the irreligious conduct of members of his household, who, on seeing the Host being carried through the streets to a dying man, turned their backs and continued their conversation.[23] Finally, during the Westminster Parliament of 1406 Robert Waterton, a Lancastrian knight, insulted Richard Alkerton as he preached at St Paul's Cross in reply to William Taylor's sermon in favour of disendowment. Waterton ordered his servant to give Alkerton a horse's curry-comb, thereby insinuating that he was trying to 'curry' favour with the ecclesiastical establishment. When Arundel complained to Henry IV, the king at first treated it as a joke, but Arundel insisted that Waterton apologize and do penance.[24]

Sir John Oldcastle must have fitted comfortably into such a milieu. His career prospered under the Lancastrians, and he became a trusted lieutenant of the prince of Wales during the campaigns against Owen Glendower. Through his marriage to Joan, Lady Cobham, in 1408 he acquired extensive estates in Kent and the south-east, and a place in the House of Lords:

---

[20] Reg. Arundel, vol. i, fo. 73[v] (*Concilia*, iii. 307): 'tanquam christianissimus et fidelissimus athleta ecclesie'.
[21] McFarlane, *Lancastrian Kings and Lollard Knights*, 162–3, 168–9, 207–15.
[22] Walsingham, *Annales Ricardi Secundi et Henrici Quarti*, 373, 414.
[23] Ibid. 395.　　　　[24] Walsingham, *St Albans Chronicle*, 1–2.

he was summoned to Parliament as Lord Cobham between 1410 and 1413. Given the stridency with which he subsequently proclaimed his beliefs, it is unlikely that Oldcastle's Lollardy went unnoticed before his marriage to Lady Cobham, but his new prominence attracted the attention of the archbishop, leading in 1410 to a temporary interdict on the Cobham estates in Kent.[25] It is also possible that Oldcastle's elevation to the peerage encouraged him to claim leadership of the Lollard movement in England, as two remarkable letters written by him to Bohemia suggest.[26] The first, dated at Cooling in September 1410, was addressed to the Hussite nobleman Wok of Waldstein, and was accompanied by a similar letter from the Lollard priest Richard Wyche to John Hus himself. The second, probably written in 1411, was addressed to King Wenzel of Bohemia. As the spokesman of the English Lollards Oldcastle offered messages of congratulation and support to both correspondents in their efforts to reform the Church and to enforce the true law of God. In his letter to Wenzel he offered his services and those of his followers against the opposition which the king might encounter from those hostile to the word of God.[27]

The letters provide valuable evidence of Oldcastle's religious and political beliefs, and help to explain the motives which led him into revolt. He regarded Wok and King Wenzel as comrades in the battle to free the Church from the clutches of the priests of Antichrist and to return it to its pristine state of apostolic poverty.[28] Following Wyclif's argument in the *Tractatus de Officio Regis*, Oldcastle assumed that the Church had been corrupted by its wealth, and that it was the Christian duty of temporal lords, and especially of kings, to reform the Church by disendowment.[29] The authorities cited in Oldcastle's letters suggest that he was familiar with the *De*

[25] Waugh, 'Oldcastle', 436–42; McFarlane, *Wycliffe*, 144–6; *Gesta Henrici Quinti*, 2–3.

[26] J. Loserth, 'Uber die Beziehungen zwischen englischen und böhmischen Wiclifiten', *Mitteilungen des Österreichischen Instituts für Geschichtsforschung*, 12 (1891), 266–9; Waugh, 'Oldcastle', 442–5. Oldcastle's letter to Wenzel also reveals that he had been in direct correspondence with Hus.

[27] Loserth, 'Beziehungen', 269.   [28] Ibid. 266, 268.

[29] John Wyclif, *Tractatus de Officio Regis*, ed. A. W. Pollard and C. Sayle, Wycliffe Society (London, 1887). See also the English Wycliffite *Tractatus de Regibus*, in *Four English Tracts*, 1–21.

Officio Regis. He quotes four texts, from Isidore, Isaiah, and John Chrysostom in the letter to Wok, and from Augustine in the letter to Wenzel. All of these except the Isaiah text appear in the *De Officio Regis*, in passages stressing the king's duty to maintain God's laws and to enforce ecclesiastical discipline.[30]

Oldcastle's letter to Wenzel was probably written in 1411, when that king must have seemed to be the champion the Lollards had been seeking. 'How delightful', Oldcastle wrote, 'that the greatest prince has proved the greatest knight of Christ.'[31] In that year Wenzel had taken the part of the Czech reformers against Archbishop Zbynek of Prague, who had ordered the public burning of Wyclif's works, excommunicated Hus, and placed the University of Prague under interdict. Wenzel secured Zbynek's eventual submission and the suspension of proceedings against Hus, first by sequestrating the revenues of the clergy and cathedral canons, and then by seizing the treasure at Prague cathedral and ordering a general visitation of the Bohemian Church.[32] This was exactly the sort of discipline by disendowment that Wyclif and the Lollards advocated. Oldcastle praised the king fulsomely:

how delightful that Wenzel king of the Romans and of Bohemia, the foremost pattern and mirror of other kings, wisely and zealously separated the tares—the false priests—from the wheat gathered in the barn, and confirmed the wheat—the true priests of Christ—in the state of apostolic poverty.[33]

There could hardly be a clearer indication of Oldcastle's hopes when Henry V became king. It is probable, as the author of the *Gesta Henrici Quinti* implies, that he raised the subject of disendowment with Henry in one of their many interviews during the spring and summer of 1413. Here,

[30] The relevant citations are as follows: (1) *Isidore*: Loserth, 'Beziehungen', 266; Wyclif, *De Officio Regis*, 84; (2) *John Chrysostom*: Loserth, 267; Wyclif, *De Officio Regis*, 79; (3) *Augustine*: Loserth, 268; Wyclif, *De Officio Regis*, 55.
[31] Loserth, 'Beziehungen', 268: 'O quam delectabile tam excelsus princeps excelsus miles Christi effectus est.' Cf. Wilks, 'Wyclif and Hus', 109–30.
[32] Leff, *Heresy in the Later Middle Ages*, ii. 629–35.
[33] Loserth, 268: 'O quam suave, quod Wenceslaus Romanorum et Boemie Rex exemplum et speculum primicieque ceterorum regum zyzaniam, falsos sacerdotes, in oreum congregatam sagaciter et studiose a tritico segregavit et triticum, veros Christi sacerdotes, in statu evangelice paupertatis corroboravit.'

following the Wycliffite theory of reformation from above, Oldcastle's views appear very much in the mainstream of Lollard doctrine.[34]

Oldcastle's hopes in the new king proved sadly misplaced. Even before his accession, Henry V had ranged himself alongside the defenders of the Church. He sponsored the petition of 1406 which attacked the advocates of disendowment, and his opposition to the Lollard bill of 1410 was noted by Walsingham.[35] The English clergy were as determined as Oldcastle to win the king over, and to impress upon him the need for decisive action against heresy.

It is arguable that the revolt of 1414 was precipitated by the demands of the clergy for sterner measures against Lollardy. Influential Lollards and their sympathizers had long enjoyed immunity from prosecution, but the convocation of 1413 insisted that the threat of heresy could not be removed until its most powerful patrons were extirpated. Oldcastle was singled out as the 'principal receiver, patron, protector, and defender' of Lollardy, and convocation called for his trial.[36]

The story of Oldcastle's trial and conviction is well known and does not need to be retold here.[37] It is worth noting, however, that the demands of the clergy for proceedings against Oldcastle placed the king in a quandary. His duty as a Christian prince to root out heresy conflicted with personal obligations of maintenance and protection towards Oldcastle as his lord. Archbishop Arundel recognized the delicacy of his position, and Oldcastle's arraignment was deferred while the king attempted to persuade him to submit to ecclesiastical discipline. These attempts failed, and after an acrimonious exchange at Windsor in August 1413 Oldcastle withdrew without licence and shut himself up in Cooling castle, upon

[34] *Gesta Henrici Quinti*, 4–5. See above at n. 5.
[35] Walsingham, *Historia Anglicana*, ii. 283. As prince of Wales Henry also demonstrated his concern about heresy through his intervention at the burning of John Badby in 1410: McFarlane, *Wycliffe*, 138; *Gregory's Chronicle*, in *The Historical Collections of a Citizen of London*, ed. J. Gairdner, Camden Soc., 2nd ser., 17 (London, 1876), 105–6; McNiven, *Heresy and Politics*, 209–18.
[36] *Foedera*, ix. 61: 'repertum fuit quod dominus Johannes Oldcastellus . . . est principalis receptator, fautor, protector, et defensor eorumdem [Lollardorum]'.
[37] For the record of Oldcastle's trial, see *Foedera*, ix. 61–6; Walsingham, *St Albans Chronicle*, 70–8. The fullest secondary accounts are Waugh, 'Oldcastle', 447–55; McFarlane, *Wycliffe*, 146–9.

which Henry instructed Arundel to proceed with the trial. Oldcastle's unauthorized departure from the king at Windsor marked the formal breach between the two men, and suggests a form of feudal *diffidatio*, or defiance. Because Henry, as his lord, had abandoned him to the humiliation of a public trial for heresy, Oldcastle may have considered himself absolved of all ties of loyalty and obedience towards him. If the Lollard revolt of 1414 foreshadowed the wars of religion,[38] it may also be seen as the rising of an injured vassal against the lord who had forsworn him.

OLDCASTLE'S REVOLT

On 25 September 1413 Oldcastle was condemned as a heretic and excommunicated at Blackfriars before Archbishop Arundel.[39] He was then handed over to the secular arm for burning, but as a mark of clemency the king deferred the execution of sentence for forty days, and Oldcastle was imprisoned in the Tower. He escaped with the aid of Lollard sympathizers on the night of 19 October,[40] and went into hiding in the house of William Fisher, a parchment-maker, in Turnmill Street, just outside the city of London near Clerkenwell priory.[41] The suburbs of Clerkenwell and Smithfield, on the north-western fringes of London, were to prove the epicentre of the revolt.[42] From this base Oldcastle organized an armed rising to remove the king, who had shown himself to be immovably opposed to Lollard schemes for Church reform, and to implement the disendowment of the Church by force.[43]

[38] Harriss, *Henry V*, 97–8.   [39] *Foedera*, ix. 65.

[40] *Gesta Henrici Quinti*, 6–7; Walsingham, *St Albans Chronicle*, 76. The Tower was an extremely insecure prison in the early fifteenth century. The traitors John Whitelock, Thomas Payn, and Sir John Mortimer all escaped from it, Whitelock in 1414, Payn and Mortimer in 1422: *CPR, 1413–16*, p. 191; J. A. F. Thomson, *The Later Lollards, 1414–1520* (Oxford, 1965), 17–18. See ch. 10 at nn. 40–7.

[41] *Memorials of London*, 641–3. Fisher must have been the 'parchemyner of Trillemelle strete' executed for treason in 1416: *A Chronicle of London from 1089 to 1483*, ed. N. H. Nicolas and E. Tyrell (London, 1827), 104; John Stow, *The Chronicles of England* (London, 1580), 597.   [42] See below at nn. 87–90.

[43] Walsingham's picture of Lollard missionaries touring the country recruiting support for Oldcastle after his escape (*St Albans Chronicle*, 76–7) is to some extent borne out by the findings of the judicial proceedings held after the revolt: see below at n. 84.

Through good intelligence Henry V soon got wind of Oldcastle's schemes. He may have known that a conspiracy was afoot before Christmas 1413: on 24 December the Parliament summoned for 29 January following was prorogued until 30 April, perhaps to allow the king time to deal with the threat of revolt.[44] Details of the plot were made known to Henry while he spent Christmas and New Year at Eltham. On 5 January John de Burgh, a carpenter, and Thomas Kentford each received an annuity of ten marks for life for revealing the Lollards' plans, and at about the same time a royal spy, Thomas Burton, was rewarded for similar information.[45] The conspirators apparently planned to appear at Eltham disguised as mummers on or shortly after Twelfth Night, and to capture the king and his brothers; they then intended to seize the government by armed force under Oldcastle's command on 10 January. The rebels' assembly-point in St Giles' Fields was strategically placed between London and Westminster.[46]

Thus forewarned, Henry ordered the arrest of all suspicious persons at Eltham and in London.[47] On the night of 6 January the mayor of London, William Crowmer, arrested a group of Lollards at John Burgate's house at the sign of the Axe outside Bishopsgate, and sent them to Eltham for interrogation.[48] Before the king they confessed their involvement in the conspiracy and implicated others; Oldcastle's plans must by now have been fully revealed.[49] He himself evaded arrest, but on 7 January a proclamation was sent to all counties

[44] *CCR, 1413–19*, p. 111.

[45] *CPR, 1413–16*, p. 157; *Issues of the Exchequer*, ed. F. Devon (London, 1837), 333; C. L. Kingsford, *English Historical Literature in the Fifteenth Century* (Oxford, 1913), 284.

[46] *Gregory's Chronicle*, 108; Stow, *Chronicles*, 584–5; Kingsford, *English Historical Literature*, 292–3; *The Brut*, ii. 373–4, 551. The magnate conspirators against Henry IV in January 1400 had planned a similar attack on the king under cover of a mumming: *The Great Chronicle of London*, ed. A. H. Thomas and I. D. Thornley (London, 1938), 83. Not surprisingly Christmas mummings were banned in London later in Henry V's reign: *Memorials of London*, 669.

[47] John Mayhew was arrested at Eltham for distributing seditious bills, and a special purchase of manacles and fetters was made for certain traitors arrested at Eltham and elsewhere: KB 29/52, m. 16d; *Issues of the Exchequer*, 330.

[48] *Gregory's Chronicle*, 108; Stow, *Chronicles*, 584–5; Kingsford, *English Historical Literature*, 292–3. Waugh, 'Oldcastle', 640, and McFarlane, *Wycliffe*, 151, assumed from Gregory's account that those arrested at the Axe were the would-be mummers. If this is true, however, their plans must already have gone awry since they were still in east London at 10 p.m. on Twelfth Night, several miles from Eltham.

[49] *CCR, 1413–19*, pp. 114–15; *Issues of the Exchequer*, 330–2; *The Brut*, ii. 373–4.

announcing the discovery of the plot and ordering the arrest of all who gathered in unlawful assemblies.[50] On 8 January King Henry returned unobtrusively to Westminster from Eltham with his brothers.[51] He allowed the conspiracy to run its course; although Oldcastle's supporters in London must have known of the arrests on Twelfth Night, contingents of rebels from various parts of the country were converging on the capital for the rendezvous at St Giles' Fields. On the evening of Tuesday 9 January Henry left Westminster with a small armed force, swept through Clerkenwell, where several rebels were captured, and set up positions guarding the routes to St Giles. The gates of London were closed to prevent Lollards from the city joining Oldcastle. About eighty rebels were captured as they approached St Giles; others, like Oldcastle himself and Sir Roger Acton, escaped, while some may have been killed resisting arrest.[52]

Legal proceedings were at once set in motion to deal with the rebels. On 10 January commissioners led by William, Lord Roos, and Henry, Lord Scrope, were given full oyer and terminer powers over treasons committed in London and Middlesex. The judges started work immediately at the Tower, fortified by a hearty breakfast. A panel of presenting jurors was assembled at considerable cost, and John Corve, a clerk of king's bench, was assigned to the commission to record proceedings.[53] According to one London source sixty-nine rebels were convicted and condemned to death on 12 January.[54] Thirty-eight were executed the following day in St Giles' Fields. Seven were burned for heresy as well as hanged.[55]

Meanwhile on 11 January provincial commissions of inquiry were issued to investigate the activities of Lollards and rebels, their findings being returnable to the king himself. On

[50] *CCR, 1413–19*, pp. 114–15.

[51] *Chronicle of London*, 96; Kingsford, *English Historical Literature*, 293; Stow, *Chronicles*, 585; Walsingham, *St Albans Chronicle*, 77.

[52] Ibid. 78; *Chronicle of London*, 96–7; *Gregory's Chronicle*, 108; Stow, *Chronicles*, 585; *The Brut*, ii. 373–4, 551; Kingsford, *English Historical Literature*, 293. See below, n. 71.

[53] *CPR, 1413–16*, p. 175; *Issues of the Exchequer*, 331.

[54] Kingsford, *English Historical Literature*, 293; Stow, *Chronicles*, 585. The loss of the oyer and terminer roll makes it impossible to verify this figure.

[55] For the names of those executed, see the list of prisoners transferred from the earl Marshal to the sheriffs of London: *CCR, 1413–19*, pp. 56–7.

the same day a proclamation was issued denouncing the revolt and offering a reward for Oldcastle's capture.[56] Finally, on Monday 15 January, the end of the emergency was signalled by an order from Archbishop Arundel to the bishop of London to hold a procession of thanksgiving to celebrate the defeat of the Lollards.[57]

The records of the legal proceedings against the rebels in 1414 are full enough to make systematic analysis worthwhile. The roll of the London and Middlesex oyer and terminer commission, before which the rebels captured at St Giles' Fields were tried, has been lost, but this can be partly reconstructed from the records of king's bench.[58] The records of the provincial commissions of inquiry are almost complete. Sixteen commissions were issued covering London, Bristol, and twenty counties. Returns survive for ten counties and Bristol.[59] In two of these counties, Hampshire and Nottinghamshire, the presenting juries made no indictments, and the blank returns were duly handed in by the commissioners. No returns of any kind survive for the remaining counties:[60] the absence of proceedings in king's bench upon commissions issued to these counties indicates that if the commissioners sat no indictments were returned before them—as in Hampshire and Nottinghamshire.

The London and Middlesex oyer and terminer commission led by Roos and Scrope rapidly completed its initial business. After the executions of 13 January the record of its proceedings was submitted to king's bench for the beginning of Hilary term, and the court took over responsibility for the prosecution of

---

[56] *CPR, 1413–16*, pp. 177–8; *Foedera*, ix. 89.

[57] Thomson, *Later Lollards*, 222.

[58] For judicial process upon indictments taken before this commission, see KB 29/52, m. 23; KB 27/611, Rex, m. 13: for the record of trial proceedings before it, see KB 27/616, Rex, m. 23; 617, Rex, m. 4 d; *CPR, 1413–16*, pp. 153, 162. It is possible that the original oyer and terminer roll may yet be discovered. In 1417 it formed part of the king's bench indictment file for Hilary term 1414: KB 9/209, m. 72. Fragments of this file were rediscovered by C. A. F. Meekings of the PRO in July 1967 during a re-examination of the debris of the king's bench file sacks, and are now classed as KB 9/991.

[59] *CPR, 1413–16*, pp. 177–8; KB 9/204/1 (Derby., Essex, Herts., Leics., Northants., Notts., Worcs.); KB 9/205/1, mm. 51–7 (Oxon.), 81–5 (Bristol and Glos.); *CIM, 1399–1422*, no. 462 (Hants.).

[60] Beds., Berks., Bucks., Devon, Dorset, Kent, Herefs., London, Shrops., Som., and War.

indicted rebels who were still at large.[61] Two leading rebels, the chaplain Walter Blake of Bristol and Sir Roger Acton, were later convicted in king's bench and executed, Blake on 27 January and Acton on 10 February.[62]

The first sessions of the provincial commissions opened in Essex, Hertfordshire, and Hampshire at the end of January 1414 and continued until the conclusion of the Nottinghamshire sessions in mid-March. The completed returns were dispatched to the king in person—an unusual provision for judicial commissions—and on 12 June 1414 they were passed on to king's bench for determination.[63] The court was then at Lichfield on tour of the north-west Midlands, and the Lollard indictments were given a fairly low priority. Process upon them was returnable in king's bench only in the following Michaelmas term.[64] From their scrutiny of the returns the king and the justices of king's bench concluded that Oldcastle had very few sympathizers in the provinces, and that the prosecution of Lollards was no longer a matter of great urgency compared with the thousands of other indictments pouring into king's bench from the Midlands.[65] The presenting juries which made returns before the Lollard commissions must have relied heavily on the authorities for information as to whom they were to indict. The Middlesex jurors, who returned indictments chiefly against rebels captured at St Giles' Fields, must simply have endorsed a schedule of accusations laid before them by the Crown. Their indictments were elaborate and carefully drafted, echoing official documents such as the proclamation against Oldcastle and the commissions of inquiry of 11 January.[66] Information leading to charges against persons not in custody, especially Lollard sympathizers amongst the gentry, had probably been obtained through the interrogation of captured rebels. The indictment

---

[61] KB 29/52, m. 23; KB 27/611, Rex, m. 13.

[62] KB 27/611, Rex, m. 7.   [63] KB 27/613, Rex, m. 6.

[64] KB 29/53, mm. 30, 36d, 37. By contrast process on the commission of inquiry into disorders in Notts. and Derby., which was delivered to king's bench at the same time as the Lollard inquiries, was made returnable at the end of June: KB 27/613, Rex, m. 6; KB 29/53, mm. 22–4.

[65] See ch. 7.

[66] KB 27/611, Rex, m. 7 (printed in *SKB* vii. 217–18). Cf. *Foedera*, ix. 89; KB 9/204/1, m. 84.

of Thomas Tickhill and Henry Booth of Derbyshire, for
example, may be explained by the capture of Walter Gilbert, a
Lollard chaplain whom Booth had harboured, and John
Green of Chaddesden, an associate of Tickhill's protégé
William Edrick.[67]

Juries before the local commissions also seem to have relied
upon information obtained by the government from the
rebels. The returns are formulaic and repetitive: in Derbyshire
William Edrick and his followers were indicted for rebellion in
the same terms by all eleven juries empanelled before the
commissioners, while in Essex Laurence Cook and his sons
John and Thomas were each indicted six times.[68] The returns
for Derbyshire, Essex, and Bristol include set formulae for
indictments. They vary from one another but are all based
upon the form of the original Middlesex indictments.[69] The
commissioners in each county were probably sent a brief
account of the revolt which they read to the jurors, together
with a list of suspects from that county whose names had been
extracted from captured rebels in London. The jurors could
then have supplemented the list from their own local
knowledge.

Table 1 summarizes the outcome of proceedings upon
indictments taken before the commissions against Lollards
and rebels.[70] A total of 231 people were indicted, including
162 who were accused of rebellion, of whom only 47 were also
indicted for Lollardy. If the names are added of those
excluded from the Lollard pardon of March 1414 or who
forfeited their possessions to the Crown for rebellion, but for
whom no legal proceedings can be traced, the total rises to
242, of whom at most 173 were rebels and at most 58 both
Lollards and rebels.[71]

[67] KB 27/611, Rex, m. 13; KB 9/204/1, mm. 58–66.
[68] KB 9/204/1, mm. 4–12, 57–67.
[69] Ibid., mm. 3–5, 57–66; KB 9/205/1, mm. 82–4. The preamble to the Derby.
indictments, which names Oldcastle, Robert Harley, Richard Morley, and John
Purvey as the leaders of the rising, is very similar to that of a Middx. indictment
returned *coram rege* in Hilary term 1414: KB 9/991, m. 4.
[70] The totals are compiled from the records described above and from the lists of
prisoners transferred from the custody of the earl Marshal to the sheriffs of London on
13 Jan. and 23 July 1414: *CCR, 1413–19*, pp. 56–7, 148. I have assumed that they were
tried before the London and Middx. oyer and terminer.
[71] For the text of the pardon, see *Foedera*, ix. 119–20. I have found no indictments

TABLE 1. *Outcomes of indictments taken before commissions against Lollards and rebels, 1414*

Indictment	Convicted	Acquitted	Pardoned	Outlawed	To Church courts	No process	Dead	Total
Lollardy and rebellion	11	2	18	15	0	0	1	47
Rebellion	33	4	42	31	0	2	3	115
Lollardy	0	0	0	9	35	8	0	52
Possession of English books	0	0	0	0	0	7	0	7
Going to London	0	0	0	0	0	6	0	6
Other	0	0	0	0	0	4	0	4
TOTAL	44	6	60	55	35	27	4	231

Sources: E 199/26, no. 30; KB 9/204/1; KB 9/205/1, mm. 51–7, 81–5; KB 27/611–60; *CCR, 1413–19*, pp. 56–7, 148.

If these figures accurately reflect the level of participation in the revolt, the response to Oldcastle's call to arms was pitifully small. Only one in three of the rebels were Lollards, and several of those involved were paid to join the rising. On the other hand the numbers are so low, especially by comparison with contemporary estimates, which counted the rebels in tens of thousands, as to suggest that we must be cautious in drawing conclusions from them.[72] The totals

against seven of the men excluded from the pardon. Four men suffered forfeiture of their lands and goods for rebellion, apparently without being indicted or convicted: E 357 (exchequer, escheators' enrolled accounts)/24, mm. 39, 49–50, 66–8, 76–7, 84. They include the well-known Lollard chaplain John Purvey, who was mentioned in the preambles to some indictments as one of the leaders of the rebellion, but for whom there is no record of indictment, conviction, or execution: KB 9/204/1, mm. 60–3; 991, m. 4. The only explanation of these facts is that Purvey and the three other forfeited rebels were killed during the revolt. For Purvey's career, see A. M. Hudson, 'John Purvey: a Reconsideration of the Evidence for his Life and Writings', *Viator*, 12 (1981), 355–80.

[72] KB 27/611, Rex, m. 7; Walsingham, *St Albans Chronicle*, 70, 78; KB 9/204/1, mm. 9, 57–63.

derived from Table 1 certainly underestimate the number of rebels: some records of judicial proceedings have been lost,[73] and local juries of presentment may have kept silent to shield suspects from prosecution. There is no evidence, however, of resistance to commissioners conducting the Lollard inquiries such as occurred in Devon in February 1414; nor is there any hint of local disturbances—comparable to the events of 1381—which might indicate widespread support for the rebels.[74] Furthermore, Oldcastle's ability to command the support even of the Lollards themselves is open to question. His rebellion was essentially a personal response to Henry's failure to protect him from prosecution in the ecclesiastical courts. It represented an abrupt departure from the long-standing Lollard policy of seeking reform through pressure in Parliament. Faced with a king who refused to reform the Church by disendowment, according to Wycliffite expectations, Oldcastle leapt to the conclusion that the only solution was that king's removal. In so doing he departed from the mainstream of Lollard thought, which not only exalted royal authority but contained a strong element of pacifism.[75] The absence of certain prominent Lollards, such as William Taylor, Richard Wyche, and John Claydon, from the rebels' ranks, indicates that although Oldcastle styled himself as its leader, some Lollards did not share his views, and were reluctant to become caught up in his personal vendetta against Henry V.[76] Although it is dangerous to argue from silence, the cumulative weight of negative evidence suggests that Oldcastle's supporters should be numbered in hundreds rather than thousands.

The rapid collapse of the rising encouraged the king to be merciful. After the mass executions of 13 January, only six rebels suffered the death penalty: John Brown, John Beverley, Walter Blake, and Sir Roger Acton were executed within a

---

[73] See above, nn. 54, 58, 71.   [74] See ch. 8 at nn. 38–41.

[75] For the exaltation of royal authority in Lollard thought, see Wycliffe's *De Officio Regis* and the English *Tractatus de Regibus* (above, n. 29). For Lollard pacifism, see *Selections from Wycliffite Writings*, 20, 28, 35; McFarlane, *Lancastrian Kings and Lollard Knights*, 177. In formulating my conclusions on Oldcastle's place in the history of the Lollard movement I have been greatly influenced by the comments of Dr Anne Hudson of Lady Margaret Hall, Oxford, on an earlier version of this chapter.

[76] McFarlane, *Wycliffe*, 163.

month of the revolt, William Fisher of Turnmill Street in 1416 and Oldcastle himself in 1417.[77] Several rebels who had been condemned to death were subsequently pardoned. The first, Henry Dene of London, received his pardon only a fortnight after the revolt.[78] On 28 March 1414 the king proclaimed a general pardon to all rebels who submitted by midsummer, with a few named exceptions.[79] In the following December thirteen rebels who had been held in the Tower and at Newgate since the rising were pardoned and released.[80]

There were sixty-nine people indicted for Lollardy and various offences which did not amount to rebellion. The latter charges were dropped and no process issued upon them (see Table 1). The king's courts could not, of course, try those accused of Lollardy, which was a matter for the Church. Process was issued summoning them before king's bench, and when they appeared they were handed over to their bishops, or to the abbot of Westminster, within whose liberty the court sat.[81] A group of Leicestershire Lollards was delivered by king's bench to the bishop of Lincoln while the court was in the Midlands in June 1414, and several Bristol Lollards indicted in 1414 made their purgation before the bishop of Bath and Wells in 1417, the result being certified to king's bench.[82]

Table 2 shows that although the known rebels were few in number, they were widely distributed geographically. The largest contingents were from Bristol, Buckinghamshire, Derbyshire, Essex, Leicestershire, and Oxfordshire, where, as McFarlane pointed out, Lollard preachers had been active and had influential patrons.[83] There are signs of rudimentary

---

[77] KB 27/611, Rex, m. 7; *Gregory's Chronicle*, 108; *The Brut*, ii. 551; *Memorials of London*, 641–3.

[78] *CPR, 1413–16*, p. 162. Dene later received back the possessions he had forfeited as a traitor: ibid. 160; E 357/24, m. 49. For other rebels pardoned after conviction, see *CPR, 1413–16*, pp. 153, 236, 237, 250; KB 27/616, Rex, m. 23; 617, Rex, m. 4d.

[79] *Foedera*, ix. 119–20; *CPR, 1413–16*, pp. 261–2.

[80] *CCR, 1413–19*, p. 148; *CPR, 1413–16*, p. 271; E 199 (exchequer, sheriffs' accounts)/26, no. 30.

[81] KB 29/54, mm. 15, 18, 20; KB 27/619, Rex, m. 2d; 620, Rex, m. 8; 627, Rex, m. 9d.

[82] KB 27/613, Rex, m. 6; 626, Rex, m. 18; *The Register of Nicholas Bubwith, Bishop of Bath and Wells, 1407–24*, ed. T. S. Holmes, Somerset Record Soc., 29–30 (2 vols.; London, 1914), ii. 283–90, 298.

[83] McFarlane, *Wycliffe*, 156–9.

organization; local agents, like William Edrick in Derbyshire, Walter Blake in Bristol, and the Cook family in Essex, recruited and led groups of rebels to join Oldcastle in London.[84] The Derbyshire rebels were given the name of William Frome, whom they were to meet when they arrived in London.[85] The Buckinghamshire rebels may have been led by Sir Roger Acton, who passed through Wycombe on his way to London and left a horse there which was later forfeited to the Crown.[86]

TABLE 2. *The geographical origin of the 1414 rebels*

Area		Area	
Beds.	1	Northants	9
Bristol	29	Notts.	1
Bucks.	13	Oxon.	13
Ches.	1	Som.	3
Derby.	14	Staffs.	1
Essex	11	War.	4
Herts.	4	Worcs.	2
Kent	3	Unknown	16
Leics.	16		
London	16	TOTAL	162
Midd.	4		
Norfolk	1		

Sources: as for Table 1.

The legal records confirm that the London suburbs of Smithfield and Clerkenwell were the heart of the revolt. Oldcastle hid in in Turnmill Street after his escape from the Tower, and after the revolt three men from the same street were accused of consorting with him and concealing his presence from the king.[87] Since one of the three, Nicholas Underwood, was serving as constable of Turnmill Street in 1427, it is possible that the real crime of these men was official

---

[84] KB 9/204/1, mm. 1–12, 57–67; 205/1, mm. 81–5; McFarlane, *Wycliffe*, 161.
[85] KB 9/204/1, m. 58.   [86] Ibid., m. 16; E 357/24, m. 68.
[87] KB 9/991, m. 12; KB 29/52, m. 20d; KB 27/616, Rex, m. 5d. Underwood was pardoned in 1415, Littleton not until 1437.

negligence in failing to detect and report Oldcastle's presence, rather than active rebellion.[88] Some of Oldcastle's possessions—two horses and two red cloaks—were found in the custody of John Joiner and Matthew Toly in St John's Street, east of Clerkenwell priory. They claimed that an unknown esquire had left the goods with them on the morning of the revolt.[89] Finally, a Smithfield inn, the Wrestlers on the Hoop, was to have been the rendezvous for William Frome and the Derbyshire rebels.[90] St Giles' Fields, little more than a mile away from Smithfield to the south-west, provided an obvious assembly-point.

The status or occupation of rebels, where it can be determined, is indicated in Table 3. Sixteen knights, esquires, and gentlemen were implicated in the rising, four of whom

TABLE 3. *The status or occupation of the 1414 rebels*

Occupation		Occupation	
Knight	5	Mercer	2
Esquire or		Miller	1
Gentleman	11	Parchment-maker	4
Brazier	1	Ploughman	4
Brewer or		Priest, Clerk,	
Taverner	5	or Chaplain	16
Carpenter	5	Scholar	2
Cooper	1	Scrivener	2
Cordwainer	4	Servant	4
Fletcher	1	Sherman	1
Fuller	4	Skinner	1
Glover	2	Smith	1
Goldsmith	2	Tailor	4
Hosier	2	Thatcher	1
Husbandman	1	Travellingman	1
Ironmonger	2	Weaver	28
Labourer	4	Unknown	37
Limner	1		
Mason	2	TOTAL	162

Sources: as for Table 1.

[88] KB 9/222/2, m. 58.
[89] KB 29/54, m. 13.   [90] See above, n. 85.

were executed: Oldcastle, Acton, Robert Harley, and Old-castle's esquire, John Brown.[91] Four others who appear to have taken part in the revolt were pardoned: Richard Colfox, Thomas Noveray, Sir Thomas Talbot, and John Wickham of Swalcliffe in Oxfordshire.[92] The remaining eight had been indicted before the London and Middlesex oyer and terminer commission and were arrested shortly after the revolt.[93] There is no other evidence that they actively supported Oldcastle, and most were later acquitted. Some were known Lollard sympathizers like Roger Cheyne of Drayton Beauchamp and his sons John and Thomas, as well as Thomas Tickhill and Henry Booth of Derbyshire, who sheltered the Lollard preachers Walter Gilbert and William Edrick.[94] Thomas Broke of Somerset was probably indicted because of his family ties with Oldcastle, while Sir Thomas Beauchamp of Somerset and Sir Thomas Chaworth, who had no known Lollard connections, may have been implicated by captured rebels.[95] Five of this group—Beauchamp, Booth, Broke, Chaworth, and Tickhill—were acquitted of rebellion in Michaelmas term 1414; Booth and Tickhill were later delivered to the bishop for ecclesiastical correction. Roger Cheyne died in prison and his sons received pardons.[96]

Unbeneficed clergy accounted for approximately one in eight of the rebels whose occupation is known. They included some of the most committed participants, like Walter Blake, William Edrick, and Walter Gilbert, who were responsible for recruiting rebels. Only one, however, came from the academic

---

[91] See above at n. 77. For Acton's career, see Waugh, 'Oldcastle', 641.

[92] KB 27/613, Rex, m. 6d; 615, Rex, m. 14; 623, Rex, m. 17; *CPR, 1413–16*, p. 250; McFarlane, *Wycliffe*, 153.

[93] KB 27/611, Rex, m. 13; *CCR, 1413–19*, pp. 54, 116, 121.

[94] KB 27/611, Rex, m. 13; KB 9/204/1, mm. 59–66. For the Cheynes, see Thomson, *Later Lollards*, 53–5. Tickhill, who had been king's attorney in the court of common pleas, was dismissed from office a few days after the revolt. His household remained a centre for Lollard activity for several years after 1414: *SKB* vi, pp. xc–xci; JUST 3/13/1, m. 1; KB 27/634, Rex, m. 34; 635, Rex, m. 15; 648, Rex, m. 4.

[95] Broke was married to Oldcastle's stepdaughter Joan Braybrooke: McFarlane, *Lancastrian Kings and Lollard Knights*, 216; Chaworth's arrest was ordered on 8 Jan. 1414, the day before the revolt, suggesting that his name had been mentioned by the conspirators arrested on 6 Jan.: *CPR, 1413–16*, p. 148.

[96] KB 27/614, Rex, mm. 15, 24d, 41; KB 29/54, m. 15; C 138 (chancery, inquisitions post mortem, Henry V)/7/2. Thomas Cheyne was excluded from the Lollard pardon but received a general pardon in Jan. 1415: C 67/37, m. 58.

milieu which had originally spawned Lollardy: he was John Mybbe, principal of St Cuthbert's Hall in Oxford.[97] Of the remainder, Oldcastle drew his support mainly from artisans and small traders, particularly those involved in the cloth trade. There were few agrarian workers: ploughmen, husbandmen, and labourers accounted for only nine of the total. McFarlane described the rebels as 'rustic simpletons', but such evidence as survives does not wholly bear out this dismissive verdict.[98] Some of the rebels, and not merely the gentry, were men of substance. Robert Cringleford, a goldsmith of St Bartholomew's, Smithfield, forfeited nearly £80's worth of goods, including gold valued at £66, as well as rents worth 7 marks in Smithfield.[99] In Buckinghamshire John Harwood (taverner), John Finch, Walter Young, and Thomas Sibley (fletcher) forfeited goods worth between £6 and £8 each.[100] If the events of 1414 are compared with the revolt of 1381, it is clear that the failure of the rebels lay more in lack of numbers than social status.

THE AFTERMATH

Although Oldcastle's rising utterly failed to achieve its aims, it did confirm the repeated warnings of the clergy that the challenge to ecclesiastical lordship inherent in Lollardy would ultimately extend to temporal lordship as well.[101] In 1414 the rebels were accused of planning to destroy the spiritual and temporal lords of the kingdom, to despoil the Church, to force the clergy into secular occupations, to establish Oldcastle as ruler, and to set up several lordships within the kingdom— nothing less, in short, than violent revolution.[102] As a result Lollardy became irredeemably tainted with treason, and laws were immediately passed proscribing it, along the lines demanded at the Parliament of 1406. The Statute of Lollards,

---

[97] KB 9/205/1, mm. 51, 57; see above at nn. 83-4.
[98] McFarlane, *Wycliffe*, 152.   [99] E 357/24, m. 49.
[100] Ibid., mm. 67-8.
[101] Aston, 'Lollardy and Sedition', 2-3, 12-13, 24, 26.
[102] KB 27/611, Rex, m. 7 (printed in *SKB* vii. 218-19); *RP* iv. 15; see also *Foedera*, ix. 89, 119-20. For the famous case of William (*recte* Richard) Morley, the Dunstable brewer who had been knighted by Oldcastle and promised the earldom of Hertford, see Walsingham, *St Albans Chronicle*, 79.

enacted by the Leicester Parliament of 1414, required all royal officials, from the chancellor to local bailiffs, to investigate heresy and to co-operate with the ecclesiastical courts in prosecuting offenders. Convicted heretics handed over to the secular arm for execution were to suffer the penalties of felony, and their lands were to be forfeit to the Crown or the feudal lord.[103] Commissions of the peace were amended to include the investigation of heresy;[104] JPs were empowered to arrest those indicted, and instructed to deliver them to the ecclesiastical authorities within ten days. The officials of private liberties and franchises were assigned similar responsibilities. The Church also introduced new measures against Lollardy at the 1416 convocation presided over by Archbishop Henry Chichele.[105] Bishops and archdeacons were instructed to investigate heresy twice a year, and in deaneries and parishes where heretics were known to reside, three or more men of good repute were to be sworn to disclose their names and whereabouts.

These measures produced a sharp increase in the prosecution of Lollards.[106] The bishops continued to shoulder the main burden, but they now received the unequivocal support of the secular power.[107] The notorious London Lollard John Claydon, who was condemned before Chichele and burned in 1415, had originally been arrested by the mayor of London for possessing heretical books.[108] Similarly, in August 1420, the mayor and sheriffs of Bristol arrested Thomas Drayton and William Taylor for preaching heresy, and bound them over to appear before the bishop of Worcester's vicar-general within ten days, in accordance with the 1414 statute.[109]

---

[103] *RP* iv. 24–5; 2 Henry V st. 1 c. 7.

[104] Putnam, *Justices of the Peace*, pp. xxii, xxiv; see also ead., *Early Treatises*, 239, 241.

[105] *The Register of Henry Chichele, Archbishop of Canterbury, 1414–1443*, ed. E. F. Jacob, Canterbury and York Soc. (4 vols.; Oxford, 1938–47), iii. 18–19.

[106] Full discussion of Lollardy and its persecution after 1414 appears in Thomson, *Later Lollards*.

[107] E.g. *Reg. Chichele*, iii. 15–19, 25, 55, 67–9, 85, 105–12, 157–73, 186–92, 195–205; iv. 132–9, 151, 155–7, 168–9, 192–3, 203–4; *The Register of Bishop Philip Repingdon, 1405–19*, ed. M. Archer, Lincoln Record Soc. (3 vols.; Lincoln, 1963–82), iii, nos. 110–11, 120, 193, 201, 224, 227, 249, 299, 346, 365, 369–70; Aston, 'Lollardy and Sedition', 26–7.

[108] *Reg. Chichele*, iv. 132–8; *Calendar of Letter Books of the City of London: Letter Book I*, ed. R. R. Sharpe (London, 1909), 139–41.

[109] Thomson, *Later Lollards*, 25, 221. For other examples of the secular authorities proceeding against Lollardy, see ibid. 24, 99, 143–4, 220–1.

While Oldcastle remained at large, however, the government's main fear was of further rebellion. It is remarkable that Oldcastle was included in the general pardon granted by the king at the end of 1414; a pardon was issued for him on 16 December, but it was not taken up, and was revoked in March 1415.[110] During 1415 and 1416 there were reports of new Lollard plots, usually in alliance with the king's enemies: the earl of Cambridge, the Scots, the supporters of Richard II. These were apparently given colour by the periodic distribution of Lollard handbills.[111] Henry V's departure for France in August 1415 was a calculated risk, for rumours were circulating at the time that Oldcastle was planning another insurrection during the king's absence. Henry's confidence was more than justified, however, as a half-hearted call to arms by Oldcastle at Hanley castle in Worcestershire was easily thwarted by local forces.[112]

Oldcastle remained elusive throughout 1415 and 1416.[113] The offer of a reward for his capture was renewed in January 1417 in a proclamation issued to the Midland and western counties,[114] and the following summer the government got wind of his movements. Accompanied by John Langacre, who had taken part in the 1414 revolt, Oldcastle was received by William and Beatrix atte Well at Byfield and Hugh and Joan Frayn at Silverstone in Northamptonshire on 15 July.[115] Their presence must have been detected, because a week later on 22 July a powerful commission was issued to hear and determine all treasons, and to inquire into heresies, in eight Midland counties, including Northamptonshire.[116] The commissioners, led by three central court justices, held sessions a month later in four of the counties named: Northamptonshire, Warwickshire, Oxfordshire, and Berkshire. The commission threw up a few accusations against coiners, but its main targets were

---

[110] Ibid. 9–10. Oldcastle's pardon is at C 67/37, m. 49.

[111] Walsingham, *St Albans Chronicle*, 88–9; Thomson, *Later Lollards*, 8–18; Aston, 'Lollardy and Sedition', 26–8.

[112] Walsingham, *St Albans Chronicle*, 88–9; *Gesta Henrici Quinti*, 20–1.

[113] He was probably hiding in the Midlands and the Welsh Marches: Thomson, *Later Lollards*, 9–15.

[114] *CCR, 1413–19*, p. 379.

[115] KB 9/209, mm. 6, 12, 20, 27; *CCR, 1413–19*, p. 148; *CPR, 1413–16*, p. 271.

[116] KB 9/209, m. 27. There is no record of this commission on the patent rolls.

those who had harboured or assisted Oldcastle. The government's frustration at its failure to capture Oldcastle was reflected in the severity of the punishments imposed upon his associates. Langacre, the Frayns and the atte Wells were indicted for treason at Northampton, and all of them except Beatrix atte Well appeared for trial on 4 September. Joan Frayn was acquitted, but the men were convicted and executed, and their heads dispatched for display at Coventry, London, and Northampton. At Oxford a chaplain, John Whitby, was convicted and hanged for receiving Oldcastle at Piddington in Oxfordshire in October 1416. Several others were indicted on similar charges at the Warwick sessions.[117] Only one, Ralph Clerk of Coventry, appeared for trial; he was acquitted of consorting with Oldcastle but was handed over to the bishop of Coventry and Lichfield as a suspected Lollard.[118]

From Northamptonshire Oldcastle returned to his manor at Almeley in Herefordshire, where he probably remained between August and October 1417. He was finally recaptured near Welshpool at the end of November by tenants of Edward Charlton, Lord of Powys, and taken to Westminster, where Parliament was in session. On 14 December he was formally condemned by the Lords in Parliament as a notorious heretic and traitor, and immediately executed.[119]

Judicial proceedings continued against Oldcastle's supporters after his death, but there was a perceptible softening of the government's policy towards them. During 1418 and 1419 three men were tried in king's bench for treason in Northamptonshire, including Sir Thomas Talbot, who was alleged to have conspired with Oldcastle at Silverstone in May 1417. All three were acquitted.[120] During 1419 investigations were also conducted against some of Oldcastle's former tenants who had consorted with him at Almeley in the autumn of 1417. The returned inquest emphasized that the accused had acted under duress, and king's bench, after consulting the council, accepted its findings, discharging the

[117] KB 9/209, mm. 27, 40, 62.
[118] Ibid., m. 50.
[119] *CCR, 1419–22*, p. 196; *CPR, 1416–22*, p. 145; *Issues of the Exchequer*, 370–1; *RP* iv. 107–8; H. G. Richardson, 'John Oldcastle in Hiding', *EHR* 55 (1940), 432–8.
[120] KB 27/630, Rex, mm. 13d, 17d; 632, Rex, m. 11d.

defendants *sine die*.[121] Clemency was also shown to John Prest, former vicar of Chesterton in Warwickshire, who in 1421 was pardoned for harbouring Oldcastle—an offence for which four men had been hanged in 1417.[122] Such merciful gestures undoubtedly stemmed from the government's confidence that, with Oldcastle's capture and execution, the threat of Lollardy had been finally extinguished. This belief was clearly expressed in the chancellor's speech to Parliament in December 1420, when the destruction of Lollardy was included in a catalogue of Henry V's many triumphs.[123]

The Oldcastle revolt has been generally regarded as a decisive turning-point for the Lollard movement.[124] After 1414 Lollardy became synonymous with sedition, and the combined judicial machinery of Church and Crown was applied to its extirpation. It was deprived of the knightly and academic support which had fostered its development from the 1380s. The debate on disendowment, so vigorous under Henry IV, was abruptly terminated: the chronicler Thomas Elmham asserted that Henry V had a certain Henry Greyndor thrown into gaol for petitioning him to confiscate the temporalities of the Church.[125] Lollards in general, and Oldcastle above all, came to be seen as agents of the devil.[126] There can be little doubt that through their insistence upon the prosecution of Oldcastle in 1413, the clergy, led by Archbishop Arundel, precipitated the crisis and collapse of Lollardy and successfully buried the issue of disendowment for over a century. The price they paid was a perceptible increase in royal authority, a *quid pro quo* accepted after a generation of papal schism as the only means of dealing with the threat of heresy.[127] Summoning the province of Canterbury to convocation in autumn 1413, after Oldcastle's escape, Arundel stressed the powerlessness of the Church to prevent the spread of Lollardy without the support of Henry V, 'the most Christian prince in Christ, our most

---

[121] Richardson, 'John Oldcastle', 432–8.

[122] *CPR, 1416–22*, p. 372; *CCR, 1419–22*, p. 206.

[123] *RP* iv. 123. Cf. Elmham, *Liber Metricus*, 165.

[124] McFarlane, *Wycliffe*, 166; Thomson, *Later Lollards*, 5.

[125] Elmham, *Liber Metricus*, 148.

[126] See below at n. 133. See Putnam, *Early Treatises*, 241, for a form of indictment for homicide, 'arte diabolica per nigromanciam, Lollardiam etc.'.

[127] See Catto, 'Religious Change', 114–15.

noble king, the zealous supporter of the law of Christ'.[128] The enforcement of religious orthodoxy at a time of widespread heresy was simply too great a task for the Church alone.

The real victor of the revolt was the king and his dynasty. The suppression of Lollardy strengthened Lancastrian claims to legitimacy, and allowed Henry V to publicize his sacramental view of kingship and his devotion to the law of God.[129] Official documents and court chroniclers made skilful use of the revolt as a vehicle for royal propaganda. The commissions and proclamations issued in the wake of the revolt emphasized that it was the king's adherence to his coronation oath to protect the Church and the Christian faith, and his steadfast refusal, as a true Christian prince, to countenance the Lollards' evil designs, that forced them into rebellion.[130] These themes were reiterated in the pardon to Lollard rebels of March 1414, through which Henry was able to display the quality of mercy expected of the just king, echoing God's mercy to sinners.[131] Thomas Elmham, in his *Liber Metricus*, and the author of the *Gesta Henrici Quinti* further elaborated the image of the king as God's agent in defeating Oldcastle and the Lollards.[132] Both writers presented Oldcastle as the 'satellite of Satan', the antitype of the Christ figure Henry V, sent by God to test His elect.[133]

The hyperbole of the *Liber Metricus* and the *Gesta* may seem out of all proportion to the events of January 1414. By comparison with the rebellions faced by Henry IV, the Lollard revolt presented no great threat to Henry V's throne, and with hindsight it is clear that Oldcastle failed to turn his quarrel with the king into the cause of Lollardy as a whole.

---

[128] *Reg. Bubwith*, i. 151–2: 'christianissimi in Christo principis, regis nostri nobilissimi, zelatoris legis Christi'.

[129] See ch. 5 at nn. 67–76.

[130] *Foedera*, ix. 89: 'They falsely and treasonably and against their due allegiance imagined our death because we took our part against them and their opinions, as a true Christian prince and as we are bound by oath' ('mortem nostram pro eo quod nos contra eos et opiniones suas hujusmodi partem nos fecimus ut verus Christianus princeps et prout vinculo juramenti astringimur contra ligeanciae suae debitum falso et proditorie imaginaverunt'). Cf. KB 9/204/1, m. 84; *CCR, 1413–19*, pp. 114–15; *SKB* vii. 218–19.

[131] *Foedera*, ix. 119–20. See ch. 5 at nn. 56–8.

[132] *Gesta Henrici Quinti*, 2–11; Elmham, *Liber Metricus*, 96–100, 156–61.

[133] e.g. *Gesta Henrici Quinti*, 2, 8. For Elmham's treatment of Oldcastle in the *Liber Metricus*, see Gransden, *Historical Writing*, 206–10.

Contemporary observers could not take such a detached view, however, and the rising provoked considerable anxiety amongst the lay and ecclesiastical establishment, recalling as it did memories of the Peasants' Revolt thirty years before. The fear generated by the threat of popular revolt is reflected in the account of the rising in the St Albans chronicle. Walsingham grossly exaggerated the numbers involved and depicted hordes of deluded rustics thronging the highways of England *en route* to join Oldcastle in London.[134] The king was expected to take firm action to restore law and order, and in the second year of his reign he addressed himself vigorously to this task.

---

[134] Walsingham, *St Albans Chronicle*, 78.

7

The Leicester Parliament and the Superior Eyre

OLDCASTLE AND the Lollards were not the only threat to public order at the beginning of Henry V's reign. Judicial activity had been revived in Wales after the Glendower rebellion through the dispatch of several special commissions, but elsewhere the king had done little to deal with the widespread disorders of which the 1413 Parliament had complained.[1] There was violent feuding among the gentry of the North and Midlands, and English mariners from the south coast ports were attacking foreign merchant vessels in the Channel in defiance of royal truces.[2] The position was all the more critical in that Henry was already planning a campaign against France. Before undertaking any expeditions abroad, a campaign against disorder at home was essential.

THE LEICESTER PARLIAMENT

With these considerations in mind, Henry made the restoration of law and order the main theme of his second Parliament, which assembled at Leicester on 30 April 1414.[3] Proceedings were opened by the chancellor, Bishop Beaufort, preaching on the text, 'He has set his heart to investigate the laws.'[4] Beaufort set out the threefold purpose of the Parliament: to root out Lollardy; to enforce maritime truces made between the Crown and foreign princes; and to restore public order within the realm—in the chancellor's words, 'for the chastisement and punishment of the rioters, murderers, and other

---

[1] See ch. 5 at nn. 91–2.
[2] These disorders are examined in ch. 8.   [3] *RP* iv. 15–33.
[4] 'Posuit cor suum ad investigand' leges.' This is probably a corruption of Ezra, 7: 10, where the Vulgate text runs: 'Esdras enim paravit cor suum ut investigaret legem domini et faceret et doceret in Israel praeceptum et judicium.'

malefactors who more than ever abound in many parts of the kingdom'.[5] Legislation was brought forward to deal with each of these matters. In a gesture calculated to appeal to the Commons, Beaufort made a point of not requesting tenths and fifteenths at this Parliament, in the hope that they might be granted more willingly to meet the king's future necessities.[6] In a marked and probably deliberate contrast with his father, Henry V was to attempt the restoration of public order without recourse to extraordinary taxation.

To show that the government was in earnest, Parliament was accompanied to Leicester by the court of king's bench, which had not left Westminster since its visit to Gloucester in 1398.[7] A house belonging to the bishop of Lincoln was requisitioned for the use of the court,[8] which opened its Easter term sessions on 23 April, sitting as a criminal court of first instance in Leicestershire in its capacity as a superior eyre.[9]

An animated debate over law and order took place at the early sessions of the Leicester Parliament. On the opening day the collectors of the 1413 subsidy in Shropshire, led by John Bruyn, submitted a petition alleging that Robert Corbet and Richard Lacon, knights of the shire for the county in 1413, had appointed them and then done everything in their power to hinder their activities. The collectors claimed they had been assaulted several times as they attempted to go about their business.[10] Further petitions reflected the breakdown of order in other Midland counties: petitions were received from Nottinghamshire concerning the oppressions of Sir Richard Stanhope, and a skirmish between rival abbots of Fountains; while Edmund Ferrers, lord of Chartley in Staffordshire,

---

[5] *RP* iv. 15.

[6] Ibid. 16. A grant of tunnage and poundage for three years was, however, made on 28 May.

[7] *SKB* vii, p. lvii. The writ ordering the dispatch of king's bench to Leicester, dated 11 Feb. 1414, survives on file in KB 37/4/2/1, unnumbered membrane.

[8] The bishop's farmer, William Norton, was later paid one mark for the use of the house: KB 27/612, fines section, m. 3.

[9] For the powers of king's bench sitting as a superior eyre, see ch. 2 at nn. 86–91. The Easter law term began on the quindene of Easter, which in 1414 fell on 22 Apr. The first recorded business of the term took place on Monday 23 Apr. when the sheriff of Leics. returned the record of assizes undetermined within the county, in accordance with a writ of 3 Apr.: KB 146 (court of king's bench, panels, assizes, and bills files)/5/2/1, unnumbered membrane.

[10] *RP* iv. 30–1. See below at nn. 35–7.

complained of the attacks of his neighbour, Hugh Erdswick of Sandon, to which Hugh made counter-charges.[11] Legislation subsequently enacted at Leicester referred to 'many serious complaints . . . made in this present Parliament',[12] and the text of the Statute of Riots makes it clear that it was framed at least in part in direct response to these petitions.[13] It was almost certainly as a result of such complaints that the decision was taken to extend the superior eyre of king's bench beyond Leicester into Shropshire and Staffordshire.

The legislation of the Leicester Parliament was largely directed towards extending the powers of royal courts and legal officials so that they could deal with the disorders outlined in the chancellor's address—Lollardy, piracy, and riot.[14] The Statute of Lollards, which has been discussed in the previous chapter, for the first time gave all royal officials the task of investigating heretical activity.[15] In effect heresy was created a felony, a breach of the king's peace, as well as an ecclesiastical offence.

The Statute of Truces declared the breach of royal truces and safe-conducts to be high treason, and provided for their enforcement through the appointment of conservators of truces in major ports.[16] The conservator, assisted by men of law where necessary, was to have jurisdiction over cases concerning breach of truces on the high seas corresponding to that of the admiral, except for capital offences. Actions could be brought both at the suit of the king and at that of the party. On leaving port all ship's captains were to swear before the conservators to observe truces then in force, and if enemy prizes were brought into port the conservator was to take a full account of the incident and the value of the goods seized. This statute reflects the king's determination to see his peace observed at sea as well as on land. Medieval truces and safe-conducts remained personal matters, guaranteed by the lord who granted them.[17] Any infringements which occurred caused the grantor effectively to break his guarantee and

---

[11] *RP* iv. 27–33.
[12] Ibid. 25: 'diverses et hidouses compleintz . . . faitz en cest present Parlement'.
[13] 2 Henry V st. 1 c. 9. [14] Ibid., cc. 1–9.
[15] Ibid., c. 7. See ch. 6 n. 103. [16] 2 Henry V st. 1 c. 6.
[17] M. H. Keen, *The Laws of War in the Later Middle Ages* (Oxford, 1965), 204–17.

called his honour into question.[18] The higher the estate of the grantor, the graver was the offence committed in flouting his truce or safe-conduct. The definition of truce-breaking as high treason was entirely consistent with Henry V's elevated sense of royal dignity.[19]

The creation of a new category of treason was the most important consequence of the statute, and one which aroused considerable disquiet.[20] Demands were made almost immediately for its modification on the grounds that the king's subjects dared not take reprisals for injuries committed against them in breach of truces for fear of being accused of treason. The grand jury summoned before the special commission of inquiry in Devon in July 1414 returned several indictments for piracy and breaches of royal truces, but refused to describe the offences as treason, and pointedly recorded that all the acts of piracy had occurred before the previous Easter, that is, before the statute's publication.[21] A petition was presented at the Parliament of November 1415 requesting that the northern counties and the coastline from Berwick to Orwell be exempt from the statute in order to allow reprisals to be taken against Scottish raids.[22] A second petition in October 1416 resulted in a statute establishing the procedure for obtaining letters of marque, licensing reprisal, in cases where peaceful attempts by the king's subjects to secure compensation for losses sustained in breach of truces had failed.[23] The general pardon issued at the same Parliament also included a clause covering all treasons committed in breach of the Statute of Truces.[24]

The Statute of Riots enacted at Leicester represented an attempt to secure the enforcement of the statute of 1411, which was acknowledged to have been ineffective.[25] The

---

[18] Cf. *RP* iv. 15.

[19] See ch. 5 at nn. 64–76. Bellamy emphasizes the Roman and continental models for this definition: *Law of Treason*, 128–9. The most immediate inspiration for the Statute of Truces appears to have been contemporary conventions governing safe-conducts and truces: Keen, *Laws of War*, 204–6.

[20] There is no indication that the elaborate scheme for establishing conservators of truces was ever put into effect; see Wylie and Waugh, *Henry V*, i. 331–2.

[21] KB 9/205/3, m. 132. See ch. 8 at n. 75.

[22] *RP* iv. 68.

[23] Ibid. 105; 4 Henry V st. 2 c. 7; Keen, *Laws of War*, 220–2.

[24] *RP* iv. 104.   [25] 13 Henry IV c. 7.

earlier legislation gave JPs and sheriffs summary powers for
the indictment and conviction of rioters; at Leicester individual
complainants were given the opportunity to invoke the statute
through a special commission to the JPs and sheriffs returnable
in chancery.[26] This statute ensured that the suppression of
riots would become a routine part of the work of the JPs.[27] An
additional, and particularly drastic, measure was enacted at
Leicester for serious cases of riot, where the offenders had fled
to avoid prosecution. The victims were to sue the rioters by
bill before the chancellor; if they failed to appear a writ of
proclamation was to be issued, returnable in king's bench,
whereby the summons was proclaimed by the sheriff throughout the county. Failure to appear upon proclamation resulted
not in the usual outlawry but in summary conviction upon the
offences alleged.[28] This procedure had been employed against
the rioters in Staffordshire in 1410, and at the Leicester
Parliament itself against those who had attacked the Shropshire
subsidy-collectors, but it had not previously received statutory
sanction.[29]

The Leicester Parliament enacted several other statutes
relating to law enforcement. One act empowered JPs to
instruct sheriffs outside their own counties to arrest persons
indicted before them under the Statutes of Labourers, a
procedure already available in cases of felony; another
ordered officials of the northern franchises of Hexhamshire
and Tyndale to co-operate in the arrest of felons indicted and
outlawed in neighbouring counties.[30] Both reflected the
fragmented jurisdictional geography of the kingdom which
continued to hinder the effective enforcement of the criminal
law.[31]

The legislation of the Leicester Parliament was ambitious
and far-reaching, but it was no more than a statement of
intent by the new king. Parliamentary opinion might be

[26] 2 Henry V st. 1 c. 8.
[27] For procedure under the Statutes of Riots and their use during the fifteenth century, see ch. 3 n. 9.
[28] *RP* iv. 26; 2 Henry V st. 1 c. 9.
[29] *RP* iii. 630–1; iv. 30–1. See ch. 8 at n. 95.
[30] 2 Henry V st. 1 cc. 4–5. For the application of this statute to the neighbouring liberty of Redesdale in 1421, see ch. 10 at n. 89.
[31] See also below, nn. 79–82.

temporarily appeased by Henry's frank acknowledgement of the need to deal with disorder, but there could be no lasting resolution of the problem without a concerted programme of law enforcement through the courts. That programme was initiated during the spring of 1414, while the Leicester Parliament was still in session.

THE SUPERIOR EYRE

The campaign of law enforcement was led by the court of king's bench, which, as we have seen, was already holding a superior eyre at Leicester when Parliament opened. Being closely associated with the king, the court was invested with a special authority. It was well suited to Henry V's purposes, bringing the full weight of royal authority to bear on those areas where disorder was most severe.

It is unlikely that the visit of king's bench to Leicester was originally conceived as the beginning of a full-scale judicial visitation of the Midlands. The first indication that king's bench was moving beyond Leicester was a writ of 8 May to the sheriff of Staffordshire ordering him to prepare for the opening of the court's sessions at Lichfield on 18 May.[32] This was followed on 14 May by the issue of a general commission of inquiry in Nottinghamshire and Derbyshire and on 4 June by the order for the dispatch of king's bench to Shropshire, following its Staffordshire sessions.[33] The timing of these measures suggests that they resulted from petitions to Parliament concerning disorder in the Midlands and elsewhere.[34] Given the overtly disturbed condition of the country, there was every reason to extend the perambulation of king's bench at short notice, thereby demonstrating the seriousness of the government's intent to restore public order.

The evidence arising from the disorders in Shropshire supports this view.[35] At the opening session of the Leicester Parliament John Bruyn of Bridgnorth complained that he had

[32] KB 37/4/2/1, unnumbered membrane.
[33] *CPR, 1413–16*, p. 222; KB 9/204/2, m. 2; KB 37/4/2/2, unnumbered membrane.
[34] See above at nn. 10–13.
[35] E. Powell, 'Proceedings before the Justices of the Peace at Shrewsbury in 1414', *EHR* 99 (1984), 535–50.

had been assaulted by Robert Corbet and Richard Lacon, members of the earl of Arundel's affinity in Shropshire, while acting as a subsidy-collector in 1413.[36] Bruyn was a leading supporter of John Talbot, Lord Furnival, Arundel's principal rival in the county, and his petition revealed one side of the feuding between the two factions. On 11 May 1414, while the parliamentary discussions over law and order were probably still in progress, Arundel, as head of the Shropshire bench, delivered to king's bench a schedule of indictments taken before the JPs of that county. It consisted almost entirely of charges against John Bruyn for offences he had committed as bailiff of Bridgnorth, and was no doubt an attempt to discredit Bruyn and cast doubt upon his petition. In dispatching the schedule of indictments to king's bench at this time Arundel must have hoped to forestall an investigation of the misdeeds of his affinity in Shropshire by blaming the disorders on its opponents. If the decision to send king's bench to Shropshire had already been taken, Arundel's action would have been pointless, since the indictments against Bruyn would automatically have been brought before the court in the course of its review of proceedings taken before shire officials.[37] Arundel's attempt to keep king's bench out of Shropshire was unsuccessful, however, and in June 1414 a county grand jury exposed in detail the offences of his servants before the superior eyre.

King's bench remained at Leicester from 23 April until 15 May.[38] Much of the first week was taken up with the preparations for the sessions, the receipt of indictments, and the issuing of process. The following week, which coincided with the opening of Parliament, saw very little business in court, no doubt because the justices, William Hankford, Robert Tirwhit, and Hugh Huls, were appointed receivers and triers of petitions in Parliament.[39] On Friday 4 May prisoners from Leicester gaol were delivered to the court, and in the third week of sessions, starting on 6 May, king's bench determined a large number of criminal cases, mainly from

[36] *RP* iv. 30–1.
[37] See below at nn. 54–5.
[38] KB 27/612, *passim.*
[39] *RP* iv. 16. The justices also received individual summonses to Parliament: *CCR, 1413–19,* pp. 108–9.

Leicestershire.[40] The Leicester sessions ended with busy days on Monday 14 and Tuesday 15 May.[41]

King's bench was active for little more than ten of the twenty-three days it sat at Leicester. Most of the cases from Leicestershire with which it dealt were drawn from coroners' inquests, which by definition recorded isolated incidents of homicide rather than widespread outbreaks of disorder. Only one case of violent feuding among the gentry emerged: the county grand jury presented William Purfrey of Warwickshire and Richard Chetwynd of Staffordshire for an assault on James Pulteney. Both were fined £20 and gave security in court to maintain the peace.[42]

After completing the sessions at Leicester, king's bench moved west into Staffordshire. On the morrow of the Ascension (Friday 18 May), which usually marked the end of Easter term, the new sessions opened at Lichfield, where the court remained until 12 June.[43] The superior eyre was now beginning to gather momentum: the commission of inquiry into the disorders in Nottinghamshire and Derbyshire, headed by Henry, Lord FitzHugh, the king's chamberlain, sat between 31 May and 5 June, and on 8 June, after examining its findings, the king ordered them to be delivered to king's bench for determination.[44] King's bench itself sat at Lichfield throughout the Easter vacation except for a brief break over Whitsun (26–30 May), running over into the beginning of Trinity term.[45] Here the court took on the brisk but searching qualities of a trailbaston commission: the first week was again

---

[40] KB 145 (court of king's bench, *recorda* and *precepta recordorum* files)/5/2/1, unnumbered membranes (*corpus cum causa* writ to the sheriff of Leics. returned with schedule of prisoners attached); KB 27/612, Rex, mm. 11–18.

[41] Ibid., mm. 17–21. The sheriff was assigned a total of £12 13*s*. 6*d*. in fines for his expenses during the sessions: ibid., fines section, mm. 1, 5, 5d, 8d.

[42] KB 9/206/1, m. 49d; KB 27/612, Rex, m. 25d; 613, fines section, m. 4d. The Pulteneys were subsequently indicted before king's bench at Lichfield for assaulting Chetwynd, and fined 40*d*. each: KB 9/113, mm. 1, 13; KB 27/613, fines section, m. 5d.

[43] Parliament and the king remained at Leicester until 29 May.

[44] *Calendar of Signet Letters of Henry IV and Henry V, 1399–1422*, ed. J. L. Kirby (London, 1978), no. 773.

[45] The octave of Trinity, the opening day of Trinity term, fell on 10 June, and king's bench was at Lichfield until 12 June: KB 27/613, Rex, mm. 1–3. In spite of the virtually continuous sessions the octave formed a strict divide between the plea rolls for Easter and Trinity terms, KB 27/612–13.

one of preparation, during which the Staffordshire coroners' and peace rolls were handed in and indictments were made *coram rege* by juries from the hundreds and liberties of the county.[46] King's bench set a cracking pace in dealing with those indictments, and by the end of the week process had been issued on most of them, returnable within ten days.[47] In the limited time available during the superior eyre the court could determine no more than a small proportion of the hundreds of indictments it received. The aim was therefore to push process through to the final stage of exaction to outlawry as soon as possible, in order to avoid undue congestion on the return days later in the visitation when the court had moved elsewhere. Most of the criminal proceedings at Lichfield were concentrated in the final week of sessions there, beginning on Monday 4 June, during which over fifty defendants from Staffordshire appeared in court. All were acquitted or pardoned.[48] By 8 June King Henry himself was at Burton-on-Trent, keeping an eye on proceedings.[49] A signet letter of that date summoned John and William Mynors to the king's presence to account for their participation in the disorders in Staffordshire during Henry IV's reign.[50]

From Lichfield king's bench moved farther west to Shrewsbury where the duke of York presided over the court.[51] Here the court sat for only a fortnight (15–30 June), but its sessions followed the pattern of Leicester and Lichfield: the first week was largely spent receiving indictments from Shropshire and issuing process upon them returnable in the second week.[52] After more than two months of continuous sessions king's bench turned back towards Westminster on 30 June, pausing

[46] JUST 2 (coroners' rolls)/159–70; JUST 1/815; KB 9/113.

[47] KB 29/53, mm. 8–10.   [48] KB 27/612, Rex, mm. 26–34.

[49] The king was still at Leicester on 4 June for negotiations with the Burgundian ambassadors: *Foedera*, ix. 137–8. While at Burton Henry put the abbey under royal control to investigate irregularities in its administration: C 1/6/50, 207–9.

[50] KB 145/5/2/1, unnumbered membrane. Three days later a second signet letter informed the justices that the Mynors brothers had been pardoned: ibid.; *CPR, 1413–16*, p. 242. The Mynors family were presented for numerous offences at Lichfield: e.g. KB 9/113, m. 27; JUST 1/815, m. 6 (Putnam, *Justices of the Peace*, 312, 315–16). William was a member of the royal household, having been appointed a yeoman of the Crown in 1413: *CPR, 1413–16*, p. 172. See ch. 8 nn. 95, 117–22.

[51] KB 27/613, m. 20; Rex, m. 36.

[52] JUST 2/142–51; JUST 1/752 (*Shrops. Peace Roll*, 52–116); JUST 1/753; KB 29/53, mm. 16–18, 20, 24.

on the way at Wolverhampton for the return days of the octave of St John (1–4 July).[53] The court arrived home for the quindene of St John (8 July), and the business of the final week of Trinity term was largely unrelated to the superior eyre.

Procedure in King's Bench during the Superior Eyre

The superior eyre of king's bench was the most powerful agency of justice available to the Crown in the late middle ages, with comprehensive jurisdiction in both civil and criminal cases. When it entered a county the proceedings of all royal judicial agencies were suspended and their unfinished business delivered to the court.[54] Shortly before the arrival of king's bench in a county, two writs were dispatched to the sheriff in preparation for the sessions. The first, dealing with the Crown side business, contained three principal instructions: to empanel juries of presentment from each hundred, borough, and liberty; to proclaim that bills of complaint for all kinds of offences would be received by the court; and to inform all JPs, coroners, and stewards of liberties that they should appear before the court with their rolls and memoranda. The sheriff was also ordered to prepare lists of shire officials for the court's use.[55] The second writ called in civil litigation to the plea side of the court. The sheriff was instructed to deliver the record of all assizes pending within the county; to proclaim, as with the Crown side writ, the receipt of bills of complaint; and to be present himself with the bailiffs.[56]

The records delivered from Leicestershire, Staffordshire, and Shropshire in response to these writs have nearly all survived among the archives of king's bench.[57] The returns on

[53] A few more Staffs. *coram rege* indictments were taken at Wolverhampton, which do not survive, and a handful of cases determined: KB 27/613, Rex, mm. 8, 18d, 20d, 21, 22.

[54] See ch. 2 at nn. 88–9.

[55] The writs for Leics., Staffs., and Shrops. survive, together with their returns, in the original Crown Side (*Brevia Regis*) files for Easter and Trinity terms 1414: KB 37/4/2/1–2, unnumbered membranes.

[56] KB 146/5/2/1–2, unnumbered membranes. Cf. *Les Reports des Cases*, pt. 5: Liber Assisarum, 28 Edward III, pl. 52. The files consist of assizes delivered to king's bench in obedience to the writ, together with private bills of trespass submitted to the court.

[57] The only exceptions are a handful of Staffs. coroners' rolls, and the *coram rege* indictments taken at Wolverhampton: see above, n. 53.

the Crown side fall into three groups: the coroners' rolls; the rolls of indictments undetermined before the JPs; and indictments made by juries summoned before the superior eyre. In all there are fifty-five coroners' rolls for the three counties, many dating from Richard II's reign, some even from that of Edward III.[58] A peace roll survives for each county.[59] They cover a shorter period than the coroners' rolls: the Shropshire peace roll runs from 1400 onwards, the Staffordshire roll from 1409, the Leicestershire roll only from 1412.[60] Each is written in a uniform hand throughout, and includes a copy of the latest peace commission, confirming that they were compiled specifically for the superior eyre.[61] The juries of presentment summoned *coram rege* made their returns to articles of inquiry which were probably similar to those drawn up for king's bench by Chief Justice Shareshull in 1353.[62] These formed the largest and most comprehensive group of indictments, with charges ranging from treason and counterfeiting to the construction of fish-weirs on the Severn.[63] The memory of the jurors was sometimes so long as to suggest access to written records: for example ten of the twenty-four offences recorded by the jury of Newcastle-under-Lyme in Staffordshire were dated before 1399.[64] In total between 800 and 900 indictments were submitted to king's bench in each county, furnishing the court with a detailed survey of criminal activity over the previous decade. The commission of inquiry held in Nottinghamshire and Derbyshire returned just under 200 indictments for the two counties which were dealt with in king's bench in the same way as those produced by the superior eyre (see Table 4).[65]

[58] R. F. Hunnisett, 'The Medieval Coroners' Rolls', *AJLH* 3 (1959), 332–3, 342–3.
[59] For the Shrops. roll (JUST 1/752), see above n. 52. The Leics. and Staffs. rolls (JUST 1/472, 815) are printed in Putnam, *Justices of the Peace*, 87–103, 295–333.
[60] The Leics. peace session dated 8 Dec. 1410 in the printed edition (Putnam, *Justices of the Peace*, 99) in fact took place two years later: JUST 1/472, m. 4.
[61] Cf. Putnam, *Justices of the Peace*, pp. lxx–lxxi.
[62] *Les Reports des Cases*, pt. 5: Liber Assisarum, Mich. 27 Edward III, pl. 44. The presentment files for Leics., Shrops., and Staffs. are KB 9/206/1, JUST 1/753, and KB 9/113 respectively.
[63] For treason, see for example JUST 1/753, m. 29(1), nos. 1–6; for illicit fish weirs, ibid., m. 22 no. 1.
[64] KB 9/113, mm. 37–8.
[65] KB 9/204/2.

TABLE 4. *Number of indictments received during the superior eyre of 1414 and related commissions*

Source	Leics.	Staffs.	Shrops.	Notts.	Derby.
Rolls of JPs	45	185	200	0	0
Coroners' rolls	625	306	285	0	0
Jury presentments	139	372	407	83	91
Total received	809	863	892	83	91
No process	500	199	280	0	0
Total processed	309	664	612	83	91

Sources: as for Tables A1–A5 in Appendix.

On receipt of the indictments, the staff of the king's attorney of king's bench carefully sorted and annotated them to prepare for the writs of summons. Offences were divided into three principal categories, felony, trespass, and accessory to felony, since the nature and timing of process differed in each case. As many cases were several years old, a rough form of limitation was imposed, and indictments dated before 1404 were usually omitted from process.[66] Certain serious offences, namely treason, murder, and rape, were excepted from this limitation, and process was issued upon them irrespective of the date of the indictment. The reason for this probably lay in the Statute of Pardons of 1390, which excluded such crimes from the scope of general pardons.[67] The result was the issue of process in several ancient cases of murder where the accused was probably long dead. For example, process was issued against four men named in the roll of a Shropshire coroner as the slayers of Richard Spencer of Wroxeter in 1367, because the record of the inquest made it clear that the crime

[66] An indictment dated earlier than 1404 was marked 'antea perdonatus' by the king's bench scribe, which indicated that the offence came within the scope of the general pardons of Richard II and Henry IV and should be omitted from process. Cf. *Shrops. Peace Roll*, 52–72, with the process lists on KB 27/613, Rex, mm. 13, 14.

[67] 13 Richard II st. 2 c. 1. It was observed throughout the reign of Henry IV, but although Henry V's first pardon, issued on 9 Apr. 1413, adhered to the statute, the second, of 8 Dec. 1414, expressly included treason, murder, and rape: C 67/37, m. 60. See below at nn. 89–93.

was premeditated, and thus defined as murder under the 1390 statute.[68]

As soon as the clerks had marked up the indictments, process was issued upon them. Separate lists of summons, *venire facias* for trespasses and *capias* for felonies, were compiled for each set of indictments, sent to the sheriff for execution, and entered on the controlment roll, the king's attorney's working copy of the plea roll.[69] It was on this copy that notes were made of the later progress of cases, through process to court appearance or outlawry.[70] By medieval standards process of summons was issued with breakneck speed, and the sheriff was given very short notice for the return of writs.[71] In Staffordshire, for example, the first return day—for *capias* writs issued on some of the coroners' rolls—was 25 May, little more than a week after the court's arrival at Lichfield.[72] Thereafter they followed in quick succession until early June.[73] In Leicestershire and Shropshire the pattern was the same, the court's aim being to transact as much business as possible during its brief sessions within each county.

Nearly all the defendants failed to answer the initial writ of summons issued against them. The sheriffs made returns that they could not be found, and the next stage of process, exaction to outlawry, was set in motion.[74] This procedure, which required summonses at five successive county courts, took several months to complete and allowed the defendants ample time to submit to the sheriff's custody. Cases from the superior eyre therefore continued to appear in large numbers during Michaelmas term 1414, and threatened to clog the machinery of king's bench for many terms to come. The issue of a comprehensive general pardon in December 1414 did much to relieve the pressure of business by enabling offenders to purchase immunity from prosecution at the suit of the

[68] JUST 2/142, m. 2d; KB 29/53, m. 17d. One of the accused, Edmund Drayton, who was outlawed in 1414, was in fact dead by 1373: *CIM, 1399–1422*, no. 449.

[69] KB 29/53, m. 8–28.

[70] These notes make it possible to compile statistics of the outcome of proceedings in king's bench during the superior eyre.

[71] See ch. 3 at nn. 46–52.

[72] KB 29/53, m. 10.   [73] Ibid., mm. 8–10, 14.

[74] Process at this second stage was enrolled on the king's bench plea roll itself, occupying several entire membranes on the rolls for Easter and Trinity terms: KB 27/612–13, Rex sections.

Crown for past offences, and it was obtained by large numbers of those who had been indicted during the superior eyre.[75]

Appearance in Court

The sheer volume of process in king's bench and the pace at which it proceeded during the summer of 1414 offered an impressive display of energetic government. If the Nottinghamshire and Derbyshire inquiries are included, nearly 2,200 persons from the Midlands were summoned before king's bench as a result of the superior eyre, at a time when the court was also handling the Lollard inquiries and special commissions from Devon. If this drive to re-establish order were to be successful it was of course essential to secure the attendance in court of a significant proportion of offenders. Table 5 summarizes the outcome of process in king's bench arising from the superior eyre.

The appearance rate fluctuated from only 29 per cent in Shropshire to 53 per cent in Nottinghamshire. The average for all counties was 37 per cent. The figures were artificially depressed for the counties of the superior eyre proper by the inclusion of indictments which were several years old in 1414.[76] In Shropshire, for example, 110 persons were summoned for offences committed over ten years before the superior eyre, of whom 99 were outlawed. As might be expected, process was far more effective on the most recent indictments. Table 6 shows that the rate of appearance for all counties improved dramatically on cases dated 1409 and after, in Leicestershire and Staffordshire rising to almost 50 per cent.

Offences under five years old were twice as likely to come to court as those over five years old. These figures suggest that where indictments were sufficiently fresh the machinery of process could be remarkably effective. The point is demonstrated by proceedings upon the Staffordshire peace roll. The latest session recorded there took place in April 1414, at which fifty-eight offenders were indicted. Forty-five, or almost 80 per cent, later appeared when summoned before king's bench.[77]

---

[75] See below at nn. 89–93.

[76] Most were cases of homicide from the coroners' rolls: see above at n. 68.

[77] Putnam, *Justices of the Peace*, 295–301.

TABLE 5. *Outcome of process issued during the superior eyre of 1414 and related commissions*

	Leics.		Staffs.		Shrops.		Notts.		Derby.		Total
	No.	%	No.	%	No.	%	No.	%	No.	%	
Appearance	145	35	362	43	203	29	49	53	40	42	799
Non-appearance	291	65	480	57	498	71	43	47	56	58	1,368
TOTAL	436	100	842	100	701	100	92	100	96	100	2,167

Note: The figures for non-appearance exclude those against whom indictments were laid, but no process issued; those summoned on indictments ruled insufficient who failed to appear; and summonses upon dead men, an offender being assumed dead if a return to that effect was accepted by king's bench. A fuller breakdown of the outcome of cases is given in Table 8.

Sources: as for Tables A1–A5 in Appendix.

TABLE 6. *Appearance rates in king's bench on indictments dated before and after 1409*

| | Leics. | | | | Staffs. | | | | Shrops. | | | |
| | Before | | After | | Before | | After | | Before | | After | |
	No.	%	No.	%	No.	%	No.	%	No.	%	No.	%
Appearance	35	18	110	46	40	23	322	48	36	16	167	35·5
Non-appearance	161	82	130	54	133	77	347	52	195	84	303	64·5
TOTAL	196	100	240	100	173	100	669	100	231	100	470	100

Note: The figures for non-appearance exclude those against whom indictments were laid, but no process issued; those summoned on indictments ruled insufficient who failed to appear; and summonses upon dead men, an offender being assumed dead if a return to that effect was accepted by king's bench.

Sources: as for Tables A1–A5 in Appendix.

Appearance rates fluctuated not only with the age of an offence, but also with its gravity. Broadly speaking, the graver an offence the less likely it was that the accused would appear in court (see Table 7). Only one in five of all those indicted for homicide during the superior eyre appeared, the rates for

TABLE 7. *Appearance rates during the superior eyre of 1414 and related commissions, analysed by type of offence*

	Homicide		Other felony		Trespass	
	No.	%	No.	%	No.	%
Leics.						
Appearance	29	17	35	28	80	57
Non-appearance	140	83	91	72	60	43
Total	169	100	126	100	140	100
Derby.						
Appearance	9	25	10	40	21	60
Non-appearance	27	75	15	60	14	40
Total	36	100	25	100	35	100
Notts.						
Appearance	4	24	8	53	37	62
Non-appearance	13	76	7	47	23	39
Total	17	100	15	100	60	100
Staffs.						
Appearance	70	25	120	37.5	169	71
Non-appearance	207	75	200	62.5	68	29
Total	277	100	320	100	237	100
Shrops.						
Appearance	39	16	63	27.5	101	46
Non-appearance	203	84	166	72.5	120	54
Total	242	100	229	100	221	100
All five counties						
Appearance	151	20	236	33	408	59
Non-appearance	590	80	479	67	285	41
TOTAL	741	100	715	100	693	100

Note: The totals of cases in some counties come to less than those of Table 5 because of the omission of treason proceedings; where a defendant was accused of several crimes the case has been categorized under the most serious offence.
Sources: As for Tables A1–A5 in Appendix.

individual counties ranging from 16 to 25 per cent.[78] For indictments on other felonies the overall rate was one in three, and for trespass it rose to nearly 60 per cent, with the Staffordshire figure exceeding 70 per cent.

The appearance rate in Shropshire was consistently lower than in other counties. Even in cases dated after 1409 only one in three of those summoned appeared in court. No doubt this is attributable to the county's exposed position on the Welsh Marches, where conditions were still disturbed after the Glendower rebellion.[79] Just over a hundred of those summoned in Shropshire were Welshmen, all but three of whom failed to appear; some must have lived within the shire, but most were described as living in Wales or the Marches, beyond the sheriff's jurisdiction. These findings confirm numerous parliamentary petitions from the border counties concerning the difficulty of obtaining redress for the depredations of the Welsh.[80] Statutes were passed in response to these complaints, but they depended for their effectiveness on the co-operation of the Marcher lords, whose jealously guarded liberties were a prime cause of the problem; in practice such legislation was unenforceable.[81] On a smaller scale, process in Shropshire and Staffordshire upon men from the palatinate of Cheshire was almost as fruitless.[82]

Bearing in mind those limitations, the superior eyre of king's bench in 1414 reveals the medieval administration of criminal justice at its most dynamic. The issue of process was remarkably swift and thorough. Indeed the court was perhaps too punctilious in pursuit of indictments so old that there was little chance of the accused appearing. Where offences were less than five years old, however, the rate of appearance was much higher, sometimes nearly half those summoned. The

[78] The low appearance rates for homicide are partly explained by the age of some indictments: see above at nn. 66–8.

[79] See ch. 8 at nn. 143–8.

[80] *RP* iii. 295, 308, 441, 474–6; iv. 10, 52, 69. The complaints refer to kidnapping and abduction of livestock, of which there are many cases among the Shrops. *coram rege* indictments.

[81] 2 Henry IV c. 16; 2 Henry V st. 2 c. 5. Parliamentary petitions of 1415 and 1442 referred specifically to the non-observance of Henry IV's legislation: *RP* iv. 69; v. 53. See also Bellamy, *Law of Treason*, 131–2.

[82] Only four appeared out of thirty men of Cheshire summoned for offences in the two counties. Cf. above at nn. 30–1.

relative gravity of offences also affected appearance rates: on average less than a quarter of those charged with homicide appeared in court, as against nearly 60 per cent in trespass cases. Within the borders of the county, the sheriff enjoyed considerable success in executing process of summons; beyond them his failure was almost complete. The greatest weakness of late medieval judicial administration was its inability to apprehend the offender who took refuge in the territorial liberties which stood outside the shire organization.[83]

Outcome of Cases: The Absence of Convictions

King's bench was moderately successful, therefore, in securing the attendance of those summoned during the superior eyre. Some 800 persons summoned from the five Midland counties appeared in court as a result of its proceedings, out of almost 2,200 against whom process had been issued.[84] What happened to all those defendants when they came into court? As we have already seen, medieval criminal trial procedure was extremely perfunctory.[85] Defence counsel were excluded from felony trials, the choice of pleas open to the defendant was restricted, and basic rules of evidence had yet to be formulated. Not many trials can have lasted more than an hour, and most probably took only a few minutes. The pressure of business which built up during the superior eyre must have reinforced those characteristics. The huge accumulation of cases which resulted in king's bench obliged the justices to deal with cases as quickly as possible, observing only the bare formalities of trial procedure. Juries were content for the most part to return verdicts of acquittal, which caused the minimum disruption within local society. A remarkable aspect of proceedings was the negligible number of convictions (see Table 8). Of the 137 defendants from all counties who opted for jury trial, only three were convicted.[86] This extraordinary lack of convictions is exceptional even by medieval standards. It has far-reaching

---

[83] See also ch. 10 at n. 89.

[84] See Table 5.   [85] See ch. 3 at n. 69.

[86] They were: Thomas Serle of Shrops., indicted for highway robbery (KB 27/613, Rex, m. 16d); John Holcotes of Leics., indicted for sheep theft and convicted upon a private appeal for the same offence (KB 9/206/1, m. 16; KB 29/53, m. 21d); and Thomas Sydewyk, indicted for highway robbery and convicted in king's bench in 1427 (KB 9/206/1, mm. 37–8; KB 29/53, m. 10d).

TABLE 8. *Analysis of proceedings in the superior eyre of 1414 and related commissions*

	Leics.	Staffs.	Shrops.	Notts.	Derby.	Total
Appearance						
Convicted	2	0	1	0	0	3
Acquitted	27	77	27	1	2	134
Pardoned	46	153	113	32	27	371
Fined	70	132	62	16	11	291
Non-appearance						
Outlawed	286	472	489	40	55	1,342
Dead	2	22	44	2	4	74
Untraced	5	8	14	3	1	31
No process	727	198	332	1	1	1,259
TOTAL	1,165	1,062	1,082	95	101	3,505

Sources: As for Tables A1–A5 in Appendix.

implications for any assessment of the purpose and effectiveness of the superior eyre, and will be considered more fully later in the chapter.

Acquittals apart, the absence of convictions during the superior eyre is largely explained by the reluctance of defendants to risk standing trial. The safest and most popular ways of bringing proceedings upon indictment to a conclusion, exploited by six defendants out of seven, were to pay a fine or buy a pardon. Only trespass cases could be settled by fine, and the offences most commonly discharged in this way were statutory, such as breaches of the Statutes of Livery. Pardons, on the other hand, might be obtained for any crime, and a striking feature of the superior eyre was the indiscriminate issue of pardons for the most serious felonies and even treason. Some of the pardons presented were for a specific offence,[87] but as Table 9 reveals, the majority were issued after Henry V's proclamation of a comprehensive general pardon in December 1414.[88]

---

[87] e.g. Adam Gerard, pardoned for the death of Henry Lancaster at Rugeley, Staffs.: *CPR, 1405–8*, p. 91; KB 27/613, Rex, m. 5.
[88] C 67/37.

TABLE 9. *Analysis of pardons presented in king's bench on indictments from the superior eyre of 1414*

Type of pardon	Leics.	Staffs.	Shrops.	Notts.	Derby.
General pardon of 1414	27	115	93	26	25
Earlier general pardons	16	10	7	6	1
Pardons for a specific offence	3	28	13	0	1
TOTAL	46	153	113	32	27

Source: KB 27/612-60.

General pardons could be obtained by individuals and corporations from chancery, for a fee of 16s. 4d., upon presentation of security to keep the peace.[89] They granted exemption from various financial liabilities and immunity from prosecution at the king's suit on a wide range of criminal offences. The Lancastrians resorted to general pardons more frequently than their predecessors: six were issued between 1399 and 1414 as against four between 1360 and 1399.[90] The pardon of 1414 was the second granted by Henry V in two years; it was proclaimed on 8 December after the grant of a generous parliamentary subsidy.[91] In two important respects it was wider than previous general pardons. The clause excluding treason, murder, and rape was dropped, contrary to the Statute of Pardons, and no time limit was set for the pardons to be sued.[92] This lack of restrictions made the pardon widely sought: just over 4,800 were granted in the following three years.[93]

[89] *Shrops. Peace Roll*, 44; Storey, *House of Lancaster*, 212. Securities for pardons form the PRO class of chancery files C 237, in which files 24–39 cover the reigns of Henry IV and V.

[90] Powell, 'Public Order', 219–21; under the Lancastrians general pardons were issued in 1399, 1403/4, 1409, 1411, 1413, and 1414: *RP* iii. 445, 544; iv. 6–7; C 67/32–7. The pardons of 1403/4 and 1411 were proclaimed outside Parliament, although the former was confirmed in the Parliament of Jan. 1404.

[91] *RP* iv. 35.

[92] C 67/37, m. 60. Almost all previous general pardons had contained clauses limiting the period of their availability.

[93] This is substantially higher than the numbers granted under the general pardons of Henry VI's reign: see Storey, *House of Lancaster*, 215–16.

THE OBJECTIVES OF THE SUPERIOR EYRE

The proclamation of the general pardon of December 1414 poses the fundamental question of the effectiveness of Henry V's campaign to re-establish public order, initiated at the Leicester Parliament. On the face of it, the offer of a full pardon to all comers, including traitors, murderers, and rapists, looks very much like an admission of failure. The statistical evidence appears to confirm that impression. From Hilary term 1415 all those who appeared in court to answer charges either presented a pardon or paid a fine.[94] Even during 1414 convictions were very rare: only three people were convicted out of some 800 who came to court. On the basis of the statistics, therefore, it is difficult to avoid the conclusion drawn by Miss Kimball from her study of the Shropshire peace roll of 1414: 'unless the majority of these indictments were not valid, serious crime was not being punished in Shropshire, or for that matter anywhere in England'.[95] If Henry V was seeking primarily to restore order by punishing crime, his plans undoubtedly failed. Indeed this failure was so complete and so uncharacteristic of the king, who had executed swift and ruthless justice upon the Lollard rebels, as to suggest that it cannot have been his primary intention to punish crime, and that the inquiries of 1414 had other objectives.

What then were these objectives? There are two obvious possibilities: firstly that the restoration of public order was merely a pretext for the inquiries, and that their real purpose was to raise revenue for military expeditions through exploiting the profits of justice; secondly that the king and his judges were unable or unwilling to restore order through the punishment of crime, and that they sought to settle the disturbances by other means.

There was ample precedent for the use of royal jurisdiction as a source of revenue. The Angevin kings, lacking an established system of national taxation, had ruthlessly exploited their judicial prerogatives, as is shown by the clauses of Magna Carta and of the Provisions of Westminster of 1259

---

[94] KB 27/615 ff.   [95] *Shrops. Peace Roll*, 45.

which attempted to curb their free exercise.[96] The value of royal judicial revenues in the thirteenth century is illustrated by the general eyre visitation of 1246–49, which raised £22,000, almost as much as the annual ordinary revenues of the Crown.[97] More direct comparison can be made with the reign of Edward III, when royal judges devised all kinds of ingenious schemes to finance the king's campaigns in France, using king's bench as the principal instrument of their exactions.[98] Between 1348 and 1353, fines and amercements levied in king's bench totalled £8,500, including almost £2,800 in two terms while the court was at York during the winter of 1348–9.[99] Penalties imposed for breaches of the Statutes of Labourers raised over £7,500 between 1352 and 1355, which helped to meet the cost of the triennial parliamentary subsidy of those years.[100] In 1353 the Black Prince ordered a general eyre in Cheshire—the first ever to be held there—which the community bought off with a fine of 5,000 marks. A general oyer and terminer commission in Devon and Cornwall in the following year raised at least another £2,500 for the Black Prince's coffers and helped to finance the Poitiers campaign of 1355–6.[101] Chief Justice Shareshull was the leading figure in this campaign of judicial fund-raising, and as his biographer makes clear, he saw the principal objective of judicial administration as the increase of royal revenue.[102]

Did the inquiries of 1414 mark a reversion to this policy, with Henry V exploiting the complaints of the Leicester Parliament to revive the use of king's bench as a fiscal device? Table 10 sets out the total of fines levied in king's bench in the Midland shires during the 1414 proceedings. The overall total comes to just over £750. The income from general pardons,

[96] *Eng. Hist. Docs., 1189–1327*, pp. 316–24, 361–76.

[97] Maddicott, 'Magna Carta and the Local Community', 47.

[98] Putnam, *Shareshull*, 65–74; Harriss, *Public Finance*, 401–6.

[99] Ormrod, 'Edward III's Government', 215–16.

[100] B. H. Putnam, *The Enforcement of the Statute of Labourers during the First Decade after the Black Death, 1349–59* (New York, NY, 1908), 127–31.

[101] P. H. W. Booth, 'Taxation and Public Order: Cheshire in 1353', *Northern History*, 12 (1976), 21–2; Putnam, *Shareshull*, 74.

[102] Ibid. 39: 'Shareshull's conviction of the financial possibilities of the profits of jurisdiction was a keynote to his policy for the king's government . . .'. Professor Putnam seems to have been oblivious to the heavy political costs of such a policy: see also Introduction at nn. 81–8.

TABLE 10. *The amounts of fines levied during the superior eyre of 1414*

	£	s.	d.
Leics.	336	7	1
Staffs.	291	0	9
Shrops.	96	7	6
Notts.	17	0	0
Derby.	10	3	0
TOTAL	750	18	4

Source: KB 27/612–60, fines sections.

which were much in demand as a result of the superior eyre, totalled a further £4,500 throughout the whole reign.[103] These were substantial sums, but in exacting them the king did not exceed the limits of what was just and reasonable. Amercements were imposed in accordance with the offence, as laid down in Magna Carta, and Henry did not resort to communal fines like those paid in the 1350s for exemption from liability to certain statutes, notably legislation on weights and measures.[104] Most significantly the visitations of Henry V's reign gave rise to no complaints in Parliament, in marked contrast to the barrage of parliamentary opposition mounted against Edward III's judicial exactions between 1343 and 1362.[105] The Parliaments of those years fought consistently to secure the cessation of general inquiries, trailbastons, and superior eyres, but in 1423, a year after Henry V's death, Parliament actually requested the dispatch of king's bench to Herefordshire to deal with disorders there.[106]

The financial motives behind the 1414 inquiries cannot be discounted entirely. The courts were not, however, straining to extort money as they had done under Shareshull in the mid-fourteenth century. The profits of justice were more an

---

[103] Roughly 5,600 general pardons were issued at a cost of 16s. 4d. each: C 67/36–7. See also Harriss, *Henry V*, 170.

[104] Putnam, *Shareshull*, 72–3; Ormrod, 'Edward III's Government', 205. In Wales, however, Henry V did impose collective fines on communities as the price of their submission after the Glendower rising: see ch. 8 at nn. 20–2.

[105] Harriss, *Public Finance*, 405–10.   [106] *RP* iv. 254.

incidental than a central feature of the inquiries. In attempting to account for the remarkably low level of convictions during 1414, we are thus left with the second hypothesis, that the king and his judges were unable or unwilling to restore order by punishing crime, and that they sought to settle the disturbances by other means.

In order to explore this hypothesis we must look beyond the bare record of the court's performance, the rates of appearance and conviction, and consider more closely the nature of the disorders with which the king was dealing. The records disclose that many of the worst offenders fell into two broad, and to some extent overlapping, groups upon which the Crown relied heavily for the administration of the realm: the county gentry, who helped run local government; and the professional administrators and servants of the house of Lancaster. The disorders in the Midlands, which had provoked the complaints to the Leicester Parliament, were chiefly the result of gentry disputes; in Devon resistance to the imposition of an oyer and terminer commission was led by county JPs; and in north Wales the effects of the Glendower rebellion were greatly exacerbated by the corrupt administration of Thomas Barnby, chamberlain of the principality from 1406 until his removal from office by the king's justices in 1414. The situation was further complicated by the fact that in some areas disorder was a legacy of the divisions of Henry IV's reign, and the abuse of power by his supporters.[107]

Table 11 provides a rough index of gentry participation in the disorders investigated during the superior eyre. Gentry were indicted in substantial numbers and formed a significant proportion of those accused in all counties except Leicestershire. Rates of appearance were noticeably higher than average, running at over 90 per cent in Staffordshire and over 80 per cent in Shropshire. It was this group which represented the principal target of the inquiries, rather than the lower classes, whose offences could be dealt with by the local judicial machinery. Although king's bench cast its nets wide and caught a large number of small fry, its real catch was the big fish, the gentry who ran the counties and whose quarrelling

[107] See ch. 8.

TABLE 11. *Outcome of process issued during the superior eyre of 1414 against men styled knight, esquire, or gentleman*

	Leics.	Staffs.	Shrops.	Notts. & Derby.
Pardoned, fined or acquitted	7	33	47	14
Outlawed	2	7	4	8
Dead	1	8	4	3
TOTAL	10	48	55	25
Percentage of total no. indicted	2.3	6.4	6.4	12.9

Source: as for Table 9.

had precipitated the outrages of which the Leicester Parliament complained.[108] The response to such disorder was as much a matter of political management as of judicial policy, and the king had to discipline offenders without alienating support for his regime at home and for the campaigns he was planning in France. Because the Crown depended on the magnates and gentry for the administration of local government, the king had to tread warily in dealing with the criminal activities of these classes. The failure of the judicial commission in Devon illustrates how the local community might withdraw its co-operation if it felt its interests threatened.[109] On the other hand, when public order appeared in danger of collapsing, as it did in the Midlands in 1413, the king was forced to intervene.

The delicacy of the problems facing Henry V is exemplified by the case of Shropshire, the county perhaps worst affected by violent disorder. Throughout Henry IV's reign the most powerful magnate in the county was Thomas FitzAlan, earl of Arundel, one of the king's most trusted supporters. Henry IV entrusted Arundel with the defence of Shropshire against the Welsh rebels, and the earl's affinity was allowed a free hand in running the shire, monopolizing the major county offices.

[108] Cf. ch. 5 at n. 47. [109] See ch. 8 at nn. 38–41.

During the second half of Henry IV's reign Arundel's servants abused this power to advance their private interests, and reacted violently when they met opposition.[110]

How did Henry V attempt to deal with such disorders? It would have been politically impossible to hang offenders of this kind or imprison them for long periods. Since the earl of Arundel was one of the Lancastrians' most valued servants, the mere indictment of his retinue in king's bench constituted an important exercise of political authority. The king's aim was not so much to punish the warring factions as to separate them, resolve their quarrels, and restore observance of his peace. His approach was firm but conciliatory: leading protagonists of the disputes were recruited for military service abroad, and the most serious offenders were made to take out recognizances for large sums binding them to keep the peace; for the rest a fine or pardon was sufficient to buy off the king's suit and gain readmittance to his peace.

Reconciliation, then, was the keynote of Henry V's policy of law enforcement. In this respect the king's methods accorded with his broader aims of disowning the legacy of faction and distrust inherited from his father's reign and reconciling the country to the new dynasty. At the local level the king's brief but decisive interventions helped to defuse the explosive hostilities which had built up during his father's reign, and to create the environment in which conciliation could be pursued through established informal procedures such as arbitration. The following chapters explore these themes by examining Henry's campaign of law enforcement in several localities.

---

[110] See ch. 8 at nn. 147–67.

The Settlement of the Realm, 1413–1415

THE SUPERIOR eyre of 1414 was the spearhead of a sustained programme for the restoration of public order which continued until the eve of the Agincourt campaign. Immediately after his accession Henry V had concentrated on the settlement of Wales, where conditions remained disturbed after the Glendower rebellion. Outside the principality, however, he had done little to reduce disorder by the end of 1413, when his attention was forcibly drawn to the problem by the Lollard revolt led by Sir John Oldcastle.[1] The need for strong measures was brought home also by the obstruction of the work of an oyer and terminer commission in Devon in February 1414, when the justices encountered a complete lack of co-operation from the local community, and returned to Westminster with their commission unfulfilled.[2] We have seen that the Leicester Parliament was concerned above all with public order, and that this gave rise to the superior eyre and the associated judicial inquiries in the Midlands. At the same time the restoration of royal authority continued in Wales, while two further commissions were dispatched to Devon to put an end to the county's defiance.[3] The purpose of this chapter is to investigate the local circumstances which gave rise to these various disorders, and to assess the effects of royal judicial intervention.

WALES IN THE AFTERMATH OF THE GLENDOWER REBELLION

The Glendower rebellion orginated as a private feud between Owen Glendower, lord of Glyndyfrdwy, and Reginald, Lord

---

[1] See ch. 6.　　　　　　　　　[2] KB 9/205/2, m. 110.
[3] *CPR, 1413–16*, pp. 263–4; KB 9/204/3, mm. 18–27; 205/3.

Grey of Ruthin, in the Marches of north Wales, but escalated into a full-scale national uprising. At its height, in 1405, Glendower controlled most of Wales and marched with his French allies to within a few miles of Worcester.[4] The rebellion collapsed in the second half of Henry IV's reign, and with the fall of his final strongholds, Aberystwyth and Harlech, in 1408 and 1409, Glendower ceased to present a serious threat to the Lancastrian regime. The principality nevertheless continued to be very disordered, especially in the northern heartlands of the rebellion, where Glendower and his son Meredith ab Owen went into hiding.[5] Grievances against the harshness and corruption of English government, which had fuelled the rebellion, remained, and there was a pressing need to reassert royal control over the civil administration.[6] Moveover, the revolt had revealed the disaffection of rising gentry families like the Tudors, the Mostyns, and the Dons of Kidwelly, who had flocked to support Glendower.[7] Although excluded from the highest levels of government, these families dominated its lower reaches, and their loyalty—or at least acquiescence—had to be regained to ensure the stability of English rule.[8]

The task facing the new king in Wales was twofold: to restore former rebels to his peace, both collectively and individually; and to investigate the activities of corrupt officials and to overhaul the machinery of government. In the

[4] The standard work on the Glendower rising remains J. E. Lloyd, *Owen Glendower* (Oxford, 1931); see also Jacob, *Fifteenth Century*, 37–65.

[5] Lloyd, *Owen Glendower*, 140–2.

[6] L. O. W. Smith, 'The Lordships of Chirk and Oswestry, 1282–1415', Ph.D. thesis (London, 1971), 385–6; G. Williams, *The Welsh Church from the Conquest to the Reformation* (Cardiff, 1962), 213–14.

[7] R. R. Davies, 'Owain Glyn Dŵr and the Welsh Squirearchy', *Transactions of the Honourable Soc. of Cymmrodorion* (1967–8), 150–69.

[8] For office-holding in south Wales, see R. A. Griffiths, *The Principality of Wales in the Later Middle Ages: The Structure and Personnel of Government*, Board of Celtic Studies, University of Wales History and Law Ser., 26 (Cardiff, 1972). Stringent statutes were passed at the time of the rebellion forbidding the appointment of Welshmen to any office in Wales, but in practice it was impossible to observe them except at the highest levels: R. A. Griffiths, 'Patronage, Politics and the Principality of Wales, 1413–61', and J. G. Jones, 'Government and the Welsh Community: The North-East Borderland in the Fifteenth Century', both in B. H. Hearder and H. R. Loyn (edd.), *British Government and Administration: Studies Presented to S. B. Chrimes* (Cardiff, 1974), 74–5 and 56–9. See also J. B. Smith, 'The Last Phase of the Glyndŵr Rebellion' *BBCS* 22 (1967), 256–7.

first two years of the reign a stream of commissions for the settlement of Wales flowed from chancery.[9] A few days after the king's accession the earl of Arundel was given full powers throughout Wales to receive rebels into the king's grace and to grant pardons according to his discretion.[10] In July 1413 separate commissions for north and south Wales were issued to investigate treasons, rebellions, and other offences committed by officials in the principality; in the north the commissioners were led by Arundel, in the south by Chief Justice William Hankford. At the same time letters patent were issued for an eyre in the Marcher lordships of the duchy of Lancaster in south Wales.[11] In 1414 Arundel led a general commission of inquiry in north Wales, with additional power to dispose of the confiscated lands of rebels.[12]

These groups of justices sat throughout Wales during the summer and autumn of 1413 and the spring of 1414.[13] The shires of the principality, after making a formal submission to the justices, were allowed to compound for their rebellion by paying collective fines. At Bala in March 1414, 600 inhabitants of Merionethshire appeared before Arundel and his fellows. Throwing themselves to the ground, they asked for the king's mercy, acknowledging that according to the strict letter of the law they deserved conviction and death as traitors.[14] The plea roll recorded that on receipt of a communal pardon, they thanked God on their knees for granting them such a magnanimous king.[15] Individual rebels were also able to buy pardons.[16] Over fifty former rebels were tried for treason in

[9] R. A. Griffiths, 'The Glyn Dŵr Rebellion in North Wales through the Eyes of an Englishman' *BBCS* 22 (1967), 152.

[10] KB 9/204/3, m. 25. This commission was not enrolled on the patent rolls.

[11] *CPR, 1413–16*, pp. 112–14; JUST 1/1152, m. 1. The justices held eyres in the lordships of Monmouth, Kidwelly, Ogmore, Ebbwy, Brecon and Hay. Cf. W. Rees (ed.) *A Survey of the Duchy of Lancaster Lordships in Wales*, Board of Celtic Studies, University of Wales History and Law Ser., 12 (Cardiff, 1953), pp. x–xviii; for the right of Marcher lords to hold eyres, see T. B. Pugh (ed.), *The Marcher Lordships of South Wales, 1415–1536*, Board of Celtic Studies, University of Wales History and Law Ser., 20 (Cardiff 1963), 4–10.

[12] *CPR, 1413–16*, p. 179. For investigations of misdeeds in the Marches conducted during the superior eyre of 1414, see the section on Shrops. below.

[13] JUST 1/1152–3; KB 9/204/3, mm. 18–27.   [14] Ibid., m. 25.

[15] Ibid.: 'omnes genuflectentes corditer et animose Deum benedicunt qui talem regem generosum eis constituit'.

[16] Wylie and Waugh, *Henry V*, i. 108–9.

the Lancastrian lordship of Kidwelly, including Henry Don, who had led the siege of Kidwelly castle in 1403. All were convicted and condemned to death by hanging and beheading, but were reprieved on payment of fines, and had their confiscated lands restored to them.[17]

To some degree, therefore, as J. H. Wylie and Professor Griffiths have observed, the Welsh felt the benefit of Henry V's general policy of conciliation.[18] In particular, pardoned rebels nearly always recovered their forfeited estates.[19] Yet they were made to pay a high price for the king's clemency. Several shires had already paid collective fines to Henry IV after their recapture from Glendower's control: Anglesey paid over £500 in 1406, Cardiganshire and Carmarthenshire comparable sums in 1407 and again in 1409.[20] In 1413, Cardigan and Carmarthen paid a further 400 and 800 marks respectively, while in the north fines of 800 marks were imposed on Anglesey, 500 on Caernarvonshire, 300 on Merionethshire and 500 on Flint.[21] Similarly the Lancastrian lordships paid a total of 2,260 marks.[22] In the following year another fine, of 1,000 marks, was imposed on Cardiganshire, while in March 1414 the northern shires paid additional sums to renegotiate the terms of their collective pardons in order to allow former rebels and their heirs to recover their estates and to confirm the tenure of land according to Welsh law.[23] Moreover, the chamberlains' account rolls for south Wales show that the fines were actually collected, and were not merely bonds for good behaviour.[24] In only two years Henry V raised just over £5,000 in collective fines from his Welsh lands, compared with a total annual income of £1,000 from the principality before the outbreak of the revolt.[25] This figure

[17] JUST 1/1152, mm. 4d, 6, 13d; 1153, m. 20.
[18] Wylie and Waugh, *Henry V*, i. 108; Griffiths, 'Glyn Dŵr Rebellion', 152–4, 166.
[19] *CPR, 1413–16*, pp. 41, 44, 195; SC 6 (ministers' and receivers' accounts)/1223/1, m. 4; Griffiths, 'Glyn Dŵr Rebellion', 153.
[20] SC 6/1222/11, mm. 1–2; 1222/12, m. 1; 1222/13, m. 3; 1222/14, m. 3d; G. Roberts, 'The Anglesey Submissions of 1406', *BBCS* 15, pt. i (1952), 39–61; Griffiths, *Principality of Wales*, 28–9; Pugh, *Marcher Lordships*, 36.
[21] SC 6/1222/13, m. 3; *CPR, 1413–16*, p. 137.
[22] JUST 1/1152, mm. 14–15; R. R. Davies, 'Baronial Accounts, Incomes and Arrears in the Later Middle Ages', *Economic History Review*, 2nd ser., 21 (1968), 223.
[23] KB 9/204/3, mm. 25–6; *CPR, 1413–16*, p. 195.
[24] SC 6/1222/13–14; 1223/1–4.   [25] Harriss, *Henry V*, 169 n. 10.

excludes the sums paid by individual rebels. Henry Don was fined 400 marks for leading the revolt in Kidwelly, but this was exceptionally heavy: the fines of up to £5 paid by his followers were more typical.[26]

The king also investigated complaints against corrupt officials. Most spectacular were the proceedings against Thomas Barnby, who as chamberlain of north Wales since 1406 had been one of the most senior financial officers in the principality during the Glendower rebellion.[27] Barnby successfully bribed jurors not to make presentments against him before Arundel's first commission to north Wales in 1413, but during the second commission in March 1414 the shires of Merioneth, Caernarvon, and Anglesey returned over thirty accusations against him. Barnby was charged with extortion and embezzlement of royal finances, as well as rallying support for the Percy rebellion in north Wales in 1403, consorting with adherents of Glendower, and procuring the malicious indictment of his enemies. After receiving indictments against him at the Caernarvon sessions on 19 March, the commissioners removed Barnby from office. He denied the accusations of treason, but confessed that in other matters he and his subordinates had not always acted correctly, and he threw himself on the king's mercy.[28] Barnby was not in disgrace for long, however: in 1416 he was selected by Henry V to be treasurer of the newly captured town of Harfleur in Normandy.[29]

In the Lancastrian lordship of Kidwelly in south Wales the eyre justices heard numerous indictments against the constable of Kidwelly castle, Walter Morton, the steward of the lordship, Sir John Scudamore, and his deputy, Rhys ap Ieuan Fychan. They were accused of selling offices, extorting cash, livestock, and labour services, and taking unauthorized fines from rebels. Fychan admitted the charges, was fined £20, and was dismissed from office. Morton and Scudamore appear to have been acquitted, but Scudamore was removed from the

---

[26] SC 6/1222/13, m. 2d; JUST 1/1152, m. 14.
[27] KB 9/204/3, mm. 22–24d. Barnby's career has been examined in detail by Griffiths, 'Glyn Dŵr Rebellion', 151–68.
[28] KB 9/204/3, m. 24d; Griffiths, 'Glyn Dŵr Rebellion', 155–66.
[29] Griffiths, 'Glyn Dŵr Rebellion', 168; see ch. 9 at nn. 45–8.

stewardship in July 1415, despite a life grant of the office.[30]

In re-establishing control over Wales and the Lancastrian Marcher lordships, Henry V relied upon a small group of military, legal, and financial administrators, many of whom were his retainers and had served under him in Wales before 1413.[31] Royal estates in Wales continued to be heavily, if not punitively, exploited: further fines, serving also as war taxes, were levied repeatedly on the shires of the principality and the Lancastrian lordships in south Wales, and became annual levies from the beginning of Henry VI's reign.[32] Under Henry V the income from the principality was three times what it had been at the beginning of Henry IV's reign.[33] The Welsh were also required to furnish troops for Henry V's French campaigns: a detachment from south Wales served with the king at Agincourt.[34]

In accepting the submission of his Welsh subjects, Henry had not forgotten the gravity of their offence, and they paid dearly for it. In view of his severity it is not surprising that Wales continued to be restive. There is evidence of resistance to royal financial demands in Merionethshire in 1416 and in Cardiganshire in 1417.[35] Glendower's son, Meredith ab Owen, lurked in north Wales, unreconciled to the king, in spite of repeated attempts to negotiate with him.[36] The threat of rebellion in the north was still serious enough in 1417 to prompt fears that the Welsh might rise in alliance with the Scots and the fugitive Sir John Oldcastle.[37] Commissions to treat with Welsh rebels were being issued as late as 1420, and it was only with the acceptance of a pardon by Meredith ab Owen in 1421 that the rebellion was finally extinguished.

[30] JUST 1/1152, mm. 5, 14; 1153, mm. 2–3, 9–10, 43. Griffiths, *Principality of Wales*, 139–41, 197–8; Davies, 'Baronial Accounts', 219–20.
[31] Griffiths, 'Patronage, Politics, and the Principality of Wales', 76–7. For Henry V's overhaul of the administration of the duchy of Lancaster, see R. Somerville, *History of the Duchy of Lancaster*, vol. i (London, 1953), 176–7, 183–9; Davies, 'Baronial Accounts', 222–3.
[32] SC 6/1223/1, mm. 1, 3d, 4d; 1223/2, m. 3; Pugh, *Marcher Lordships*, 36–42; Griffiths, *Principality of Wales*, 28–9; Davies, 'Baronial Accounts', 226.
[33] See above, n. 25.   [34] See ch. 9 at n. 26.
[35] Smith, 'Glyndŵr Rebellion', 254; Pugh, *Marcher Lordships*, 42.
[36] *CPR, 1413–16*, pp. 342, 404; *1416–22*, p. 89.
[37] Smith, 'Glyndŵr Rebellion', 253–60; Richardson, 'Oldcastle in Hiding', 433.

DEVON AND THE ENFORCEMENT OF MARITIME TRUCES

Late in February 1414 a general oyer and terminer commission
for Devon opened at Exeter. The presiding justice was Richard
Norton, chief justice of common pleas, and the terms of the
commission were comprehensive, covering treason, rebellion,
felony, and trespass.[38] A fortnight later the commissioners
returned to Westminster, having secured a grand total of four
indictments from over forty juries summoned before them by
the sheriff, Sir Thomas Pomeroy.[39] Only two of those accused
had been tried and both were acquitted. In order to protect
themselves from accusations of negligence, the justices noted
in the enrolment of proceedings the refusal of the presenting
juries to make indictments. The justices had even dismissed
the first county grand jury and summoned a second, but it
proved no more co-operative; with remarkable unanimity the
jurors of Devon said that they knew of no one guilty of the
offences under inquiry.[40]

We may quickly dismiss any notion that those jurors were
telling the truth. In the Parliament of 1410 Devonshire was
singled out as one of the most disorderly shires in England,
and later events proved that the county's response to the oyer
and terminer commission was a concerted act of resistance.[41]
What, then, were the reasons for this remarkable display of
defiance, and how did Henry V respond to it?

A clue to the purpose of the commission lies in two of the
four indictments laid before the February oyer and terminer,
which accused Stephen Sherman, master of a ship called the
Marie of Rye, of seizing a Breton vessel and its cargo in breach
of the truce between England and Brittany.[42] This appears
to have been the kind of indictment which the justices
expected, but the Devon juries were not prepared to indict
their own mariners, whose commercial activities and freelance
privateering must have contributed substantially to the local

[38] KB 9/205/2.
[39] Four more bills of indictment were submitted, but were returned *ignoramus* by
the presenting juries and were thus invalid: ibid., mm. 10, 26–7, 32.
[40] Ibid., m. 110.
[41] *RP* iii. 624. C. J. Tyldesley, 'The Crown and the Local Communities in Devon
and Cornwall, 1377–1422', Ph.D. thesis (Exeter, 1978), 217–21.
[42] KB 9/205/2, mm. 3, 8.

economy. The south Devon ports, above all Dartmouth, were important centres of maritime trade for the Atlantic and North Sea coasts.[43] The trade was run largely by merchant shipowners like the two John Hawleys of Dartmouth, father and son,[44] but the local aristocracy and gentry also had a stake in it. The Courtenay earls of Devon had their own port at Topsham, and their maritime interests were recognized in their frequent appointment as admirals.[45] During the French wars of the early fifteenth century the Lancastrian kings relied heavily for naval support upon Devon ships and sailors,[46] and the county was accustomed to look to its own defence against periodic coastal raids.[47]

The oyer and terminer commission of February 1414 must be understood against this background, and particularly in the light of the diplomatic activity which followed Henry V's accession. Henry's aim was to isolate France by forming alliances with the dukes of Brittany and Burgundy, who were vassals of the French king but ruled semi-independent principalities and pursued autonomous foreign policies.[48] On

[43] C. L. Kingsford, *Prejudice and Promise in Fifteenth-Century England* (Oxford, 1925), 78–87; F. A. Mace, 'Devonshire Ports in the Fourteenth and Fifteenth Centuries', *TRHS* 4th ser., 8 (1925), 98–126; *A Calendar of Early Chancery Proceedings Relating to West Country Shipping*, ed. D. A. Gardiner, Devon and Cornwall Record Soc., New Ser., 21 (Exeter, 1976).

[44] For John Hawley senior, see D. A. Gardiner, 'John Hawley of Dartmouth', *Transactions of the Devonshire Association*, 98 (1966), 173–205; S. P. Pistono, 'Henry IV and John Hawley, Privateer', *Transactions of the Devonshire Association*, 111 (1979), 145–63.

[45] Cherry, 'Political Community in Devonshire', 47; Tyldesley, 'Devon and Cornwall', 7.

[46] C. J. Ford, 'Piracy or Policy: the Crisis in the Channel 1400–1403', *TRHS* 5th ser., 29 (1979) 63–78; *Cal. . . . West Country Shipping*, pp. xii–xvii; Gardiner, 'Hawley', 194–204.

[47] In 1403 the Bretons attacked Plymouth and the following year they were repulsed in a skirmish at Blackpool outside Dartmouth. The men of Devon retaliated with a raid on Brittany led by the mayor of Exeter, William Wilford: see Tyldesley, 'Devon and Cornwall', 203; Walsingham, *Historia Anglicana*, ii. 259–60; *CIM, 1399–1422*, no. 282; Wylie, *Henry IV*, i. 434–6. Periods of war between England and France in the late fourteenth and early fifteenth centuries were accompanied by extensive privateering and raids on enemy shipping in the Channel, which have usually been seen as unauthorized 'pirate wars'. It has recently been argued, however, that privateering was far more closely controlled by the government than has been thought, and formed part of a wider military strategy: Ford, 'Piracy or Policy', 63–5.

[48] G. A. Knowlson, *Jean V, Duc de Bretagne, et L'Angleterre* (Cambridge, 1964), 78–125; R. Vaughan, *John the Fearless* (London, 1966), 158–63, 205–27; Jacob, *Fifteenth Century*, 135–43; Wylie and Waugh, *Henry V*, i. 82–106, 147–59, 403–46.

3 January 1414 Henry had concluded a treaty of mutual defence with John V of Brittany.[49] The ten-year truce of 1412 was confirmed, and each party agreed not to harbour the enemies of the other. The implications of this agreement were seen immediately in Anglo-French negotiations: at the end of January the French listed the duke of Brittany as one of the allies of the king of England.[50]

The Devon oyer and terminer commission offered an early opportunity for Henry to show good faith to his new ally by investigating attacks on Breton shipping in breach of previous truces between the duke and Henry IV. Medieval truces were often broken, and their effectiveness was therefore gauged not so much by the absence of infractions as by the provision of restitution for those that inevitably occurred.[51] Henry V was determined to make the truce work, and to stamp out the unauthorized taking of reprisals which might undermine it.[52] The January treaty explicitly provided for prompt action against infractions by arrest and punishment of the offender and seizure of his goods, 'as an example to all others'.[53] Conservators of the truces were named, who were to take custody of Breton prizes brought to English ports, list the cargoes, and determine whether there had been a breach of the truce.[54] Arrangements were made for the conservators to meet in Guernsey to consider complaints from both sides.[55] The truce was formally proclaimed in England on 4 February, and a week later a special commission was appointed to inquire into breaches of royal truces with Flanders and Brittany.[56] On 10 February, the oyer and terminer commissioners sent their precept to the sheriff of Devon instructing him to prepare for the opening of the sessions on 26 February.[57]

The events at Exeter late in February 1414 provide a textbook example of the conflict between central authority and local self-interest. The justices were trying to condemn

---

[49] *Foedera*, ix. 80–5.
[50] Ibid., ix. 94, 101; Knowlson, *Jean V*, 81–5.
[51] Keen, *Laws of War*, 214–15.   [52] Knowlson, *Jean V*, 86.
[53] *Foedera*, ix. 83: 'tellement que ce soit a tous autres exemple'.
[54] Ibid.   [55] Ibid., ix. 85, 114, 163, 194.   [56] Ibid. 112, 116.
[57] KB 9/205/2, m. 105. The commission itself had been issued on 20 Nov. 1413: ibid., m. 108; *CPR, 1413–16*, p. 148.

activities which the men of Devon regarded as perfectly legitimate, that is the seizure of ships of foreign merchants on the high seas in reprisal for the capture of English vessels by mariners of the same nationality. The line between piracy and legitimate reprisal was extremely difficult to draw at this time. Medieval international law recognized the right of private parties to reprisal where peaceful attempts to obtain restitution had failed. In such circumstances the complainant's sovereign was obliged to grant letters of marque: failure to do so would have constituted a denial of justice.[58] To take reprisals without specific authorization, in time of peace or truce, was a breach of the peace which the king had guaranteed by treaty with foreign powers, and was thus piracy. In practice, however, the mariners of Devon were accustomed to obtaining restitution by self-help, without waiting to exhaust the formal channels of redress.[59] In the face of such unwonted royal interference the county community closed ranks, and maintained a wall of silence against the baffled justices.

The resistance of the Devon juries may have been partly responsible for the Statute of Truces enacted at the Leicester Parliament of 1414. This act declared truce-breaking to be high treason, and provided for the appointment of conservators of truces.[60] During this Parliament Sir Thomas Pomeroy, who, as sheriff of Devon, had been responsible for empanelling the juries before the February commission, was dismissed from office after only six months, and replaced by Sir John Arundel, steward of the duchy of Cornwall and a trusted Lancastrian retainer.[61] In July two new commissions of inquiry were issued to a single set of commissioners, who

[58] Keen, *Laws of War*, 214–31. For letters of marque granted by Henry IV and V, see *CPR, 1408–13*, pp. 323, 351–2, 354; *1413–16*, pp. 17, 444. Some fifteenth-century treaties contained clauses forbidding the use of letters of marque by the powers concerned: Vaughan, *John the Fearless*, 161–2; *Cal. . . . West Country Shipping*, xv; *CCR, 1409–13*, p. 381.

[59] See above, n. 47. Cf. Ford, 'Piracy or Policy', 67–9. For inquiries into breaches of truces, many involving ships from Devon, see *CPR, 1408–13*, pp. 65, 231–2, 235, 316–17, 373, 381, 432–3, 474; *1413–16*, pp. 35–6, 110, 115, 147–8, 179, 192, 203, 209, 224, 267, 388; *CCR, 1409–13*, pp. 133, 369, 381, 385; *CIM, 1399–1422*, nos. 350, 376; *Cal. . . . West Country Shipping*, nos. 15–16.

[60] 2 Henry V st. 1 c. 6; see ch. 7 at nn. 16–24.

[61] Tyldesley, 'Devon and Cornwall', 219; C. Given-Wilson, *The Royal Household and the King's Affinity* (London, 1986), 233.

included the two western circuit assize judges, William
Cheyne and William Skrene, and John Tiptoft, one of the
king's closest advisers, but no local men.[62] As commissions of
inquiry, rather than oyer and terminer, their findings were to
be returned to Westminster and determined centrally before
king's bench. The first repeated the terms of the unsuccessful
oyer and terminer commission; the second ordered an
investigation of the obstruction of that commission by John
Boson, Henry Fulford, and Robert Kirkham.

The commissioners held their sessions at Exeter from 30
July to 1 August 1414, at the same time as the regular summer
assizes.[63] No systematic attempt was made by Arundel, the
new sheriff, to exclude from jury panels those who had failed
to co-operate with the oyer and terminer in February. The
jury of presentment from Haytor hundred, for example,
included five men who had served in February, that of
Woneford hundred four, that of Clifton hundred seven.[64] This
time, however, the juries were more co-operative, and some
150 indictments were returned.[65] Most involved the common
run of homicide, larceny, and trespass, but a significant
minority concerned acts of piracy.[66] About twenty shipmen
were indicted, including three of the leading Dartmouth
shipowners: John Hawley, several times mayor and member
of Parliament for the town, feodary and escheator of the duchy
of Cornwall from 1422;[67] Edmund Arnold, who had been
mayor and MP of Dartmouth, a frequent recipient of royal
commissions, and deputy admiral in Devon;[68] and John
Foxley, also a former mayor of Dartmouth, and MP for
Barnstaple in 1410.[69]

---

[62] *CPR, 1413–16*, pp. 263–4.
[63] KB 9/205/3; cf. JUST 1/196, m. 12; JUST 1/1527, m. 16.
[64] Cf. KB 9/205/2, mm. 73–5, with KB 9/205/3, mm. 7, 32, 39.
[65] KB 9/205/3, mm. 91–132.
[66] There were twenty indictments for piracy and associated offences: ibid., mm. 92, 112, 121, 131–2.
[67] Tyldesley, 'Devon and Cornwall', 10–11; Gardiner, 'Hawley', 199–204; Pistono, 'Hawley', 155–9; *Return of Members of Parliament, 1213–1876* (London, 1878), 274–321. He was pardoned in Michaelmas 1414: KB 27/614, Rex, m. 58.
[68] KB 9/205/2, m. 3; *CCR, 1405–9*, p. 142; *CPR, 1408–13*, p. 228; *Return of MPs*, 274, 283. He was pardoned in 1416: KB 27/621, Rex, m. 20d.
[69] *CCR, 1405–9*, p. 437; *Return of MPs*, 274. He was pardoned in 1415: KB 27/615, Rex, m. 13d.

Most important of these was John Hawley, who had inherited a sizeable merchant fleet from his father, John Hawley senior, and was perhaps the wealthiest shipowner in the west of England.[70] Because of the scale of his operations, Hawley's vessels were frequently involved in the seizure of foreign shipping, some of it legitimate action against the king's enemies—notably the French.[71] This involved Hawley in endless litigation with Breton, Flemish, and Spanish merchants demanding restitution from him through petitions to the king's council and chancery.[72] He regularly ignored royal summonses to answer such complaints, causing the government to order his arrest and distraint upon his goods.[73] Hawley's indictment for piracy by the grand jury of Devon, and his subsequent appearance in king's bench to present a pardon, was thus an important assertion of the king's political authority.[74]

In July 1414, the king's commissioners at last won their point and secured the indictment of several Devon shipmen for piracy. Yet even now the shire community did not concede completely. The Statute of Truces, enacted in May, had decreed the breach of royal truces to be high treason. In making their returns, however, the grand jury noted explicitly that all the acts of piracy recorded had occurred before Easter (that is, before the opening of the Leicester Parliament), so that they could only be classed as felony.[75] By so doing they registered their alarm at the severity of the new statute, which was to be expressed more generally in subsequent parliamentary petitions, and led to its relaxation in 1416.[76]

The commissioners' inquiry into the obstruction of the earlier oyer and terminer followed a similar pattern.[77] The inquest returned that Fulford, Boson, and Kirkham, the men named in the commission, had talked with Robert Cary and

[70] See above, n. 44.

[71] Gardiner, 'Hawley', 179–83; Ford, 'Piracy or Policy', 69–70; *Cal. . . . West Country Shipping*, no. 14.

[72] Pistono, 'Hawley', 145–7, 154–9; *Cal. . . . West Country Shipping*, nos. 11, 14–16, 24–5; *CPR, 1408–13*, pp. 316, 381, 474; *1413–16*, p. 35; *CCR, 1405–9*, pp. 24, 34–5; *1409–13*, p. 381; *1413–19*, pp. 8, 67, 501, 503.

[73] *CCR, 1405–9*, pp. 24, 34–5, 166, 177; *1409–13*, pp. 129–30, 135, 433; *1413–19*, pp. 8, 67; *CFR, 1405–13*, p. 207; *1413–22*, p. 245; *CPR, 1413–16*, p. 116.

[74] KB 9/205/3, m. 132; KB 27/614, Rex, m. 58.

[75] KB 9/205/3, m. 132.   [76] *RP* iv. 68, 105; see ch. 7 at nn. 22–3.

[77] Tyldesley, 'Devon and Cornwall', 219–20.

John Copplestone at the opening of the oyer and terminer sessions. They expressed concern at the damage the commission might do, and agreed that it would be good governance if the county could be kept without harm.[78] If these five men were indeed the ringleaders of the county's resistance in February, then its success is not surprising. All five were prominent 'administrative' gentry, not in the first rank of landed families, but active in local government as JPs, escheators, and subsidy-collectors.[79] Three of them—Cary, Copplestone, and Kirkham—served on the county grand jury and were thus well placed to give a lead to the hundred and borough juries.[80] Boson, Fulford, and Kirkham were indicted of trespass as a result of the inquest, and process was issued against them returnable in king's bench. The staff of the sheriff's office quietly ignored writs against the three men for the whole of Henry V's reign, and, when king's bench finally caught up with them in 1428, made a false return that they were dead. John Boson finally presented a pardon for his offence in Michaelmas term 1429, but Fulford and Kirkham never did appear in court, and proceedings against them were formally ended only in Michaelmas 1439 when a genuine return of their deaths was accepted.[81]

The contest between the Crown and the local community in Devon during 1414 ended in something of a draw. The king secured indictments for piracy which acknowledged that his writ ran at sea as well as on land, but not to the extent of recognizing earlier piracy as treason. The ringleaders of the resistance to royal justices in February were identified and indicted, but never effectively brought to justice. They continued to be active in local administration, Boson joining Fulford on the peace commission barely a year later.[82] In the following years the king does appear to have succeeded in enforcing maritime truces and providing restitution through legal channels rather than self-help, and Devon's seamen

[78] KB 9/205/3, m. 91: 'dixit . . . quod esset bona gubernacio quod patria custodiretur absque dampno'.

[79] Tyldesley, 'Devon and Cornwall', 72, 218, 223. The disenchantment of Cary and Copplestone with the new regime was no doubt coloured by their exclusion from the peace commission in January 1414: *CPR, 1413–16*, p. 418.

[80] KB 9/205/2, m. 56.

[81] KB 29/53, m. 39; KB 27/670, Rex, m. 7d.   [82] *CPR, 1413–16*, p. 418.

contributed substantially to Henry V's war effort.[83] There were occasions, however, when they showed the obstinate individualism they had displayed in 1414. In July 1415, as the king's army was gathering at Southampton for the Agincourt campaign, a ship from Dartmouth, the *Katherine* of Kingswear, left the muster without permission. The crew had been bribed by John Southam, prior of Totnes, who led them on a raid up the river Dart to Totnes, where they captured and held the castle.[84] On another occasion, in 1420, Hugh Courtenay, earl of Devon and admiral of the West, at first refused to muster his fleet for the summer patrol of the Channel. On the flagship, the *Gracedieu*, one of the quartermasters, William Duke of Dartmouth, seized the muster roll and threatened to throw it overboard. After the fleet had set sail some of the Devon seamen mutinied and insisted on being put ashore on the Isle of Wight.[85] Henry V's assertion of authority over the men of Devon thus seems to have had only a limited effect in curbing their independent-mindedness.

THE MIDLANDS

Staffordshire

Underlying the disturbances in Staffordshire lay a struggle for local power which was in part a reaction against the Lancastrian domination of the county. Throughout the reign of Henry IV the county administration had been monopolized by the Lancastrian affinity, based in the duchy honors of Tutbury and Duffield which straddled the Staffordshire—Derbyshire border.[86] The extent of Lancastrian control is clear from the careers of retainers like Sir John Blount, Sir John Bagot, Sir Robert Francis, and Roger Leach, who

---

[83] *RP* iv. 88–90; *PPC* ii. 152, 186–7, 234, 243, 248, 347; *CPR, 1413–16*, pp. 147–8, 179, 192, 223–4, 292, 344–5, 410; *1416–22*, pp. 135, 202–4, 209, 267, 324, 388; *CCR, 1413–19*, pp. 180, 311, 398, 500, 502–3, 513. See also ch. 9 at nn. 29–30.

[84] Tyldesley, 'Devon and Corwall', 222–3. Southam was arrested by the mayor of Totnes and imprisoned at Exeter gaol; he was pardoned in 1416.

[85] S. Rose (ed.), *The Navy of the Lancastrian Kings*, Navy Records Soc. (London, 1982), 50–1; E 101 (exchequer accounts various)/49/33. The reasons for these acts of defiance are not explained, but were probably connected with terms of payment.

[86] Somerville, *Duchy of Lancaster*, i. 7.

between them ran Staffordshire under Henry IV.[87] In a county with substantial Lancastrian landholdings such predominance was natural in the years after 1399. Its effects were intensified, however, by the death in 1403 of Edmund, earl of Stafford, which was followed by the twenty-year minority of his son Humphrey.[88] Other magnates with land in the county—Hugh, Lord Burnell, John Talbot, Lord Furnival, Richard Beauchamp, earl of Warwick—had their main estates elsewhere. They were appointed to the Staffordshire peace commission, but took little part in county politics.[89] Good lordship—so essential to the career of an ambitious gentleman—was thus a scarce commodity in Staffordshire at the beginning of the fifteenth century; control over office and patronage had fallen almost entirely into the hands of the Lancastrian affinity.

This state of affairs probably explains the series of attacks on Lancastrian retainers in the second half of Henry IV's reign. They were committed by a band of gentry led by Hugh Erdswick of Sandon. Hugh's father Thomas was the grandson of Sir James Stafford, through whom he had inherited Sandon and a claim to the manor of Bramshall.[90] The family had connections in Cheshire through Hugh's mother Helen, daughter of Hugh Venables of Kinderton.[91] Erdswick's chief accomplices were the Mynors brothers, William, John, and Thomas, of Uttoxeter. The Mynors were an old Lancastrian

---

[87] Ibid. 419; *RP* iii. 630; DL 28 (duchy of Lancaster accounts various)/27, nos. 3, 5, 6, 9; J. G. Bellamy, 'The Parliamentary Representation of Nottinghamshire, Derbyshire and Staffordshire during the Reign of Richard II', MA thesis (Nottingham, 1961), xxxiv, 16–32, 270–7.

[88] C. Rawcliffe, *The Staffords, Earls of Stafford and Dukes of Buckingham, 1394–1521* (Cambridge, 1978), 12, 18–19. Families of baronial status or above were scarce in Staffs. at the turn of the fourteenth and fifteenth centuries. The family of Bassett, lords of Drayton, had died out in 1390, that of Audley, lords of Heighley castle, in 1391; the Audley barony was revived for John Tuchet in 1405, but he died in 1408, leaving as his heir James Tuchet, a minor of ten: G. E. Cokayne, *The Complete Peerage of England* . . . (new edn., London, 1910–59), i. 340–1, ii. 2.

[89] *CPR, 1405–8*, p. 497; *1408–13*, p. 485; *1413–16*, p. 423; *1416–22*, p. 459; for Burnell, see *Shrops. Peace Roll*, 19; for Talbot, see below at n. 159. Beauchamp's influence in Staffs. increased in the 1420s and 30s as the connections of his affinity spread across the border from War. See Carpenter, 'Political Society', 90–1.

[90] J. C. Wedgwood, *Staffordshire Parliamentary History, 1213–1603*, Staffordshire Historical Collections., 3rd ser., 8 (London, 1917–18), 177; cf. JUST 1/814, m. 3.

[91] CHES 3 (Palatinate of Chester, inquisitions post mortem (Chester and Flint))/26/4. Thomas Erdswick died in March 1410, when Hugh was 24.

family that had fallen into obscurity and had failed to profit from Henry IV's largesse after his accession.[92]

In October 1408 Erdswick and his followers were indicted at the Newcastle-under-Lyme court leet before Robert Waterton, chief steward of the duchy north of the Trent. A warrant for their arrest was issued to Sir John Blount, who took surety from Erdswick to appear before the king and council when summoned. Far from ending the disturbances, however, this merely provoked renewed assaults on Lancastrian targets. In February 1409 Erdswick and the Mynors brothers raided the house of John Pasmere of Uttoxeter, a forester of the duchy and a lifelong Lancastrian servant. On the same day they attacked the manor of Sir Nicholas Montgomery at Cubley, for no other reason, as Montgomery alleged, but that he was a tenant of the duchy. At the end of February four Lancastrian knights were commissioned to arrest Erdswick and the Mynors brothers and to bring them before the council.[93] Erdswick gathered a large band of supporters, rode to Rocester, and sent messengers to Sir John Blount at his nearby manor of Barton, challenging him to resolve their differences either in single combat or by battle between a number of gentlemen chosen from each side.[94]

Erdswick's violent provocation of the Lancastrian establishment in Staffordshire, and his defiance of the royal commission for his arrest, called forth drastic measures from the central government. A long catalogue of his misdeeds was presented in a petition to Parliament in January 1410. Henry IV sprang to the defence of his affinity, ordered the conversion of the petition into an indictment, and referred it to king's bench for determination. It was to be proclaimed in the county court that if they defaulted in king's bench, Erdswick and his followers were to stand convicted of the offences alleged in the petition, and to forfeit their lands and chattels to the Crown. Under this threat most of the offenders soon submitted and were granted pardons. Erdswick himself was pardoned in

---

[92] Maddicott, *Thomas of Lancaster*, 42, 46, 339.

[93] *RP*, iii. 630–1; KB 9/113, mm. 2, 46, 47d; *CPR, 1408–13*, p. 64. An indictment from the FitzHugh commission in Derby. in 1414 suggests that Blount gathered a substantial force in his own defence against Erdswick: KB 9/204/2, m. 41.

[94] *RP* iii. 630–1.

February 1411, but John and William Mynors remained unreconciled to the Crown.[95]

The peace thus imposed on Staffordshire by the intervention of the king and Parliament was short-lived. Henry IV's reaction to the disorders was narrowly partisan: he accepted without question the allegations of his retainers in Staffordshire, and failed to remove the cause of the disturbances by broadening his support in the county to create a royal, as opposed to a merely Lancastrian, affinity. This task remained for Henry V to conclude.

Disorder continued unabated in Staffordshire in the last two years of Henry IV's reign. In 1411 Thomas and Robert Mynors broke into Wolverhampton church and assaulted the parson. The constable arrived and tried to arrest them. The brothers resisted and the local posse—'tota patria'—enraged at the desecration of their church, set upon and killed them.[96] The two surviving brothers, John and William Mynors, embarked on a virtual siege of Wolverhampton. Early in 1412 they gathered a group of supporters and wrecked six mills near the town. At the same time they warned men of the neighbouring villages, on pain of mutilation or death, not to take food supplies into Wolverhampton.[97]

Hugh Erdswick was not involved in these outrages. In the closing months of Henry IV's reign he was building up his influence in Staffordshire, and, aided by his brothers, Robert, Roger, and Sampson, established a sizeable following. Most of his recruits were yeomen from the villages outside the duchy of Lancaster, for whom the proximity of the duchy perhaps raised hopes of patronage without satisfying them.[98] Erdswick was clearly determined to become a force in local politics, and to break the Lancastrian monopoly of power in Staffordshire.[99]

---

[95] KB 27/597, Rex, m. 11; *CPR, 1408–13*, pp. 269, 275–7.

[96] JUST 2/162, m. 1d; KB 9/113, m. 11.

[97] Putnam, *Justices of the Peace*, 314–17. The deaths at this time of Richard Featherstone and Roger Ring of Wolverhampton, both at the hands of the Mynors, were no doubt part of the same vendetta: JUST 2/162, m. 1d; KB 9/113, mm. 34, 42; Putnam, *Justices of the Peace*, 312, 315.

[98] For example Thomas Pakeman of Gayton, Ralph Say of Stone, Robert and Ralph Orchard of Milwich, and Ralph Vickers of Stone: KB 9/113, mm. 2, 40. See DL 28/27, nos. 3, 5, 6, 9, for lists of wages paid to numerous parkers, foresters, and other officers of the honor of Tutbury.

[99] A mark of his success was his election to represent the county at Henry V's first Parliament in 1413, alongside his supporters Thomas Barber and Hugh Wildblood,

Within a month of Henry V's accession political rivalries in Staffordshire were complicated by the entry of Edmund Ferrers, lord of Chartley, who was given livery of his lands in April 1413, shortly after the death of his father Robert.[100] Apart from Chartley in Staffordshire, he inherited lands in Warwickshire, Gloucestershire, and several other Midland counties.[101] He was a direct descendant of Robert Ferrers, earl of Derby, who had been stripped of his lands and titles to provide an apanage for Edward I's younger brother Edmund.[102] Ferrers's father and grandfather had served with distinction in the French wars,[103] and he himself had been a member of the household of Henry V while he was prince of Wales.[104]

Edmund Ferrers clashed with Hugh Erdswick within months of inheriting his father's lands. The cause of the conflict is unknown, but since the two were near neighbours it was probably a land dispute. The scale of the disturbances which followed, however, makes it clear that something more was at stake. Erdswick saw Ferrers as a threat to his growing power. Ferrers's ancestry and personal ties with the new king made him an attractive alternative to Erdswick as a leader of the Staffordshire gentry outside the duchy of Lancaster, and he quickly secured the support of several gentlemen who had stood aloof from Erdswick.[105] Hostilities broke out in the middle of 1413, when the Erdswicks gathered at Amerton near Sandon and descended on Chartley park a few miles away. There they captured John Bythewater, a tenant of Ferrers, and held him to ransom.[106] A few days later Robert Erdswick and two followers broke into the houses of Ralph Aleyn and Roger Baxter, retainers of Ferrers, and assaulted them.[107]

who served for Stafford and Newcastle respectively: Wedgwood, *Parliamentary History*, 160, 177–9.

[100] *CFR, 1413–22*, pp. 1, 16. Cokayne, *Complete Peerage*, v. 305.

[101] Ibid.; R. H. Hilton, *A Medieval Society: The West Midlands at the End of the Thirteenth Century* (Cambridge, 1967), 181; Carpenter, 'Political Society', 12–13.

[102] McFarlane, *Nobility*, 254–6.

[103] Cokayne, *Complete Peerage*, v. 305; Edmund's grandfather was killed at Najera in 1367.

[104] *CCR, 1402–5*, p. 456; *1405–9*, p. 422.

[105] Ferrers's supporters included John Meverel of Throwley, Ralph Bassett of Cheadle, Edmund Bassett of Blore, John Draycott of Paynesley, and William Lichfield of Lichfield: KB 9/113, m. 41.

[106] Ibid., mm. 14, 26.   [107] Ibid., m. 1.

An attempt was made in the autumn of 1413 to bring an early end to the dispute through arbitration.[108] In the event neither side observed its undertakings to keep the peace, and the attempted award broke down amid mutual recrimination and renewed violence.[109] The dispute spread to London, where Ferrers's men assaulted Sampson Erdswick as he was on his way to obtain writs from chancery, leaving him with his toes stuffed in his mouth.[110] On Palm Sunday, 1 April 1414, the Erdswicks, accompanied by several adherents from Cheshire and most of their Staffordshire following, broke into Chartley park while Ferrers was away on royal service and murdered Ralph Page, one of Ferrers's servants.[111] A few weeks later both sides submitted petitions against their opponents to the Leicester Parliament,[112] and during the superior eyre the dispute gave rise to many indictments from the Staffordshire juries summoned before king's bench. The protagonists were indicted on several charges of granting unlawful liveries.[113] The murder of Ralph Page was presented six times,[114] and Page's widow, no doubt under Ferrers's direction, brought an appeal against her husband's slayers.[115]

The proceedings in king's bench against the chief trouble-makers in Staffordshire were low-key compared with those in Shropshire, which are described below.[116] John and William Mynors had already found favour with the new king: in 1413 William was made a yeoman of the king's household and John was appointed a bailiff of the duchy of Lancaster in Staffordshire.[117] They had not, however, secured reversal of the conviction and forfeiture proclaimed against them in 1410.[118] Formal reconciliation with the Crown was completed during the superior eyre. The brothers were summoned to appear before the king in person at Burton abbey on 8 June, and three days later Henry sent a signet letter to king's bench,

---

[108] See ch. 9 at nn. 53–9.   [109] KB 9/113, mm. 3, 4.

[110] *RP* iv. 33; see also *CPR, 1413–16*, p. 180.

[111] *RP* iv. 32; JUST 2/170. See also KB 9/113, mm. 1, 24, 32, 39, 47.

[112] *RP* iv. 32–3.

[113] KB 9/113, mm. 2, 11, 28, 40–3.   [114] See above, n. 111.

[115] KB 27/613, m. 25. The appeal was discontinued when Beatrix, Page's widow, defaulted in Hilary term 1415.

[116] See next section.

[117] Somerville, *Duchy of Lancaster*, i. 548; DL 28/27, no. 6; *CPR, 1413–16*, p. 172.

[118] See above at n. 95.

ordering that the Mynors be pardoned for their previous default in court.[119] A few days later the two brothers appeared in court with pardons covering the offences committed during their feud with Wolverhampton.[120] William Mynors accompanied the king to Agincourt and took part in the conquest of Normandy.[121] John Mynors remained at home in Staffordshire, surviving long enough to pass his Lancastrian office on to his son.[122]

Edmund Ferrers appeared in king's bench in Trinity term 1414, pleaded exemption from prosecution under the Statutes of Livery, and gave security of the peace towards Sampson Erdswick.[123] He eventually presented a pardon in Trinity 1415, when twenty of his followers paid fines for receiving unlawful liveries.[124] Sampson Erdswick also appeared in Trinity 1414, and was mainperned to trial at Michaelmas. The trial jury defaulted and he was later pardoned.[125] Hugh Erdswick did not appear until Michaelmas 1414, when he was made to give security of £200 not to harm Ferrers's attorney Richard Norman,[126] no doubt because Norman had been prominent in securing the indictment of the Erdswicks before king's bench.[127] No proceedings are recorded against Erdswick before Hilary 1415, when he presented a general pardon obtained after the proclamation of 8 December 1414.[128] Erdswick's two remaining brothers were outlawed after failing to appear in court, but this did not prevent one of them, Robert, from serving on the Agincourt campaign.[129]

The arrival of king's bench ended the violent feuding in Staffordshire, although the parties continued their fight in the courts until 1415.[130] Whatever the resolution of the immediate

[119] KB 145/5/2/1, unnumbered membranes.
[120] KB 27/612, Rex, m. 34.   [121] See ch. 9 at n. 24.
[122] Somerville, *Duchy of Lancaster*, i. 548.
[123] KB 27/613, Rex, mm. 9, 30; McFarlane, *Nobility*, 106–7, 123–4.
[124] KB 27/618, fines section, m. 1d.
[125] KB 27/613, Rex, m. 15.   [126] KB 27/614, Rex, m. 64.
[127] Numerous presentments against the Erdswick brothers were made by the jury of bailiffs from the bishop of Lichfield's liberty in Staffs., on which Norman sat: KB 9/113, mm. 2, 46–7; KB 27/613, attorneys section, m. 3.
[128] KB 27/614, Rex, m. 4d.
[129] N. H. Nicolas, *History of the Battle of Agincourt* (London, 1827), 345.
[130] In Michaelmas term 1414 Ferrers was suing in common pleas for the return of the bonds of arbitration from their custodian, Walter Bullock (later vicar-general to the bishop of Coventry and Lichfield): see ch. 9 at nn. 54–5.

dispute, its longer-term result is clear. Despite Ferrers's greater landed wealth and connections with the king, Erdswick got the better of him, probably by attacking him before Ferrers could create an effective power-base in the county. For although Ferrers was liberal in the granting of liveries during 1413, the support he attracted was not yet solid and coherent enough to counter Erdswick's repeated assaults.

Erdswick was henceforth established as a leading member of the county gentry: in 1415 he was appointed a JP, and during the next thirty years he held all the major county offices and often served as royal commissioner.[131] Ferrers went off to France, serving at Agincourt and throughout the conquest of Normandy.[132] On returning to England in the 1420s his activities were centred on Warwickshire. There he joined the affinity of Richard Beauchamp, earl of Warwick, whose support enabled him successfully to pursue his wife's claims to the manors of Birmingham and Castle Bromwich.[133]

Both sides in the Erdswick–Ferrers dispute were indicted on numerous counts of illegal retaining, and many other Staffordshire gentlemen, like Sir William Newport, Thomas Stanley, and Thomas Marchington were prosecuted for the same offence during the superior eyre.[134] The growth of such retinues at the end of Henry IV's reign reflected the absence of magnate interests in Staffordshire outside the duchy of Lancaster. It should not, however, be taken simply to illustrate the innately anarchic tendencies of the gentry. These retinues grew up to challenge the hegemony of the Lancastrian faction. Men like Erdswick recruited followings to increase their standing and further their own interests. In return they offered their retainers protection, maintenance,[135] and the possibility of future advancement into magnate service. In 1416 Thomas Stanley took his retinue abroad to serve under

[131] Wedgwood, *Parliamentary History*, 177–8; *CPR, 1413–16*, p. 423; *1416–22*, pp. 251, 416, 459; *1422–9*, p. 569; *1429–36*, pp. 137, 154, 200; *1436–41*, pp. 145, 249, 369, 505; *CFR, 1413–22*, pp. 315, 365; *1422–30*, p. 53; *1430–7*, pp. 186, 190, 260; *CCR, 1429–35*, p. 271.

[132] Cokayne, *Complete Peerage* v. 305.

[133] Carpenter, 'Political Society', 112–14.

[134] KB 9/113, mm. 11, 28, 41–3.

[135] Hugh Erdswick, for example, brought a bill in chancery against John and William Draycott for assaulting his retainer Robert Barnevile: C 1/6/12.

the earl of Warwick at Calais, and as a result secured
remission of the fines imposed upon them during the superior
eyre.[136] When Humphrey, earl of Stafford, later duke of
Buckingham, attained his majority in 1423, Hugh Erdswick
was an obvious choice for membership of his affinity, and
some of his former retainers also entered the earl's service.[137]

There was method, then, in the madness of the disturbances
which Henry V was quick to recognize. The gentry of
Staffordshire and their retainers were not simply indulging in
mindless thuggery, but were seeking patronage and advancement, from which they had been excluded under Henry IV.
Through the king's masterful intervention and shrewd management, Hugh Erdwick, Edmund Ferrers, and the Mynors
brothers, the *enfants terribles* of Staffordshire at his accession,
became trusted servants of the Crown in war and local
government.

Shropshire

The pattern of shire politics in Shropshire during Henry IV's
reign resembles that of Staffordshire, in that there were
outbreaks of disorder provoked partly by a reaction against
the concentration of local power in the hands of a small clique
of gentry, in this case the retainers of Thomas FitzAlan, earl of
Arundel. The exposed position of Shropshire on the Welsh
Marches made it particularly prone to lawlessness, however,
and the county felt the direct effect of the Glendower rebellion.

The earl of Arundel was the most powerful magnate in the
region. Besides holding large estates in Shropshire, he was
master of Chirk, Oswestry, and Clun, the Marcher lordships
on the county's western borders.[138] He was a leading
Lancastrian, and Henry IV allowed him a free hand in
Shropshire in order to defend the county against the Welsh
rebels. Eventually, however, the predatory behaviour of his
Marcher captains aroused opposition, which in 1413 found a
leader in the young John Talbot, Lord Furnival, later earl of

---

[136] *CPR, 1413–16*, p. 403.

[137] Rawcliffe, *Staffords*, 81, 216, 222; followers of Erdswick who entered the duke's
service included Thomas Barber, William Sandbach, and Ralph Vickers: ibid., 201,
215, 237–8; cf. KB 9/113, m. 2.

[138] They were incorporated into the county by Henry VIII: W. Rees, *An Historical
Atlas of Wales* (London, 1951), 51–2 and plate 56.

Shrewsbury, whose family had recently acquired lands in Shropshire.

Shropshire, like Staffordshire, was plagued with minorities among its great landowning families in the first years of the fifteenth century,[139] and responsibility for the defence of the county fell heavily upon Arundel.[140] During the second half of Henry IV's reign, however, Arundel himself was rarely present in Shropshire, as is apparent from the frequent demands of king and Parliament that he should defend his Welsh lands in person.[141] In practice the county's defence devolved upon Arundel's officers in the Marches, notably John Wele, captain of Oswestry, and Richard Lacon, captain of Clun. Wele was also constable of Shrewsbury castle by 1409, and controlled the strategic bridge across the Severn at Montford, which carried the main road from southern England to north Wales.[142]

Shropshire suffered the full impact of the Glendower rebellion, which broke out in the northern Marches in 1400.[143] Early in Henry IV's reign the rebels carried out a series of damaging raids, which were particularly serious in 1404, when the Talbot lordship of Blackmere was devastated and the suburbs of Shrewsbury ravaged by the rebels.[144] The nature of Glendower's rebellion made Shropshire particularly vulnerable, for it had its very roots in the Marches, and found

---

[139] The heirs to the Marcher lordship of Whittington, the Stafford barony of Cause, and the Mortimer lordships of Montgomery, Ludlow, and Wigmore, were all minors. During the minority of Fulk FitzWarin, Whittington was held in wardship by Elizabeth, Lady Botreaux and her son-in-law, William, Lord Clinton, whom Arundel accused of neglecting the defence of the lordship: JUST 1/753, m. 3(1); KB 27/613, Rex, m. 33. For the minority of Humphrey Stafford, Lord of Cause, see above, n. 88; for that of Edmund Mortimer, see McFarlane, *Lancastrian Kings and Lollard Knights*, 62.

[140] Ibid., 65; *CPR, 1401–5*, pp. 138–9, 438; *1405–8*, p. 80.

[141] *CCR, 1405–9*, pp. 453–4; *1409–13*, p. 15; *RP* iii. 552 (cf. ibid., 476, 610).

[142] Lacon and Wele were in office by Jan. 1408, when they were elected to the Shrewsbury gild merchant: 'Shrewsbury Gild Merchant Rolls', ed. C. H. Drinkwater, *TSAS* 3rd ser., 5 (1905), 48. See also JUST 1/753, m. 32d; C. H. Drinkwater, 'Montford Bridge', *TSAS* 3rd ser., 7 (1907), 71–4.

[143] Jacob, *Fifteenth Century*, 37–8; Smith, 'Chirk and Oswestry', 376 ff. See also *SKB* vii. 114–17.

[144] Pollard, 'Family of Talbot', 15, 344, 358; *RP* iii. 597. Cf. Jacob, *Fifteenth Century*, 54–5. Oswestry was sacked and burnt in 1400, and left so impoverished that in 1407 Arundel waived repayment of a £100 loan he had made to the town: Smith, 'Chirk and Oswestry', 399; J. Parry-Jones, 'Owen Glyndŵr and the Battle of Shrewsbury', *TSAS* 3rd ser., 3 (1903), 170.

much support among the Welsh tenants of Marcher lords. Glendower himself had held lands in Chirk of Richard FitzAlan, earl of Arundel, father of earl Thomas, and served in his war retinue. Most of the Arundel tenantry in Chirk and Oswestry rebelled with him, partly in reaction against the earls' increasingly harsh exploitation of their Welsh possessions.[145] Furthermore, many of the officials who administered the Marcher lordships had relatives who were rebels, and openly or covertly supported the revolt.[146] This collapse of seigneurial authority in the Marches left border castles like Oswestry and Clun as isolated English outposts, exposing Shropshire directly to rebel assaults.

It is in this context that we must place the accusations made against Lacon and Wele in 1414. They undoubtedly faced a difficult task in defending Shropshire, and the exigencies of their position, remote and isolated from the central government, may have justified the seizure of provisions without payment and the maintenance of close contacts with the rebels. It is clear, however, that they were often motivated more by personal gain than by military necessity. In 1414 Wele was indicted on several counts of treasonable dealings with the Welsh in 1408–9.[147] He was accused of sending provisions to Glendower and to the rebels besieged at Harlech, and of levying fines to allow rebels to live unmolested within Oswestry lordship. Rumours of such dealings had prompted the government in November 1409 to order Marcher lords to defend their lordships in person, and some plausibility is lent to the charges against Wele by a letter written in about 1412 to Lord Grey of Ruthin by Griffith ap David ap Griffith, a rebel in the service of Meredith, son of Owen Glendower.[148]

Both Lacon and Wele provisioned their garrisons with produce plundered from the surrounding countryside. In May

---

[145] Smith, 'Chirk and Oswestry', 377, 384–91.
[146] Lord Grey of Ruthin pointed this out in a letter to Henry, prince of Wales: Smith, 'Glyndŵr Rebellion', 252, 256.   [147] JUST 1/753, mm. 29(1).
[148] *CCR, 1409–13*, p. 15; Smith, 'Glyndŵr Rebellion', 250–2, 257. Griffith complained that Wele had tried to capture him through false promises of a royal pardon in return for military service abroad. Wele was, however, sufficiently trusted by Henry IV to be given custody of the members of Glendower's family captured at Harlech: *Issues of the Exchequer*, 321.

1413, for example, Wele carried off grain and livestock from Lord Burnell's manor at Pitchford.[149] The bishop of Hereford's liberty of Bishop's Castle was a favourite target for Lacon's men, and suffered repeated cattle raids from Clun.[150] Indictments for such offences were more common in the *coram rege* files for 1414 than those for raids carried out by the rebels, so that if their testimony is to be believed Shropshire at the end of Henry IV's reign was suffering more heavily from the Marcher captains than from Welsh raiders.[151]

Arundel's servants dominated the civil as well as the military administration of Shropshire. John Burley of Broncroft and David Holbache, both lawyers prominent in the earl's service, were among the busiest members of the Shropshire peace commission.[152] The commission also included John Wele, Arundel's brother-in-law Sir Roland Lenthall, John Winsbury, a tenant of the earl in Clun, and Robert Corbet of Moreton Corbet, one of Arundel's most active supporters in the dispute with Talbot in 1413.[153] Holbache and Burley also dominated the parliamentary representation of the county: one of them served for Shropshire at every Parliament between 1403 and 1414, except 1413, when Lacon and Corbet were knights of the shire.[154]

Arundel's commanding position on the Marches, his close links with the Lancastrian regime, and the long minorities in the FitzWarin, Stafford, and Mortimer families ensured the overwhelming predominance of his affinity in Shropshire.[155] There is no evidence that the earl's most experienced servants, Burley and Holbache, were not honest and efficient as county administrators. It was not their example, however, but that of Lacon and Wele, which was followed by the more junior members of Arundel's affinity. Burley's son, also called John, was implicated in the murder of John Stanton, the bailiff of Munslow hundred, and various lesser offences.[156] Robert

[149] JUST 1/753, m. 3(2).   [150] Ibid., mm. 1, 19(1), 19(3).
[151] For indictments involving Welsh border raids, see ibid., mm. 1, 8(1), 9, 22, 25(1), 25(5).
[152] *Shrops. Peace Roll*, 22–6.
[153] Ibid.; Shrops. Record Office, 552/1 (Clun court rolls)/45, m. 1.
[154] H. T. Weyman, 'Shropshire Members of Parliament, 1393–1584', *TSAS* 4th ser., 11 (1928), 4–12.
[155] See above, n. 139.   [156] JUST 1/753, mm. 6, 7(2), 11, 25(4), 27, 33.

Corbet's brother Roger was indicted in 1414 on several counts of demanding money with menaces, and of destroying the house of an opponent in a property dispute.[157] In August 1413 Lacon himself, with a band of followers, interrupted the summer assizes at Shrewsbury and rescued William Bridge, a prisoner in the sheriff's custody.[158]

By contrast with Staffordshire, where the Lancastrian gentry proved incapable of crushing the Erdswicks with a decisive show of force, Arundel's following in Shropshire, with its strong Marcher element, was well organized and aggressive, resorting readily to arms. When John Talbot had the temerity to challenge Arundel's supremacy at the beginning of Henry V's reign, the reaction of the earl's supporters was vigorous and dramatic.

The Talbots had recently acquired an interest in Shropshire through John's mother Ankaret, heiress to the Lestrange lordship of Blackmere.[159] John and his elder brother Gilbert spent their youth fighting the Welsh, and with their Shropshire lands and Marcher credentials they posed a threat to Arundel's domination of the county. Conflict arose as early as 1409 when John Talbot, on his way to Caernarvon at the head of a force to combat the Welsh rebels, was refused entry to Shrewsbury by Wele and Lacon.[160] In 1413 contention again arose between Talbot and Arundel's affinity. The conflict originated in a territorial dispute between Arundel and the prior of Wenlock over the enclosure of a piece of land at Powkesmoor near Ditton Priors in Corvedale. The prior turned to Talbot for protection and leased Powkesmoor to him.[161] In May 1413, on hearing that Lacon and Wele were preparing to break down the enclosure, a group of Talbot's followers led by the former bailiff of Bridgnorth, John Bruyn, rode to defend the disputed land.[162] A fortnight later Arundel's men descended on Powkesmoor and threw down the enclosure previously erected by the prior.[163] Leading this raid were seven members

---

[157] JUST 1/753, mm. 11, 12(2), 25(2), 29(1); C 1/6/124. The Corbets also patronized the counterfeitors Roger and Thomas Adams: JUST 1/753, m. 23(1).

[158] Ibid., m. 31(1).

[159] The following paragraph is drawn from Pollard, 'Family of Talbot', 1–30.

[160] JUST 1/753, m. 32.

[161] *CCR, 1413–19*, p. 43.

[162] JUST 1/753, m. 29(1).   [163] Ibid., m. 32.

of the Shropshire gentry who were indicted together before king's bench at Shrewsbury in June 1414: Lacon, Wele, Robert Corbet and his brother Roger, John Burley junior, John Winsbury, and Ralph Brereton.[164] From Powkesmoor the band rampaged through nearby manors belonging to Wenlock priory: at Ditton Priors, Eaton, and Oxenbold they attacked the prior's tenants, particularly those who had ridden in support of Talbot earlier in the month.[165]

Talbot's decision to challenge Arundel was rash and provocative. With his good record of service in defence of the Marches under Henry IV, he may have thought he could rely on royal support. But his influence with Henry V could hardly match that of Arundel, who had recently been appointed treasurer of England by Henry V.[166] Nor was Talbot's following in Shropshire cohesive enough to be called an affinity. Its leading member was John Bruyn, formerly bailiff of Bridgnorth, who led the defence of Powkesmoor in May. As bailiff Bruyn had made many enemies in the town, and he was to be indicted before king's bench on many counts of corruption and extortion.[167]

There was a lull in the dispute over the summer of 1413, but it flared up again in the autumn when the time came for the collection of the subsidy granted by Henry V's first Parliament. Shropshire's representatives at that assembly—Richard Lacon and Robert Corbet—nominated for the unpopular office of subsidy-collector John Bruyn and four other adherents of Talbot: Roger Lyney, Henry Hordley, Thomas Marshall, and Robert Swynnerton of Poynton.[168] When the latter attempted to collect the subsidy they were constantly harassed by Arundel's retainers. At the same time Bruyn's enemies in Bridgnorth, led by Richard Hord and William Palmer, had procured a commission for the arrest of Bruyn to give security of the peace towards them.[169] The Shropshire JP John

---

[164] KB 27/613, Rex, mm. 36 ff.   [165] JUST 1/753, mm. 27, 30, 32.

[166] McFarlane, *Lancastrian Kings and Lollard Knights*, 65; *CCR, 1413–19*, p. 4.

[167] Powell, 'Justices of the Peace', 535–50. Other adherents of Talbot in Shropshire, like Henry Hordley of Ludlow and Roger Lyney of Newport, were also townsmen. For sterner support Talbot was obliged to draft in family retainers such as John Abrahall from Herefordshire: JUST 1/753, mm. 15, 29(1); KB 27/613, Rex, m. 39; cf. Pollard, 'Family of Talbot', 29.

[168] *RP* iv. 30–1, 87–8.   [169] Cf. C 1/6/189.

Winsbury issued a warrant for the arrest to Hord, now himself bailiff of Bridgnorth, who served it on Bruyn at Oldbury in November, while the collection of the subsidy was in full swing. Bruyn, accompanied by the other subsidy-collectors and a band of servants from Bridgnorth, resisted arrest, and later claimed that Hord was trying to impede the collection of the subsidy.[170]

By now the disturbances had come to the ears of the king, who took drastic action: on 16 November 1413 Arundel, John Talbot, and his brother Gilbert were made to take out recognizances to maintain the peace, Arundel for 10,000 marks, the Talbots for £4,000 apiece.[171] On the same day John Talbot was committed to the Tower, and although no reason for his arrest was given, there can be little doubt that it stemmed from his defiance of Arundel.[172] On 1 February 1414 Powkesmoor was taken into the king's hand, and on 24 February, no doubt under pressure from Arundel, the king appointed John Talbot as lieutenant of Ireland for six years.[173] Arundel pressed home his advantage a few days later. At the Shrewsbury peace sessions on 6 March he presided with several of his followers over the indictment of John Bruyn, Talbot's leading supporter, by a jury composed of his enemies in Bridgnorth.[174]

The conflict had ceased to be a purely internal Shropshire affair, however. Complaints were made at the Leicester Parliament about the disorder in the county. The attacks on Bruyn and his fellow subsidy-collectors aroused particular concern, and Parliament authorized stern measures to deal with the offenders. It was in the light of these complaints that the decision was taken to send king's bench to Shropshire.[175]

The Shrewsbury sessions were full of drama. In the presence of the duke of York, Chief Justice Hankford harangued the county grand jury about the lamentable state of public order in Shropshire, and reminded them of their duty to present a full and impartial account of the disturb-

---

[170] *RP* iv. 31; JUST 1/753, m. 15; KB 9/206/1, m. 18.
[171] *CCR, 1413–19*, pp. 97–9.   [172] Ibid. 40.
[173] Ibid. 43; *CPR, 1413–16*, p. 164.
[174] KB 9/206/1, mm. 18–19; printed in Powell, 'Justices of the Peace', 542–50.
[175] Ibid. 535–41.

ances.[176] The jurors, mindful of the power of the Arundel affinity, requested that all offenders they indicted should, on appearing in court, offer security to keep the peace towards them, and this request was granted by the court. Their subsequent indictments comprised a remarkable catalogue of the misdeeds of Arundel's affinity over the previous years: indictments concerning Arundel's leading adherents—Lacon, Wele, the Corbet brothers, Winsbury, Brereton, and John Burley junior—were entered on the plea roll, where they filled the face and dorse of five membranes.[177] These seven men appeared in court together at the end of Trinity term, 1414, and each made recognizances of £200 to keep the peace, especially towards the grand jurors. Arundel himself was made to take out bonds totalling £3,000 as pledges of their good behaviour.[178]

Since the earl of Arundel was one of the king's most trusted servants, Henry V's decision to prosecute his affinity in king's bench represented a notable exercise of royal authority. It demonstrated that Arundel's support for the Lancastrian regime no longer guaranteed him nor his retainers judicial immunity. This no doubt was the message that the king intended to convey by singling out Arundel's following for exemplary treatment at Shrewsbury. Yet Arundel's supremacy in Shropshire was not affected. Talbot was sent to cool his heels in Ireland, where Arundel, as treasurer, kept him short of money.[179] All Arundel's leading supporters obtained pardons, and six of them later served in the earl's retinue on the Agincourt campaign.[180]

It may appear surprising that pardons were allowed even to Lacon and Wele, who had been charged with treason. The explanation is probably that they were experienced Marcher captains too valuable to be discarded. Neither suffered a permanent setback in his career as a result of the superior eyre; at the time of the Agincourt campaign Wele was one of the captains left in charge of the Welsh Marches. Lacon took part in the campaign itself, and on his return served as sheriff

[176] *SKB* vii. 227. [177] KB 27/613, Rex, mm. 37 ff.
[178] Ibid., Rex, m. 36d. [179] Pollard, 'Family of Talbot', 114.
[180] E 101/47/1. See ch. 9 at nn. 18–21.

of Shropshire in 1415–16. Both subsequently participated in the conquest of Normandy.[181]

The Talbot faction lay low during and after the superior eyre. When John Talbot left for Ireland in November 1414, accompanied by John Bruyn, neither had appeared in king's bench on the indictments laid against them. Talbot presented a pardon by attorney in 1415, but Bruyn remained outlawed.[182] A few months after the superior eyre, in October 1415, the political complexion of Shropshire was suddenly transformed by the death of the earl of Arundel of disease contracted at the siege of Harfleur.[183] He left no direct male heir, and the way was clear for the Talbots to assume a dominant position in Shropshire, culminating in the elevation of John Talbot to the earldom of Shrewsbury in 1442. In 1416 there were important changes in the county peace commission: Wele, Robert Corbet, and John Winsbury were omitted and servants of Talbot substituted for them.[184] In 1417 Bruyn was able to return from Ireland and the quarrels with his enemies in Bridgnorth were settled by arbitration. Bruyn subsequently presented a pardon in king's bench in 1419.[185] Most significant as an indication of the Talbots' growing authority in Shropshire was the fact that Arundel's former servants began to transfer their allegiance to them. William Burley, the son of John Burley senior, began his distinguished administrative career in Arundel's service, but upon the earl's death he joined the Talbots.[186] So also did Richard Lacon and his sons, which suggests that although the Arundel–Talbot dispute of 1413–14 was hard fought, its enmities were rapidly forgotten in the changed circumstances after 1415.[187]

Nottinghamshire

Nottinghamshire was the third Midland shire whose disorders came to the attention of the Leicester Parliament.[188] Three

[181] See ch. 9 at n. 19. [182] KB 27/616, Rex m. 26.
[183] Walsingham, *St Albans Chronicle*, 92.
[184] *The Victoria County History of Shropshire*, vol. iii, ed. G. C. Baugh (Oxford, 1979), 56–7.
[185] Nat. Lib. Wales, Pitchford Hall Deeds, no. 2492; KB 27/634, Rex, mm. 6, 14.
[186] Pollard, 'Family of Talbot', 229–30; J. S. Roskell, 'William Burley of Broncroft', *TSAS* 66 (1960), 264–5.
[187] Pollard, 'Family of Talbot', 231–2. [188] *RP* iv. 27–30.

petitions were received against the oppressive activities of Sir Richard Stanhope, a Lancastrian retainer and leading member of the county gentry, and two concerning a dispute between rival claimants to the abbacy of Fountains in Yorkshire, which had led to violence in northern Nottinghamshire.[189] As in Shropshire and Staffordshire, the king acted promptly: Stanhope was summoned before Parliament to answer the petitions and was then imprisoned, and on 14 May a general commission of inquiry was issued to investigate offences in Nottinghamshire and Derbyshire.[190] The commission was led by two of the most senior members of the king's household, Henry, Lord Fitzhugh, and Sir John Rothenale.

The indictments taken before this commission confirmed that the disputed election at Fountains abbey had degenerated into open violence.[191] The dispute had begun in 1410, and the two contenders, Roger Frank and John Ripon, formerly abbot of Meaux, pursued their claims vigorously in both royal and ecclesiastical courts. In December 1413 the king sequestrated the abbey and placed it in the keeping of the archbishop of York and the bishop of Durham pending a resolution of the dispute. In 1413 Frank brought an action in chancery against Ripon under the Statute of Praemunire. The court decided in Ripon's favour, but he was unable to secure entry to the abbey. Frank continued to act as abbot, disposing of the abbey's valuables and property and carrying off its common seal. The tenants of Fountains appear to have been divided in their loyalties, and in Lancashire at about this time there were attacks on Ripon's supporters by men loyal to Frank. In March 1414 the duke of Bedford and the earl of Westmorland were instructed to put Ripon in possession of the abbey. On 5 May, while passing through Nottinghamshire on his way to king's bench to claim restitution of the abbey's possessions, Ripon was attacked at Norton Cuckney near Welbeck park by Frank, his brother Oliver, his cousin Robert Frank, and several monks of Fountains and their followers.[192] In June

---

[189] Ibid.; SC 8 (ancient petitions)/97/4081.

[190] KB 9/204/2, m. 2.

[191] E. F. Jacob, 'The Disputed Election at Fountain's Abbey, 1410–16', in id., *Essays in Later Medieval History* (Manchester, 1968), 79–97.

[192] *RP* iv. 27–8. The attack took place while the Leicester Parliament was in session, and Ripon must therefore have framed his petition almost instantaneously.

1414 and again in October, commissions were issued for the arrest of Frank and his confederates, and for their delivery to Ripon for chastisement according to the Cistercian rule. The ecclesiastical nature of the dispute made it impossible for the king's courts to render an authoritative verdict, and it was not until 1416, after a further parliamentary petition and appeals to the council of Constance, that the matter was finally resolved in Ripon's favour. Only three of the eleven men accused of the attack on Ripon came to court; Roger Frank himself was one, although he did not appear until Trinity 1424, when he presented a pardon.[193]

Apart from the Fountains incident, the worst of the disorder in Nottinghamshire stemmed from a territorial dispute between two gentlemen, Alexander Meering and John Tuxford, over the ownership of part of the manor of Little Markham.[194] Meering occupied the disputed lands by force in 1410, and in August 1411 the dispute was referred to arbitrators nominated by the parties. Sir John Zouche, Sir John Leek, and Hugh Willoughby acted for Meering; Sir Thomas Chaworth, Sir Richard Stanhope, and Henry Pierrepont for Tuxford. The loveday broke up without agreement, however, and Meering departed asserting his determination to retain the disputed land. A few days later Tuxford, accompanied by Stanhope and Ralph Cromwell, Stanhope's brother-in-law, with a large band of their followers, re-entered Little Markham. Meering in turn, with his sons William and Thomas, and supported by Leek and Zouche, raised a large armed force to recover the land, and a violent confrontation was only averted by the arrival of William, Lord Roos.[195]

As a result of these incidents Stanhope and Zouche were indicted for maintenance before the commission of inquiry. They were also accused of extortion and intimidation.[196] In addition to his support for Tuxford, Ralph Cromwell was indicted for forcibly rescuing a confessed felon from sanctuary at Woodborough.[197] The indictment file was delivered to

---

[193] KB 29/53, m. 22. The other two were John Faghley and John Judde of Derby., who paid fines at Trinity 1416: KB 27/617, fines section, m. 1.

[194] KB 9/204/2; *CCR, 1413–19*, pp. 50–4; Payling, 'Lancastrian Nottinghamshire', 245–50.

[195] KB 9/204/2, mm. 6, 7, 26.   [196] Ibid.   [197] Ibid., m. 6.

king's bench in mid-June 1414, during the court's proceedings at Lichfield, and process was issued without delay.[198] Sir Richard Stanhope, who had been held in Kenilworth castle since the Leicester Parliament, appeared in court on 23 June to present a general pardon.[199] Zouche, Cromwell, Alexander Meering and his sons had all appeared and submitted pardons by Easter 1415.[200]

Meanwhile the disputing parties reverted to peaceful means to seek a settlement over Little Markham. Early in 1412, with Tuxford in control of the land, Meering brought an action of novel disseisin against him. The case came before the assize justices of the Midland circuit, headed by Robert Tirwhit; but in October, while the action was still pending, both sides submitted to the arbitration of Tirwhit, Chief Justice William Gascoigne, and William, Lord Roos.[201] This award was not made within the stipulated term, however, and in February 1414 Meering obtained a royal licence to proceed anew with the assize.[202] This time a verdict was reaching establishing that Meering had indeed been disseised, and he was awarded fifty marks in damages. Final judgement was never rendered, however, owing to clerical error, and Meering was forced to petition Parliament to seek a remedy.[203] Finally, in November 1416, an award was successfully concluded in which the disputed lands were divided equally between the two parties.[204]

The level of violence and disorder in Nottinghamshire was far lower than in Shropshire and Staffordshire, and it might not have been subjected to a special commission but for the spate of judicial activity which stemmed from the Leicester Parliament. On a smaller scale, nevertheless, the pattern of the proceedings elsewhere was repeated. Sir Richard Stanhope, a pillar of the Lancastrian establishment who had fought

---

[198] See ch. 7 at n. 44.

[199] SC 8/97/4081; KB 27/613, Rex, m. 9d; Payling, 'Lancastrian Nottinghamshire', 242–7.

[200] KB 27/614, Rex, mm. 9, 12; 616, Rex, mm. 17d, 28d. Tuxford appeared in court but apparently defaulted before trial.

[201] *CPR, 1408–13*, pp. 431–2; *CCR, 1409–13*, p. 397; *CIM, 1399–1422*, no. 443. Powell, 'Arbitration and the Law', 57–8.

[202] *CCR, 1413–19*, pp. 50–4.

[203] *RP* iv. 73.   [204] *CPR, 1416–22*, pp. 54–5.

against the Percies at the battle of Shrewsbury, was disciplined and rebuked in Parliament for a career of petty lawlessness and intimidation under Henry IV.[205] Royal intervention defused the Tuxford—Meering dispute and led to its settlement by arbitration under the auspices of Parliament. After 1414 Stanhope served Henry V in local government as a frequent commissioner of array and for loans, and after 1417 as a JP.[206] Ralph Cromwell, who had aided Stanhope in the maintenance of Tuxford, served on the Agincourt campaign and on the subsequent conquest of Normandy, where for a time he commanded the garrison at Harfleur. William Meering, indicted with his father Alexander in 1414, also served with the king at Agincourt and in Normandy.[207]

[205] Given-Wilson, *Royal Household*, 233.
[206] *CPR, 1416–22*, pp. 143, 197, 252, 389, 417, 457; *CCR, 1419–22*, p. 179.
[207] See ch. 9 at n. 28.

9

Henry V's Policy of Conciliation and Recruitment

THE JUDICIAL inquiries of 1413 and 1414 left no doubt that the king was intent upon restoring public order throughout the realm, as his first Parliament had requested.[1] In marked contrast to his father, Henry V brought the full weight of royal judicial authority to bear upon the shires through a battery of special commissions. The consequent proceedings revealed extensive local feuding, official corruption, and contempt for the king's peace, at sea as well as on land. Supporters of the Lancastrian regime, who had been virtually immune from prosecution under Henry IV, found their offences exhaustively catalogued before royal justices, and had to make their peace with the new king.

It has already been suggested that it was not Henry V's primary intention to punish crime in 1414, and that his main instruments in restoring public order were conciliation and recruitment for military service.[2] The problems facing him were political rather than merely judicial. The worst disorders of Henry IV's reign had been caused by the magnates and gentry—precisely those upon whom the Crown relied most for support in war and government. These groups were the primary targets of Henry V's inquiries. Like other medieval kings, however, Henry could not have punished noble offenders with hanging or lengthy terms of imprisonment: any attempt to do so would have made the country ungovernable. Instead the king made generous use of his prerogative of mercy by promulgating general pardons. At the same time he took many of the offenders into his service, and channelled their aggressive energies into his foreign war.

Conciliation has long been recognized as one of the

---

[1] See ch. 5 at nn. 91–2.   [2] See ch. 7 at nn. 107–10.

keynotes of Henry V's early years as king, a policy dictated by his determination to disown the legacy of faction and distrust inherited from his father's reign and to reconcile the country to the Lancastrian regime. It is most obvious in his restoration of the heirs of nobles who had rebelled against his father, but has been noted also in his dealings with former Welsh rebels, and in the ceremonial reburial of Richard II in Westminster abbey.[3] Henry's conciliatory approach to law enforcement was thus consistent with this broader policy.

For such a policy to succeed it was essential that it be presented, and perceived, as an assertion of the king's authority, not an admission of weakness. The threat of the iron hand had to be felt beneath the velvet glove. The examples mentioned above show this double-edged quality quite clearly: Richard II was honoured in death, but his reburial was an emphatic riposte to the conspirators who in 1413 were still plotting Richard's restoration;[4] while in granting to the heirs of noble families such as Percy, Montague, and Holland the lands and titles their forebears had forfeited by rebelling against Henry IV, the king upheld the attainders of his father's reign, and stressed that such restorations were totally dependent on his grace.[5] Henry V was adept at exercising the kingly quality of mercy in such a way as to emphasize and exalt his authority, as is evident from the terms of his first general pardon and the pardon to the Lollards after the revolt of 1414.[6]

Henry V adopted similar methods in re-establishing public order throughout the realm. The disciplining of unruly magnates and gentry, and in particular the bringing to heel of Lancastrian supporters, had to precede the process of conciliation. Much depended on the sheer force of the king's personality, and such was Henry's success in this regard that it gave rise to a story, probably apocryphal, related in the *Brut* chronicles.[7] During the first year of his reign two knights, one of Lancashire and one of Yorkshire, prosecuted a fierce quarrel in which many of their supporters were killed. On

[3] Jacob, *Fifteenth Century*, 128–9; Harriss, *Henry V*, 33–9; Griffiths, 'Glyn Dŵr Rebellion', 152–4.
[4] See ch. 5 at nn. 100–8.
[5] Harriss, *Henry V*, 38–9.
[6] See ch. 5 at nn. 76, 87.
[7] *The Brut*, ii. 595 (spelling modernized).

hearing of this the king summoned them to his presence at Windsor. They appeared before him as he was about to sit down to a dish of oysters. Henry upbraided them roundly for their conduct and asked by what authority they raised up his liege men to fight and slay each other. The two men begged for mercy, and the king replied: 'by the faith that he owed to God and to Saint George, but if they agreed and accorded by the time that he had eaten his oysters, they should be hanged both two or ever he supped'. The knights withdrew, and when recalled a few minutes later, had come to terms to settle their quarrel.

The *Brut* tale conveys admirably the spirit of Henry V's approach to law enforcement. In Shropshire, where the disorder was perhaps most severe, Henry took drastic measures. Huge recognizances for the maintenance of the peace were extracted from the earl of Arundel, Gilbert Talbot, and his brother John, while the latter was imprisoned in the Tower and subsequently sent off to Ireland. Powkesmoor, the land in dispute between the two factions, was taken into the king's hands, and during the superior eyre itself the extraordinary step was taken of making a formal enrolment on the king's bench of the indictments against Arundel's leading retainers. The settlement of north Wales was expedited by the dismissal of the corrupt chamberlain, Thomas Barnby, at the clamour of the local communities. In Staffordshire William and John Mynors were called before the king to account for their long defiance of the law courts, while from Nottinghamshire Sir Richard Stanhope was summoned before the Leicester Parliament and was thrown into prison in spite of denying the charges against him. Likewise the Statute of Truces, promulgated at Leicester, was an attempt to secure respect for the king's peace at sea through the observation of his treaties.[8]

Henry V's general pardons must therefore be seen in the light of his dynamic reassertion of royal authority. Comprehensive in scope and simple to apply, they provided a speedy and convenient means of dealing with the vast number of cases which were clogging the courts in the early years of

[8] See ch. 8, *passim*.

the reign. But whereas the numerous general pardons of Henry IV's reign sprang primarily from the king's financial weakness, those of Henry V formed part of a wider strategy in which domestic peace, dynastic stability, and foreign war were closely linked. Many pardons were undoubtedly granted on the understanding that the beneficiaries should perform military service, and they provided the king with valuable leverage to recruit those who might otherwise have been reluctant to risk their lives and fortunes abroad.

RECRUITMENT TO MILITARY SERVICE

All medieval kings faced the problem of inducement in raising military forces; the potential rewards in terms of prestige, booty, and royal favour were enormous, but the risks involved were correspondingly great.[9] Apart from the obvious danger of death, injury, or disease, war was a financial gamble. The initial outlay for equipment, whether of an earl, a knight, or a man-at-arms, was substantial and could not be met entirely out of royal wages;[10] on campaign the threat of capture was always present, and with it the prospect of a ransom which could cripple a family's finances.[11] Such considerations did not deter the nobility from military service. Throughout the Hundred Years' War it was they, rather than mercenary captains, who furnished the king's 'general staff' for his campaigns in France.[12] Even as early as Edward I's reign, however, the risks and expenses of warfare may have discouraged the knightly and gentry classes from serving in sufficient numbers to satisfy the Crown's military needs.[13] The problem was particularly acute if the king was waging a prolonged war of conquest, like Edward I in Scotland and

---

[9] McFarlane, *Fifteenth Century*, 175–97; id., *Nobility*, 19–40.

[10] Harriss, *Henry V*, 41–2; A. E. Goodman, 'Responses to Requests for Military Service under Henry V', *Northern History*, 17 (1981) 246–51.

[11] McFarlane, *Nobility*, 29–31, 126–8; id., *Fifteenth Century*, 41; M. K. Jones, 'John Beaufort, Duke of Somerset, and the French Expedition of 1443', in R. A. Griffiths (ed.), *Patronage, the Crown and the Provinces in Later Medieval England* (Gloucester, 1981), 81–2; C. T. Allmand, *Lancastrian Normandy, 1415–1450* (Oxford, 1983), 69–70, 76–8.

[12] McFarlane, *Nobility*, 40; Harriss, *Henry V*, 44.

[13] N. Denholm-Young, *Collected Papers on Medieval Subjects* (Cardiff, 1969), 63; Harriss, *Public Finance*, 52–4, 391–400.

Henry V in France, as opposed to individual campaigns or *chevauchées*. Two or three years after embarking on the conquest of Normandy in 1417, Henry V was already running short of knights and gentlemen skilled in the arts of war and the leadership of men—in effect soldiers of the 'officer class'— and was obliged to mount an intensive recruitment campaign, with only limited success.[14]

The granting of royal pardons to offenders on condition of military service was a well established method of recruitment in medieval England.[15] Edward I often used it in his wars against Wales, France, and Scotland. Between 1294 and 1307 thousands of fugitives, outlaws, and felons enlisted in return for general pardons, or provided substitutes to perform military service for them. This recruitment by pardon was aimed at common criminals as much as offenders of gentle birth, and soon gave rise to demands for curbing the exercise of the royal prerogative of mercy.[16] The practice continued, in spite of several statutes to the contrary, under Edward III. During the 1330s members of the Folville and Coterel gangs— the most notorious of late medieval criminal gentry—received pardons for service in the Scottish wars.[17]

By offering pardons in return for military service, therefore, Henry V adopted a well established and familiar method of recruitment. The judicial investigations of 1414 provided ample scope for such a policy, and many of the leading offenders were recruited for service on the Agincourt campaign and in the conquest of Normandy. The most striking link between the disorders and subsequent service in France is the muster roll of the earl of Arundel's retinue at the siege of Harfleur.[18] The roll reads like a catalogue of those indicted in

---

[14] Goodman, 'Requests for Military Service', 240–52. Altogether 96 gentlemen were approached, producing pledges for the military service of only 15 men; cf. *PPC* ii. 246–8, where similar attempts to recruit Norfolk gentry were entirely unsuccessful.

[15] For similar practices in the early modern period, see J. M. Beattie, *Crime and the Courts in England, 1660–1800* (Oxford, 1986), 498, 532–3.

[16] Hurnard, *King's Pardon*, 311–26.

[17] Stones, 'Folvilles', 128–9; Bellamy, *Public Order*, 86–7, 193; H. J. Hewitt, *The Organization of War under Edward III* (Manchester, 1966), 29–31. The general pardons of 1362 and 1377 were granted in peacetime and were not associated with recruitment: see Powell, 'Public Order', 219–20.   [18] E 101/47/1.

king's bench for their misdeeds in Shropshire. The list of esquires included Ralph Brereton, John Burley, Robert and Roger Corbet, Richard Lacon, and John Winsbury, six of the seven Arundel retainers whose offences were enrolled on the plea roll of king's bench at Shrewsbury. Only John Wele, the constable of Oswestry, was missing, because he was then serving on the Welsh Marches.[19] Other esquires in Arundel's retinue were William Steventon of Preston-on-the-Weald Moors, pardoned for murder in 1415; Ughtred Dod, indicted for riot in 1412; and Nicholas Peshall of Chetwynd, accused of various offences in Shropshire and Staffordshire, including assaults on the subsidy-collectors.[20] Still more revealing is the fact that these followers of Arundel were accompanied in the earl's retinue by their own servants. Among the men-at-arms and archers named in the muster roll are Roger Onslow, Thomas Pendale, and Hugh Purce, all servants of Richard Lacon; and Richard Leach and Richard Pykestoke, who served the Corbet brothers. All these men had taken part in the Shropshire disturbances and were prominent in the indictments submitted to king's bench.[21]

The superior eyre in Staffordshire also proved a successful recruiting exercise, especially among those who had participated in the Erdswick–Ferrers dispute. Edmund Ferrers led his own retinue at Agincourt, and was on active service in Normandy between 1417 and 1422, serving at the sieges of Rouen, Melun, and Meaux.[22] Hugh Erdswick's brother Robert fought under Lord Talbot at Agincourt, while his principal confederate, Thomas Giffard of Chillington, served in the earl of Arundel's retinue with two of Erdswick's retainers, Thomas Pakeman and Ralph Vickers.[23] William Mynors, who was summoned before Henry V at Burton abbey to answer for his attacks on

---

[19] Wylie and Waugh, *Henry V*, i. 456 n. 4. Wele later participated in the conquest of Normandy: E 404 (exchequer, writs and warrants for issue)/35/276; *DKR* 44, p. 616.

[20] E 101/47/1, m. 1; *Shrops. Peace Roll*, nos. 169, 173, 183, 194; JUST 1/753, mm. 11, 13, 23, 25, 33; KB 9/113, mm. 3–4; KB 27/615, Rex, m. 36d., 617, Rex, m. 26.

[21] JUST 1/753, mm. 19–33; KB 27/619, Rex, m. 28.

[22] Cokayne, *Complete Peerage*, v. 305; *DKR* 44, pp. 569, 571, 581, 589, 592, 609.

[23] Nicolas, *Agincourt*, 345; E 101/47/1, mm. 1, 2d. For Erdswick's retainers, see KB 9/113, m. 2. For Giffard's offences, see ibid., mm. 32, 41–2; KB 27/614, Rex, m. 16. Giffard's brother John also served under Arundel. He had been indicted for murder before the superior eyre in 1414 and was pardoned in the summer of 1415: KB 9/113, mm. 32, 46; KB 27/617, Rex, m. 15.

Lancastrian tenants in Staffordshire, served at Agincourt in the king's household retinue. He took part in the conquest of Normandy, and after Henry's death remained in France to become a mainstay of the Lancastrian occupation and one of Lord Talbot's chief lieutenants.[24] Thomas Stanley of Elford, who was fined £60 at Lichfield in 1414 for unlawful retaining, had the fine remitted when he took his entire retinue with him to serve in the garrison of Calais in 1416.[25]

A similar pattern of recruitment can be seen in all the regions visited by the king's justices in 1413–14. In 1415 a force of 10 men-at-arms and 500 archers was sent from the newly reconciled shires of Cardigan and Carmarthen in south Wales, led by three former rebels, Griffith Don, David ap Ieuan ap Trahaiarn, and Meredith ab Owen ap Griffith.[26] Griffith Don, the grandson of Henry Don, a leading supporter of Glendower in the south, was pardoned in 1413, fought at Agincourt, and went on to enjoy a long and successful military career in France, acquiring estates in Alençon from the duke of York.[27] Two of the protagonists in the Tuxford–Meering dispute in Nottinghamshire, William Meering and Ralph Cromwell, gave long and distinguished service in France.[28] Several of the Devon men indicted before the commissions of 1414 served the king at sea.[29] John Hawley of Dartmouth donated one of his ships, the *Craccher*, to the navy, served in the king's retinue on the Agincourt campaign, and commanded

---

[24] Nicolas, *Agincourt*, 351; SC 1 (ancient correspondence)/43/60; Pollard, 'Family of Talbot', 289.

[25] KB 9/113, mm. 11, 28, 41; KB 27/613, fines section, m. 4; *CPR, 1413–16*, p. 403.

[26] E 101/46, m. 20; Griffiths, *Principality of Wales*, 201, 273–4, 298. Other former Welsh rebels who served in France were John Lloyd and John ap Rhys ap David: ibid. 292, 326–7.

[27] Don was lieutenant of Cherbourg by 1424, and successively captain of Carentan, Tancarville, Lisieux, and Neufchâtel. His three sons all fought in France, and one, Sir John Don, rose in Yorkist service to become a councillor of Edward IV: Griffiths, *Principality of Wales*, 187, 201.

[28] Nicolas, *Agincourt*, 378, 382; E 101/45/4, m. 11; 45/18, m. 5; 50/6, 9; *DKR* 41, pp. 715, 717–18, 720, 797.

[29] Tyldesley, 'Devon and Cornwall', 11, 202, 222–3; Cherry, 'Political community in Devonshire', 211–13. John Foxley, William Tracy, John Sampson, Thomas Rake, and Robert Tiler, mariners indicted for piracy and other offences, served in Henry V's navy, as did Stephen Sherman of Rye (see ch. 8 at n. 42): KB 9/205/2, m. 3; 205/3, mm. 112, 131–2; E 101/44/30/1; 48/9, mm. 3, 7d; *DKR* 44, pp. 570, 572, 579, 604, 609.

Channel patrol fleets later in the reign.[30] Finally Richard
Colfox, Oldcastle's accomplice in the Lollard revolt, and Sir
Thomas Chaworth, also implicated in the rising, both fought
on the Agincourt campaign—Chaworth in the king's retinue
and Colfox under the duke of Gloucester.[31] A clear correlation
therefore exists between criminal prosecution and subsequent
military service during Henry V's reign. We must, however,
guard against exaggerating the significance of this phenomenon,
and assuming a simple cause and effect between indictment
and recruitment. Henry V did not have to rely on convict
armies. The king's authority and abilities were such as to
persuade virtually the entire able-bodied aristocracy to serve
with him in France.[32] Magnates like John Talbot and Ralph
Cromwell would probably have joined royal expeditions
abroad even if they had not fallen foul of the law courts, and
the muster-lists for Agincourt and the Norman campaigns
carry the names of thousands of men for whom no criminal
record can be traced. Unlike Edward I, Henry V did not
resort to the large-scale recruitment of common criminals. Yet
he did face shortages of manpower as the campaigns wore on,
particularly among the 'officer class' of knights and gentry.
These were exactly the classes over whom Henry was
determined to reassert control through the judicial visitations
of 1413–15, and indictments against them provided the king
with leverage to enlist them for long spells of military service.
The pardoning of rebels and other serious offenders was a
calculated risk, but one which was often repaid, not merely by
attendance on a single campaign, but by years of loyal and
strenuous service. Henry V's successful use of this policy is
exemplified by the rehabilitation of two notorious offenders,
Nicholas Burdet and Thomas Barnby, whose careers deserve
detailed examination.

Sir Thomas Burdet of Arrow in Warwickshire, and his son
Nicholas, were members of a substantial Midland knightly
family with long-standing ties of service to the earls of

---

[30] *Navy of the Lancastrian Kings*, 36–7, 50–1, 250; Tyldesley, 'Devon and Cornwall',
11; *DKR* 44, pp. 566, 610, 616.
[31] See ch. 6 at nn. 92, 95; Nicolas, *Agincourt*, 333; E 101/44/30/1; *DKR* 44, p. 561.
[32] Harriss, *Henry V*, 40–4; Allmand, *Lancastrian Normandy*, 246–51.

Warwick.[33] During the reign of Henry V they became embroiled in a series of violent disputes with other landowners in the west Midlands which brought them constantly before the courts.[34] In June 1413, Nicholas Burdet and his followers murdered two of the tenants of Worcester cathedral priory at Shipston-on-Stour.[35] Nicholas fled to Ireland, returning only after his father had submitted to arbitration supervised by the earl of Warwick. Sir Thomas made out a recognizance to the earl for 300 marks that he and his son would keep the peace towards the prior and his tenants, and Nicholas was made to perform an elaborate penance in Worcester cathedral.[36] Nicholas presented a general pardon in king's bench at Easter 1415, and was recruited into the retinue of the duke of Gloucester for the Agincourt campaign.[37] After his return from France, however, the Burdets were soon in trouble again. Late in 1417 they raided the manors of Evesham abbey at Lenchwick, Offenham, and Norton in Worcestershire, wrecking the abbot's mill at Lenchwick and assaulting his servants. They were immediately indicted before the justices of the peace, and in February 1418 a special oyer and terminer commission was issued, before which the abbot sued the Burdets and their servants for damages.[38] The two sides came to terms in September 1418.[39] The suit of the Crown against the Burdets remained to be resolved; given the growing shortage of gentlemen on active service in France, they were obvious candidates for recruitment. Indictments against them

[33] W. Dugdale, *The Antiquities of Warwickshire* (2nd edn., revised by W. Thomas; London 1730), ii. 846–9. Sir Thomas was a life retainer of Richard Beauchamp: BL Egerton Roll, 8772 (foreign expenses).

[34] Putnam, *Early Treatises*, 68–72, 89–90; Carpenter, 'Political Society', 125. I am indebted to Dr Carpenter for providing me with much valuable information on the Burdets. In 1408 Sir Thomas Burdet had been involved in a violent brawl in Alcester market with tenants of his master, Richard Beauchamp, from Tanworth, which necessitated the mediation of the earl's council: BL Egerton Roll 8772 (foreign expenses).

[35] KB 9/202, mm. 42–4. *CPR, 1413–16*, p. 111.

[36] HMC, *Fifth Report* (London, 1876), i. 303.

[37] E 101/45/13, m. 3d.

[38] *CPR, 1416–22*, p. 147; KB 9/1038/3; KB 9/1056, mm. 3–7; *CCR, 1413–19*, p. 448.

[39] Proceedings against the Burdets before the oyer and terminer were dropped after the grant of a *licencia interloquendi*, but the abbot was awarded 1,000 marks in damages against several of their servants, who were arrested and gaoled at Worcester: KB 9/1038/3, mm. 27–8.

were summoned into king's bench in 1419. When Sir Thomas
and Nicholas appeared, in Hilary 1420, they were bailed on
condition that they served in France with the duke of
Bedford.[40]

In Bedford's service Nicholas Burdet's career underwent a
dramatic transformation. He saw almost continuous service in
France until his death at the siege of Pontoise in 1441,
establishing a reputation as one of the most redoubtable of
Lancastrian captains. He served with distinction at the battle
of Verneuil in 1424, and was rewarded with the offices of chief
butler of Normandy and *bailli* of the Cotentin. Immediately
after Verneuil he was given command of the siege of Mont-St-
Michel on the border between Normandy and Brittany.[41] His
most famous exploit, which became legendary, was the rout of
a large force under Arthur de Richemont, brother of the duke
of Brittany and constable of France, at the siege of St James de
Beuvron in March 1426. With about eighty men Burdet led a
sortie which threw the French into headlong retreat, leaving
behind some 800 casualties and their entire artillery and
baggage train.[42] Burdet became a trusted servant of Bedford's,
acting as the Regent's lieutenant at Rouen and witnessing his
will in 1435.[43] His martial exploits won him a considerable
posthumous reputation as a paragon of chivalry, so that, by a
pleasing irony, the former bane of the Worcestershire JPs was
glorified in the sixteenth-century *Mirror for Magistrates*.[44]

The conquest and defence of Normandy required able
administrators as well as good soldiers, and an obvious choice
was Thomas Barnby, who as chamberlain of north Wales
from 1406 until his dismissal in 1414 had extensive experience
of wartime administration. Henry V clearly thought well of

[40] KB 27/635, Rex, mm. 9, 22; Putnam, *Early Treatises*, 72. They were finally tried
and acquitted *nisi prius* at Worcester in 1422.

[41] BL Harley MS 782, fos. 51b, 53; BL Add. Ch. 320–1, 6820; Allmand, *Lancastrian
Normandy*, 30; Jacob, *Fifteenth Century*, 244–5.

[42] Jean de Waurin, *Recueil des Croniques et Anchiennes Istories de la Grant Bretaigne à
Present Nommé Engleterre, 1422–1431*, ed. W. Hardy, Rolls Ser. (London, 1879), 228–30;
The Mirror for Magistrates, ed. L. B. Campbell (Cambridge, 1938), 467–9; A. H.
Burne, *The Agincourt War* (London, 1956), 220–1.

[43] BL Add. Ch. 11827; *Testamenta Vetusta*, ed. N. H. Nicolas (2 vols.; London, 1826)
ii. 243; R. A. Newhall, *Muster and Review* (Cambridge, Mass., 1940), 20, 86–7, 110.

[44] Allmand, *Lancastrian Normandy*, 267; *Mirror for Magistrates*, 463–82; Putnam, *Early
Treatises*, 69–72.

his abilities, in spite of the charges of treason and corruption levelled against him in 1414.[45] In January 1416, less than two years after his ignominious dismissal at Caernarvon, the king appointed him to the onerous post of treasurer of Harfleur, the Norman port captured the previous September.[46] The office carried a salary of £100 per annum, the same as the treasurer of Calais, with travel expenses of 10s. a day for journeys on royal business. As treasurer Barnby was responsible for the muster and payment of the garrison, and for supervising the reconstruction and maintenance of the town's fortifications. The post also involved frequent consultation with the council and sometimes with the king himself. In April 1416, as the French prepared to besiege the town by land and sea, Barnby was sent by the captain of Harfleur, Thomas Beaufort, earl of Dorset, to report to the king and council and to bring back wages for the garrison. Owing to the French blockade, which was not lifted until Bedford's naval victory in mid-August, Barnby did not return to Harfleur until early September; when he did so, it was with nearly £3,000 in cash for the garrison's wages. When Henry V made his second landing in Normandy in August 1417, Barnby met him at Touques to report on Harfleur and its defences.[47] He was treasurer of Harfleur until January 1420, serving occasionally on commissions of array in Normandy. Early in Henry VI's reign he was appointed constable of Bordeaux and treasurer of Gascony, posts which he held until his death in 1427.[48]

Burdet and Barnby were not the only men who redeemed their offences by loyal service in France: other serious offenders in 1414—Edmund Ferrers, William Mynors, Griffith Don, and William Meering—pursued lengthy military careers in France, some for the duration of the Lancastrian occupation. At a higher level Henry secured a similar commitment from the heirs of old opponents of his father; for both Thomas Montague, earl of Salisbury, and John Holland, earl of Huntingdon, loyal service in the French wars was the means

---

[45] See ch. 8 at nn. 27–9.

[46] *DKR* 44, p. 576; Griffiths, 'Glyn Dŵr Rebellion', 168; Nicolas, *Agincourt*, 53–63. Barnby's accounts as treasurer of Harfleur survive at E 101/48/7–8.

[47] E 101/48/7, fos. 26–7; 48/8, m. 1. See *Gesta Henrici Quinti*, 144–9.

[48] Griffiths, 'Glyn Dŵr Rebellion', 168; *DKR* 44, pp. 314, 324, 372; E101/48/7, fo. 26.

of recovering the estates and titles forfeited by their fathers.[49] Such a long-term commitment was what the Lancastrians required for the consolidation of their hold on France, and in these terms Henry V's policy of conciliation paid off handsomely.[50]

Henry's firm but conciliatory policy was equally successful in keeping the peace at home, as is shown by the lack of serious disorder in England during the king's long absences abroad between 1415 and 1422.[51] His programme of law enforcement was greatly facilitated by the judicious use of pardons conditional upon military service, which removed troublemakers from the localities and provided a constructive outlet for their energies. It would be an exaggeration to say that the battle of Agincourt was won in the courtrooms of king's bench, but there is no doubt that in order to explain Henry's successes in France we must first assess his achievement in restoring order in England.

PUBLIC ORDER AND CONCILIATION IN LOCAL SOCIETY

Thus far this chapter has adopted a 'king's-eye view' of the restoration of public order, and considered the problem largely in terms of the reassertion of royal authority. But what was the impact of Henry's policies upon local society? Did the judicial visitations of 1413–15 have a purely cosmetic effect, creating the illusion of vigorous action without any substantial results, or did they genuinely benefit the shires in which they took place by reducing the levels of violence and disorder? If public order were to be restored, it was not enough for conciliation to take place merely between the king and those who broke his peace; it also had to take place locally, amongst the warring parties whose feuding had first given rise to the disorder. The local communities of late medieval England were largely self-governing.[52] The Crown relied upon the co-operation of local society at all levels, and in particular the landowning classes, to keep the peace and administer the legal system. Extra-judicial procedures such as arbitration were used extensively and were useful in settling complex territorial

[49] Harriss, *Henry V*, 38–40.   [50] Allmand, *Lancastrian Normandy*, 1–80.
[51] See ch. 10.   [52] See ch. 4 at nn. 2–21.

disputes. If the local community failed to contain and resolve conflicts arising within it, it was the king's duty to intervene as an impartial arbiter, and to create conditions in which disputes could be settled peacefully.

The success of such interventions by Henry V may be gauged by examining a number of attempts at local conflict resolution which took place both before and after 1414. Mediation and arbitration procedures were often used in an effort to settle the disputes which had arisen. But whereas they were ineffective or inconclusive in their results before 1414, they appear to have succeeded after the king's intervention. At the height of the Erdswick–Ferrers dispute in Staffordshire in the autumn of 1413 an unsuccessful attempt was made to persuade the parties to accept arbitration.[53] Preliminary negotiations leading to a loveday were carried out by mediators, who included the Lancastrian retainers Sir William Newport and Robert Babthorpe, and the prominent diocesan official, Walter Bullock.[54] Six arbitrators were chosen, each side selecting three, and the earl of Warwick was nominated *nonpar* or umpire. This arbitration was also intended to resolve differences which had arisen between the Erdswicks and Richard Peshall of Chetwynd, who was associated with Ferrers, and between Ferrers and Thomas Giffard of Chillington, one of Erdswick's main allies. Erdswick and Ferrers both took out bonds of 500 marks to observe the award and to keep the peace until it had been made. The bonds were deposited with Walter Bullock for safe-keeping. A time and place was fixed for the arbitration. Each side was to bring no more than fifty supporters, of whom not more than four were to be knights and not more than twenty gentlemen. The arbitrators were prominent in local society: Erdswick chose his uncle William Venables, and the leading Derbyshire knights Sir Thomas Gresley and Sir John Cockayne; on Ferrers's side there were Sir Humphrey Stafford, predisposed against Erdswick by property disputes,[55] the powerful Lancastrian Sir

[53] CP 40/615, m. 342, calendared in *Collections for Hist. of Staffs.*, 51.

[54] *RP* iv. 32. Bullock was appointed a custodian of the see of Lichfield during the vacancy of 1414–15, and was the vicar-general of Bishop John Catterick between 1415 and 1419: *CPR, 1413–16*, p. 191; Lichfield Joint Record Office, B/A/1/8.

[55] JUST 1/814, m. 3.

John Bagot, whose manor at Blithbury Erdswick had raided a few years earlier,[56] and a lawyer, John Savage.

These negotiations between Erdswick and Ferrers represented a concerted effort on the part of the gentry community to contain a violent dispute and to exert pressure on the protagonists to accept a peaceful solution.[57] The effort failed. Before the arbitrators were able to determine their award, feuding again broke out, culminating in the murder of Ferrers's servant Ralph Page by Erdswick's men at Easter 1414.[58] It took the visit of king's bench to Staffordshire and the king's enlistment of Edmund Ferrers on the Agincourt campaign to put an end to the violence. No record survives of a formal reconciliation between Erdswick and Ferrers, but there was no recurrence of the feuding later in Henry V's reign, and the abandonment of the appeal of Page's widow against the Erdswicks in Hilary term 1415 may indicate that some form of compensation was made.[59]

Shropshire and Nottinghamshire provide two good examples of arbitration completed after 1414 which put an end to disorder dating from Henry IV's reign. In Nottinghamshire the initial course of the Tuxford–Meering dispute in 1410–11 was similar to the Erdswick–Ferrers case in Staffordshire. Lovedays were held and arbitrators were named, but these negotiations, far from promoting peace, increased tension between the parties.[60] The arbitrators nominated by each side were partisan, and appear to have exploited the dispute for their own ends. By contrast with Staffordshire, however, the violence did not continue to escalate, although the case was actively pursued both inside and outside the courtroom. The assize of novel disseisin brought by Meering against Tuxford in 1412 was accompanied by inconclusive attempts at arbitration. In 1416, after further litigation and a petition submitted by Meering on the matter to the Parliament of March 1416, the parties were apparently prevailed upon to attempt arbitration once more: the arbitrators chosen, Sir

[56] KB 9/113, m. 47d.

[57] Cf. the claim made by Erdswick in his petition to Parliament in 1414 that a murderous assault on him by Ferrers was averted only through the mediation of Sir Thomas Gresley.

[58] See ch. 8 at nn. 108–14.

[59] KB 27/613, m. 25–6d.	[60] See ch. 8 at nn. 194–5.

Thomas Rempstone and Sir John Ashton, were knights of the shire present at this Parliament.[61] Meering non-suited in the assize, in which judgment had been rendered in his favour but never executed, and in November 1416 an award was concluded which, while it favoured Merring, allowed Tuxford a life estate in a moiety of the disputed lands with reversion to Meering and his heirs.[62]

A notable arbitration award survives from Shropshire in the aftermath of the superior eyre. In 1414 and 1415 the king sent most of the malcontents abroad. John Talbot was accompanied to Ireland by his servant John Bruyn, who had been the particular object of attack by the Arundel affinity. After Arundel's death Bruyn felt it safe to return to Shropshire, and in 1417 was able to make peace with his enemies in Bridgnorth.[63] Through the mediation of mutual friends, the parties submitted their differences to four arbitrators, the abbot of Shrewsbury, the prior of Wenlock, George Hawkstone, and William Burley.[64] Mutual bonds of £200 to observe the award were exchanged, and placed in the safe-keeping of the prior. Completing their award at Bridgnorth on 30 July 1417, the arbitrators ordered that peace should henceforth be maintained between the men of Bridgnorth and John Bruyn, his servants, and followers. They then awarded Bruyn twenty marks in compensation for the malicious indictments which his enemies had laid against him in 1414. Bruyn and his servant John Cardmaker were ordered to pay a total of nine marks in damages for injuries inflicted on their opponents. All the damages awarded were to be paid within a prescribed period.

The completion of this award was undoubtedly facilitated by the death of Arundel and the new ascendancy of the Talbots in Shropshire.[65] Three of the arbitrators had close links with Talbot: the prior of Wenlock had enjoyed his support over Powkesmoor in 1413, while Hawkstone and

---

[61] *RP* iv. 73; *CCR, 1413–19*, pp. 373–4.

[62] *CPR, 1416–22*, pp. 54–5; CP 25(1) (court of common pleas, feet of fines)/186/38/6.

[63] Nat. Lib. Wales, Pitchford Hall Deeds, no. 2492.

[64] Hawkstone was a leading member of the affinity of John Talbot, Lord Furnival, and prominent in Shrops. county administration: Pollard, 'Family of Talbot', 233–4. For Burley, see ch. 8 at n. 186.

[65] See ch. 8 at nn. 183–7.

Burley were members of his affinity.[66] The award thus illustrates how shifts in the balance of power in local politics could influence the resolution of conflict. Nevertheless the settlement, though leaning in Bruyn's favour, was not totally one-sided. The falsity of the indictments previously laid against him was acknowledged, and financial compensation paid, but nearly half the sum awarded had to be returned as damages for injuries committed by Bruyn and his men. The emphasis, above all, was upon the restoration of peace and harmony.

The king himself was not actively involved in arranging the awards in Nottinghamshire and Shropshire, but there were occasions, as the story from the *Brut* chronicle suggests, when he intervened personally in settling particularly intractable disputes. A case in point was the struggle for power in King's Lynn in Norfolk. Lynn had long been ruled by a merchant oligarchy, known as the *potentiores*, who controlled elections to office and appointments to the town council. In the early fifteenth century, however, they were challenged by an alliance of the *mediocres*, or burgesses outside the mercantile elite, and the *inferiores*, or non-burgesses. The efforts of these groups to gain a say in the town's government were supported by the bishop of Norwich, the traditional opponent of the *potentiores*.[67] In 1411 the parties submitted their differences to eighteen arbitrators selected from each group, and their award was confirmed by a decree in chancery in 1412.[68] The most contentious issue was the procedure for election of the mayor, which was the subject of a separate arbitration award in 1412.[69]

The two mayors elected under the new procedure in 1412 and 1413 were drawn from the *mediocres*, and they proceeded to admit large numbers of *inferiores* as burgesses without the customary payment. The *potentiores*, fearing that they might permanently lose their traditional authority, challenged these

---

[66] Pollard, 'Family of Talbot', 229–34.

[67] M. Green, *Town Life in the Fifteenth Century* (2 vols.; London, 1894), ii. 403–20.

[68] William Asshebourne, *William Asshebourne's Book*, ed. D. M. Owen, Norfolk Record Soc., 48 (Norwich, 1981), nos. 31, 109, 146–7; D. M. Owen (ed.), *The Making of King's Lynn*, British Academy, Records of Social and Economic History, New Ser., 9 (London, 1984), no. 443; HMC, *Eleventh Report* (London, 1887), Appendix, iii. 191–4.

[69] *Asshebourne's Book*, nos. 136, 144.

admissions, and when one of their number, John Lakenheath, was elected in 1414, set up an inquiry.[70] There were riots in the town in January 1415, and the mayor was summoned to appear before the king and council. Upon receiving an account of the disorders, Henry ordered that the dispute be settled through negotiations conducted by six from each party, and that the result be reported to him a fortnight after Easter.[71] These negotiations, if attempted, were inconclusive, and in June the men of Lynn submitted their disputes to the award of the bishop of Norwich and the earl of Dorset, Thomas Beaufort.[72] The town was now so divided that, in an attempt to prevent the disturbances which an election might provoke, the government appointed Thomas Hunt, one of the *potentiores*, as mayor. This action merely exacerbated tension, however, and when a royal serjeant-at-arms appeared at Lynn on election day (29 August) to enforce the order, he was assaulted by a mob of *inferiores* and forced to proclaim the election of their candidate, John Bilney.[73] The government tried to prevent further irregularities by ordering the incumbent, Robert Brunham, to remain in office, but at Michaelmas, when the new mayor was traditionally installed, the *inferiores* again gathered and forced Brunham to swear in Bilney as his successor.[74]

It may be significant that the disorders in Lynn occurred while Henry V was abroad on the Agincourt campaign. If he had been at home he would hardly have tolerated such defiance of royal authority twice within a month. After the king's return, Hunt was finally recognized as mayor and a commission of inquiry was dispatched to investigate the disturbances. In 1416 more than forty offenders were indicted, of whom thirty were brought before king's bench and fined.[75] The king summoned representatives of the disputing factions

[70] Ibid., nos. 29, 236, 280; *King's Lynn*, nos. 444, 446.

[71] Ibid., no. 445; *Asshebourne's Book*, nos. 212–13, 284.

[72] Ibid., nos. 232, 319.   [73] KB 9/188, mm. 9–11.

[74] The riotous installation of Bilney was graphically related by William Asshebourne, the common clerk of Lynn: *Asshebourne's Book*, no. 282; *King's Lynn*, no. 447.

[75] *CPR, 1413–16*, p. 411; KB 9/188, mm. 9–11; KB 27/621, fines section, m. 1d; *Asshebourne's Book*, nos. 269, 273, 314, 322–3; *King's Lynn*, no. 447 (p. 400). The accused were all craftsmen, and almost half had been admitted as burgesses between 1412 and 1414; cf. ibid., no. 446, with KB 9/188, m. 9.

before him and instructed them to reach a quick settlement.[76] In June 1416, after five years of conflict, the warring factions in Lynn finally made peace, on terms highly favourable to the *potentiores*. The new ordinances for the town's government and for mayoral elections were revoked, and the traditional procedures restored. The claims of the *mediocres* were recognized by the establishment of a common council consisting of three burgesses from each of the town's nine wards, and this detached them from their alliance with the *inferiores*, who lost the voice they had briefly enjoyed in Lynn's affairs.[77]

Henry V's judicial visitations therefore served as a catalyst for the restoration of order and stability in local society. Since the Crown as yet lacked the power to enforce order by coercion, the maintenance of the peace depended upon a fragile consensus involving the king, the magnates, and the gentry communities in the shires. The full penalties of the law were not routinely invoked except for the most heinous of crimes, as witness the executions of the Lollard rebels and the conspirators in the earl of Cambridge's plot. Otherwise the royal judicial machinery was principally directed towards creating the stable and ordered conditions in which conciliation and the private resolution of disputes could flourish. The king represented the final guarantor of order, the ultimate *nonpar* in the settlement of disputes. As in 1414, he might use the judicial machinery to urge the warring factions in local society towards peaceful reconciliation; in the last resort, however, public order rested not on institutions but on the character and the personal authority of the king. The proceedings of 1413–15 are infused with Henry V's personality, and it was largely through his vigour and shrewd political management that order and 'bone governance' were restored throughout the realm.

---

[76] HMC, *11th Report*, 197; Green, *Town Life*, ii. 417–18.

[77] HMC, *11th Report*, 195–203; Green, *Town Life*, ii. 417–20. For a similar dispute in Norwich settled by arbitration in 1415, see ibid., ii. 371–86; *The Records of the City of Norwich*, ed. W. Hudson and J. C. Tingey (2 vols.; Norwich and London, 1906), i, pp. lviii–lxxiii.

The Administration of Justice, 1415–1422: The Limits of Law Enforcement

THE WINTER of 1414–15 marked the end of the first phase of Henry V's reign. Until then the king had concentrated on establishing his authority and restoring public order. At the Westminster Parliament of November 1414 the chancellor's speech signalled Henry's intention to recover his inheritance in France, and a double subsidy was granted for that purpose in return for a general pardon.[1] For the remainder of the reign, the king was preoccupied with the war. All other business, including judicial administration, was subordinated to this over-riding goal.[2] Never again was Henry V able to devote so much of his attention to law and order as in 1414.

JUDICIAL ADMINISTRATION DURING THE FRENCH WARS

The judicial visitations of 1413–14 were themselves a necessary preparation for war in that, by settling the realm, they were designed to enable the king to wage war abroad without fear of insurrection or disorder at home. Henry did not need reminding of the dangers of leaving an unsettled realm to seek foreign conquests. As a boy he had accompanied Richard II on his expedition to Ireland in 1399, an absence which allowed his father, Henry of Lancaster, time to slip back into England and acquire support sufficient to usurp the throne.[3] In this respect the visitations, coupled with the twin policies of conciliation and recruitment, were outstandingly successful, as the years after 1415 were to show.

---

[1] *RP* iv. 35; C 67/37, m. 60. See ch. 7 at n. 91.
[2] For the course of the war, see Jacob, *Fifteenth Century*, 141–210; Allmand, *Lancastrian Normandy*, 1–23.
[3] See E. Powell, 'The Restoration of Law and Order', in G. L. Harriss (ed.), *Henry V: the Practice of Kingship*, (Oxford, 1985), 53.

As the king turned his energies towards military matters from 1415 onwards, a slackening in the pace of judicial activity was inevitable. The recruitment for foreign service of many of the leading protagonists in the local disturbances before 1414 also served to relieve the pressure on the courts. The diversion of royal interest from the problem of law and order is reflected by the comparative slackness of business in king's bench during 1415 and 1416. Cases arising from the 1414 inquiries gradually worked their way through the system, their passage eased by the free availability of the general pardon, but there was no new business on the same scale.[4]

In one important respect, the reopening of the French war disrupted judicial administration during the remainder of Henry V's reign. In the summer of 1415, and again between 1417 and 1421, the king's council issued ordinances suspending all possessory assize proceedings, in order to protect the legal interests of those landowners serving in France.[5] Although the ordinances were directly concerned only with civil litigation, they indirectly affected criminal justice because assize business was associated with gaol delivery in the work of the biannual judicial circuits, which formed one of the principal links between central government and the localities. The suspension of assize proceedings disrupted the routine of circuit visitations and consequently the delivery of county gaols in spring and summer by judges of the central courts.[6]

[4] KB 27/615–22, Rex sections, *passim*.

[5] *PPC* ii. 166–7; 9 Henry V st. 1 c. 3; 'Calendar of General and Special Assize and General Gaol Delivery Commissions on the Dorses of the Patent Rolls: Henry IV and Henry V', unpublished PRO list, 226–7. Dr R. F. Hunnisett of the PRO kindly allowed me to consult this list, which has been completed but is not yet available in the search rooms. The suspension was removed at the request of Parliament in 1421: see below at n. 77.

[6] While the assizes were suspended, civil assize business was dealt with in chancery, a phenomenon which contributed to the development of the chancellor's equitable jurisdiction. For examples of individual cases, see C 1/5/39 (*CCR, 1419–22*, p. 74); C 1/5/129 (*CCR, 1419–22*, pp. 72–3); C 1/5/151 (*CCR, 1419–22*, p. 169); C 1/5/171 (*CCR, 1419–22*, p. 85). See also L. O. Pike, 'Common Law and Conscience in the Ancient Court of Chancery', *LQR* 1 (1885), 443–54; A. D. Hargreaves, 'Equity and the Latin Side of Chancery', *LQR* 68 (1952), 489–90. Miss Avery, in her study of the early history of equity, asserted that until the mid-1420s chancery dealt with large numbers of cases involving violence and riot: 'Equitable Jurisdiction', 132–3. In fact very little criminal business appears in the proceedings before Henry V's chancellors, Henry Beaufort and Thomas Langley (C 1/4–6). The annual total of surviving

The dislocation of the assize circuits is most apparent from the fragmentary survival of their proceedings during Henry V's reign.[7] Circuit records were not systematically kept between 1415 and 1421, an omission which apparently reflects the temporary interruption or discontinuation of the circuits themselves. No gaol delivery records of any kind survive for the home circuit under Henry V, and only on the Midland circuit is there clear evidence that sessions continued with any regularity between 1415 and 1422, albeit only once a year.[8] Some circuit activity, however, did continue. Throughout the reign the customary practice was maintained whereby two central court judges or serjeants were appointed to the bench of each county within a given circuit. Thus John Cockayne and James Strangways were appointed JPs in every shire of the Midland circuit between 1413 and 1422; while Robert Tirwhit and William Lodington served on the northern circuit from 1413 until Lodington's death in 1420, when he was replaced by John Preston, formerly on the Oxford circuit.[9] The involvement of these judges in judicial administration at local level, even after 1417, is suggested by their appointment to various circuit commissions and their involvement in criminal trials referred back to the locality from king's bench under *nisi prius* proceedings.[10]

petitions averages less than fifty during these years, and in so far as criminal matters came into chancery they most frequently took the form of allegations of maintenance and corruption of justice: e.g. C 1/5/40, 44, 47, 51, 54, 65, 85–7, 100. See R. L. Storey, *Thomas Langley and the Bishopric of Durham, 1406–1437* (London, 1961), 41–2; G. L. Harriss, *Cardinal Beaufort: A Study of Lancastrian Ascendancy and Decline* (Oxford, 1988), 72–6. See also below at n. 17

[7] JUST 1/1524–33; D. Crook, 'List of Assize Rolls, 1206–1481', unpublished PRO reading room list (1984), 184–7; JUST 3/195–200.

[8] JUST 3/195: circuit justices delivered the gaols of Leicester, Northampton, Nottingham, and Warwick annually during the Lent vacation between 1416 and 1420, although Lincoln, which was normally part of the circuit, was separately administered. Cf. *CPR, 1416–22*, pp. 205–6.

[9] *CPR, 1413–16*, pp. 416–26; *1416–22*, pp. 449–63. Cf. Powell, 'Criminal Justice', 49–59.

[10] *CPR, 1416–22*, pp. 205–6; C 66 (chancery, patent rolls)/401, mm. 11d, 12d; 402, m. 31d. For criminal proceedings at *nisi prius*, see KB 27/628, Rex, m. 18; 630, Rex, mm. 10d, 16d; 631, Rex, m. 9d; 632, Rex, mm. 4, 12d, 14, 16d. Central court judges might also hold *nisi prius* proceedings in their own home counties where they were JPs but not circuit judges, e.g. William Hankford in Devon and Robert Tirwhit in Lincs: KB 27/626, Rex, m. 20; 627, Rex, m. 8 (Hankford); 629, Rex, m. 13; 630, Rex, m. 6d (Tirwhit). During the early fifteenth century the government had great difficulty in

The paucity of records makes it very difficult to assess what provision was made after 1415 for the exercise of the Crown's jurisdiction over felony, which was normally handled through gaol delivery commissions to the assize justices.[11] It seems likely that during the intervening periods felony trials were being conducted either by JPs exercising their recognized determining powers, or by *ad hoc* commissions empowered to conduct a single gaol delivery.[12] The evidence of the Worcestershire JPs' manual of *c*.1422 suggests that JPs played an important part in gaol delivery during Henry V's reign, while commissions to local men for single deliveries became increasingly frequent from the second half of 1416 onwards.[13]

The disruption of the assizes and the lack of circuit records imply a decline in central supervision over the administration of criminal justice between 1415 and 1421. On the other hand, there is evidence that the king and his council took measures to maintain central control. Between 1418 and the end of the reign the terms of the peace commission were modified to ensure that a justice of the central courts or of assize, and not merely a member of the quorum, should be present for the determination of all cases of felony.[14] The rule must have been enforced, for in the Parliament of May 1421 the Commons complained of its restrictiveness, and requested the observance of the statute of 1394, which provided that two local men of law should be appointed to the quorum of peace commissions to deliver thieves and felons.[15] In addition many royal judges

securing the appointment of serjeants at law, who assisted central court judges in assize work, and from whose ranks judges were selected. Under Henry V a group of apprentices-at-law resisted appointment for several years until summoned before Parliament in 1417 and compelled to assume the office: Baker, *Serjeants at Law*, 28–38. Possibly this state of affairs resulted from the campaign against the retaining of royal judges in the late fourteenth century, which may have reduced the income of serjeants from private clients, and thus made the office financially unattractive: see Introduction at nn. 84–8.

[11] See ch. 2 at nn. 46–69. Circuit visitations were probably conducted as usual during the Lent vacation in 1415, 1416, and 1417, and began again in the summer of 1421: JUST 1/1524, 1528–31; JUST 3/195, 197, 198.

[12] Gollancz, 'Gaol Delivery', 85–96.

[13] Putnam, *Early Treatises*, 88–9; *CPR, 1416–22*, p. 81; C 66/399–403. The enrolment of gaol delivery commissions on the dorses of the patent rolls virtually ceases after 1420.

[14] Putnam, *Justices of the Peace*, p. xxvi.

[15] 17 Richard II c. 10; *RP* iv. 146. A justice of the quorum was added as an alternative to the other justices in May 1422: Putnam, *Justices of the Peace*, p. xxvi.

and serjeants were very active within their own home counties as JPs, special commissioners, and judges at *nisi prius*.[16]

Further evidence of the government's determination to maintain its supervision of local justice lies in its concern with cases involving judicial corruption and malpractice.[17] King's bench and the king's council were actively involved in the investigation of such abuses, summoning suspects and officials for interrogation, and examining documentary evidence. A full-scale judicial inquiry was precipitated by the parliamentary petition of an Oxfordshire gentleman, Thomas Clare, in 1417.[18] He complained that he had been falsely indicted and outlawed in Northamptonshire, and in response to his petition the JPs, coroners, under-sheriff, and indicting jurors were called before king's bench, together with the records relating to the case. The justices noticed that the original indictment had been tampered with.[19] An examination of the officials pointed to the misconduct of the under-sheriff, John Thornton, who eventually confessed that he had conspired to secure Clare's outlawry on false charges in order to obstruct his lawsuits against Thornton's master Sir Thomas Green, the sheriff of Northamptonshire in 1416–17.[20]

Officials were examined before the king's council in two other cases involving forged indictments. In 1421 the chancellor himself interrogated Thomas Whitley, a Northumberland coroner, who had indicted a fellow coroner, Nicholas Turpin, as accessory to the murder by Scottish raiders of Walter Michelson, a steward of the duke of Bedford.[21] The Worcestershire coroner William Spetchley had been examined by the council the previous year over a false indictment returned in

---

[16] See above, n. 10.
[17] Cf. McFarlane, *Nobility*, 118, and below at n. 72.
[18] KB 27/629, Rex, m. 9.
[19] The indictment survives in KB 145/5/6/1, unnumbered membrane.
[20] *List of Sheriffs for England and Wales*, PRO Lists and Indexes, 9 (London, 1898), 93. The indictment against Clare was declared null and void. See ch. 3 at nn. 23–5, 49–50.
[21] KB 9/216/2, m. 5; KB 27/644, Rex, m. 4; 649, Rex, m. 16; *PPC* ii. 308. This is a baffling case. Turpin claimed to have held the inquest upon Michelson's body himself, and that Whitley's inquest was unauthorized and malicious. The notes of Whitley's examination are so abbreviated as to make their meaning obscure. The charges against Turpin were dismissed, but he was removed from office shortly afterwards: *CCR, 1419–22*, p. 247.

his name by John Russell and Roger Oliver.[22] The forgers were charged with attempting to undermine Henry V's rule by delivering to king's bench another fictional coroner's inquest which purported to record an armed incursion into Yorkshire by supporters of Richard II.[23]

All late medieval governments were ostensibly concerned to stamp out judicial corruption and malpractice, but it is rare to find central judicial bodies investigating complaints with such meticulous care as they showed in Henry V's reign. Moreover, offenders might face heavy penalties for what, by late medieval standards, must be considered minor transgressions. In 1421 Richard Cheddar of Somerset was fined 300 marks by the council for intimidating a peace sessions jury of present-ment.[24] This may be contrasted with the lenity shown during Henry IV's reign to John Freeman, who was bailed and later pardoned on the much more serious charge of breaking into the royal treasury of receipt at Westminster and stealing legal records.[25] Although the hectic judicial pace of the early years of Henry V's reign could not be maintained after 1415, the momentum was not wholly lost; even while the king was abroad his dynamism continued to make itself felt throughout the judicial system.

THE PROSECUTION OF TREASON

During the king's absences between 1415 and 1422 his government was concerned less with the routine administration of criminal justice than the investigation and prosecution of treasonable offences. Until 1417 the main emphasis was on hunting down Lollard rebels and other enemies of the Lancastrian regime. After Oldcastle's execution the crushing of sedition took second place to a determined campaign

---

[22] KB 27/642, Rex, m. 20.
[23] KB 27/637, Rex, m. 12; 642, Rex, m. 35 (*SKB* vii. 248–53, 254–7). Oliver died in prison; the case against Russell remained unconcluded. He may be the same as the John Russell who was an inveterate conspirator against the Lancastrians and was eventually executed for his part in the Lollard revolt in 1431: Aston, 'Lollardy and Sedition', 32–3.
[24] KB 27/640, Rex, m. 5; 641, Rex, m. 7 (*SKB* vii. 253–4).
[25] KB 9/192, m. 8; KB 27/567, Rex, m. 18d. Freeman was protected by John, Lord Lovell, a member of Henry IV's council: see ch. 4 at nn. 109–10.

against the counterfeiting of coin, which had increased sharply after 1415 as the financial demands of the war created an acute shortage of specie.

When Henry V embarked upon the Agincourt campaign, he and his advisers must have been acutely aware of the continuing threat to his throne posed by the opponents of the Lancastrian dynasty. The earl of Cambridge's plot, revealed only days before the king's departure from Southampton, roused fears that the king's enemies—Ricardian loyalists, Oldcastle and the Lollards, the Welsh rebels, the Scots— might launch a co-ordinated rising in the king's absence.[26] According to one source, some of the king's counsellors even urged him to abandon the expedition at the last minute. Henry was not to be deflected, however, and his confidence proved to be justified.[27] In the following years the government's vigilance and good intelligence resulted in the capture and conviction of several leading traitors and rebels.

During these years, as Dr Aston first observed, Lollardy became closely identified with sedition.[28] While Sir John Oldcastle remained at large the regime, with some justification, suspected virtually all rebels and conspirators of connections with Lollardy. Two notorious heretics executed in 1415, John Claydon and Richard Gurmyn, had no known involvement in seditious activities, but in 1416 Benedict Wolman, who had participated in the Lollard revolt, and Thomas Lucas, an Oxford MA and long-standing Wycliffite, were accused of treasonably presenting bills to the Emperor Sigismund which advocated clerical disendowment and alleged that Richard II was still alive in Scotland. Wolman was convicted before a

[26] Walsingham, *St Albans Chronicle*, 86–8; *Gesta Henrici Quinti*, 18–19; *The Brut*, ii. 375–6; Wylie and Waugh, *Henry V*, i. 513–39. The earl of Cambridge's plot has recently been re-examined by Pugh, 'Southampton Plot', 62–89. Pugh plays down the seriousness of the plot, arguing that the earl's conspiracy had virtually collapsed even before its betrayal to the king by Edmund Mortimer, earl of March. The alliance that Cambridge was trying to effect between the dynastic claims of the earl of March and the military resources of the Percies was potentially a grave threat, however, and the kidnap of Murdoch, earl of Fife, by the plotters in May 1415 suggests that it was not merely an armchair conspiracy: see Harriss, *Henry V*, 36–8; *SKB* vii. 236–9. See ch. 5 at nn. 100–8.

[27] A Scottish invasion was repulsed late in July, and there was also a half-hearted rising by Oldcastle in the west: Walsingham, *St Albans Chronicle*, 88–9; Wylie and Waugh, *Henry V*, i. 527–8; Nicholson, *Scotland*, 248.

[28] Aston, 'Lollardy and Sedition', *passim*.

special oyer and terminer commission at Newgate and executed, Lucas later acquitted in king's bench.[29] At the same time Wiliam Fisher, who had helped Oldcastle to escape from the Tower in 1413, was also convicted and executed for treason.[30]

Anti-Lollard anxiety reached its height in 1417, when the king's departure for France again raised fears of rebellion during his absence. In Parliament the Commons petitioned against criminal gangs of 'Lollards, traitors, and rebels' who were said to be invading parks and forests and planning insurrection.[31] Oldcastle does indeed appear to have made a final effort to rally opposition to the king at this time. He travelled to north Wales to meet Meredith ab Owen, the son of Glendower, and was rumoured to have made contact with the Scots at Pontefract. He is also said to have promised Sir William Douglas a large sum of money to encourage a Scottish invasion of the North to support the return of the pseudo-Richard II, Thomas Ward of Trumpington.[32] The Ricardian conspirator Henry Talbot, who had been implicated in the earl of Cambridge's plot in 1415, and was now attempting to foment rebellion in the North, may have had links with Oldcastle through his brother, Sir Thomas Talbot.[33] At about the same time the constable of Harlech castle, John Salghall, reported rumours of an imminent landing of Scottish forces in north Wales to support another rebellion led by Meredith ab Owen.[34] The Scots did indeed invade northern England shortly after Henry V's departure for France, but

---

[29] *Memorials of London*, 617–18, 638–41; KB 27/624, Rex, m. 9; Stow, *Chronicles*, 586, 597; Thomson, *Later Lollards*, 15–19, 139–43; Aston, 'Lollardy and Sedition', 27–8. For Wolman's involvement in the Lollard revolt, see KB 27/611, Rex, m. 13. Lucas was accused of consorting with the Ricardian conspirator, John Whitelock: see ch. 5 at nn. 101–5.

[30] *Memorials of London*, 641–3; Walsingham, *St Albans Chronicle*, 89.

[31] *RP* iv. 113–14.

[32] Smith, 'Glyndŵr Rebellion', 254–5; Richardson, 'Oldcastle in Hiding', 437; Walsingham, *St Albans Chronicle*, 114; Wylie and Waugh, *Henry V*, iii. 87–9.

[33] KB 27/624, Rex, m. 4 (*SKB* vii. 236–9); Kightly, 'Early Lollards', 27. For the indictment and acquittal of Thomas Talbot on charges of conspiring with Oldcastle in 1417, see KB 9/994, mm. 41–3; KB 27/630, Rex, m. 13d; and see also below, n. 80. The possibility that Oldcastle made common cause with Ricardian plotters is strengthened by the declaration of allegiance to Richard II which, according to Walsingham, he made at his trial: Walsingham, *St Albans Chronicle*, 117.

[34] Smith, 'Glyndŵr Rebellion', 254–5, 259.

were repulsed by troops under Bedford and Exeter after unsuccessfully besieging Berwick and Roxburgh.[35]

If Oldcastle really was trying to forge a coalition of the king's enemies in 1417, he was unsuccessful. Indeed his efforts to rouse the Welsh and Scots suggest that he lacked any significant following in England, and that since 1414 the government had eradicated the threat of rebellion from Lollardy. Perhaps it was this last-ditch attempt to rally support that led to Oldcastle's detection and arrest. At any rate the authorities picked up his trail in the Midlands during the summer. In September several Lollards were executed for harbouring him in Northamptonshire, shortly before Oldcastle himself was recaptured near Welshpool in the Welsh Marches.[36]

After Oldcastle's execution the government was more inclined to be merciful to Lollard rebels and sympathizers. In 1421 John Prest, former vicar of Chesterton in Warwickshire, was pardoned for harbouring Oldcastle,[37] while a group of Oldcastle's former tenants from Almeley in Herefordshire, suspected of the same offence, had the charges against them dismissed in king's bench on the grounds that they had acted under duress.[38] At the same time trial juries became more reluctant to convict on charges of sedition, principally because of the growing number of unsubstantiated accusations, but also because of the government's attempts to extend the scope of treason.[39] In the spring of 1422 two mass escapes of prisoners occurred within a month, one from the marshalsea prison of king's bench, the other from the Tower.[40] The fugitives from the marshalsea included two criminal approvers, John Painter, a coiner, and Thomas Exeter, a Scottish spy.

---

[35] Walsingham, *St Albans Chronicle*, 114. This was the so-called Foul Raid: see Nicholson, *Scotland*, 249; Wylie and Waugh, *Henry V*, iii. 87–90.

[36] See ch. 6 at n. 119.

[37] KB 9/209, mm. 27, 40, 62; KB 27/641, Rex, mm. 17d; *CPR, 1416–22*, p. 372.

[38] Richardson, 'Oldcastle in Hiding', 432–8.

[39] See ch. 5 at nn. 64–6. For the acquittal of Sir Thomas Talbot of treason charges, see above, n. 33. The increased use of approvers' appeals as the basis for treason prosecutions is a noticeable feature of the later years of the reign: see below, n. 61.

[40] KB 27/644, fines section, mm. 1–2; Rex, m. 11; *CPR, 1422–9*, p. 186. The escapes occurred on 18 March and 18 April 1422 respectively. Documents relating to the marshalsea escape appear in *Year Books of Henry VI: 1 Henry VI, 1422*, ed. C. H. Williams, Selden Soc., 50 (London, 1933), 69–76.

The escape from the Tower was led by two suspected traitors, Sir John Mortimer and Thomas Payn of Glamorgan. Although most of the prisoners were soon recaptured, such incidents confirmed the inadequacy of security in London gaols demonstrated earlier in the reign by the escapes of Oldcastle and John Whitelock. The government was undoubtedly shocked and angered by the affair, and attempted to discourage any recurrence of the escapes by extending the scope of the law of treason. Prison breach by persons indicted or suspected of treason was declared to be treason in itself, as was breach of a gaol where traitors were held, which had formerly been mere felony.[41]

The new doctrine, which lacked statutory authority, was tested almost immediately in the trial in king's bench of Mortimer and Payn after their recapture in May 1422. Both were suspected traitors: the reasons for Mortimer's detention were probably dynastic, while Payn was an associate of Oldcastle and was said to have plotted to rescue King James of Scotland from captivity at Windsor.[42] The council apparently had little evidence of sedition against them, for the indictments concentrated on their escape from the Tower accompanied by two prisoners of war.[43] Both men were tried, on the same day, before juries chosen and sworn in the presence of the king's serjeants, and both were acquitted of treason. The verdicts caused consternation in king's bench. The justices asked the jurors in Mortimer's case whether they understood their obligation to return a true verdict. Refusing to be browbeaten, the jurors replied that they had, and repeated their verdict. Despite his acquittal Mortimer was sent back to the Tower pending consideration of his case by the king and council. Payn's jury was also closely questioned, and, choosing its words with great care, found him not guilty of the charges of treasonable escape brought against him, but guilty of fleeing from royal custody. He was sent to Newgate while the court considered their judgment.[44]

---

[41] *Year Book 1 Henry VI*, 69; Bellamy, *Law of Treason*, 131 n. 2.

[42] Thomson, *Later Lollards*, 17–18; *PPC* v. 105. For Mortimer's links with the earls of March, see below, n. 48.

[43] KB 27/644, Rex, m. 11–11d.

[44] Ibid.

The acquittals of Mortimer and Payn represented sharp rebuffs to the government. The terms of the verdict in Payn's case suggest that the trial juries were concerned by the extension of treason without statutory authority to cover prison breach. Their reservations may have stemmed from the weakness of the government's original case against the two men, evidenced by the lack of indictments laid against them before the escape. Should the fearful penalties of treason be visited upon those who had been held in prison without any formal accusation of the crime?

Rather than accept these verdicts, the king's council and the judiciary decided to impose the new category of treason by circumventing trial procedure. Indictments were laid against several prisoners of the marshalsea of king's bench implicated in the escapes of Exeter, Painter, and others, the charges framed as treason.[45] One of the accused, William Bridge, a canon of Hastings priory, was arraigned in Michaelmas 1422, the term after Henry V's death, and pleaded not guilty. Significantly the case did not come to trial; Bridge later confessed his crimes and turned approver, and in the following term he was condemned to a traitor's death.[46] Prison breach as a treasonable offence thus entered the legal record without being put to a jury, and it was noted as a point of law in the first year book of Henry VI's reign.[47]

Having won its point by avoiding the inconvenience of jury trial, the regime was still more ruthless in dealing with Sir John Mortimer. Little is known about Mortimer; he claimed to be related to the Mortimer earls of March, and had been arrested in 1418, apparently for plotting to advance the Mortimer claim to the throne.[48] In February 1424 a government agent helped him to escape from the Tower; he was immediately recaptured, indicted for treasonable prison breach, and brought before Parliament, where a temporary statute had just been enacted declaring that anyone breaking gaol while indicted, appealed, or suspected of treason was a traitor.

[45] *Year Book 1 Henry VI*, 70–1, 75–6. Exeter was recaptured and executed as a confessed traitor.

[46] KB 27/646, Rex, mm. 18, 20d; 647, Rex, m. 2d.

[47] *Year Book 1 Henry VI*, 69.

[48] *CCR, 1413–19*, p. 483; *Chronicles of London*, ed. C. L. Kingsford (Oxford, 1905), 282–3.

The Commons, followed by the Lords, unanimously confirmed the indictment, and Mortimer was sentenced and executed forthwith.[49]

The violent reaction of the government in these cases betrays a feeling of insecurity within the Lancastrian establishment which even Henry V's triumphs in France had not dispelled. In attempting to extend the law of treason the government was acting as Henry IV had done in 1402, when Ricardian agitators were convicted of the novel offence of treasonable words.[50] The persecution of Mortimer, which must have been ordered by Henry V himself, shows that he remained acutely sensitive to any hint of dynastic rivalry.[51]

One form of treasonable activity which aroused increasing concern in the second half of the reign was the counterfeiting of coin. Counterfeiting was an endemic problem in medieval and early modern England, but it particularly concerned rulers who embarked on continental wars. According to the bullionist principles upon which the monetary policies of all medieval governments were based, the gold and silver of which coin was made were of intrinsic value; they were the basis of a realm's wealth and power. Throughout the Hundred Years' War the rulers of England, France, and Flanders competed to attract bullion to their mints, and to prevent its free circulation to their enemies.[52]

Gold and silver were by axiom the sinews of war, and as a prudent monarch one of Henry V's first priorities when

---

[49] *RP* iv. 202, 260.

[50] Thornley, 'Treason by Words', 556–61; Bellamy, *Law of Treason*, 116–18.

[51] Although Mortimer's second trial and execution took place after Henry V's death, he had been arrested in 1418 and held without trial on the king's special order until his escape in 1422. In 1421 he petitioned the Lords in Parliament to intercede with the king on his behalf. After acquittal at his first trial in May 1422 he was sent back to the Tower to await the decision of the king and council: KB 27/644, Rex, m. 11; *CCR, 1413–19*, pp. 456–7, 483; *RP* iv. 160.

[52] J. Feaveryear, *The Pound Sterling* (2nd edn.; Oxford, 1963), 21–45; J. H. Munro, *Wool, Cloth and Gold* (Toronto, 1972), 11–41. There was no fixed bullion standard of coin in the middle ages: the monetary value of silver and gold fluctuated according to demand. In time of war the price of bullion went up and rulers were forced to debase their currencies accordingly. Minted coin had to circulate at a slight premium to the value of its bullion content, in order to attract bullion to the mint and to cover the costs of production and the ruler's mintage tax or *seignorage*. If it circulated at a discount to its bullion value, coin would be heavily clipped at home and exported to overseas mints where its exchange value was higher.

planning his campaigns was the accumulation of a large war-chest. In 1415 he gathered over £130,000 in cash, in 1417 over £160,000.[53] To protect the value of these huge cash resources and to encourage the flow of bullion to the mints, it was essential to prevent the excessive debasement of the coinage through the clipping of good coin and the circulation of bad. The king and council had considered the problem as early as 1414, and in 1416 statutory measures were taken to protect the currency.[54] The import and circulation of debased continental and Scottish silver coins were forbidden on pain of indictment for felony. Such coins already in use were to be handed in and the good silver reminted. The Statute of Treasons was extended by construction so that in addition to the making of false coin, the clipping, washing, and filing of good coin were held to be treason. JPs were empowered to investigate counterfeiting, and such offences were to be determined by the justices of assize in their provincial sessions.

This legislation was accompanied by concerted judicial action through special commissions and in king's bench,[55] and until 1417 the government clearly regarded such measures as sufficient. Recorded prosecutions at this period suggest that coiners were confined to London and large towns like Coventry, Exeter, Bristol, and Southampton. Most of the coiners were goldsmiths or mercers, for whom currency offences were a profitable sideline, rather than professional counterfeitors.[56] After 1417 the government became increasingly preoccupied with the problem. The conquest of Normandy involved a vast outflow of coin from England, and the shortage of currency soon became acute. Parliament petitioned the king to buy provisions for Normandy within England, and suggested a 'hosting' system for foreign merchants to restrict

---

[53] Harriss, *Henry V*, 164.

[54] *RP* iv. 35, 82; Stat. 3 Henry V; 4 Henry V cc. 6, 7; Putnam, *Justices of the Peace*, p. xxii.

[55] *CPR, 1413–16*, pp. 262, 266, 293, 343, 414; *1416–22*, pp. 80, 81, 86; KB 9/71, mm. 38–44; 207/2, mm. 5–9, 45–7; 208, mm. 91–8; *CIM, 1399–1422*, nos. 537, 539.

[56] KB 27/617, Rex, mm. 7, 27; 618, Rex, m. 1; 620, Rex, m. 20; 621, Rex, m. 7d; 622, Rex, mm. 2d, 4d, 11, 20d; 623, Rex, mm. 11, 16d; 624, Rex, mm. 2d, 6d, 13, 13d, 16d.

the export of bullion.[57] Gold bullion was particularly scarce, and by 1421 gold coins were so heavily clipped that they were accepted by weight rather than face value.[58]

Between 1418 and the end of the reign there was a spate of counterfeiting cases.[59] At the height of the crisis in 1419, the unprecedented step was taken of arresting and arraigning suspected coiners without indictment; suspects were released only if they were found to be of good fame by a jury.[60] The surge of prosecutions was further fuelled by the revelations of several criminal approvers, some of whom were undoubtedly skilled professional counterfeitors.[61] Their confessions revealed a thriving criminal underworld of coiners throughout the country, which must have alarmed the king's judges and spurred them to redouble their efforts. The Herefordshire coiner William Carswell, interrogated by the king's council in 1418, accused over thirty of his associates. His approver's appeal suggests that he had been a coiner for over five years; he claimed an extensive network of accomplices and clients running along the Welsh border, including Dominican friars at Hereford, monks at Shrewsbury and Malvern, and the prior of Wenlock.[62] The appeal of William Baret, rector of

---

[57] *RP* iv. 118, 125–6. The proposed 'hosting' system envisaged that each alien merchant entering the country should be assigned to an English merchant who was to ensure that he exported goods rather than bullion. A statute of 1420 compelled Spanish and Italian merchants to pay for exports of wool and tin in gold or silver bullion: 8 Henry V c. 2.

[58] *RP* iv. 130, 150–1; *The Brut*, ii. 448. The crisis was only resolved by a recoinage of gold nobles (with the king forgoing the traditional *seignorage*) and by the successful establishment of the Calais mint in 1422: Munro, *Wool, Cloth and Gold*, 73–4.

[59] The number of persons indicted in king's bench for counterfeiting in the four-year period between 1418 and 1421 was 114, compared with 54 between 1414 and 1417: KB 27/611–27, Rex sections, *passim*. After 1417 counterfeiting was also being dealt with at assizes: see above at n. 54.

[60] KB 27/634, Rex, mm. 15, 18, 32; 635 Rex, m. 6; 643, Rex, m. 6d.

[61] The appeals of twelve approvers survive among the records of king's bench between 1417 and 1423: see KB 9/206/2, m. 1 (William Buxum); 212/2, mm. 23–4, 40 (Nicholas Stokes, William Carswell); 213, m. 70 (John FitzHarry); 216/2, m. 27; 995, m. 1 (William Baret); KB 27/624, Rex, m. 2d, 6d, 13 (Thomas Butler); 640, Rex, m. 9, 9d (Thomas Exeter, John Painter); 650, Rex, mm. 11–33 (David Trefnant, Richard Swallow, John Sperling, William Benet).

[62] KB 9/212/2, m. 40; KB 27/631, Rex, mm. 7d–9d; *SKB* vii. 244–6. Carswell also accused the prior of Wenlock of harbouring Sir John Oldcastle early in 1417. He alleged that the prior introduced him to Oldcastle, who retained him to make false coin. The prior was acquitted in 1419. The charges sound far-fetched, but Carswell may have been embroidering upon a rumour circulating at the time that Oldcastle

Wortham in Suffolk, in 1420, revealed that he had been involved in counterfeiting on a large scale in Bristol, with contacts in the Midlands and East Anglia.[63]

The evidence of such approvers' appeals must be treated with considerable caution, but they can sometimes be corroborated from other sources. William Carswell's colourful and unlikely tale of his encounter with Sir John Oldcastle at Wenlock priory must be set against his more prosaic dealings with known Shropshire coiners such as Maurice and Roger Weston, who operated under the protection of Sir Richard Lacon;[64] while it was the appeal of a professional thief, John FitzHarry of Ireland, which revealed the existence of a gang of counterfeitors in Northamptonshire and led to the superior eyre of king's bench in the county at Easter 1421, during which nine of the gang were convicted and executed and a tenth turned approver.[65]

On balance, therefore, the growth of official anxiety over counterfeiting after 1417 seems justified. As with the Lollard rebels, the government's level of concern was reflected by the frequency of conviction and the severity of punishment. Only two counterfeitors were convicted between 1413 and 1416, and both were pardoned.[66] From 1417 onwards over twenty were convicted, and none pardoned.[67] Only after Henry V's death was the problem resolved, following the successful gold recoinage of 1421 and the kingdom's temporary respite from taxation.[68]

HENRY'S LAST VISIT TO ENGLAND, 1421

Throughout his long absences abroad King Henry remained in close contact with the domestic administration. Items of government business were frequently submitted to him for decision, and he kept up with his paperwork even while

had found help from a Shrops. monastery. In 1421 another approver made similar charges against the abbot of Shrewsbury: KB 27/640, Rex, m. 13d.

[63] KB 9/216/2, m. 71; 995, m. 1.
[64] Powell, 'Public Order', 235–6.
[65] KB 9/213, m. 70; KB 27/640, Rex, mm. 9–10, 13.
[66] KB 27/616, Rex, m. 11d; 620, Rex, m. 20.
[67] JUST 3/195–9; KB 27/623–45, Rex sections, *passim*.
[68] Munro, *Wool, Cloth and Gold*, 73–4.

actively campaigning.[69] During the siege of Rouen he sent a peremptory letter to the duke of Bedford, ordering him to deal with an enclosed list of complaints from the duke of Brittany concerning infractions of maritime truces.[70] Henry maintained a close watch on the proceedings of Parliament, insisting in 1420 that common petitions should not be answered by the council, but rather referred to him directly.[71] He even found time to consider petitions from private individuals. In July 1420, for example, at the siege of Montereau, Henry dealt with the petition of one Ralph atte Ree, a tenant of the king at Ramsden Crays in Essex, who had been ousted from his inheritance by John Wethy and John Tyrell. The king ordered the chancellor to do right to the petitioner, and to take care that no injustice be done through the powerful maintenance of atte Ree's enemies.[72]

The king's attention to domestic administration while on active service, though impressive, was a poor substitute for his presence at home. When the treaty of Troyes was concluded in May 1420, Henry had been away for nearly three years. The Parliament of December 1420, anxious to discuss with him the implications of the treaty, and unsettled by his long absence, pressed for his immediate return.[73] Henry V and Queen Katherine finally landed at Dover on 1 February 1421. Parliament was immediately summoned for May 1421, and after Katherine's coronation at Westminster late in February she accompanied her husband on a tour of the country, ostensibly on a pilgrimage of major shrines. Their progress

---

[69] McFarlane, 'Henry V, Beaufort and the Red Hat', 338 (*Fifteenth Century*, 103); id., *Lancastrian Kings and Lollard Knights*, 118–19; Harriss, *Henry V*, 13.

[70] *PPC* ii. 243: 'as we suppose it is not out of youre remembraunce in what wise and how ofte we have charged yow by oure lettres that good and hasty reparacion and restitucion were ordeined and maad at al tymes . . .'.

[71] *RP* iv. 128; Harriss, *Henry V*, 149.

[72] *Calendar of the Proceedings in Chancery in the Reign of Elizabeth*, ed. J. Caley and J. Bayley (3 vols.; London, 1827–32), i, pp. xvi–xviii: the king ordered 'that he be not wrongfully ousted by maintenance of lordship ner other wyse, for as we have been enfourmed, beside that that is contened in the saide supplication, the personnes whiche he compleineth hym upon be gretely maintened ayenst him . . .'. For other minor judicial matters dealt with by the king in Normandy, see *Cal. Signet Letters, 1399–1422*, nos. 818, 838, 845, 870–1, 886. On the other hand the king's military commitments often forced him to refer petitions to the chancellor for decision: Storey, *Thomas Langley*, 41.

[73] *RP* iv. 125; Harriss, *Henry V*, 148–9.

through the kingdom enabled Henry not only to show off his new bride but also to recruit troops and raise funds for campaigns in France.[74] News in late March of the disaster at Baugé, where the king's brother Thomas, duke of Clarence, was killed, cut short Henry's visit, and he returned to France in early June, shortly after the dissolution of Parliament.

Committed to a continuing war of conquest against Dauphinist France by the treaty of Troyes, the king was preoccupied with military affairs throughout his few months in England in 1421. Public order had been well maintained during his absence, and there was little call for the extraordinary measures which had been necessary at the beginning of the reign. Nevertheless Henry found time to attend to judicial business: one chronicler relates how he heard the petitions of poor men during his 'pilgrimage', while a number of magnate disputes were submitted to him for decision, including the case of the Berkeley inheritance between James, Lord Berkeley, and the earl of Warwick.[75] The theme of the chancellor's speech to Parliament in May was the redress of wrongs committed since the king's departure, particularly those against men serving in France.[76] Parliament enacted several judicial measures, the most important of which was the revival of the assize circuits, which had been suspended on the king's departure in 1417.[77]

One county, Northamptonshire, had been a constant source of concern to the government since 1417. As we have seen, the government's chief judicial preoccupations at this time were treason, particularly counterfeiting, and judicial malpractice, and all three flourished in Northamptonshire. The chicanery of John Thornton, under-sheriff of Northamptonshire, was exposed at length before king's bench in 1418.[78] The trail of the fugitive traitor Sir John Oldcastle had been detected in the

---

[74] Monstrelet, *Chronique*, iv. 25; Wylie and Waugh, *Henry V*, iii. 265–92; Harriss, *Henry V*, 150–1.

[75] *Gesta Henrici Quinti*, ed. B. Williams, English Historical Soc. (London, 1850), 148; McFarlane, *Nobility*, 118–19; Harriss, *Henry V*, 46–7.

[76] *RP* iv. 129.

[77] 9 Henry V st. 1 c. 3. Other statutes dealt with bogus indictments, the arrest of outlaws who took refuge in the northern liberties of Hexham and Tyndale, and the criminal activities of Oxford scholars: ibid., cc. 1, 7, 8; *RP* iv. 131–47.

[78] See above at nn. 18–20.

county shortly before his recapture in 1417, and several of his accomplices executed for treason.[79] Further treason inquiries in 1418 and 1419 produced indictments for coining and fresh charges against Lollard sympathizers, including Sir Thomas Talbot.[80] Finally, late in 1420, a ring of counterfeitors was discovered at Overstone, Farthingstone, and Hargrave in Northamptonshire, and a special order was made for their arrest.[81] One of the suspects, John Taillard, was brought to Westminster in the custody of the JP Thomas Billing, apparently without authorization, for on 10 December Billing was ordered by Parliament, on pain of his life and goods, to take Taillard back to Northampton and to deliver him to the sheriff's custody to await trial.[82] Billing's dismissal from the peace commission in January 1421 probably resulted from this incident, but it may also have been connected with his earlier negligence in allowing the theft of records from his custody while he was keeper of the rolls in 1418.[83] Confidence in the judicial administration of the shire cannot have been strengthened by the murder of Thomas Beeston, a JP and clerk of king's bench, by his wife Katherine in June 1420.[84]

These disorders explain the decision to hold a superior eyre of king's bench at Northampton during Easter term 1421.[85] The court sat for three weeks from 7 April, and conducted its customary review of the local machinery of criminal justice. The surviving records are far less comprehensive than those of the superior eyre of 1414. The *coram rege* indictment file appears complete, but the peace roll is fragmentary, and only one coroner's roll survives out of fourteen delivered to king's

---

[79] KB 9/209, mm. 1–27. See ch. 6 at nn. 115–17.

[80] KB 9/83, m. 51; 994, mm. 41–3; 215/1, mm. 26–7; KB 27/630, Rex, mm. 13d, 17d; 632, Rex, m. 11d. See also above, n. 33.

[81] *CPR, 1416–22*, pp. 321, 328; KB 9/93, m. 60d. See also the approver's appeal of the counterfeitor John FitzHarry: KB 9/213, m. 70; KB 27/640, Rex, mm. 2, 10.

[82] *RP* iv. 124; *CCR, 1419–22*, p. 95.

[83] KB 9/93, m. 59; KB 27/640, Rex, m. 12. Billing was first appointed to the peace commission in 1417, dropped from it in 1419, and reappointed by a commission of 1420 which was not entered on the patent rolls: *CPR, 1416–22*, p. 456; KB 9/93, m. 59d.

[84] KB 9/216/2, m. 21. Katherine Beeston was convicted and burned for petty treason at Hilary 1421 and her accomplice John Colles convicted at the suit of the party the following term: KB 27/638, Rex, m. 20d; 640, m. 32, Rex, m. 13.

[85] KB 27/640. This was the last superior eyre ever to be held. Putnam, *Justices of the Peace*, p. lviii.

bench.[86] A systematic analysis of proceedings is therefore not possible, but the king's bench plea roll entries confirm that the main object of the exercise was to stamp out counterfeiting. Two deliveries of Northampton gaol were held, on 10 and 26 April, at which nine counterfeitors were convicted and another, John Painter, turned approver.[87] The remaining offenders dealt with before the superior eyre faced routine charges of felony and trespass, apart from Thomas Exeter of Ireland who was accused of spying for the king's enemies in 1415. He also turned approver, escaped from the marshalsea prison in the mass break-out of 1422, and was recaptured and executed for treason in 1423.[88]

THE LIMITS OF LAW ENFORCEMENT

The success of Henry V's law enforcement policy is demonstrated by the lack of serious disorder in England during his long absences between 1415 and 1422. The king never found it necessary to interrupt his French campaigns in order to deal with outbreaks of violence and lawlessness at home. Nevertheless it would be quite wrong to assume that public order was perfectly maintained. As is evident from petitions to Parliament, there were regions of the country, notably the Scottish and Welsh borders, where the king's peace was still freely broken. Such petitions tended to associate outbreaks of disorder with jurisdictional liberties—the great territorial lordships of the Marches, and the lesser franchises within the realm. In 1414, for example, the commons of Northumberland complained against the depredations of the 'intakers and outputters' of the liberties of Tyndale and Hexhamshire, and requested that the lords and officials of those liberties be ordered to assist in the punishment of such malefactors. A statute was passed to that effect, but it merely shifted the problem to the neighbouring liberty of Redesdale, and complaints were renewed in 1421.[89]

---

[86] The indictment file is KB 9/93, which includes the peace roll fragments at mm. 59–60; the coroner's roll is JUST 2/119C. For the rolls submitted to the court which do not survive, see KB 27/640, fines section, mm. 1–5; 641, fines section, m. 1d.

[87] KB 27/640, Rex, mm. 9, 13.

[88] KB 27/640, Rex, m. 9d; 647, Rex, m. 2d; 654, Rex, m. 10. See above, nn. 41, 45.

[89] *RP* iv. 21, 143; for similar problems regarding the liberties of the Welsh Marches and Oxford University, see ibid. 52, 69, 131.

In 1417, shortly after the king's departure for Normandy, the Commons submitted a petition in general terms against armed criminal bands composed, it was alleged, of Lollards, traitors, and rebels, who assembled to break into forests and parks, and whom the local officials dared not prosecute.[90] Attempts were made to arrest the leader of one of these gangs, nicknamed Friar Tuck, who had been active in Surrey and Sussex, but he was still at large as late as 1429.[91] William Wawe, another notorious outlaw leader, operated with impunity from the latter years of Henry V's reign until his capture after a manhunt in 1427, committing offences in places as far apart as London, Bedfordshire, Hampshire, and Worcestershire.[92] These disorders did not, however, compare with the lawlessness which faced Henry V at his accession. Although problems of law enforcement remained after 1415, public order ceased to be the serious political issue that it had been throughout Henry IV's reign and at Henry V's accession.

Henry V's success in the sphere of public order was a triumph of personal authority, and like his military and diplomatic triumphs it was a precarious one. Its consolidation after his death depended upon the abilities of his brothers and son. The fragility of Henry V's achievement was revealed barely a decade after his death, when public order again rose to the top of the political agenda, and the government had to resort to extraordinary measures such as the oaths of 1429 and 1433 against the maintenance of law-breakers.[93]

The essentially personal quality of Henry V's peace is best illustrated by a number of minor incidents which occurred within a few months of his death in August 1422. The settlement imposed by Henry on Lord Berkeley and the earl of Warwick over the Berkeley inheritance broke down as soon as the king's death became known, and during September 1422

[90] *RP* iv. 113–14.
[91] *CPR, 1416–22*, pp. 84, 141; Holt, *Robin Hood*, 58–9. See KB 27/642, fines section, m. 1d, for Richard Herring, *alias* Juliana, wife of Friar Tuck.
[92] R. A. Griffiths, 'William Wawe and his Gang, 1427', *Proceedings of the Hampshire Field Club and Archaeological Soc.*, 33 (1977), 89–93; KB 9/222/2, mm. 34–7. The charges against Wawe included treason and Lollardy.
[93] Griffiths, *Henry VI*, 128–53.

Warwick's forces besieged Berkeley castle.[94] In the Midlands and on the Welsh Marches troublemakers curbed by the superior eyre of king's bench in 1414 suddenly became active again. During Henry VI's first Parliament a proclamation was issued against Sir Richard Lacon, a leading figure in the Arundel–Talbot feuding in Shropshire at the beginning of Henry V's reign, summoning him to appear in chancery on a charge of forcible entry into the lordship of Whittington, near Oswestry, in November 1422.[95] Lacon's old adversary John Talbot was the subject of a petition from Herefordshire less than a year later, which asked for a superior eyre to be held in that county to deal with the disturbances arising from Talbot's dispute with a former retainer, John Abrahall.[96] Edmund Ferrers of Chartley, a protagonist of the disorders in Staffordshire before 1414, had been drafted into Henry V's service for the Agincourt expedition, and saw several years' campaigning in France. He returned to England soon after Henry V's death, and in 1423 became embroiled in a violent struggle with Sir William Birmingham over the inheritance to the manor of Birmingham, for which he was indicted in king's bench.[97]

None of these incidents is very significant in itself, but taken together they suggest that Henry V's death caused an immediate slackening of central judicial control. Disorder had been kept in check for the past decade by the sheer force of Henry V's personality; the elaborate machinery of justice and the web of social and political obligation within the local community was insufficient to contain them. The peace of the infant Henry VI, proclaimed in September 1422, signalled a new period of uncertainty which restless opportunists like Lacon, Talbot, and Ferrers immediately sought to exploit.[98]

[94] J. Smyth, *Lives of the Berkeleys*, ed. J. MacLean (2 vols.; Gloucester, 1883), ii. 66. The Berkeley dispute has been re-examined by Ms Alexandra Sinclair in a paper entitled 'The Great Berkeley Lawsuit Revisited, 1417–39', delivered to the Fifteenth-Century History Conference at the University of Keele in 1985.

[95] *RP* iv. 192. In 1423 the approver David Trefnant appealed Lacon of organizing a ring of counterfeitors in Shrops.: KB 27/650, Rex, mm. 23d, 30d. The appeal was dismissed as insufficient at law.

[96] *RP* iv. 254; cf. Griffiths, *Henry VI*, 131, 136, 150, 162–7.

[97] KB 27/654, Rex, mm. 19d, 20. Carpenter, 'Political Society', 112–14; Griffiths, *Henry VI*, 142, 148.

[98] *Foedera*, x. 254; *CPR, 1422–9*, p. 35; Griffiths, *Henry VI*, 128–53.

Conclusion

HENRY V died on 31 August 1422, a little over a year after his final departure from England. His passing was marked in the minutes of the king's council by a brief epitaph breathless with superlatives:

Henry the Fifth, king of England, the most Christian warrior of the Church, the sun of prudence, the exemplar of justice, the most invincible king, flower of knighthood, passed away.[1]

This verdict is typical of most English assessments of Henry V after his death: a conventional and uninformative eulogy, emphasizing his military prowess.[2] For contemporary French and Burgundian chroniclers, however, Henry was above all a paragon of justice. Monstrelet wrote that his magnates and captains regarded him with such awe that they dared not break his laws; another Burgundian chronicler, Fenin, noted that the poor particularly loved him because he was determined to protect them from the oppressions of the great.[3] Jean Juvenal des Ursins, a servant of the Valois kings and the author of a treatise refuting English claims to the throne of France, was no less fulsome in his praise: 'the said king', he wrote, 'was a great administrator of justice, who without respect for persons gave as good justice to the mean as to the great.'[4]

On the English side the fullest appreciation of Henry V's judicial achievements came a generation after his death. John Hardyng completed the first recension of his chronicle in the

---

[1] *PPC* iii. 3: 'Decessit christianissimus pugil ecclesie prudencie jubar et exemplar justicie ac invictissimus rex flos et decus omnis milicie Henricus Quintus post conquestum rex Anglie.'

[2] Wylie and Waugh, *Henry V*, iii. 423; Gransden, *Historical Writing*, 196–8, 216–17; *Vita et Gesta*, 331–2, 334; *The Brut*, ii. 493–4; Walsingham, *Historia Anglicana*, ii. 344; John Strecche, 'The Chronicle of John Strecche for the Reign of Henry V', ed. F. Taylor, in *BJRL* 16 (1932), 187.

[3] Monstrelet, *Chronique*, iv. 116; Wylie and Waugh, *Henry V*, iii. 424.

[4] Ibid., n. 6; I have used the translation in McFarlane, *Lancastrian Kings and Lollard Knights*, 130; P. S. Lewis, 'War Propaganda and Historiography in Fifteenth-Century France and England', *TRHS* 5th ser., 15 (1965), 11–18.

1450s, when Henry VI's incapacity and the bitter enmity between the dukes of York and Somerset led to a breakdown of public order.[5] The work was presented to the king in 1457, and included a lengthy panegyric of Henry V emphasizing his success in law enforcement:

> Above all thynge he kept the lawe and pese
> Thurgh all Englonde, that none insurreccion
> Ne no riotes than wer withouten lese,
> Ne neyghbours werre in fawte of his correccion.[6]

The maintenance of public order at home was, in Hardyng's view, the foundation of Henry V's victories in France:

> Whan he in Fraunce dayly was conversaunt
> His shadow so abowmbred all Englonde
> That pese and lawe wer kept contynuant.
>
> .   .   .   .
>
> The pese at home and lawe so wele conserved
> Wer rote and hede of all his grete conqueste . . .[7]

Hardyng urged Henry VI to follow his father's example and take firm action to stem the rising tide of disorder: offenders should be sent overseas to use their martial energies constructively by recovering the king's right in France.[8]

The chaos in which Henry VI's reign ended, while enhancing Henry V's reputation for justice at that time, underlines the short-lived nature of his achievement. It cannot be said that Henry V found a permanent solution to the problem of public order. He made no striking institutional innovations, no change in the balance between central and local power such as occurred during the reigns of Edward I and Henry VIII. He offered no radical solution to the structural deficiencies of the medieval judicial system as historians have traditionally perceived them, notably the lack of central coercive power and the vulnerability of the legal system to corruption and intimidation. His true achievements lay in fulfilling contemporary expectations of justice through a more effective use of the existing machinery, and in adapting his judicial policy so successfully to the demands of his

---

[5] Gransden, *Historical Writing*, 276–7; John Hardyng, 'The First Version of Hardyng's Chronicle', ed. C. Kingsford, in *EHR* 27 (1912), 462–82, 740–53.
[6] Hardyng, 'Chronicle', 744.   [7] Ibid. 745.   [8] Ibid. 745–6, 749–50.

military campaigns. Recruitment for war provided a vital safety-valve which allowed malefactors to redeem their offences and earn their pardons in royal service. As Hardyng observed, domestic peace and foreign conquest were inextricably linked; but it took a king of extraordinary ability to combine the two so effectively, and, working within the limitations of his slender resources, to make each serve the interests of the other.

The administration of criminal justice under Henry V clearly illustrates the strengths and weaknesses of the judicial system in late medieval England. It shows what could be achieved by a vigorous king with a coherent judicial policy, but it also reveals the constraints upon royal power to enforce the law. Henry V demonstrated that England was not ungovernable in the fifteenth century. There was no shortage of legal machinery available, provided that the king could exploit it effectively. Henry did so in 1414 by co-ordinating the whole programme of law enforcement through king's bench: the court itself sat as a superior eyre in the north-west Midlands; all the proceedings held in other counties, including the Lollard commissions of January 1414, were commissions of inquiry rather than oyer and terminer. This meant that the commissioners were empowered only to receive indictments and order arrests, whereas justices of oyer and terminer could try offenders locally. The findings of those inquiries were returned to king's bench for determination. A degree of speed and flexibility in dealing with the disorders was lost through restricting the commissioners' powers, but on the other hand, by using king's bench as a general clearing-house for the commissions, Henry was able to exercise closer supervision of the localities and to gauge more accurately the extent and severity of disorder throughout the kingdom in order to formulate an appropriate response.

The methods adopted to restore order were determined by the Crown's limited resources. Like other medieval rulers, Henry V could not afford a standing army and permanent police force with which to implement a primarily coercive system of justice. His programme of law enforcement was carried out largely without resort to punitive measures such as imprisonment or execution, relying rather on the threat of coercion as a spur to participation in the royal policy of conciliation; a process neatly illustrated by the story in the *Brut* chronicle of the king settling a dispute between two quarrelsome knights over a dish of oysters.[9] In such circumstances the bare statistics of criminal justice offer a poor guide to the effectiveness of law enforcement. The records of king's bench in 1414 reveal a negligible conviction rate and the indiscriminate use of general pardons, features which are usually interpreted as symptoms of a lax and inefficient judicial system, but which under Henry V accompanied the successful restoration of public order. The inadequacy of the statistical evidence confirms the need to look beyond the narrow institutional framework to the wider social and political context of judicial administration.

In its efforts to enforce the law and maintain public order the Crown relied heavily on the support and co-operation of the local community; not only the nobility and gentry who filled the commissions of the peace and the local administrative offices of the Crown, but also the yeomen and substantial villagers who served as constables and jurors. The system had obvious weaknesses. Where a community closed ranks against central government and refused to co-operate in the investigation of crime, even a king as forceful as Henry V was virtually powerless, as we have seen in the case of Devon in 1414. Similarly, the strict course of justice might be diverted by sectional interests. Justices of the peace often used their powers as a tool of faction or class interest, while trial jurors were extremely reluctant to return convictions for homicide, even if the defendant's guilt was apparent.

Royal judicial power was particularly weak in the areas most remote from Westminster, along the Welsh and Scottish borders. This was partly the result of distance and poor communications: the judges of the northern circuit visited the border shires only once a year. More significant, however, were the substantial judicial liberties of the Marcher lordships which stood outside the administrative framework of the shires. By Henry V's reign such liberties were increasingly seen as hindrances to sound judicial administration, but the

---

[9] See ch. 9 at n. 7.

cumbersome procedures adopted to deal with the problem did little to reduce their reputation as criminal havens.

The effect of local influence in the administration of justice was not, however, purely negative: the surest way for a locality to avoid external interference was to police itself effectively. Unlike visiting royal justices, the local community had to live with the settlement imposed after conflict and disorder. Its primary concern, therefore, was to reconcile hostile parties and re-establish peace and concord, rather than to punish offenders. The leading regional magnate or a group of county gentry would act as arbitrators between disputants and attempt to settle the issues in contention in a form acceptable to both sides. Arbitration of this kind flourished in England throughout the late middle ages. It had well-defined procedures which functioned independently of the law courts, though often in conjunction with them. For the local communities where it thrived it was the ideal mechanism for the internal resolution of conflict.

What functions, then, did the legal system serve in late medieval England? Why, if so few criminals were convicted and so many legal actions left unconcluded, did indictments continue to be returned and lawsuits filed in such large numbers? First, the law courts represented in insitutional form the structure of authority, a structure that was seen as ordained by God. The legal system was therefore closely linked to the social and political hierarchy, and helped maintain the stability of the existing order. The law was also a repository of norms governing social behaviour. The courts provided means for enforcing those norms as a last resort, but paradoxically their effectiveness relied more on the general habit of obedience: over-use of the legal sanction might weaken their force. The climate of opinion did not, of course, remain static, and legislation during the late middle ages reflects changing social attitudes, particularly with regard to the professional morality of lawyers and judges.

Perhaps the most important function of the legal system, however, was to bring about the peaceful mediation of conflict. The slow-moving procedures of the law and the formalized encounters in court allowed ample time and opportunity for negotiation between the disputing parties, of

which they took full advantage. Furthermore the law offered
disputants an immense variety of resorts by which they could
wage their quarrels. Litigation in the late middle ages was
highly complex: suits and counter-suits could be pursued
simultaneously in different courts, all with the aim of securing
a tactical advantage with which to exert pressure on an
opponent out of court. One main objective of the legal system
was to reduce violence, and although it is evident that the
law's delays sometimes aggravated disputes, the alternative—
a rapid judicial decision leaving one side empty-handed and
dissatisfied—was a certain recipe for conflict. The success of
medieval law courts must be assessed less according to the
number of actions concluded and criminals convicted than
according to their contribution to social peace and harmony
and their continuing popularity. During the fourteenth and
fifteenth centuries new courts proliferated to meet the
demands of litigants, and lawyers, as always, grew rich
exploiting the technicalities and loopholes of the law.

Above all, justice in the late middle ages was a co-operative
enterprise involving the king and his people, a continuous
dialogue between central authority and local autonomy. The
king's responsibility for law enforcement had greatly increased
in the three centuries before 1400, but even in the fifteenth
century he did not impose justice upon a passive subject
populace. Rather the king's subjects participated actively in
judicial administration, and in the process helped to mould its
distinctive character. The machinery of royal justice would
have broken down without the co-operation of the king's
subjects; on the other hand the king was the ultimate
guarantor of the system, bound by his coronation oath to
uphold the laws and do justice. It was his task to foster the
conditions in which local courts could work smoothly and
disputes could be settled with the minimum of central
interference.

Justice and politics were inextricably connected in the
fifteenth century because both turned so much on the king's
relations with his greatest subjects. Justice was the personal
quality most needed in a king, as the 'mirrors of princes' never
tired of stressing. It was through his example and at his
command that justice was done throughout the realm, and the

manner in which he dealt with the rivalries and disputes of his nobility set the tone for litigation and dispute settlement in every shire. This concept of justice in late medieval England was clearly defined in the light of the constitutional developments of preceding centuries; it touched every aspect of government and was grounded in the belief that the king held his office as a sacred trust for the common welfare of the realm. No king came closer to embodying the contemporary ideal of the just king than Henry V. His success in the administration of justice must rank with his greatest achievements, alongside the battle of Agincourt, the conquest of Normandy, and the treaty of Troyes, which established the union of the crowns of England and France. On the continent, indeed, his reputation for justice proved more enduring than his conquests. For the chronicler Chastellain, writing after the expulsion of the English from France, Henry remained 'the prince of justice, both in himself, for the sake of example, and towards others, according to equity and right; he upheld no one through favour, nor did he allow any wrong to go unpunished out of kinship.'[10]

---

[10] Georges Chastellain, *Œuvres*, ed. K. de Lettenhove (8 vols.; Brussels, 1863–6), i. 334; Wylie and Waugh, *Henry V*, iii. 424: 'il estoit prince de justice tant envers soy meme, par exemple, comme envers aultruy par equite droituriere; ne supportoit personne par faveur, ne torfais ne laissoit impugnit par affinite de sang.'

Appendix: Analysis of Criminal Offences brought before King's Bench and Associated Commissions in the Midlands in 1414

TABLE A1. *Treason and felony: numbers of cases and accused*

	Leics.		Staffs.		Shrops.		Notts.		Derby.	
	Cases	Accused	Cases	Accused	Cases	Accused	Cases	Accused	Cases	Accused
Treason	1	2	8	9	26	26	0	0	0	0
Homicide[a]	641	723	377	483	358	499	16	17	30	38
Rape	9	9	33	34	18	20	0	0	0	0
Larceny	43	59	148	175	157	235	3	5	7	6
Robbery	11	17	21	43	39	59	1	1	4	5
Other felony	1	3	7	16	7	14	1	3	0	0
Accessory to felony	182	217	95	175	103	159	5	5	9	17
TOTAL	888	1,030	689	935	708	1,012	26	31	50	66

[a] The large number of homicide cases from the counties visited by the superior eyre of king's bench is due chiefly to the numerous coroners' rolls submitted to the court. Many of these dated from the reigns of Edward III and Richard II.

Sources: JUST 1/472, 752, 753, 815; JUST 2/48–63, 142–51, 159–70, 255/9; KB 9/112, 113, 200, m. 45, 204/2, 206/1; KB 27/612–60; KB 29/53.

TABLE A2. *Trespass: numbers of cases and accused*

	Leics.		Staffs.		Shrops.		Notts.		Derby.	
	Cases	Accused	Cases	Accused	Cases	Accused	Cases	Accused	Cases	Accused
Assault & abduction	47	119	99	192	94	231	36	54	26	34
Extortion & corruption	3	5	12	10	57	50	20	10	14	8
Breaches of livery laws	0	0	26	133	12	35	0	0	0	0
Breaches of labour laws	8	14	11	24	15	58	0	0	0	0
Miscellaneous	8	11	2	2	11	39	0	0	0	0
TOTAL	66	149	150	361	189	413	56	64	40	42

Sources: as for Table A1.

TABLE A3. *Outcome of homicide indictments*

	Leics.	Staffs.	Shrops.	Notts.	Derby	Total
Convicted	0	0	0	0	0	0
Acquitted	7	16	2	0	0	25
Pardoned	22	54	37	4	9	126
Outlawed	140[a]	207	203	13	27	590
Dead	0	8	9	0	2	19
Untraced	0	3	0	0	0	3
No process[b]	554	195	248	0	0	997
TOTAL	723	483	499	17	38	1,760

[a] This figure includes 43 defendants who had previously appeared at gaol delivery at Leicester on the same charge. Of these, 18 had been acquitted, 12 pardoned, and 13 convicted.
[b] Most 'no process' cases came from indictments on coroners' rolls dated before 1404.
Sources: as for Table A1.

TABLE A4. *Outcome of felony indictments excluding homicide*

	Leics.	Staffs.	Shrops.	Notts.	Derby.	Total
Convicted	1	0	2	0	0	3
Acquitted	6	55	19	0	0	80
Pardoned	10	24	53	4	3	94
Fined	0	1	0	0	0	1
Outlawed	65	183	169	5	7	429
Dead	0	1	9	0	0	10
Untraced	0	2	1	0	1	4
No process	6	2	75	0	0	83
TOTAL	88	268	328	9	11	704

Note: Excluding homicide, felony covers rape, larceny, robbery, arson, and burglary.
Sources: as for Table A1.

TABLE A5. *Outcome of indictments for common law trespass*

	Leics.	Staffs.	Shrops.	Notts.	Derby.	Total
Convicted	0	0	0	0	0	0
Acquitted	6	1	1	0	0	8
Pardoned	6	33	52	14	9	114
Fined	52	65	30	17	6	170
Outlawed	48	87	120	17	16	288
Dead	1	4	19	2	2	28
Untraced	5	1	0	4	1	11
No process	1	1	9	0	0	11
TOTAL	119	192	231	54	34	630

Note: Common law trespass covers ambush, assault, abduction, riot etc.
Sources: as for Table A1.

TABLE A6. *Outcome of indictments for statutory trespass*

	Leics.	Staffs.	Shrops.	Notts.	Derby.	Total
Convicted	0	0	0	No indictments		0
Acquitted	0	0	0	—	—	0
Pardoned	0	36	18	—	—	54
Fined	10	87	39	—	—	136
Outlawed	4	28	28	—	—	60
Dead	0	0	12	—	—	12
Untraced	0	5	2	—	—	7
No process	0	1	0	—	—	1
TOTAL	14	157	99	—	—	270

Note: Statutory trespass covers breaches of the statutes of labourers, livery, and weights and measures.
Sources: as for Table A1.

Select Bibliography

A. MANUSCRIPT SOURCES

British Library
Additional charters, 320, 321, 6820, 11827
Additional MS 35205
Egerton roll 8772
Harley MS 782

Burton on Trent Public Library
D 27, Burton abbey deeds

Lambeth Palace Library
Register of Archbishop Thomas Arundel

Lichfield Joint Record Office
B/A/1/8, Register of Bishop John Catterick

National Library of Wales
Pitchford Hall deeds

Public Record Office
C 1, early chancery proceedings
C 66, chancery, patent rolls
C 67, chancery, patent rolls supplementary (pardon rolls)
C 138, chancery, inquisitions post mortem, Henry V
C 237, chancery, bails on special pardons
CHES 3, Palatinate of Chester, inquisitions post mortem (Chester
    and Flint)
CP 25(1), court of common pleas, feet of fines
CP 40, court of common pleas, plea rolls
DL 28, duchy of Lancaster accounts (various)
E 101, exchequer accounts (various)
E 163, exchequer miscellanea
E 199, exchequer, sheriffs' accounts
E 357, exchequer, escheators' enrolled accounts
E 404, exchequer, writs and warrants for issue
JUST 1, eyre rolls, assize rolls, etc.
JUST 2, coroners' rolls
JUST 3, gaol delivery rolls
JUST 4, eyre, assize etc., writ files

KB 9, court of king's bench, ancient indictments
KB 27, court of king's bench, plea rolls
KB 29, court of king's bench, controlment rolls
KB 37, court of king's bench, *brevia regis* (crown side) files
KB 145, court of king's bench, *recorda* and *precepta recordorum* files
KB 146, court of king's bench, panels, assizes, and bills files
SC 1, ancient correspondence
SC 6, ministers' and receivers' accounts
SC 8, ancient petitions

Shropshire Record Office

552/1, lordship of Clun and Purslow hundred court rolls

B. PRINTED SOURCES

Primary Sources

AMUNDESHAM, JOHN, *Annales Monasterii Sancti Albani*, ed. H. T. Riley, Rolls Ser. (2 vols.; London, 1870–1).

AQUINAS, THOMAS, *De Regimine Principum*, tr. G. B. Phelan as *On Kingship to the King of Cyprus* (Toronto, 1949).

—— *Selected Political Writings*, ed. A. P. D'Entrèves (Oxford, 1959).

—— *Summa Theologica*, tr. the Fathers of the English Dominican Province (25 vols.; London, 1911–22).

ASSHEBOURNE, WILLIAM, *William Asshebourne's Book*, ed. D. M. Owen, Norfolk Record Soc., 48 (Norwich, 1981).

Bracton on the Laws and Customs of England, ed. S. E. Thorne (4 vols.; Cambridge, Mass., 1968–77).

The Brut, ed. F. W. D. Brie, Early English Text Soc., 131, 136 (2 vols.; London, 1906–8).

Calendar of the Close Rolls, 1272–1485 (45 vols.; London, 1892–1954).

A Calendar of Early Chancery Proceedings Relating to West Country Shipping, ed. D. A. Gardiner, Devon and Cornwall Record Soc., New Ser., 21 (Exeter, 1976).

Calendar of the Fine Rolls, 1272–1509 (22 vols.; London, 1911–63).

Calendar of General and Special Assize and General Gaol Delivery Commissions on the Dorses of the Patent Rolls, 1377–99 (London, 1977).

Calendar of Inquisitions Miscellaneous, 1216–1422 (7 vols.; London, 1916–69).

Calendar of Letter Books of the City of London: Letter Book I, ed. R. R. Sharpe (London, 1909).

Calendar of London Trailbaston Trials under Commissions of 1305 and 1306, ed. R. B. Pugh (London, 1975).

Calendar of the Patent Rolls, 1216–1509 (55 vols.; London, 1891–1916).

Calendar of the Proceedings in Chancery in the Reign of Elizabeth, ed. J. Caley and J. Bayley (3 vols.; London, 1827–32).

Calendar of Signet Letters of Henry IV and Henry V, 1399–1422, ed. J. L. Kirby (London, 1978).

CESSOLIS, JACOBUS DE, *The Game of Chess* (tr. and printed by William Caxton; repr. London, 1976).

CHASTELLAIN, GEORGES, *Œuvres*, ed. K. de Lettenhove (8 vols.; Brussels, 1863–6).

A Chronicle of London from 1089 to 1483, ed. N. H. Nicolas and E. Tyrell (London, 1827).

Chronicles of London, ed. C. L. Kingsford (Oxford, 1905).

CLÉMANGES, NICHOLAS DE, *Opera Omnia* (Leyden, 1613; repr. Farnborough, 1967).

Collections for a History of Staffordshire, William Salt Archaeological Soc., 17 (London, 1896).

Concilia Magnae Britanniae et Hiberniae, ed. D. Wilkins (4 vols.; London, 1737).

Crown Pleas of the Wiltshire Eyre, ed. C. A. F. Meekings, Wiltshire Record Soc., 16 (Devizes, 1960).

Decretum Gratiani, ed. E. Friedberg (Leipzig, 1879).

Early Registers of Writs, ed. E. De Haas and G. D. G. Hall, Selden Soc., 87 (London, 1970).

ELMHAM, THOMAS, *Liber Metricus de Henrico Quinto*, printed in *Memorials of Henry the Fifth*, ed. C. A. Cole, Rolls Ser. (London, 1858), 77–166.

English Historical Documents, 1189–1327, ed. H. Rothwell (London, 1975).

English Historical Documents, 1327–1485, ed. A. R. Myers (London, 1969).

English Wycliffite Sermons, vol. i, ed. A. M. Hudson (Oxford, 1983).

The Eyre of Northamptonshire, 1329–30, ed. D. W. Sutherland, Selden Soc., 97–8 (2 vols.; London, 1981–2).

The First English Life of King Henry the Fifth, ed. C. L. Kingsford (Oxford, 1911).

FITZNEALE, RICHARD, *The Dialogue of the Exchequer*, ed. C. Johnson (London, 1950).

Foedera, Conventiones, Litterae, ed. T. Rymer and R. Sanderson (20 vols.; London, 1704–35).

FORTESCUE, JOHN, *De Laudibus Legum Anglie*, ed. S. B. Chrimes (Cambridge, 1942).

—— *De Natura Legis Naturae*, ed. Lord Clermont (London, 1864).

—— *On the Governance of England*, ed. C. Plummer (Oxford, 1885).

Four English Political Tracts of the Later Middle Ages, ed. J.-P. Genet, Camden Soc., 4th ser., 18 (London, 1977).

Gesta Henrici Quinti, ed. B. Williams, English Historical Soc. (London, 1850).

Gesta Henrici Quinti, ed. F. Taylor and J. S. Roskell (Oxford, 1975).

GILES OF ROME, *De Regimine Principum*, tr. as *Li Livres du Gouvernement des Rois*, ed. S. P. Molenaer (London, 1899).

GOWER, JOHN, *The Major Latin Works of John Gower*, tr. E. W. Stockton (Seattle, Wash., 1962).

The Great Chronicle of London, ed. A. H. Thomas and I. D. Thornley (London, 1938).

Gregory's Chronicle, in *The Historical Collections of a Citizen of London*, ed. J. Gairdner, Camden Soc., 2nd ser., 17 (London, 1876).

HALE, M., *A History of Pleas of the Crown* (London, 1736).

HARDYNG, JOHN, 'The First Version of Hardyng's Chronicle', ed. C. Kingsford, in *EHR* 27 (1912), 462–82, 740–53.

HISTORICAL MANUSCRIPTS COMMISSION, *Reports of the Royal Commission on Historical Manuscripts: Fifth Report* (London, 1876); *Eighth Report* (London, 1881); *Eleventh Report* (London, 1887).

Historical Poems of the Fourteenth and Fifteenth Centuries, ed. R. H. Robbins (New York, NY, 1959).

HOCCLEVE, THOMAS, *The Regement of Princes*, ed. F. J. Furnivall, Early English Text Soc., Extra Ser., 72 (London, 1897).

Issues of the Exchequer, ed. F. Devon (London, 1837).

JOINVILLE, JEAN DE, *The Life of St Louis*, in *Chronicles of the Crusades*, tr. M. R. B. Shaw (Harmondsworth, 1963).

Kent Keepers of the Peace, 1316–17, ed. B. H. Putnam, Kent Records, 13 (Canterbury, 1933).

LAMBARDE, WILLIAM, *Eirenarcha* (London, 1599).

LANGLAND, WILLIAM, *The Vision of William Concerning Piers the Plowman*, ed. W. W. Skeat (2 vols.; Oxford, 1886).

Letters and Papers of John Shillingford, ed. S. A. Moore, Camden Soc., New Ser., 2 (London, 1871).

The Lisle Letters: An Abridgement,. ed. M. S. Byrne (London, 1983).

The Making of King's Lynn, ed. D. M. Owen, British Academy, Records of Social and Economic History, New Ser., 9 (London, 1984).

The Memoranda de Parliamento of 1305, ed. F. W. Maitland, Rolls Ser. (London, 1893).

Memorials of Bury St Edmunds, ed. T. Arnold, Rolls Ser. (3 vols.; London, 1890–6).

Memorials of London and London Life, 1276–1419, ed. and tr. H. T. Riley (London, 1868).

The Mirror of Justices, ed. W. J. Whittaker, Selden Soc., 7 (London, 1893).

The Mirror for Magistrates, ed. L. B. Campbell (Cambridge, 1938).

MONSTRELET, ENGUERRAND DE, *Chronique*, ed. L. Douët-d'Arcq, Société de l'Histoire de France (6 vols.; Paris, 1857–62).

The Navy of the Lancastrian Kings, ed. S. Rose, Navy Records Soc. (London, 1982).

Original Letters Illustrative of English History, ed. H. Ellis, 1st ser. (3 vols.; London, 1824).

Paston Letters and Papers of the Fifteenth Century, ed. N. Davis (2 vols.; Oxford, 1971–6).

Placita Corone, ed. J. M. Kaye, Selden Soc., Suppl. Ser., 4 (London, 1966).

Proceedings and Ordinances of the Privy Council of England, ed. N. H. Nicolas (7 vols.; London, 1834–7).

The Records of the City of Norwich, ed. W. Hudson and J. C. Tingey (2 vols.; Norwich and London, 1906).

The Register of Nicholas Bubwith, Bishop of Bath and Wells, 1407–24, ed. T. S. Holmes, Somerset Record Soc., 29–30 (2 vols.; London, 1914).

The Register of Henry Chichele, Archbishop of Canterbury, 1414–1443, ed. E. F. Jacob, Canterbury and York Soc. (4 vols.; Oxford, 1938–47).

The Register of Bishop Philip Repingdon, 1405–19, ed. M. Archer, Lincoln Record Soc. (3 vols.; Lincoln, 1963–82).

Registrum Omnium Brevium Tam Originalium Quam Judicialium (London, 1687).

Les Reports des Cases (11 pts; London, 1678–80).

Reports of the Deputy Keeper of Public Records (120 vols.; London, 1840–1958): *Forty-First Report* (London, 1880); *Forty-Second Report* (London, 1881); *Forty-Fourth Report* (London, 1883).

The Reports of Sir John Spelman, ed. J. H. Baker, Selden Soc., 93–4 (2 vols.; London, 1976–7).

Return of Members of Parliament, 1213–1876 (London, 1878).

The Roll of the Shropshire Eyre of 1256, ed. A. Harding, Selden Soc., 96 (London, 1980).

Rolls of Northamptonshire Sessions of the Peace, ed. M. Gollancz, Northamptonshire Record Soc., 11 (Northampton, 1940).

Rotuli Parliamentorum, 1278–1503 (6 vols.; London, 1783–1832).

Rymes of Robyn Hood, ed. R. B. Dobson and J. Taylor (London, 1976).

ST GERMAN, CHRISTOPHER, *Doctor and Student*, ed. T. F. T. Plucknett and J. L. Barton, Selden Soc., 91 (London, 1974).

Secretum Secretorum: Nine English Versions, ed. M. A. Manzalaoui, Early English Text Soc., 276 (Oxford, 1977).

Select Cases in Chancery, 1364–1471, ed. W. P. Baildon, Selden Soc., 10 (London, 1896).
Select Cases in the Council of Henry VII, ed. C. G. Bayne and W. H. Dunham, Selden Soc., 75 (London, 1958).
Select Cases in the Court of King's Bench, ed. G. O. Sayles, Selden Soc., 55, 57, 58, 74, 76, 82, 88 (7 vols.; London, 1936–71).
Select Cases before the King's Council, ed. I. S. Leadam and J. F. Baldwin, Selden Soc., 35 (London, 1918).
Select Charters, ed. W. Stubbs (9th edn.; Oxford, 1913).
Select Documents of English Constitutional History, 1307–1485, ed. S. B. Chrimes and A. L. Brown (London, 1961).
Select Passages from the Works of Azo and Bracton, ed. F. W. Maitland, Selden Soc., 8 (London, 1894).
Selections from English Wycliffite Writings, ed. A. M. Hudson (Cambridge, 1978).
'Shrewsbury Gild Merchant Rolls', ed. C. H. Drinkwater, *TSAS* 3rd ser., 5 (1905), 35–54.
The Shropshire Peace Roll, ed. E. G. Kimball (Shrewsbury, 1959).
SMITH, THOMAS, *De Republica Anglorum*, ed. M. Dewar (Cambridge, 1972).
Snappe's Formulary, ed. H. E. Salter, Oxford Historical Soc., 80 (Oxford, 1924).
The Song of Lewes, ed. C. L. Kingsford (Oxford, 1890).
Statutes of the Realm, 1101–1713, ed. A. Luders *et al.* (11 vols.; London, 1810–28).
STOW, JOHN, *The Chronicles of England* (London, 1580).
STRECCHE, JOHN, 'The Chronicle of John Strecche for the Reign of Henry V', ed. F. Taylor, in *BJRL* 16 (1932), 137–87.
A Survey of the Duchy of Lancaster Lordships in Wales, ed. W. Rees, Board of Celtic Studies, University of Wales History and Law Ser., 12 (Cardiff, 1953).
The Tale of Gamelyn, ed. W. W. Skeat (Oxford, 1884).
Testamenta Vetusta, ed. N. H. Nicolas (2 vols.; London, 1826).
Thomae de Elmham Vita et Gesta Henrici Quinti, ed. T. Hearne (London, 1727).
The Treatise on the Laws and Customs of . . . England Commonly Called Glanvill, ed. G. D. G. Hall (London, 1965).
The 1235 Surrey Eyre, ed. C. A. F. Meekings, Surrey Record Soc., 31 (Guildford, 1979).
Twenty-Six Political and Other Poems, ed. J. Kail, Early English Text Soc., 124 (London, 1904).
WALSINGHAM, THOMAS, *Annales Ricardi Secundi et Henrici Quarti*, in *Johannis de Trokelowe Annales*, ed. H. T. Riley, Rolls Ser. (London, 1866).

—— *Historia Anglicana*, ed. H. T. Riley, Rolls Ser. (2 vols.; London, 1863–4).

—— *The St Albans Chronicle, 1406–20*, ed. V. H. Galbraith (Oxford, 1937).

WAURIN, JEAN DE, *Recueil des Croniques et Anchiennes Istories de la Grant Bretaigne à Présent Nommé Engleterre, 1422–31*, ed. W. Hardy, Rolls Ser. (London, 1879).

Wiltshire Gaol Delivery and Trailbaston Trials, 1275–1306, ed. R. B. Pugh, Wiltshire Record Soc., 33 (Devizes, 1977).

WYCLIF, JOHN, *Tractatus de Officio Regis*, ed. A. W. Pollard and C. Sayle, Wycliffe Society (London, 1887).

Year Books 30 and 31 Edward I, ed. A. J. Horwood, Rolls Ser. (London, 1863).

Year books of Henry VI: 1 Henry VI, 1422, ed. C. H. Williams, Selden Soc., 50 (London, 1933).

Year Books of Richard II: 11 Richard II, 1387–8, ed. I. D. Thornley, Ames Foundation (Cambridge, Mass., 1937).

Secondary Sources

ALLMAND, C. T., *Lancastrian Normandy, 1415–1450* (Oxford, 1983).

ASTON, M., 'Lollardy and Sedition, 1381–1431', *Past and Present*, 17 (1960), 1–44; repr. in ead., *Lollards and Reformers* (London, 1984), 1–44.

—— '"Caim's Castles": Poverty, Politics and Disendowment', in R. B. Dobson (ed.), *The Church, Politics and Patronage in the Fifteenth Century* (Gloucester, 1984), 45–81.

AVERY, M. E., 'The History of the Equitable Jurisdiction of Chancery before 1460', *BIHR* 42 (1969), 129–44.

AVRUTICK, J. B., 'Commissions of Oyer and Terminer in Fifteenth-Century England', M.Phil. thesis (London, 1967).

BAKER, J. H., 'Criminal Courts and Procedure at Common Law, 1550–1800', in J. S. Cockburn (ed.), *Crime in England, 1550–1800*, (London, 1977), 15–48.

—— *An Introduction to English Legal History* (2nd edn.; London, 1979).

—— *The Order of Serjeants at Law*, Selden Soc., Suppl. Ser., 5 (London, 1984).

BALDWIN, J. F., *The King's Council in England during the Later Middle Ages* (Oxford, 1913).

BALFOUR-MELVILLE, E. W. M., *James I, King of Scots, 1406–37* (London, 1936).

BARLOW, F., 'The King's Evil', *EHR* 95 (1980), 3–27.

BARNES, P. M., 'The Anstey Case', in P. M. Barnes and C. F. Slade (edd.), *A Medieval Miscellany for Doris Mary Stenton*, Pipe Roll Soc., New Ser., 36 (London, 1960), 1–24.

BEATTIE, J. M., *Crime and the Courts in England, 1660–1800* (Oxford, 1986).

BELLAMY, J. G., 'The Parliamentary Representation of Nottinghamshire, Derbyshire and Staffordshire during the Reign of Richard II', MA thesis (Nottingham, 1961).

—— *The Law of Treason in England in the Later Middle Ages* (Cambridge, 1970).

—— *Crime and Public Order in England in the Later Middle Ages* (London, 1973).

—— *Criminal Law and Society in Late Medieval and Tudor England* (Gloucester, 1984).

BENNETT, H. S., *The Pastons and Their England* (2nd edn.; Cambridge, 1932).

BENNETT, J. W., 'The Medieval Loveday', *Speculum*, 33 (1958), 351–70.

BENNETT, M. J., 'A County Community: Social Cohesion amongst the Cheshire Gentry, 1400–1425', *Northern History*, 8 (1973), 24–44.

—— *Community, Class and Careerism: Cheshire and Lancashire Society in the Age of Sir Gawain and the Green Knight* (Cambridge, 1983).

BERGES, W., *Die Fürstenspiegel des Höhen und Späten Mittelalters* (Leipzig, 1938).

BLATCHER, M., 'The Workings of the Court of King's Bench in the Fifteenth Century', Ph.D. thesis (London, 1936).

—— *The Court of King's Bench, 1450–1550* (London, 1978).

BLOCH, M., *Les Rois Thaumaturges* (new edn.; Paris, 1983).

BOOTH, P. H. W., 'Taxation and Public Order: Cheshire in 1353', *Northern History*, 12 (1976), 16–31.

BORN, L. K., 'The Perfect Prince: A Study in Thirteenth- and Fourteenth-Century Ideals', *Speculum*, 3 (1928), 470–504.

BRAND, P., 'Chief Justice and Felon: The Career of Thomas Weyland', in R. Eales and D. Sullivan (edd.), *The Political Context of Law* (London, 1987), 27–47.

BUCK, M. C., *Politics, Finance and the Church in the Reign of Edward II* (Cambridge, 1983).

BURNE, A. H., *The Agincourt War* (London, 1956).

CAM, H. M., *Studies in the Hundred Rolls*, Oxford Studies in Social and Legal History, 6 (Oxford, 1921).

—— *The Hundred and the Hundred Rolls* (London, 1930).

—— 'Shire Officials: Coroners, Constables and Bailiffs', in J. F. Willard, W. A. Morris, and W. H. Dunham (edd.), *The English*

Government at Work, 1327–1336 (3 vols.; Cambridge, Mass., 1940–50), iii. 165–83.

—— 'Stubbs Seventy Years After' in ead., *Law-Finders and Law-Makers in Medieval England* (London, 1962), 188–211.

CARPENTER, M. C., 'The Beauchamp Affinity: A Study of Bastard Feudalism at Work', *EHR* 95 (1980), 515–32.

—— 'Law, Justice and Landowners in Late Medieval England', *Law and History Review*, 1, no. 2 (1983), 205–37.

—— 'Political Society in Warwickshire, c.1401–72', Ph.D. thesis (Cambridge, 1976).

CATTO, J., 'Religious Change under Henry V', in G. L. Harriss (ed.), *Henry V: the Practice of Kingship*, (Oxford, 1985), 97–115.

CHERRY, M., 'The Courtenay Earls of Devon: The Formation and Disintegration of an Aristocratic Affinity', *Southern History*, 1 (1979), 71–97.

—— 'The Crown and the Political Community in Devonshire, 1377–1461' Ph.D. thesis (Swansea, 1981).

—— 'The Struggle for Power in Mid-Fourteenth Century Devonshire', in R. A. Griffiths (ed.), *Patronage, the Crown and the Provinces in Later Medieval England* (Gloucester, 1981), 123–44.

CHRIMES, S. B., *English Constitutional Ideas in the Fifteenth Century* (Cambridge, 1936).

—— *Henry VII* (London, 1972).

—— Ross, C. D., and GRIFFITHS, R. A. (edd.), *Fifteenth-Century England, 1399–1509* (Manchester, 1972).

CLANCHY, M. T., 'Did Henry III Have a Policy?', *History*, 53 (1968), 203–16.

—— 'Remembering the Past and the Good Old Law', *History*, 55 (1970), 165–76.

—— 'Law, Government and Society in Medieval England', *History*, 59 (1974), 73–8.

—— 'Highway Robbery and Trial by Battle in the Hampshire Eyre of 1249', in R. F. Hunnisett and J. B. Post (edd.), *Medieval Legal Records Edited in Memory of C. A. F. Meekings* (London, 1978), 25–61.

—— *From Memory to Written Record: England 1066–1307* (London, 1979).

—— 'Law and Love in the Middle Ages', in J. Bossy (ed.), *Disputes and Settlements* (Cambridge, 1983), 47–67.

CLARKE, M. V., and GALBRAITH, V. H., 'The Deposition of Richard II', *BJRL* 14 (1930), 125–81.

CLOUGH, C. H. (ed.), *Profession, Vocation, and Culture in Later Medieval England: Essays Dedicated to the Memory of A. R. Myers* (Liverpool, 1982).

COCKBURN, J. S., *A History of English Assizes, 1558–1714* (Cambridge, 1972).

—— 'Early Modern Assize Records as Historical Evidence', *Journal of the Soc. of Archivists*, 5 (1975), 215–31.

—— 'Trial by the Book? Fact and Theory in the Criminal Process, 1558–1625', in J. H. Baker (ed.) *Legal Records and the Historian* (London, 1978), 60–79.

COKAYNE, G. E. (ed.), *The Complete Peerage of England* . . . (new edn., 12 vols.; London, 1910–59).

COLEMAN, J., *English Literature in History, 1350–1400: Medieval Readers and Writers* (London, 1981).

CROOK, D., 'The Later Eyres', *EHR* 97 (1982), 241–68.

—— *Records of the General Eyre* (London, 1982).

—— 'List of Assize Rolls, 1206–1481', unpublished PRO reading room list (1984).

DAVIES, R. R., 'Owain Glyn Dŵr and the Welsh Squirearchy', *Transactions of the Honourable Soc. of Cymmrodorion* (1967–8), 150–69.

—— 'Baronial Accounts, Incomes and Arrears in the Later Middle Ages', *Economic History Review*, 2nd ser., 21 (1968), 211–29.

DENHOLM-YOUNG, N., *Collected Papers on Medieval Subjects* (Cardiff, 1969).

DOBSON, R. B. (ed.), *The Peasants' Revolt of 1381* (2nd edn.; London, 1983).

—— (ed.), *The Church, Politics and Patronage in the Fifteenth Century* (Gloucester, 1984).

DRINKWATER, C. H., 'Montford Bridge', *TSAS* 3rd ser., 7 (1907), 71–4.

DUBY, G., *The Three Orders*, tr. A. Goldhammer (Chicago, Ill., 1980).

DUGDALE, W., *The Antiquities of Warwickshire*, revised by W. Thomas (2nd edn., 2 vols.; London, 1730).

DYER, C. C., 'The Social and Economic Background to the Rural Revolt of 1381', in R. H. Hilton and T. H. Aston (edd.), *The English Rising of 1381* (Cambridge, 1984), 9–42.

ELTON, G. R., 'Crime and the Historian', in J. S. Cockburn (ed.), *Crime in England, 1550–1800* (London, 1977), 1–14.

ERNST, D. R., 'The Moribund Appeal of Death: Compensating Survivors and Controlling Jurors in Early Modern England', *AJLH* 28 (1984), 164–88.

EVERITT, A., *The Community of Kent and the Great Rebellion* (London, 1966).

FAITH, R., 'The "Great Rumour" of 1377 and Peasant Ideology', in R. H. Hilton and T. H. Aston (edd.), *The English Rising of 1381* (Cambridge, 1984), 43–73.

FEAVERYEAR, J., *The Pound Sterling* (2nd edn.; Oxford, 1963).

FLETCHER, A., *A County Community in Peace and War: Sussex, 1600–1660* (London, 1975).

FORD, C. J., 'Piracy or Policy: The Crisis in the Channel, 1400–1403', *TRHS* 5th ser., 29 (1979), 63–78.

FRYDE, N. M., 'A Medieval Robber Baron: Sir John Molyns of Stoke Poges, Buckinghamshire', in R. F. Hunnisett and J. B. Post (edd.), *Medieval Legal Records Edited in Memory of C. A. F. Meekings* (London, 1978), 197–222.

GABEL, L. C., *Benefit of Clergy in England in the Later Middle Ages* (Northampton, Mass., 1929).

GARDINER, D. A., 'John Hawley of Dartmouth', *Transactions of the Devonshire Association*, 98 (1966), 173–205.

GILLESPIE, J., 'Sir John Fortescue's Concept of Royal Will', *NMS* 23 (1979), 47–65.

GIVEN, J. B., *Society and Homicide in Thirteenth-Century England* (Stanford, Cal., 1977).

GIVEN-WILSON, C., *The Royal Household and the King's Affinity* (London, 1986).

GOLLANCZ, M., 'The System of Gaol Delivery as Illustrated in the Extant Gaol Delivery Rolls of the Fifteenth Century', MA thesis (London, 1936).

GOODMAN, A. E., 'Responses to Requests for Military Service under Henry V', *Northern History*, 17 (1981), 240–52.

GRANSDEN, A., *Historical Writing in England: c.1307 to the Early Sixteenth Century* (London, 1982).

GREEN, M., *Town Life in the Fifteenth Century* (2 vols.; London, 1894).

GREEN, T. A., 'The Jury and the English Law of Homicide, 1200–1600', *Michigan Law Review*, 74 (1976), 413–99.

—— *Verdict According to Conscience* (Chicago, Ill., 1985).

GRIFFITHS, R. A., 'Some Partisans of Owain Glyn Dŵr at Oxford', *BBCS* 20 (1963), 282–92.

—— 'The Glyn Dŵr Rebellion in North Wales through the Eyes of an Englishman', *BBCS* 22 (1967), 151–68.

—— *The Principality of Wales in the Later Middle Ages: the Structure and Personnel of Government*, Board of Celtic Studies, University of Wales History and Law Ser., 26 (Cardiff, 1972).

—— 'Patronage, Politics and the Principality of Wales, 1413–61', in B. H. Hearder and H. R. Loyn (edd.), *British Government and Administration: Studies Presented to S. B. Chrimes* (Cardiff, 1974), 69–86.

—— 'William Wawe and his Gang, 1427', *Proceedings of the Hampshire Field Club and Archaeological Soc.*, 33 (1977), 89–93.

GRIFFITHS, R. A., (ed.), *Patronage, the Crown and the Provinces in Later Medieval England* (Gloucester, 1981).

—— *The Reign of King Henry VI* (London, 1981).

—— and SHERBORNE, J. W. (edd.), *Kings and Nobles in the Later Middle Ages: a Tribute to Charles Ross* (Gloucester, 1986).

GUENÉE, B., *Tribunaux et Gens de Justice dans le Bailliage de Senlis à la Fin du Moyen Age* (Paris, 1963).

—— *States and Rulers in Later Medieval Europe*, tr. J. Vale (Oxford, 1985).

Guide to the Contents of the Public Record Office (2 vols.; London, 1963).

GUTH, D. J., 'Enforcing Late-Medieval Law: Patterns in Litigation during Henry VII's Reign', in J. H. Baker (ed.), *Legal Records and the Historian* (London, 1978), 80–96.

HAINES, R. M., ' "Our Master Mariner, Our Soveraign Lord": a Contemporary Preacher's View of King Henry V', *Medieval Studies*, 38 (1976), 85–96.

—— *The Church and Politics in Fourteenth-Century England: the Career of Adam Orleton* (Cambridge, 1978).

HALL, G. D. G., 'Three Courts of the Hundred of Penwith', in R. F. Hunnisett and J. B. Post (edd.), *Medieval Legal Records Edited in Memory of C. A. F. Meekings* (London, 1978), 169–96.

HALLAM, E. M., *Domesday Book through Nine Centuries* (London, 1986).

HAMIL, F. C., 'The King's Approvers', *Speculum*, 11 (1936), 238–58.

HAMMER, C. I., 'Patterns of Homicide in Fourteenth-Century Oxford', *Past and Present*, 78 (1978), 1–23.

HANAWALT, B. A., 'Fur Collar Crime: The Pattern of Crime among the Fourteenth-Century English Nobility', *Journal of Social History*, 8, no. 4 (1975), 1–17.

—— *Crime and Conflict in English Communites, 1300–1348* (Cambridge, Mass., 1979).

HARDING, A., 'The Origins and Early History of the Keeper of the Peace', *TRHS* 5th ser., 10 (1960), 85–109.

—— *A Social History of English Law* (Harmondsworth, 1966).

—— *The Law Courts of Medieval England* (London, 1973).

—— 'Plaints and Bills in the History of English Law', in D. Jenkins (ed.), *Legal History Studies 1972* (Cardiff, 1975), 65–86.

—— 'Early Trailbaston Proceedings from the Lincoln Roll of 1305', in R. F. Hunnisett and J. B. Post (edd.), *Medieval Legal Records Edited in Memory of C. A. F. Meekings* (London, 1978), 143–68.

—— 'The Origins of the Crime of Conspiracy', *TRHS* 5th ser., 33 (1983), 89–108.

—— 'The Revolt against the Justices', in R. H. Hilton and T. H. Aston (edd.), *The English Rising of 1381* (Cambridge, 1984), 165–93.

HARGREAVES, A. D., 'Equity and the Latin Side of Chancery', *LQR* 68 (1952), 481–99.

HARRISS, G. L., *King, Parliament, and Public Finance in England to 1369* (Oxford, 1975).

—— 'Theory and Practice in Royal Taxation', *EHR* 97 (1982), 811–19.

—— (ed.), *Henry V: the Practice of Kingship* (Oxford, 1985).

—— *Cardinal Beaufort: A Study of Lancastrian Ascendancy and Decline* (Oxford, 1988).

HASTINGS, M., *The Court of Common Pleas in Fifteenth-Century England* (Ithaca, NY, 1947).

HEWITT, H. J., *The Organization of War under Edward III* (Manchester, 1966).

HICKS, M. A., 'Restraint, Mediation and Private Justice: George, Duke of Clarence as "Good Lord"', *Journal of Legal History*, 4, no. 2 (1983), 56–71.

HIGHFIELD, J. R. L., and JEFFS, R. (edd.), *The Crown and the Local Communities in England and France in the Fifteenth Century* (Gloucester, 1981).

HILTON, R. H., *A Medieval Society: The West Midlands at the End of the Thirteenth Century* (Cambridge, 1967).

HOLDSWORTH, W., *A History of English Law* (12 vols.; London, 1922–38).

HOLMES, G. A., *The Good Parliament of 1376* (Oxford, 1975).

HOLT, J. C., *Magna Carta* (Cambridge, 1965).

—— *Robin Hood* (London, 1982).

HUDSON, A. M., 'John Purvey: A Reconsideration of the Evidence for his Life and Writings', *Viator*, 12 (1981), 355–80.

—— *Lollards and Their Books* (London, 1985).

HUNNISETT, R. F., 'The Medieval Coroners' Rolls', *AJLH* 3 (1959), 95–124, 205–21, 324–59.

—— *The Medieval Coroner* (Cambridge, 1961).

HURNARD, N. D., *The King's Pardon for Homicide before 1307* (Oxford, 1969).

HYAMS, P. R., 'Trial by Ordeal: The Key to Proof in the Early Common Law', in M. S. Arnold, T. A. Green, S. A. Scully, and S. D. White (edd.), *On the Laws and Customs of England: Essays in Honor of Samuel E. Thorne* (Chapel Hill, NC, 1981), 90–126.

IVES, E. W., *The Common Lawyers of Pre-Reformation England* (Cambridge, 1983).

JACOB, E. F., 'Sir John Fortescue and the Law of Nature', *BJRL* 18 (1934), 359–76.

—— *The Fifteenth Century* (Oxford, 1961).

JACOB, E. F., 'The Disputed Election at Fountain's Abbey, 1410–16', in id., *Essays in Later Medieval History* (Manchester, 1968), 79–97.

JANEAU, H., 'L'Arbitrage en Dauphiné au Moyen Age', *Revue Historique de Droit Français et Étranger*, 4th ser., 24–5 (1946–7), 229–71.

JONES, J. G., 'Government and the Welsh Community: The North-East Borderland in the Fifteenth Century', in B. H. Hearder and H. R. Loyn (edd.), *British Government and Administration: Studies Presented to S. B. Chrimes* (Cardiff, 1974), 55–68.

JONES, M. (ed), *Gentry and Lesser Nobility in Late Medieval Europe* (Gloucester, 1986).

JONES, M. K., 'John Beaufort, Duke of Somerset, and the French Expedition of 1443', in R. A. Griffiths (ed.), *Patronage, the Crown and the Provinces in Later Medieval England* (Gloucester, 1981), 79–102.

KAEUPER, R. W., 'Law and Order in Fourteenth-Century England: the Evidence of Special Commissions of Oyer and Terminer', *Speculum*, 54 (1979), 734–84.

—— 'An Historian's Reading of the Tale of Gamelyn', *Medium Aevum*, 52 (1983), 51–62.

KANTOROWICZ, E., *Laudes Regiae* (Berkeley, Cal., 1946).

—— *The King's Two Bodies* (Princeton, NJ, 1957).

KEEN, M. H., *The Laws of War in the Later Middle Ages* (Oxford, 1965).

—— *England in the Later Middle Ages* (London, 1973).

—— *Chivalry* (London, 1984).

KERN, F., *Kingship and Law in the Middle Ages*, tr. S. B. Chrimes (Oxford, 1939).

KIGHTLY, C., 'The Early Lollards: A Survey of Popular Lollard Activity in England, 1382–1428', Ph.D. thesis (York, 1975).

KINGSFORD, C. L., *English Historical Literature in the Fifteenth Century* (Oxford, 1913).

—— *Prejudice and Promise in Fifteenth-Century England* (Oxford, 1925).

KIRBY, J. L., *Henry IV of England* (London, 1970).

KNOWLSON, G. A., *Jean V, Duc de Bretagne, et L'Angleterre* (Cambridge, 1964).

LANGBEIN, J. H., 'The Origins of Public Prosecution at Common Law', *AJLH* 17 (1973), 313–35.

—— *Prosecuting Crime in the Renaissance* (Cambridge, Mass., 1974).

LAPSLEY, G. T., 'Bracton and the Authorship of the "Addicio de Cartis"', *EHR* 62 (1947), 1–19.

—— 'Some Recent Advance in English Constitutional History', in id., *Crown, Community, and Parliament* (Oxford, 1951), 1–33.

LEFF, G., *Heresy in the Later Middle Ages* (2 vols.; Manchester, 1967).

LEGG, L. G. W., *English Coronation Records* (London, 1901).

LEWIS, P. S., 'War Propaganda and Historiography in Fifteenth-Century France and England', *TRHS* 5th ser., 15 (1965), 1–21.

—— 'Two Pieces of Fifteenth-Century Political Iconography', in id., *Essays in Later Medieval French History* (London, 1985), 191–2.

List of Sheriffs for England and Wales, PRO Lists and Indexes, 9 (London, 1898).

LLOYD, J. E., *Owen Glendower* (Oxford, 1931).

LLOYD, T. H., *The English Wool Trade in the Middle Ages* (Cambridge, 1977).

LOSERTH, J., 'Über die Beziehungen zwischen englischen und böhmischen Wiclifiten', *Mitteilungen des Österreichischen Instituts für Geschichtsforschung*, 12 (1891), 254–69.

McFARLANE, K. B., 'Henry V, Bishop Beaufort and the Red Hat', *EHR* 60 (1945), 316–48; repr. in id., *England in the Fifteenth Century* (London, 1981), 79–114.

—— *John Wycliffe and the Beginnings of English Nonconformity* (London, 1952); repr. as *Wycliffe and English Nonconformity* (London, 1972).

—— *Lancastrian Kings and Lollard Knights* (Oxford, 1972).

—— *The Nobility of Later Medieval England* (Oxford, 1973).

—— *England in the Fifteenth Century: Collected Essays* (London, 1981).

McKENNA, J. W., 'The Coronation Oil of the Yorkist Kings', *EHR* 82 (1967), 102–4.

McNIVEN, P., 'Prince Henry and the English Political Crisis of 1412', *History*, 65 (1980), 1–16.

—— 'The Problem of Henry IV's Health, 1405–13', *EHR* 100 (1985), 747–72.

—— *Heresy and Politics in the Reign of Henry IV: The Burning of John Badby* (Woodbridge, 1987).

MACE, F. A., 'Devonshire Ports in the Fourteenth and Fifteenth Centuries', *TRHS* 4th ser., 8 (1925), 98–126.

MADDERN, P., 'Violence, Crime and Public Disorder in East Anglia, 1422–42', D.Phil. thesis (Oxford, 1985).

MADDICOTT, J. R., *Thomas of Lancaster* (Oxford, 1970).

—— 'The Birth and Setting of the Ballads of Robin Hood', *EHR* 93 (1978), 276–99.

—— 'The County Community and the Making of Public Opinion in Fourteenth-Century England', *TRHS* 5th ser., 18 (1978), 27–43.

—— *Law and Lordship: Royal Justices as Retainers in Thirteenth- and Fourteenth-Century England*, Past and Present Supplement 4 (Oxford, 1978).

—— 'Magna Carta and the Local Community, 1215–1259', *Past and Present*, 102 (1984), 25–65.

MADDICOTT, J. R., 'Poems of Social Protest in early Fourteenth-Century England', in W. M. Ormrod (ed.), *England in the Fourteenth Century* (Woodbridge, 1986), 130–44.

MEEKINGS, C. A. F., 'King's Bench Files', in J. H. Baker (ed.), *Legal Records and the Historian* (London, 1978), 97–139.

MILSOM, S. F. C., *The Legal Framework of English Feudalism* (Cambridge, 1976).

—— *Historical Foundations of the Common Law* (2nd edn.; London, 1981).

MORRILL, J. S., *The Revolt of the Provinces* (London, 1976).

MORRIS, W. A., *The Frankpledge System* (New York, NY, 1910).

MUNRO, J. H., *Wool, Cloth and Gold* (Toronto, 1972).

NADER, L., and TODD, H. F. (edd.), *The Disputing Process: Law in Ten Societies* (New York, NY, 1978).

NEWHALL, R. A., *Muster and Review* (Cambridge, Mass., 1940).

NICHOLSON, R., *Scotland: The Later Middle Ages* (Edinburgh, 1974).

NICOLAS, N. H., *History of the Battle of Agincourt* (London, 1827).

NOONAN, J. T., *Bribes* (London, 1984).

ORME, N., *From Childhood to Chivalry* (London, 1984).

ORMROD, W. M., 'Edward III's Government of England, *c.*1346 to 1356', D.Phil. thesis (Oxford, 1984).

OWST, G. R., *Literature and Pulpit in Medieval England* (2nd edn.; Oxford, 1961).

PALMER, R. C., *The County Courts of Medieval England, 1150–1350* (Princeton, NJ, 1982).

—— *The Whilton Dispute, 1264–1380* (Princeton, NJ, 1984).

PARRY-JONES, J., 'Owen Glyndŵr and the Battle of Shrewsbury', *TSAS* 3rd ser., 3 (1903), 163–70.

PAYLING, S. J., 'Inheritance and Local Politics in the Later Middle Ages: the Case of Ralph, Lord Cromwell and the Heriz Inheritance', *NMS* 30 (1986), 67–96.

—— 'Political Society in Lancastrian Nottinghamshire', D.Phil. thesis (Oxford, 1987).

PHILLIPS, J. R. S., *Aymer de Valence, Earl of Pembroke* (Oxford, 1972).

—— 'Edward II and the Prophets', in W. M. Ormrod (ed.), *England in the Fourteenth Century* (Woodbridge, 1986), 189–201.

PIKE, L. O., 'Common Law and Conscience in the Ancient Court of Chancery', *LQR* 1 (1885), 443–54.

PISTONO, S. P., 'Henry IV and John Hawley, Privateer', *Transactions of the Devonshire Association*, 111 (1979), 145–63.

PLUCKNETT, T. F. T., 'A Commentary on the Indictments', in B. H. Putnam (ed.), *Proceedings before the Justices of the Peace in the Fourteenth and Fifteenth Centuries: Edward III to Richard III*, Ames

Foundation (Cambridge, Mass., 1938), cxxxiii–clxi.

—— *A Concise History of the Common Law* (5th edn.; London, 1956).

POLLARD, A. J., 'The Family of Talbot, Lords Talbot and Earls of Shrewsbury, in the Fifteenth Century', Ph.D. thesis (Bristol, 1968).

—— 'The Richmondshire Community of Gentry during the Wars of the Roses', in C. D. Ross (ed.), *Patronage, Pedigree and Power in Late Medieval England* (Gloucester, 1979), 37–59.

—— (ed.), *Property and Politics: Essays in Later Medieval English History* (Gloucester, 1984).

POLLOCK, F. M., and MAITLAND, F. W., *The History of English Law before the Time of Edward I* (2nd edn.; repr. Cambridge, 1968).

POST, J. B., 'Some Limitations of the Medieval Peace Rolls', *Journal of the Soc. of Archivists*, 4 (1973), 633–9.

—— 'Criminals and the Law in the Reign of Richard II', D.Phil. thesis (Oxford, 1976).

—— 'Courts, Councils and Arbitrators in the Ladbroke Manor Dispute, 1382–1400', in R. F. Hunnisett and J. B. Post (edd.), *Medieval Legal Records Edited in Memory of C. A. F. Meekings* (London, 1978), 289–339.

—— 'Equitable Resorts before 1450', in E. W. Ives and A. H. Manchester (edd.), *Law, Litigants and the Legal Profession* (London, 1983), 68–79.

—— 'Local Jurisdictions and Judgment of Death in Later Medieval England', *Criminal Justice History*, 4 (1983), 1–21.

—— 'The Admissibility of Defence Counsel in English Criminal Procedure', *Journal of Legal History*, 5, no. 3 (1984), 23–32.

—— 'The Evidential Value of Approvers' Appeals: The Case of William Rose, 1389', *Law and History Review*, 3, no. 1 (1985), 91–100.

POWELL, E., 'Public Order and Law Enforcement in Shropshire and Staffordshire in the Early Fifteenth Century', D.Phil. thesis (Oxford, 1979).

—— 'Social Research and the Use of Medieval Criminal Records', *Michigan Law Review*, 79 (1981), 967–78.

—— 'Arbitration and the Law in England in the Later Middle Ages', *TRHS* 5th ser., 33 (1983), 49–67.

—— 'The King's Bench in Shropshire and Staffordshire in 1414', in E. W. Ives and A. H. Manchester (edd.), *Law, Litigants and the Legal Profession* (London, 1983), 94–103.

—— 'List of Special Oyer and Terminer Proceedings, 1262–1443', unpublished PRO reading room list (1984).

—— 'Proceedings before the Justices of the Peace at Shrewsbury in 1414', *EHR* 99 (1984), 535–50.

POWELL, E., 'Settlement of Disputes by Arbitration in Fifteenth-Century England', *Law and History Review*, 2, no. 1 (1984), 21–43.
—— 'The Restoration of Law and Order', in G. L. Harriss (ed.), *Henry V: the Practice of Kingship* (Oxford, 1985), 53–73.
—— 'The Administration of Criminal Justice in Late Medieval England: Peace Sessions and Assizes', in R. Eales and D. Sullivan (edd.), *The Political Context of Law* (London, 1987), 49–59.
—— 'Jury Trial at Gaol Delivery in the Late Middle Ages: The Midland Circuit, 1400–29', in J. S. Cockburn and T. A. Green (edd.), *Twelve Good Men and True: The English Criminal Trial Jury, 1200–1800* (Princeton, NJ, 1988), 78–116.
POWICKE, F. M., and FRYDE, E. B. (edd.), *Handbook of English Chronology* (2nd edn.; London, 1961).
POWICKE, M. R., and SANDQUIST, T. A. (edd.), *Essays in Medieval History Presented to Bertie Wilkinson* (Toronto, 1969).
PRESCOTT, A. J., 'The Judicial Records of the Rising of 1381', Ph.D. thesis (London, 1984).
PRESTWICH, M. C., *War, Politics and Finance under Edward I* (London, 1972).
—— 'The Piety of Edward I', in W. M. Ormrod (ed.), *England in the Thirteenth Century* (Harlaxton, 1985), 120–8.
PUGH, R. B., *Imprisonment in Medieval England* (Cambridge, 1968).
—— 'Some Reflections of a Medieval Criminologist', *PBA* 59 (1973), 83–103.
—— 'The Duration of Criminal Trials in Medieval England', in E. W. Ives and A. H. Manchester (edd.), *Law, Litigants and the Legal Profession* (London, 1983), 104–15.
—— 'Early Registers of English Outlaws', *AJLH* 27 (1983), 319–29.
PUGH, T. B. (ed.), *The Marcher Lordships of South Wales, 1415–1536*, Board of Celtic Studies, University of Wales History and Law Ser., 20 (Cardiff, 1963).
—— 'The Southampton Plot of 1415', in R. A. Griffiths and J. W. Sherborne (edd.), *Kings and Nobles in the Later Middle Ages* (Gloucester, 1986), 62–89.
PUTNAM, B. H., *The Enforcement of the Statute of Labourers during the First Decade after the Black Death, 1349–59* (New York, NY, 1908).
—— (ed.), *Early Treatises on the Practice of the Justices of the Peace in the Fifteenth and Sixteenth Centuries*, Oxford Studies in Social and Legal History, 7 (Oxford, 1924).
—— 'The Transformation of the Keepers of the Peace into Justices of the Peace, 1327–80', *TRHS* 4th ser., 12 (1929), 19–48.
—— (ed.), *Proceedings before the Justices of the Peace in the Fourteenth and Fifteenth Centuries: Edward III to Richard III*, Ames Foundation (Cambridge, Mass., 1938).

—— *The Place in Legal History of Sir William Shareshull* (Cambridge, 1950).

RAMSAY, N., 'Retained Legal Counsel, *c*.1275–*c*.1475', *TRHS* 5th ser., 35 (1985), 95–112.

RAWCLIFFE, C., *The Staffords, Earls of Stafford and Dukes of Buckingham, 1394–1521* (Cambridge, 1978).

—— 'Baronial Councils in the Later Middle Ages', in C. D. Ross (ed.), *Patronage, Pedigree and Power in Later Medieval England* (Gloucester, 1979), 87–108.

—— 'The Great Lord as Peacekeeper: Arbitration by English Noblemen and Their Councils in the Later Middle Ages', in J. A. Guy (ed.), *Law and Social Change* (London, 1984), 34–54.

REES, W., *An Historical Atlas of Wales* (London, 1951).

REYNOLDS, S., *Kingdoms and Communities in Western Europe, 900–1300* (Oxford, 1984).

RICHARDSON, H. G., 'John Oldcastle in Hiding', *EHR* 55 (1940), 432–8.

—— 'The English Coronation Oath', *Speculum*, 24 (1949), 44–75.

—— 'The Coronation in Medieval England', *Traditio*, 16 (1960), 111–202.

—— and SAYLES, G. O., *The Governance of Medieval England from the Conquest to Magna Carta* (Edinburgh, 1963).

RICHMOND, C. F., 'After McFarlane', *History*, 68 (1983), 46–60.

ROBERTS, G., 'The Anglesey Submissions of 1406', *BBCS* 15, pt. i (1952), 39–61.

ROBERTS, S., *Order and Dispute* (Harmondsworth, 1979).

—— 'The Study of Disputes: Anthropological Perspectives', in J. Bossy (ed.), *Disputes and Settlements* (Cambridge, 1983), 1–19.

RÖHRKASTEN, H., 'Some Problems of the Evidence of Fourteenth-Century Approvers', *Journal of Legal History*, 5, no.3 (1984), 14–22.

ROSENTHAL, J. T., 'Feuds and Private Peace-Making: A Fifteenth-Century Example', *NMS* 14 (1970), 84–90.

ROSKELL, J. S., 'William Burley of Broncroft', *TSAS* 66 (1960), 263–72.

—— *The Commons and their Speakers in English Parliaments, 1376–1523* (Manchester, 1965).

—— *The Impeachment of Michael de la Pole, Earl of Suffolk* (Manchester, 1984).

ROSS, C. D., *Edward IV* (London, 1975).

—— (ed.), *Patronage, Pedigree and Power in Later Medieval England* (Gloucester, 1979).

—— *Richard III* (London, 1981).

ROWNEY, I., 'Arbitration in Gentry Disputes in the Later Middle Ages', *History*, 67 (1982), 367–76.

SANDQUIST, T. A., 'The Holy Oil of St Thomas of Canterbury', in M. R. Powicke and T. A. Sandquist (edd.), *Essays in Medieval History Presented to Bertie Wilkinson* (Toronto, 1969), 330–44.

SAUL, N., *Knights and Esquires: The Gloucestershire Gentry in the Fourteenth Century* (Oxford, 1981).

SCATTERGOOD, V. J., *Politics and Poetry in the Fifteenth Century* (London, 1971).

SCHNEEBECK, H. N., 'The Law of Felony in Medieval England from the Accession of Edward I to the Mid-Fourteenth Century', Ph.D. thesis (Iowa, 1973).

SCHULZ, F., 'Bracton on Kingship', *EHR* 60 (1945), 136–76.

SEYMOUR, M. C., 'The Manuscripts of Hoccleve's *Regiment of Princes*', *Edinburgh Bibliographical Soc. Transactions*, 4, pt. 7 (1974 for 1968–71), 253–97.

SHARPE, J. A., *Crime in Early Modern England, 1550–1750* (London, 1984).

SIMPSON, A. W. B., 'The Penal Bond with Conditional Defeasance', *LQR* 82 (1966), 392–422.

SMITH, A., 'Litigation and Politics: Sir John Fastolf's Defence of his English Property', in A. J. Pollard (ed.) *Property and Politics: Essays in Later Medieval English History* (Gloucester, 1984), 59–75.

SMITH, J. B., 'The Last Phase of the Glyndŵr Rebellion' *BBCS* 22 (1967), 250–60.

SMITH, L. O. W., 'The Lordships of Chirk and Oswestry, 1282–1415', Ph.D. thesis (London, 1971).

SMYTH, J., *Lives of the Berkeleys*, ed. J. MacLean (2 vols.; Gloucester, 1883).

SOMERVILLE, R., *History of the Duchy of Lancaster*, vol. i. (London, 1953).

STONE, L., *The Crisis of the Aristocracy* (Oxford, 1965).

STONES, E. L. G., 'The Folvilles of Ashby Folville, Leicestershire, and their Associates in Crime', *TRHS* 5th ser., 7 (1957), 117–36.

STOREY, R. L., *Thomas Langley and the Bishopric of Durham, 1406–1437* (London, 1961).

—— 'Liveries and Commissions of the Peace, 1388–90', in F. R. H. Du Boulay and C. M. Barron (edd.), *The Reign of Richard II: Essays in Honour of May McKisack* (London, 1971), 131–52.

—— *The End of the House of Lancaster* (London, 1966; 2nd edn., Gloucester, 1986).

STUBBS, W., *Constitutional History of England* (3 vols.; 5th edn., Oxford, 1903).

SUTHERLAND, D. W., *Quo Warranto Proceedings in the Reign of Edward I* (Oxford, 1963).

—— 'Mesne Process upon Personal Actions in the Early Common Law', *LQR* 82 (1966), 482–96.
TAYLOR, M. M., 'The Justices of Assize', in J. F. Willard, W. A. Morris, and W. H. Dunham (edd.), *The English Government at Work, 1327–1336* (3 vols.; Cambridge, Mass., 1940–50), iii. 219–47.
THAYER, J. B., *A Preliminary Treatise on Evidence at the Common Law* (London, 1898).
THOMSON, J. A. F., *The Later Lollards, 1414–1520* (Oxford, 1965).
THORNLEY, I. D., 'Treason by Words in the Fifteenth Century', *EHR* 32 (1917), 556–61.
TIERNEY, B., 'Bracton on Government', *Speculum*, 38 (1963), 295–317.
TILLOTSON, J. H., 'Peasant Unrest in the England of Richard II: Some Evidence from Royal Records', *Historical Studies*, 16 (1974), 1–16.
TOUT, T. F., *Chapters in the Administrative History of Medieval England* (6 vols.; Manchester, 1920–30).
TURNER, R. V., *The King and His Courts* (Ithaca, NY, 1968).
TYLDESLEY, C. J., 'The Crown and the Local Communities in Devon and Cornwall, 1377–1422', Ph.D. thesis (Exeter, 1978).
ULLMANN, W., 'Thomas Becket's Miraculous Oil', *Journal of Theological Studies*, 8 (1957), 129–33.
VAUGHAN, R., *John the Fearless* (London, 1966).
The Victoria County History of Shropshire, vol. iii, ed. G. C. Baugh (Oxford, 1979).
The Victoria County History of Wiltshire, vol. v, ed. R. B. Pugh and E. Crittall (Oxford, 1957).
VIRGOE, R., 'The Death of William de la Pole, Duke of Suffolk', *BJRL* 47 (1964–5), 499–501.
WAUGH, S. L., 'The Profits of Violence: the Minor Gentry in the Rebellion of 1321–2 in Gloucestershire and Herefordshire', *Speculum*, 52 (1977), 843–69.
WAUGH, W. T., 'Sir John Oldcastle', *EHR* 20 (1905), 434–56, 637–58.
WEDGWOOD, J. C., *Staffordshire Parliamentary History, 1213–1603*, Staffordshire Historical Collections, 3rd ser., 8 (London, 1917–18).
WEYMAN, H. T., 'Shropshire Members of Parliament, 1393–1584', *TSAS* 4th ser., 11 (1928), 1–48.
WHITE, S. D., ' "Pactum . . . Legem Vincit et Amor Judicium": The Settlement of Disputes by Compromise in Eleventh-Century Western France', *AJLH* 22 (1978), 281–308.
WHITTICK, C., 'The Role of the Criminal Appeal in the Later Middle

Ages', in J. A. Guy (ed.), *Law and Social Change* (London, 1984), 55–72.

WILKINSON, B., 'The Authorization of Chancery Writs under Edward III', *BJRL* 8 (1924), 107–39.

—— *The Constitutional History of Medieval England, 1216–1399* (3 vols.; London, 1948–58).

WILKS, M., *The Problem of Sovereignty in the Later Middle Ages* (Cambridge, 1963).

—— 'Royal Priesthood: the Origins of Lollardy', in *The Church in a Changing Society: Proceedings of the CIHEC Conference, 1977* (Uppsala, 1978), 63–70.

—— '*Reformatio Regni*: Wyclif and Hus as Leaders of Religious Movements', in D. Baker (ed.), *Studies in Church History IX* (Cambridge, 1972), 109–30.

WILLIAMS, G., *The Welsh Church from the Conquest to the Reformation* (Cardiff, 1962).

WOLFFE, B. P., *Henry VI* (London 1981).

WRIGHT, S. M., *The Derbyshire Gentry in the Fifteenth Century*, Derbyshire Record Soc., 8 (Chesterfield, 1983).

WYLIE, J. H., *History of England under Henry the Fourth* (4 vols.; London, 1884–98).

—— and WAUGH, W. T., *The Reign of Henry the Fifth* (3 vols.; Cambridge, 1914–29).

Glossary

AMERCEMENT. A fine.

APPEAL OF FELONY. A private prosecution for felony brought by the victim or (in the case of homicide) the victim's kin.

ASSIZE OF NOVEL DISSEISIN. A form of legal action dealing with recent dispossession of freehold.

ASSIZES. The twice-yearly visitations of royal judges into the shires to determine civil and criminal business.

CAPIAS. A writ ordering arrest and appearance in court: the first stage of legal process upon an indictment for felony.

CORAM REGE. Literally, 'in the king's presence': the term given to proceedings in the court of king's bench.

DEFEASANCE. The rendering null and void (e.g. of a conditional bond or recognizance).

ENFEOFFMENT TO USE. A form of trust enabling landlords to escape liability to the king's feudal rights. Legal ownership of the land was vested in a group of feoffees (or trustees), who then conveyed the land back to the 'use' of the lord.

ESCHEAT. A forfeiture of lands or goods to the king.

EXIGENT. Legal process leading to outlawry.

EYRE. *See* general eyre.

FEET OF FINES. Records of agreements, or final concords, concluded in court to terminate legal actions.

FELONY. Serious crime punishable by death (e.g. homicide, robbery).

GAOL DELIVERY. The trial of prisoners held in a gaol upon the charges for which they had been arrested and imprisoned.

GENERAL EYRE. The periodic visitation in the twelfth and thirteenth centuries of royal justices empowered to hear all manner of pleas, civil and criminal.

INDICTMENT. A formal, written accusation of crime recorded by a presenting jury before a court. *See also* presentment.

MAINPERNOR. A surety responsible for the appearance of a man in court, or for his future good behaviour.

NISI PRIUS. The process by which a case was referred for trial from Westminster to the locality.

NOVEL DISSEISIN. *See* assize of novel disseisin.

OYER AND TERMINER. A commission which empowered justices to 'hear and determine' certain cases or categoiics of cascs.

PLAINT. An oral or written statement of grievance made to a court of law.

PRESENTMENT. A formal, written accusation of crime recorded by a presenting jury from their own knowledge before a court. *See also* indictment.

QUITCLAIM. To give a formal discharge or release.

RECOGNIZANCE. A bond entered into before a court, by which a person undertakes to perform some act, on pain of a financial penalty.

TOURN. The court held by the sheriff twice a year in each hundred or wapentake, at which indictments and presentments were taken.

TRAILBASTON. Powerful commissions of oyer and terminer issued to deal with violent breaches of the peace and abuses of legal procedure. The first such commissions were issued in 1305.

TRESPASS. An actionable wrong committed against the person or property of another. In criminal law, a misdemeanour, or offence less serious than felony.

VENIRE FACIAS. A writ ordering that a person be summoned to appear in court. The first stage of legal process upon an indictment for trespass.

WRITS *DE CURSU.* Writs obtainable from chancery in standard form, without the special authorization of the king or chancellor.

Index

Spalding (Lincs.) 44 n.
Spencer, Richard 179
Sperling, John 260 n.
Spetchley, William 251
Sprowston (Norfolk) 93
Stafford (Staffs.) 212 n.
Stafford, Edmund, earl of Stafford
   (d. 1403) 209
Stafford, Humphrey, earl of Stafford and
   duke of Buckingham (d. 1460) 103,
   209, 216, 217 n., 219
Stafford, Sir Humphrey 241
Stafford, Sir James 209
Staffordshire 51 n., 53, 55, 58, 121,
   123-4, 139, 169-70, 172-3, 175-8,
   180-5, 192-3, 208-16, 220, 234-5,
   242, 267
   see also Abbots Bromley; Amerton;
   Blithbury; Blore; Bramshall;
   Burton; Chartley; Cheadle;
   Chillington; Gayton; Lichfield;
   Milwich; Newcastle; Paynesley;
   Rocester; Rugeley; Sandon; Stone;
   Tamhorn; Throwley; Tutbury;
   Uttoxeter; Wolverhampton
Stanhope, Sir Richard 169, 225-8, 231
Stanley family 90 n.
Stanley, Thomas 215, 235
Stansbatch, Thomas 125 n.
Stanton, John 219
star chamber, court of 52
Statutes 83, 250, 265
   of Additions (1413) 67, 136
   on bail and committal (1554-5) 78, 80-2
   of Forcible Entry (1391) 53, 59, 124
   of Labourers (1351, 1361, 1388) 59,
      111, 172, 190
   of Livery (1377, 1390, 1400, 1401,
      1406) 59, 124, 187, 214-16
   of Lollards (1414) 144, 161-2, 170
   of Northampton (1328) 59
   of Pardons (1390) 84, 179-80, 188
   of Praemunire (1353) 225
   of Riots (1411, 1414) 52 n., 53, 59,
      65 n., 67 n., 124, 170, 171-2
   of Treasons (1352) 50, 131, 259
   of Truces (1414) 131, 170-1, 204, 206,
      231
   of Westminster (1361) 59
   of Winchester (1285) 15, 43, 59, 76-7
Steventon, William 234
Stewart, Murdoch, earl of Fife and duke
   of Albany (d. 1425) 137, 139, 253 n.

Stewart, Robert, duke of Albany
   (d. 1420) 137
Stillington, Robert, bishop of Bath and
   Wells (1466-91), chancellor of
   England 28
Stokes, Nicholas 260 n.
Stone (Staffs.) 211 n.
Storey, R. L. 58 n.
Strangways, James 249
Stubbs, W. 2
Suffolk, duke of see Pole
   see also Bury St Edmunds; Ipswich;
   Orwell; Wortham
Summa Theologica 29
   see also Aquinas
summons 74-5, 176-86, 207
   see also arrest; outlawry
superior eyre see king's bench
Surrey 266
   see also Bermondsey; Kingston
Sussex 266
   see also Rye
Swalcliffe (Oxon.) 160
Swallow, Richard 260 n.
Swynnerton, Robert 221
Sydewyk, Thomas 186 n.

Taillard, John 264
Talbot, Henry 137, 254
Talbot, Gilbert, Lord (d. 1418) 220, 222,
   231, 234
Talbot, John, Lord Furnival, Lord
   Talbot, and earl of Shrewsbury
   (d. 1453) 94-5, 101 n., 139-40, 174,
   209, 216, 220-4, 231, 235-6, 243,
   267
Talbot, Sir Thomas 160, 164, 254, 264
Tale of Gamelyn 39, 41
Tamhorn (Staffs.) 55
Tancarville (Seine-Maritime) 235 n.
Tanworth (War.) 237 n.
Taylor, William 143, 157, 162
Thomas of Canterbury, St 37
Thomas, duke of Gloucester see
   Gloucester
Thornton, John 70-1, 74-5, 95, 111,
   251, 263
Thorp, William, chief justice of king's
   bench (1346-50) 108, 113
Throwley (Staffs.) 212 n.
Tickhill, Thomas 154, 160
Tiler, Robert 235 n.
Tiptoft, John 205